# The Long March of the French Left

*By the same author*

HOW LONG WILL SOUTH AFRICA SURVIVE?

# The Long March of the French Left

R. W. Johnson

St. Martin's Press    New York

# For Claude and Simone

ISBN 0 – 312 – 49645 – 1

**Library of Congress Cataloging in Publication Data**

Johnson, Richard William.
The Long March of the French Left.

Includes bibliographical references and index.
1. Communism – France. 2. Socialism in France.
3. France – Politics and government – 1945 –
I. Title
HX269.J63        1981        324.24407        80 – 24518
ISBN 0 – 312 – 49645 – 1

# Contents

# List of Tables and Figures

TABLES

FIGURES

# Preface

Ever since 1789 French radicalism has had an importance and an audience which has stretched far beyond the confines of France itself. The Revolution of 1789 not merely transformed Europe and, finally, the world: it altered basic intellectual conceptions of what was politically possible or even desirable. Its shadow and its 'lessons' dominated the nineteenth century. Only with the Russian Revolution of 1917 did any real alternative focus for radical hopes and fears come into existence. Even so, the Bolsheviks of 1917 were quite self-consciously the children of 1789 – their debates are strewn with references to 'Thermidorean reaction', the possibilities of Bonapartism, and the like.

Long before then, however, the Paris Revolution of 1848 and the Commune of 1871 had reinforced the universalist claims of the French radical tradition in a way which has made the similar claims of later would-be universal states – the British in the nineteenth-century, the Americans in the twentieth – seem almost paltry by comparison. The proud boasts of these latter that they had bequeathed Westminster parliamentarism to the world or made it 'safe for democracy' quickly turned to ashes as it became clear that such models depended more on the (transitory) power of those who bestowed them than on their genuine acceptability to others. But the world beyond France has not merely accepted the universality of the French tradition but often seized eagerly upon it. The first Soviet space vehicle to land on the moon contained a Communard flag. Modern egalitarians and populist politicians of all stripes quote (not always consciously) Rousseau on equality and the general will. Embattled social democrats echo Léon Blum's classic repudiation of modern Communism at Tours in 1920. Anarchists and syndicalists (and, sometimes, fascists) have, in the long run, probably drawn greater sustenance from Sorel than Kropotkin.

Defeat, Occupation and the rise of the super-powers saw a dramatic reduction in the global significance of France and of French culture and traditions. Politically and economically the new post-1945 world belonged, it seemed clear, to Moscow, Washington and Peking. Culturally, Anglo-Saxon dominance was so complete that for the first time even the French language – which had known only expansion since the time of Charlemagne – began to retreat. France was economically and politically weak, was losing its empire, mattered less. The French Left was monopolised by the most Stalinist Communist Party outside the Soviet Union and by the equally smothering blanket of a threadbare, time-serving Socialist Party. One could have been forgiven for believing, in such a world, that the French radical and revolutionary tradition would peter out into parochial insignificance.

This tradition had, however, never depended very much on its practical successes, on French power, or, indeed, on propitious circumstance of any kind. The Great Revolution lasted only a decade before it was expropriated by Napoleon and the 1848 Revolution only three years before it met a similar fate at the hands of his nephew, while the Paris Commune was a rather aimless nine-week wonder in a badly beaten and dismembered country. Indeed, failure at home has not merely never hindered the influence of the French Left abroad, but has often seemed inversely related to it. Babeuf, the 'father of modern communism', was executed for an attempted coup which never got off the ground and which lacked popular support. Louis Blanc, despite the influence of his *Organisation du Travail* (1839), was a disaster in the few months in 1848 when he was asked to put his ideas into practice and ended his days as a wordy old bore who could empty the National Assembly of the Third Republic just by rising to speak in it. Auguste Blanqui, the greatest revolutionary of the nineteenth-century, spent most of his life behind bars and was even under arrest when his day finally came in 1871: the Commune was made, in part, by Blanquistes, but not by Blanqui. Sorel, for all his *ouvrieriste* glorification of the world of proletarian struggle, was never fully accepted into the anarcho-syndicalist movement, always remaining an intellectual outsider looking in. Léon Blum's stirring oration against totalitarianism at Tours was given, it is sometimes forgotten, by a man who had just been democratically out-voted 3:1 and was seeking to justify his refusal to accept this decision. Luckier than most, he had two chances to implement his ideas: first, during the Popular Front government of 1936 which he led, ditheringly, to disaster; and again in 1946, when he ended his career hawking about pathetically for an American loan.

It is only when this imperviousness to *realpolitik* is taken into account that it seems unsurprising that the French Left has continued to enjoy a wider than national audience and significance. In the new post-war France the rise of a Stalinist Communist Party to overwhelming predominance on the Left enthroned an 'official' Marxism at the centre of the intellectual stage, displacing an older, more individualist radical tradition which stretched back in apostolic succession all the way to Voltaire. The resulting clash of opposites produced the phenomenon of Jean-Paul Sartre, whose centrality in post-war intellectual life depended essentially on the fact that he, almost alone, attempted to synthesise the two currents. The consequent polemics between Sartre, the official Marxists, Camus, Aron, Merleau-Ponty and others produced a debate of peculiar intensity and fascination for a world well beyond France. Again, so attracted was this international audience by the apparent grandeur of the debate that it passed almost without notice that Camus had become a straightforward apologist for the most bestial practices of French colonialism in Algeria, that Sartre's own tiny party was no more than an outlandish and short-lived political joke, and that Aron had settled comfortably into providing standard conservative pap for *Le Figaro*.

In the 1960s and 1970s the same little world of the Paris Latin Quarter continued to enjoy an extraordinary international resonance. It remained true throughout this period that the easiest way to know what radical intellectuals across the world would be discussing tomorrow was to stroll through the bookshops off the Boulevard

Saint-Michel – particularly 'La Joie de Lire', the little bookshop in the Rue Saint-Severin run by the left-wing publisher, François Maspero. Here one would first have come across the works of Frantz Fanon, of Amilcar Cabral, Régis Debray and other prophets of Third World revolution; it was through this filter that the works of Antonio Gramsci and other Continental Marxists were fed into the mainstream of 1960s radical culture; here too the works of Althusser, Balibar, Gorz, Poulantzas and a host of other French Marxist *philosophes* were first to be found. It was entirely fitting that some of the fiercest street fighting of the May Events of 1968 should have swirled round these same shops – they are, after all, only a stone's throw from the Sorbonne and in 1968 that was, literally, the most significant way to measure things . . .

And, once again, all these phenomena were seized upon by external audiences with an enthusiasm almost devoid of discrimination. Régis Debray was hailed so loudly as the prophet of Latin American revolution that it was some time before it was widely noticed that the guerrilla movements he espoused had already collapsed everywhere in bloody shambles. Again, the ease with which Fanon was assimilated into the French Marxist tradition drew surprisingly little notice given that it was the obverse side to his almost complete neglect in Algeria and the rest of the Third World. The bitterness of his rejection of the metropole merely succeeded in making Fanon a cult figure for metropolitan radicals, a comprehensive and ironic failure of his proclaimed intent. Similarly, the sheer freakishness of Althusser's position was hardly noticed, either, in the welter of critical attention devoted to him abroad. That the doctrine of proletarian dictatorship, at the very point when it was being abandoned with barely a dissenting voice by the French Communist Party, should have found its most doughty defender in the impeccably bourgeois figure of a Sorbonne professor was, after all, a rare piece of pantomime. By this stage, however, lovers of this form of theatre had perhaps been already sated by the sight of Régis Debray being extracted from the Latin American prison in which the attempted application of his theories had landed him by the formidable maternal *démarches* of Mme Debray, a prominent former Gaullist deputy who still enjoyed a useful influence with the Rothschild's banker who was then President of France . . .

Most of all, of course, the 1968 May Events were greeted abroad as yet a further example of Paris leading the way to revolution, just as it had in 1789 and 1848. There was certainly no doubt that the student radicalism of the 1960s reached its flamboyant highpoint in those heady days in and around the Sorbonne. But foreign enthusiasts almost invariably missed the cardinal point that what had made the Events so significant was the greatest general strike in European, possibly world, history. The challenge mounted to the regime by the students themselves, however photogenic they and their slogans were, was in itself nugatory. None the less, for years thereafter – and to some extent still today – the Events were used abroad to erect extraordinary theories in which the radical intelligentsia, not the working classes, were taken to be the new revolutionary class of the technetronic era. More staggering still, the Events were taken by many radicals in the West as proof of the possibility of revolution in even the most advanced capitalist society, while, if anything, they proved the opposite. The intelligentsia and the proletariat had done all that any

revolutionary theory might ever have asked of them; the state machine trembled –
but was unharmed; the Right triumphed. Curiously, the idea that a revolutionary
situation truly existed in the Paris of 1968 but was somehow 'thrown away' still has
considerable currency in Britain and America, though hardly any at all in France
itself.

All of which conspires to place anyone who writes about the French Left in a
somewhat difficult situation. Despite the fact that France has, save for brief inter-
ludes, been almost invariably ruled by the Centre or the Right,[1] his subject, the Left,
is, in one sense, already far too 'famous'. In Gaullism France gave to the world, and
particularly to Europe, a political model which is still far from fully understood and
whose ultimate consequences, even if it fails (as it still may not) to become the
generalised voice of a resurgent Europe, may well be incalculable. Nevertheless,
anyone working or living in a university in the English-speaking world in the 1970s
was likely to hear little about Gaullism but papers *ad nauseam* about French Marxism.
The French Left, to some extent within France and overwhelmingly outside France, is
hidden in its own mystique, cloaked in revolutionary rhetoric and theorising, its
physique obscured by its ideas and its myth.

There is, though, another, more mundane, French Left, one that is not glimpsed in
the Fifth *arrondissement*. Just as the Right may talk of a *'pays réel'*, so there is, too, a
*gauche réelle*. It is the Left one sees if one wanders further out into the industrial
wasteland of the Paris *banlieu*, where the great blocks of cheap multi-storey housing,
the *habitations à loyer modéré* (HLM), march like some gaunt column of soldiers
through the even less salubrious *bidonvilles* of immigrant workers and the great
fortress-like factories of French industrial life. Out here, beyond the Metro's reach,
no one much has heard of Althusser and no one at all about Poulantzas. What matters
here is *saisis* and *expulsions* (rent-evictions) and *coupures* (electricity and gas cut-offs
for unpaid bills). Here Trotskyite slogans fade on the wall: *'Lutte Ouvrière – Votez la
plus à la gauche possible'*, competing with racist slogans aimed at immigrant
workers, and torn old Communist and Socialist posters telling one how different it
might be if the Left should win. It is difficult, in such surroundings, to believe.
Beyond this there is the Left of poor peasants eking out a miserable and almost
timeless existence on the *Massif Central*; of young civil servants, *cadres* and media
men, infuriated to the point of despair by their superiors' institutionalised deference to
*le pouvoir*; and of white-collar workers and technocrats goaded by the equally
institutionalised jobbery of a Right grown fat and complacent in power.

By all save a few tiny fragments of this Left it is assumed that the only hope of
deliverance from the *status quo* lies in voting the *Majorité* out of power (the Right's
term for itself has been as universally accepted as was the Bolsheviks' self mis-
description in an earlier time). True, the PCF (*Parti Communiste Français*) still talks
of itself, loosely, as a 'revolutionary' party, but it did not require the Party's formal
abandonment of the doctrine of proletarian dictatorship in 1976 to convince even its
own supporters that it had long since placed all its eggs in an electoral basket. By the
1970s, indeed, there were probably fewer real revolutionaries in France than at any
time this century. Instead, voters have flocked to the polls in numbers (84.9 per cent in

1974, 84.7 per cent in 1978)[2] which not only far surpass British and American levels of political participation but which are at or near record levels even for the traditionally more participant French. Moreover, the small membership, divisions and organisational weakness of French trade unions means that the Left is in no position to mount a sustained challenge to the Right on the industrial front as, for example, the British and German labour movements are capable of doing. The Left's best hope – indeed, almost its only hope – lies on the electoral battleground and the Left knows it.

Such a perspective is at considerable variance with that of many of the non-French enthusiasts for French left-wing culture. This is not merely – though it is partly – because the inhabitants of such *milieux* are generally interested in abstract debate, sometimes to the point where any empirical reference is dismissed as 'mere empiricism'. Nor is it simply – though again it is partly – that such *milieux* have such meagre prospects within their own countries' electoral arenas that they have found it convenient to affect a grand contempt for elections and electoral politics as being somehow intrinsically part of a system they oppose. (The rather odd species of elections held in, say, Cuba, Vietnam or Guiné-Bissao are normally passed over in pregnant silence.)

Rather, there is often a half-conscious though none the less deep-seated realisation that the serious study of electoral politics may have a most subversive effect on one's ability to describe the political process in the broad brush-strokes of class analysis. To take an obvious example: in 1979 it was a fairly well accepted dictum in the upper reaches of the PCF that the current phase of world history is one in which international monopoly capital had found its interests best served by placing in power 'enlightened' and social democratic regimes – Carter in the USA, Callaghan in Britain, Schmidt in West Germany, and so on. Any serious analysis of the elections which brought such governments to power will not merely show that the vast preponderance of business support went to the conservative oppositions to such regimes, but will also throw up facts which, awkwardly, do not sit easily with any sort of class analysis. The British election of February 1974 which placed Labour in power, and the West German and American elections of 1976 were all extremely close-run contests, after all. The critical margins of support which settled them were probably provided by Enoch Powell's paradoxical support of Labour in the British case, by Reagan's refusal to campaign for Ford in the American case, and by the successful insistence of the West German Social Democrats (the SPP) that 'our Helmut [Schmidt] is better than their Helmut [Kohl]'. Thus in all three cases the bourgeoisie solidly backed the losing side – and lost for oddly flukish and personal reasons in the end. Such facts of political life become awkwardly present to one if electoral politics are seriously looked into. Better, most radicals seem to conclude, to leave the whole ghastly elections business alone . . .

The syndrome of reactions discussed above was, naturally, much in evidence in the wake of the Left's defeat in the 1978 French election. The *New Left Review*, probably the most influential Marxist journal in the English-speaking world, greeted this sad event in the following way:

The defeat of the left in the 1978 French general elections has had repercussions far beyond the national frontiers of France. The imperialist powers have been reassured by the unexpected prospect of renewed stability in a key country. The French working-class, which in May 1968 showed itself capable of a far higher degree of coordinated mobilization than any of its peers in the advanced capitalist world since 1945, has been – at least temporarily – demoralized and disoriented. Yet what was formerly the most monolithic of the mass Communist Parties of Western Europe has generated, in defeat, a public debate within its own ranks whose plain speaking and substantive stakes have no parallel since the twenties. In this debate, the most dramatic and eloquent intervention to date has been that of Louis Althusser, the most eminent living Communist philosopher. In the text published here . . . Althusser indicts – from the Left – the strategy, organizational practice and ideology of the PCF leadership . . .[3]

This paragraph has almost everything. A terrible event has taken place. The Left has been defeated in France which, because it's the *French* Left, means it's an event of world historical importance. The imperialists are, anonymously, happy. The French proletariat, which ten years before had experienced a great spasm quite atypical of its history, is unhappy. One might, perhaps, ask how and why exactly this defeat was effected – in fact hopes of future success may depend on asking these questions now. This, however, might be depressing and anyway leave one trapped in bourgeois empiricism. But – what luck! – here comes the philosophical cavalry riding over the hill. Better still, a *public debate*. With one of the acknowledged Great Men leading it! Not only great, but eloquent and dramatic! Best of all, he's attacking *from the Left* and right across the board too! No tepid hole-in-the-corner empiricism from *him*. He makes a fine sight, one thrills to his charge. It is, after all, charges like this which explain one's whole fascination with the French Left. Indeed, if electoral defeat can conjure up something so excitingly fine then it was almost worthwhile Our Side getting beaten . . .

Perhaps it would help if some radicals were to read Trotsky on the subject of elections. Having, in his youth, joined in the general (and by no means unjustified) chorus against 'parliamentary cretinism', the prophet in exile came to believe, too, in the sin of 'anti-parliamentary cretinism'. Writing of Comintern policy in Spain in 1931 on the eve of crucial elections to the Cortes, Trotsky was appalled at the manner in which Marxists were being encouraged to feel the elections were irrelevant:

By speaking *only* of the seven hour day, of factory committees and arming the workers, by ignoring 'politics' and by not having a single word to say in all its articles about elections to the Cortes, *Pravda* goes all the way to meet anarcho-syndicalism, fosters it, covers up for it . . . To counter-pose the slogan of *arming the workers* to the reality of the political processes that grip the masses at their vitals means to isolate oneself from the masses . . .[4]

This book attempts, at least, to take such strictures to heart. The rise of the French

Left from the dénouement of 1968 to an apparently invincible position in 1975–7 and its sudden collapse to defeat in 1978 is a story of no little interest, the more so since it poses the question of whether the Left could *ever* win. These developments took place almost exclusively within the world of political parties and electoral politics. To understand and explore them one needs at least some history and some knowledge of the changing social structure and political sociology of contemporary France. Such information this book seeks to provide, however inadequately. The great debates of the post-election period have their interest, too, but I have attempted to situate them in their real political environment rather than leave them hanging abstractly as mere philosophical contributions to the greater goal of theory. It is possible that the author's own political prejudices will show from time to time and for this he apologises in advance to all to whom they may give offence.

Finally, this preface affords me the occasion to thank a number of people. Most of all, of course, I am grateful to a large number of French friends of a variety of political persuasions who have helped me, perhaps more than they know, in the dozen years during which I have trespassed on their hospitality in order to learn about their country's politics. They are, in truth, too numerous to mention and I hope that others will forgive me if I cite only Alain Bidaut and Bernard and Marianne Maigrot by name. Among academic colleagues my debts are greatest to Philip Williams and David Goldey. It has been impossible for some time now for anyone writing about French politics to acknowledge properly the diffuse debt they owe to Philip but, in addition to that, I owe him thanks for many personal acts of patience and kindness. To David my debt is even greater. He knows much more than I do and has been unfailingly generous in sharing his knowledge with me, as with others. I should also like to thank Keith Griffin and Bob Townsend for providing me with room, and both Keith and Dixie for managing to provide a splendid and cheering event during the time I was writing, one which greatly invigorated me for the task ahead. As always I am grateful to my colleagues at Magdalen for providing me with an environment within which it is not hard to write. My particular thanks go to Frank Parkin and Andreas Boltho, both of whom read chapters of this book in draft and made extremely useful criticisms thereon. They will both have reason to feel that I have less than answered all their points. Andreas, whose exact nationality always remains something of a mystery, would probably like me to state that he is not, in the last analysis, a Frenchman. I hereby do so.

Finally, my thanks and more go to Anne, Rebecca and Dicken. They have all put up with me while I was writing, were endlessly patient, and have helped in more ways than they know. On the other hand, since they are my family, I feel safe in saying that all mistakes which may occur in this book are directly their fault, while any good bits are entirely to my own credit.

*Magdalen College,*　　　　　　　　　　　　　　　　　　　　　R. W. JOHNSON
*Oxford*
*November 1979*

# List of Abbreviations

ACO        Action Catholique Ouvrière
AFL        American Federation of Labour
AFP        Agence France Presse
CD         Centre Démocrate
CDP        Centre Démocratie et Progrès
CDS        Centre des Démocrates Sociaux
CERC       Centre d'Etudes des Revenus et des Coûts
CERES      Centre d'Etudes, de Récherches et d'Education Socialistes
CERM       Centre d'Etudes et de Récherches Marxistes
CEVIPOF    Centre d'Etudes de la Vie Politique Française
CFDT       Confédération Française Démocratique du Travail
CFTC       Confédération Française des Travailleurs Chrétiens
CGC        Confédération Génerále des Cadres
CGIL       Confederazione Generale Italiana del Lavoro
CGT        Confédération Générale du Travail
CGTU       Confédération Générale du Travail Unifaire
CIA        Central Intelligence Agency
CIR        Convention des Institutions Républicaines
CNIP       Centre National des Indépendants et Paysans
CNPF       Conseil National du Patronat Français
CPSU       Communist Party of the Soviet Union
CREP       Centre de Récherche Economique sur l'Epargne
CRS        Compagnies Républicaines de Sécurité
DIFE       Défense des Interêts de la France en Europe
DOM-TOM    Départements d'Outre-Mer et Territoires d'Outre-Mer
EEC        European Economic Community
FEN        Federation de l'Education Nationale
FFI        Forces Françaises de l'Intérieur
FGDS       Fédération de la Gauche Démocratique et Socialiste
FI         Front de l'Indépendance
FLN        Front de Libération Nationale
FNSEA      Fédération Nationale des Syndicats d'Exploitants Agricoles
FO         Force Ouvrière
HLM        Habitations à Loyer Modéré
IFOP       Institut Français d'Opinion Publique
JAC        Jeunesse Agricole Chrétienne
JEC        Jeunesse Etudiante Chrétienne

| | |
|---|---|
| JJSS | Jean-Jacques Servan-Schreiber |
| JOC | Jeunesse Ouvrière Chrétienne |
| KPD | Kommunistische Partei Deutschlands |
| LCR | Ligue Communiste Révolutionnaire |
| LO | Lutte Ouvrière |
| MDSF | Mouvement Démocrate Socialiste de France |
| MJCF | Mouvement de la Jeunesse Communiste Française |
| MRG | Mouvement des Radicaux de Gauche |
| MRP | Mouvement Républicain Populaire |
| NATO | North Atlantic Treaty Organisation |
| OAS | Organisation Armée Sécrète |
| OAU | Organisation for African Unity |
| OECD | Organisation for Economic Co-operation and Development |
| PCE | Partido Comunista de España |
| PCF | Parti Communiste Français |
| PCI | Partito Communista Italiano |
| PDM | Progrès et Démocratie Moderne |
| PPF | Parti Populaire Français |
| PR | Parti Républicain |
| PRL | Parti Républicain de la Liberté |
| PS | Parti Socialiste |
| PSU | Parti Socialiste Unifié |
| RDA | Rassemblement Démocratique Africain |
| RI | Républicains Indépendants |
| RPF | Rassemblement du Peuple Français |
| RPR | Rassemblement pour la République |
| SE | Sections d'Entreprise |
| SFIO | Section Française de l'Internationale Ouvrière |
| SHAPE | Supreme Headquarters Allied Powers Europe |
| SOFRES | Société Française d'Enquêtes par Sondages |
| SPD | Sozialedemokratische Partei Deutschlands |
| UDF | Union pour la Démocratie Française |
| UDR | Union des Démocrates pour la République; later, Union pour la Défense de la République |
| UDSR | Union Démocratique et Socialiste de la Résistance |
| UEC | Union des Etudiants Communistes |
| UFE | Union pour la France en Europe |
| UGSD | Union de la Gauche Socialiste et Démocratique |
| UNEF | Union Nationale des Etudiants Français |
| UNR | Union pour la Nouvelle République |
| UNR-RI | Union pour la Nouvelle République – Républicain Indépendant |
| URP | Union des Républicains de Progrès (pour le soutien au President de la République) |
| WFTU | World Federation of Trade Unions |

# PART ONE

## The Long March

# 1 Scenes from French Life, 1977–9

It was just after 10 a.m. on 17 May 1977 when a large metal-grey Renault 30 drew up in the Rue de Grenelle in the sixth *arrondissement* of Paris. Before its doors had opened the vehicle was assailed by a great crowd of photographers, journalists and cinema and television cameras. The car's principal occupant, and object of this frenzied interest, Georges Marchais, was, however, well used to dealing with such scenes even without the ominously burly bodyguards who surrounded him on this occasion. The press interest was perfectly understandable for ever since Marchais, at the age of fifty, became leader of the French Communist Party (the PCF) in 1970 whatever he does is news. His beetling black eyebrows and powerful, combative figure (he is a former metalworker and looks it) are, thanks to his formidable television performances, known to every French household. In many of them he is, almost literally, a bogeyman – one survey has shown that as many as three-quarters of French children have heard of him by the age of eight and, by a 3:1 majority, don't like him.[1] But among his own faithful, the 5.8 million who voted Communist in 1978, Marchais is a revered and commanding figure – young workers who approach him at meetings address him spontaneously as '*tu*' and 'Georges'. Nobody – least of all his political enemies – doubts Marchais's power with such meetings, for his ability to combine biting sarcasm and a masterful irony with moving evocations of the hardships and wrongs of the poor make him a formidable public orator.

There was, though, a special reason for the press attention on this occasion, for in the preceding week Marchais's party had done two astonishing things. First, on the eve of the Socialist leader Mitterrand's television debate with the Prime Minister, Raymond Barre, it had released a barrage of figures which, to most eyes, had the effect of casting grave doubts on the viability of the Common Programme the Socialists (the PS), the Left Radicals (the MRG) and the PCF had signed in 1972, when they had formed the Union of the Left. Second, the PCF Politburo, without warning or even any show of consultation with a Party congress, had suddenly reversed its position of thirty years' standing on the nuclear deterrent, arguing that France must, after all, keep the *force de frappe* so dear to Gaullist hearts. Given that the renunciation of the nuclear deterrent was written large and clear into the Common Programme (with full PCF agreement), this too had had an extremely damaging impact on the entire credibility of the Union of the Left. These moves had, moreover, astonished and disoriented the Left's electorate. Only two months before, after all, the allied parties of the Left had swept to a triumph of unprecedented proportions in the municipal elections – a pointer of very real significance in a country where great power is still held by local mayors and where, accordingly, electoral turnout is very high (in March 1977, indeed, it had reached the record level of 78.8 per cent). It had seemed then that it would be well-nigh impossible for either the President, Giscard d'Estaing, or the Gaullists, led by Giscard's bitter rival, Jacques Chirac, to prevent the Left sweeping to power in the elections scheduled for March 1978. But such calculations had not allowed for such aberrant behaviour by one of the major partners to the Left alliance. What on earth, the press wanted to know, were Marchais and the PCF up to?

There was, of course, scant chance that Marchais was going to unburden himself of the answers to this question to the journalists crowding on the pavement. He had come now to the MRG headquarters in the Rue de Grenelle for a summit meeting with Mitterrand and the MRG leader, Robert Fabre, in an attempt to reach agreement on the Common Programme and its application. Fabre and Mitterrand were already there, waiting for Marchais to arrive. Fabre opened the proceedings with a strong condemnation of the way in which the PCF, with no prior consultation with its partners, had driven a coach and horses through the Common Programme.[2] Other delegations held their breath. The fact was that Fabre was a minnow amongst whales – his party was only a tenth of the size of either of the other two – and Marchais would hardly take kindly to such public castigation at his hands. To the general surprise Marchais took it all in rather subdued form, replying weakly that it was just a matter of modifying the Programme to bring it up to date, and making precise the details for its ultimate application. After a quarter of an hour of such question-begging banalities from the Communist leader, the astonishing surmise had run right round the table that, for all his apparent dominance, Marchais was sounding very like a man who had been outvoted in his own Politburo and who, with a notable lack of enthusiasm, was now having to defend policies he himself did not believe in. Despite the PCF's vociferous denials of internal divisions within its leadership it had seemed for some time that the politburo had a hard-line group – centring on its doyen, Gaston Plissonnier, and, more particularly, Roland Leroy, the editor of *L'Humanité*. Despite the Party's recent moves towards liberalisation this group had, it was rumoured, regained its ascendancy over the 'doves' such as Paul Laurent – largely because of the Party's poor recent performance in polls and by-elections in the face of the dramatically expanding PS. It certainly began to sound as if Leroy was calling the tune which Marchais was now attempting, with little conviction, to put words to.

As Marchais tailed off all heads turned towards François Mitterrand. He, more than any other single person, was the architect of the Union of the Left. Mitterrand had had to countenance severe opposition to his takeover of the PS leadership in 1971 (succeeding mainly because the party had been too weak and divided to stop him) and even more when, in 1972, he had tied the PS firmly to the Common Programme. A general chorus of opinion had gone up from all political observers that such a step would be disastrous to the Socialists, leaving them to trail along in the wake of the Communist juggernaut. Within two years Mitterrand had utterly confounded such critics. The PS had gone from strength to strength. In 1974 Mitterrand had come within an ace of winning the presidential election against Giscard and every indication since then had been that he would win a re-run quite decisively. Meanwhile all indications were that the PS had actually by far overhauled the PCF in popular support. The Union of the Left and the Common Programme on which it was based were synonymous with Mitterrand's almost miraculous political success – and now both were in mortal danger. If they were to be saved, now, surely, the PS leader must pull something rather special out of the hat.

'I have no preliminary declaration to make', he said. 'I made it in 1972 when we signed the Common Programme. There will be no second Common Programme before the first has been applied. Certainly, we must take new facts into account. We agree about putting it into practice. But there will be no re-making of the Common Programme or re-negotiation of it. A calendar for putting it into effect, yes. But, as for putting figures to it, we don't see the point of that.'[3]

He stopped. A silence grew as the room, riveted by the tone of calm announcement, waited for him to go on. Only slowly – and to Marchais's visible consternation – did it dawn that Mitterrand had finished. That was it. The silence spoke for him. It meant, decoded: If the PCF has decided to break the union of the Left, we cannot stop you. But the PCF, after its recent extraordinary moves, will bear the full weight of responsibility for such a rupture in the eyes of everyone, including its own electorate. From a self-inflicted wound of such proportions the PCF may well never recover. but there is no point in the other Left parties making concessions or doing the talking. The initiative is yours, whether you like it or not – and so is the responsibility.

Marchais was thrown heavily on the defensive, by turns pleading and blustering that this was no good, that there must be discussion. Mitterrand refused to soften – until the following exchange took place:

MARCHAIS: But if we can't discuss things before opening negotiations, then your position is one of a veritable *diktat*!

MITTERRAND: I don't accept that word.

MARCHAIS: The Common Programme must be made precise. One can't, after all, give a blank cheque to tomorrow's government.

MITTERRAND: An excellent formula.

MARCHAIS: ... Some people doubt whether we [the PCF] want to win.

MITTERRAND: We have never doubted it.

MARCHAIS: The question has been posed, I want to answer it. We want to win. We want to govern together with you. We want to succeed right to the very end.[4]

At this, perhaps fatefully, Mitterrand weakened. Very well, they could set up a joint commission of the three parties to work out details of how the Programme could be put into practice. But it must hurry and get its job finished quickly. To decode again: It's clear that if the door is slammed now there is a majority of hawks on your

Politburo who will be happy to lead the PCF back into the ghetto. You clearly don't want that but, as you can see, the PS and MRG will make you take full responsibility for any breakdown. Here is a proposal to give you enough time to somehow whip your Politburo into line. But don't take long about it.

Marchais, clearly much relieved at this outcome, was quick to realise that, having opened this door, Mitterrand had surrendered a tremendous hostage to fortune. If negotiations now dragged on, the PS and MRG were in effect conceding that the PCF had a genuine case, worthy of discussion. Responsibility for any breakdown would become more clouded and ambiguous – and would probably land on the Socialists if negotiations dragged on long enough and they were foolish enough to be the ones who finally broke them off. Meanwhile, the one certainty was that the PCF wouldn't want the talks to go quickly – indeed, all options could best be kept open if they were spun out as long as possible. Marchais quickly seized his opportunity: 'Well, I'm going on holiday in July and I've already got my plane ticket.' With this, he left, as if having already to join the queue at Orly airport . . . He was, indeed, to take an extravagantly long holiday, conveniently secluded in Corsica where he was well out of reach of his Left 'allies', and didn't return to Paris until 3 August. When he did return, it was to go on television with a long list of new and intransigent demands for Mitterand to swallow . . . The Left was on the slippery slope but things were never to be as clear again as they had been during the tense confrontation of 17 May.

April 3 1978. Another spring, another Paris. In the year which had elapsed since the theatrical set-piece of 17 May a great deal of very muddied water had flowed under the bridges. The elections were over, the Left had lost. On the Right – in government, the business community and the upper middle classes in general – an always strong trait of self-satisfaction mingled with simple delight at the sheer outrageous luck of it all. Such feelings were only slightly tempered by the consciousness of the deep divisions within the Majority between Giscard and Chirac, the Gaullist leader. This rivalry seemed certain to produce a long guerrilla war which could only end in confrontation between the two men in the presidential election of 1981. But that was far ahead. The main thing – the relief was almost tangible – was that there would, after all, be business as usual.

There could have been no surer sign of this blessed resumption of business normalcy than the pale figure of the eighty-six-year-old man waiting to receive journalists that April morning at the Rond Point, midway down the Champs-Elysées between the Arc de Triomphe and the Place de la Concorde. For Marcel Dassault, whose headquarters these were, having just been re-elected as the Gaullist deputy for Beauvais-Nord (Oise), the seat he had held since 1951, was now the doyen of the National Assembly and he, accordingly, would deliver the formal opening address of the new parliamentary session. How better to commemorate the triumph of the Right than to have the Assembly's new term inaugurated by the richest and most powerful arms manufacturer in the world? What more fitting send-off for a government which was, by far, his best and most faithful client?

The myth of Marcel Dassault was, as the journalists were well aware, many times larger than life. In part, perhaps, this was due simply to the lethal glamour of his famous aeroplanes – the Ouragan, the Mystère, the Super-Mystère, and, above all, the delta-winged Mirage which, in its various types, commanded the skies of southern Africa and the Middle East, as well as of France. But, even more, it was due to the fact that the installation in power of De Gaulle – whom Dassault had faithfully followed and supported from the 1940s on – had seen the creation of a vast military-industrial complex in France, a symbiosis of business and government in which Dassault had been the central figure – and the main beneficiary (he owned 98 per cent of his company's shares).[5] De Gaulle had shown himself deeply appreciative of Dassault's unwavering support, giving him a copy of his memoirs with the inscription 'To Marcel Dassault, in memory of our struggle and of the part he has played in giving stature to France'.[6] More to the point, De Gaulle had made the creation of a French independent nuclear strike force – the *force de frappe* – a cornerstone of his policy, and Dassault's planes became that force. Dassault's planes – particularly the Mirage – were, moreover, in great demand abroad and De Gaulle was able to use his ability to supply or withold them as a major political and military bargaining counter. They became, as Sampson notes, 'one of the most phenomenal of all French exports'[7] and French governments came to regard the promotion of Dassault's sales as a major national interest. In the successive great international competitions for arms contracts, the whole weight of the French government and diplomatic service was placed behind Dassault. A contract for Mirages was a victory for France or even, if the Americans were the rivals, as they usually were, a victory for Europe. The choice of an alternative warplane was seen as a grave affront to national prestige, not just a setback for the national exchequer. Needless to say, such governmental efforts merely topped up on the very considerable private inducements offered and pressures exerted by Dassault's company itself.

Oddly, perhaps the chief opponent of Dassault had sat alongside him on the government benches in the National Assembly, General Paul Stehlin, former chief of staff of the Armée de l'Air. To Dassault's fury Stehlin had decried the claims of the Mirage F.1E to become the main NATO combat plane of the 1970s, pleading instead the superior virtues of the American Northrop F.17 Cobra. Stehlin's claims that, once again, the French taxpayer was being fleeced to buy inferior planes at inflated costs merely in order to swell Dassault's profits had been regarded by Dassault and his friends in the government as an act almost of treason and Stehlin had been forced to resign as Vice-President of the Assembly. In the end, however, Stehlin and Dassault's efforts had been self-cancelling and the 'deal of the century', as it was popularly termed, had finally gone to another American rival, General Dynamics. But Dassault had a revenge of sorts: in June 1975 it was revealed that for the past eleven years Stehlin had secretly been on the Northrop payroll . . . When the news reached Paris Stehlin had walked in front of a bus and been killed.

Dassault, on the other hand, was apparently indestructible. Brought up as a French Jew in the era of the Dreyfus Affair (his real name was Bloch, Dassault merely his Resistance name which he adopted permanently), he had been inspired by Bleriot's air crossing of the channel in 1909 to launch his own mass-production aviation company during the First World War. By the 1930s he had already become a major figure in the French aviation world and carried on running his company even after it was nationalised by the Popular Front government in 1936. In 1940, to his everlasting credit, he had refused to design planes for the Nazis even though they had offered him his freedom in return. This refusal he had maintained even when, as a Jew, he was incarcerated in Buchenwald; even, indeed, when the Nazis sentenced him to death. Saved by the arrival of the Allies, his honourable Resistance record stood him in good stead when compared, for example, with those of men like Louis Renault and Marius Berliet, who had built tanks and trucks for the Germans.[8] Thanks in part to this record the reborn Dassault company had received highly favourable treatment from post-war governments, receiving large injections of Marshall Aid money. He had prospered mightily, stuffing his Rond Point headquarters with antique furniture and Impressionist masterpieces and building himself his own Petit Trianon, a $10 million marble palace outside Paris.

But what made Dassault so awesome a representative of French capital was not merely his prosperity: it was his survival. He had lived through the Dreyfus Affair. He had survived the First World War and built aeroplanes for Clemenceau. His planes had carried Daladier to negotiate with Hitler at Munich in 1938. He had survived nationalisation at the hands of his fellow Jew, Léon Blum, and then survived the Nazis and Buchenwald too. He had seen the Fourth Republic come and go, and had built the planes which Mollet unleashed upon Suez. He had been a major figure before De Gaulle; had supported him; and survived him. The happy relationship had continued under Pompidou. Dassault had survived him, too. Now he subsidised a newspaper for the man Pompidou had fondly called 'my bulldozer', Jacques Chirac. Chirac had fallen from power as Prime Minister; Dassault continued, serene. In 1976 a great scandal had burst over his companies' highly questionable financial practices. Dassault appeared on television to explain cheerfully that he would do just what he liked with his money. With the constitution of a new Popular Front in the 1970s – the Union of the Left – Dassault's empire naturally headed the list of enterprises the Left was determined to nationalise. Now, with the defeat of the Left in March 1978, Dassault had survived that threat too. And here he was, accompanied as always by his right-hand man and fellow deputy, General de Bénouville (a chief executive in Dassault's company),[9] getting ready to ride off in his huge black Rolls-Royce to open the National Assembly: a pale, genial little leprechaun of a man who was the authentic voice of French capital right down the century. Journalists could hardly miss the point as they gathered at the Rond Point – for this was, after all, the head office of *Jours de France* – which Dassault owned. He had founded the newspaper in 1951, he explained, 'to amuse myself. One can't build aeroplanes *all* the time'.[10]

Dassault had not always been a Gaullist, a journalist began; in his youth he'd been a Radical-Socialist. 'It was the fashion. Everybody was a Radical-Socialist.' Well then, did his enormous wealth give him great political power? 'No. The best proof is that I don't have any at all,' he explained, adding that politics was something that gave him something to do when he got 'bored with managing' his wealth. But, his questioners persisted, didn't he find political ways to spend his money? This was, as everyone knew, a loaded question, for Dassault's heavy-handed and high-pressure salesmanship with foreign governments had been equalled only by his prodigious disbursements to the voters of Beauvais and to elected officials in a wide circle around his constituency. Even victorious Communist mayors swept into power in the 1977 municipal elections had found large and gracious gifts from Dassault in their mail – though probably the Communists were alone in sending them back. It might have been supposed that the institution of universal suffrage had prevented the possibility of elections being influenced by the distribution of largesse, but such supposition failed faced with the resources of a tycoon of Dassault's magnitude. In 1976 the press had revealed the existence of a secret Dassault political fund amounting to no less than $6 million a year. A great deal of this was undoubtedly spent in Beauvais and in March 1978 his grateful voters had returned their deputy comfortably on the first ballot, although on paper the seat 'should' probably have been won by the Socialists and certainly ought, at the least, to have been highly marginal.

M. Dassault felt that his questioners didn't realise how onerous it was to be a businessman. After all, at the end of a month an employee just took his salary and was happy, but a businessman was never free from care, had always to worry about showing the necessary politeness to his clients, and so forth . . . But, they continued, what about his 'generosity' during the election campaign? 'That, well that's only normal. When one has money, one's friends must benefit from it . . . I went into some municipal buildings where there was no washroom, well . . . since I was able to do something about it . . . There were some country roads which were badly maintained. My car would stop at the side of the road and there would be children floundering through the mud . . . These poor people, it's only normal to help them. And then . . . they are very attached to their Church, and yet there'd be a belfry open to the four winds, with all the slates falling off . . .' M. Dassault continued with a long catalogue of the small and humble kindnesses he had been able to effect with his cheque book. 'And didn't those cheques bring you votes?' he was asked. 'Not votes, perhaps, but friendships.' But did he feel he could really talk about how poor people might feel? 'Having been in Buchenwald, I have been in worse circumstances than any unfortunate in my constituency, than any worker.'

Faced with this ace of trumps, the journalists moved on. Which great men had fascinated him – De Gaulle, Onassis? 'De Gaulle. Fascinated . . . if you mean like at Lourdes, like the little shepherdess who saw the Holy Virgin, no . . . I was astonished by him. But he, too, had his luck . . . Onassis? He's a nobody. He's just a businessman who built boats, he'd do business with anyone . . .' He only really admired Thomas Edison, he said. He'd been a newspaper-seller but he'd made a big business out of electricity and had invented the gramophone. He, Marcel Dassault, had been only fifth in class at school but he'd invented a flight recorder for jet planes 'because I used to enjoy playing with electrical apparatus'. But really, he continued, he'd like to have been a government minister – that was the only way to get things done. As it was he was only a deputy and 'a deputy has no power at all'. But he would be opening the National Assembly, wouldn't he? 'That's just what they call the benefit of age . . . I'll do the best I can. It's a lot of fat to chew. I'll talk about unity, about industry, about the young . . . No, no I won't be talking politics.'

It was time to go. Dassault shook hands with the journalists as if with affectionate intimates of old. Twinkling brown eyes behind tortoiseshell glasses, an implacably amiable old man huddled in a fur coat which displayed the Legion of Honour on its front, he was a friend of all the world. He moved towards the waiting Rolls and was gone. Things were back to normal all right. Indeed, it was difficult to imagine now that they might ever have changed . . .

February 21 1979. Another year, another spring – or, more precisely, a winter which refused to turn into spring. The snow and bitter cold which had descended over all of Europe made life as difficult and miserable in France as anywhere else. In the grimy, grey little steel towns of Lorraine stretching along the Belgian and Luxembourg borders the weather merely added to the general climate of depression which had settled over the region since the previous December when official plans had been disclosed for swingeing cuts in the French steel industry. The world-wide steel surplus, the employers and the government had declared, provided France with no real alternative to such contraction. Thousands of jobs – ultimately tens of thousands – would have to go. This was, naturally, regrettable at a time when unemployment was already at record levels, but there was nothing else to be done.

The whole episode provided a rich example of the inimitable style of French executive authority. What the government might have said (but of course didn't) was that the problem was largely of its own making. For years there had been voices saying that the French steel industry should (following the German example) be slimmed down and that this should be done while the boom of the 1960s and early 1970s lasted so that there would be other jobs for the workers to go to. But governments had enjoyed the idea of a large steel industry as part of the national *grandeur*, a symbol of French industrial virility in the face of the *défi américain*. The long-term need to shrink the industry down to sustainable size had been blindly, even blandly, ignored.

Now these chickens had come to roost. The government, for its part, was enjoying a new, post-electoral mood of executive decisiveness. Since one had to be cruel to be kind, it would be best to cut deep: 30,000 jobs must go. Since neither the unions of the affected workers nor the several communities thus virtually sentenced to death could be expected to like such a plan, the decision was reached without their being consulted at all. Instead the government and the employers together drew up a plan which talked euphemistically of 'the need for restructuring the industry', as if this somehow mitigated the massive blow it implied for the population of Lorraine. Finally, it was decided to release this bombshell just before Christmas as if, absurdly, it were a minor administrative change the government hoped to 'slip through' during the holiday season. It was government by bland fiat – a tone which, once challenged, modulated only to a distant, rather haughty, self-righteousness.

In Lorraine the news had been received at first with sheer stupefaction and then, as the Christmas and New Year season tailed dismally away, with a slow, rising fury. The anger had several targets. First, of course, were the employers. True, they had issued warnings of the need for contraction long before the government had decided to apply the EEC's Davignon plan to cut back European steel production across the board. But, like the government, they had done nothing much about it. What the workers could see was that the employers had carried on making profits out of steel while they could and that once the profits evaporated it was they, the workers, who were to be sacrificed. The fact that rationalisation had not been carried out earlier – despite all the preaching – made many workers suspicious of how real the need for it now was. (The PCF and its allied trade union, the *Confédération Générale du Travail* (CGT), catered to these suspicions by coming up with schemes of great ingenuity but dubious realism whereby production levels could be maintained intact.) But this was not the nub of the argument. What counted was that the employers were rich and more or less definitionally the enemy, while the workers were simply victims. Whatever the rights of the argument over surplus capacity, the human fact was that the workers were trapped in a region of high unemployment and old, declining indutstries. Many of the younger and more mobile, seeing the writing on the wall, had left some time before; those who had stayed were usually those with least alternative. If, now, the steel plants were to be closed, what on earth were they and their families to do? And what of the communities in which many of them had grown up? However small the hope of life, Lorraine was, as the workers rather pathetically put it, a region 'which did not want to die'.

The second – and equally obvious – target was the government of M. Raymond Barre. Quite apart from the government's policies towards the steel industry in the past and its arrogant tactics now, the Barre government was deeply unpopular with the workers on general grounds. For the last three years the country had been subjected to Barre's austerity plan, the Blois Programme. In its main objectives – the shrinking of the trade deficit and the consolidation of the franc on the exchange markets – the plan had had considerable success: but at great cost. Inflation had stuck around 10 per cent, growth fell to 2.6 per cent in 1978 (against a 5.5 per cent average in the 1960s), investment stagnated and unemployment had soared at the rate of 250,000 a year. In the face of the rising tide of protest Barre, a portly academic economist entirely innocent of grassroots experience of any kind, had displayed a cheerful and autocratic inflexibility. Indeed, he had gone rather out of his way to advertise his cavalier disregard for mere 'carriers of placards' and 'the choir of cry-babies' (the unemployed). Barre enjoyed stressing how entirely willing he was to consult with anyone, even the opposition, but in practice was too convinced of his own rectitude to listen to anything less than full agreement. The steelworkers of Lorraine needed little encouragement to see such a man as their natural enemy.

In the period preceding the 1978 election Giscard had betrayed an understandable nervousness about the political impact of the Blois Programme and Barre had been forced to rein in on his eager pursuit of austerity. (During the election itself, of course, the government had somehow neglected to publish the latest unemployment figures.) But since March 1978 Barre had had his head and had embarked with fresh vigour on his campaign to make the French economy respond to the 'logic of capitalism'. Hugely encouraged by the election result, the government had pushed through a sweeping abolition of industrial price controls. The result could only be inflationary, but it would do wonders for company profits and thus, it was piously hoped, for business investment. To workers the logic seemed dubious: with the dole queues lengthening, in part as the result of official government policy, Barre's response was to hand more money to his friends, the employers. They *were* his friends too: François Ceyrac, the head of the employers' organisation, the Conseil National du Patronat Français (CNPF), was a close associate of Barre's and was frequently pictured with him in the press (the two men dined together on a regular private basis, quite apart from official functions). Indeed, it seemed quite likely that the Barre plan was really the Ceyrac plan – it was well known, for example, that Ceyrac had played the key role in initiating and framing the new price decontrol policy. It was difficult, in a word, for workers to feel that their interests were anywhere close to the government's heart. After all, *their* political and trade union representatives only saw Barre when he appeared on television . . .

It would be unfair to claim that the steelworkers of Lorraine had ever expected much of such a government. It wasn't *their* government anyway. The towns where they lived tended to elect Communist deputies and hardly expected political favours as a result. But nor were their feelings for the Left entirely uncomplicated, either. Like most other workers they had supported the Left strongly and from 1974 to 1977 had been swept along in a mood of almost euphoric unity. While the Left had stayed united it had seemed almost certain that its *dynamique unitaire* would sweep it to victory in the 1978 elections. But the bitter quarrel which had opened up between the leaders of the Left parties had ended that hope. These divisions and the terrible disappointment of March 1978 had led many workers virtually to despair of political action. The Left had let the workers down; it was all just dirty politics after all. When Edmond Maire[11] said that the trade unions had been wrong to count so heavily on the political victory of the Left, that they should have remained more detached from the game of parties and concentrated on trade unionism pure and simple, he found a strong echoing response in such milieux. Not that the workers could quite say 'a plague on all their houses'. They were of the Left, would – less enthusiastically – vote for it again, and looked back with bitter nostalgia to the days of Left unity. In any case, only a Left victory could have saved them. The PCF had been determined to nationalise the steel industry and despite considerable wavering on the issue by Michel Rocard,[12] the Socialists had finally come out in favour of it, too. With nationalisation and a Left government, the workers knew, plant closures would have been virtually inconceivable. The quarrels of the Left had cost them their hopes and were now costing them their jobs and the life of the communities in which they lived.

After the election there had been much wild talk of a 'long hot summer' or a 'hot autumn' in which the trade unions and workers might vent their disappointment on the government. This had been absurd – the workers were far too demoralised, confused and disoriented to consider such strong initiatives. Hearing themselves already depicted in such talk as politically motivated aggressors, many workers had concluded – quite rightly – that it was the prelude to a renewed offensive against them. The government, after all, was anxious to reward its friends in the *patronat* for their prodigious financial support at election time and, after March 1978, it was a government which felt it could get away with almost *anything*. Of course, Barre and Ceyrac – government and bosses, they were the same thing, *le pouvoir* – didn't put it that way. They continually preached the need for sacrifice in the national interest and the necessity for Frenchmen to look across the Rhine and try to emulate the miracles of German industrial achievement. What this meant was: work harder, a moral difficult to apply to the steelworkers' current plight. It seemed a tasteless joke, particularly when French employers had not waited for German levels of achievement before paying themselves salaries larger than their German counterparts received.[13] While the steelworkers had spent their family Christmas and New Year holiday anxiously worrying whether they would be employed next year, their employers had been off skiing or on holidays in tropical climes which cost a worker's whole annual pay packet. So the Communists said, anyway.

Since the election the Communists had, in effect, been attempting to recover ground lost to the Socialists by transforming themselves into a sort of super-trade union. Such efforts were almost entirely negated by the prevailing mood of cynicism towards all politicians, particularly since many workers felt the PCF was probably the main culprit in the quarrel which had cost the Left the election. The PCF had, however, discovered a fruitful new line in its furiously anti-EEC stance, aimed at distancing itself from the (more pro-European) PS. With the European direct elections of June 1979 looming in its sights, the PCF had seized on the fact that the steel redundancies were the result of the EEC's Davignon plan and referred to the EEC only as '*l'Europe du chomage*'. In Lorraine this made a certain sense. Belgium and Luxemburg were only a stone's throw away, and three times in the last century German armies had rolled through the area in wars which had Alsace-Lorraine as one of the main prizes. The great battlefields of 1870 were right there, after all – Metz and Sedan. One knew about the Germans. All these neighbouring countries had steel industries of their own and some of that steel was being sold into France. It was a new sort of war in its way, one in which towns like Longwy and Denain might suffer greater damage now than they had in the blitzkrieg of 1940. The government, the workers felt, should be keeping foreign steel out, not getting together with foreign governments to co-ordinate plans to make more French workers unemployed. The whole situation, they felt, was grotesque. It was too much, far, far too much.

This mood of anger and comprehensive bitterness mounted throughout January 1979, with a growing wave of protests, demonstrations and spectacular incidents, often of a quite spontaneous nature. The unions were keenly aware that they were not in control of this mood, much as they attempted to put themselves forward as the spokesmen of grievance. The union leaders could recognise better than anyone the welling up of the anarcho-syndicalist habits of thought and behaviour which still provide the last recourse of the French working-class. In times of relative industrial peace such habits lay dormant or in the background and, despite the unions' small membership and political divisions, they were able to exercise a steady influence, if seldom real power. But if the workers were provoked too far, if they felt their backs against the wall, there would be a danger of a major social explosion which, the unions knew, they would be unable to channel or control. The government, for its part, nervously began to feel that it might have miscalculated. Normally, both it and the employers evinced an easy satisfaction at the weakness of the trade unions and helped weaken them further by their contemptuous refusal to accord them real consultative status. Now it was agreed that the Minister for Industry, M. André Giraud, would meet the leaders of the steel unions in Paris on 23 February. In the steel towns the whole population waited anxiously upon this last chance. As the date approached, tension mounted.

On 21 February the tension snapped .[14] During the afternoon a group of workers occupied the Longwy offices of Credit Lyonnais (the bank had nothing to do with the crisis and was apparently chosen simply as a symbol of French capitalism). In the evening some 100 CFDT militants occupied the local television transmitter and, announcing their disgust with the media coverage of the crisis on the eve of the crucial talks, forced the nineteen local journalists they found there to broadcast programmes putting the workers' point of view. The Prefect of Meurthe-et-Moselle, doubtless acting on orders from Paris, quickly requisitioned a team of electricians who, under heavy police guard, managed to cut off the transmitter's power supply, bringing the broadcasts to a dead halt at 9 p.m. The workers stayed put and only released the journalists at 2 a.m. following a desperate phone-call to them by Michel Rolant, a national secretary of the CFDT. M. Rolant put out a statement saying that, while all mass actions were justified in the circumstances, no interference with the freedom of the press or the individual could be tolerated. In effect this amounted to saying that the union would attempt to legitimate what it was powerless to stop – for the occupation itself continued.

Early next morning workers moved into the railway stations at Valenciennes, Denain and Aulnoye-Aymeries, preventing any further movement of rail traffic. At the same time roadblocks sprang up, cutting traffic dead in all three towns. The particular object of these measures was to prevent the movement not only of foreign steel into the area, but of any products used in steel manufacture. At a routine meeting of the joint factory committee at Fonderies de Gorcy at Longwy, the workers' delegates pounced on the management representatives and held them prisoner, while at the Usinor plant CGT militants invaded the offices of the plant director and personnel chief, hurling their furniture and papers out of the window.

It was against this background that the crucial meeting between M. Giraud and the steel unions began on 23 February. After ten hours of fierce but fruitless discussion the Minister announced a series of measures already decided on by the government, badly shaken by the ferocity of the workers' response. With the aim of preventing any 'special' rise in unemployment in Longwy or Denain in 1979 the retirement age would be lowered from fifty-five to fifty and (since few workers were expected to take advantage of that option) the government would set up 'reconversion companies' to retrain steelworkers. The unions were bitterly dissatisfied, viewing such companies as mere 'unemployment ghettos' and 'parking lots for the workless'. The CGT announced that, as far as they were concerned, 'nothing was settled' and CFDT spoke of 'an opportunity of avoiding a social explosion' being thrown away. Such pronouncements ignored the not inconsiderable fact that the government was promising, on the face of it, to shelve the redundancy programme for a whole year. The unions, pushed hard from below, were hardly able to sound grateful for such small mercies: the appearance of anything less than uncompromising militancy would risk loss of control over their own members.

The news reached Longwy and Denain on Friday evening. Since the government had now played its hand, the local Prefect moved to end the occupation of the Longwy television transmitter, which had, by then, lasted for three days. At 2.30 a.m. on Saturday morning 150 *gendarmes mobiles*, backed up by large numbers of police, stormed the transmitter, surprised the fifty workers inside, confiscated their films and equipment, and turned them out on the street. No arrests were made and the police dispersed quickly, eager to avoid any further confrontations. The workers hastened off to the surrounding steel plants to tell their story to their fellow workers on night-shift duty at the furnaces. One group returned almost immediately with such reinforcements and, finding the transmitter unguarded by police, reoccupied it without difficulty.

Meanwhile, unaware that this objective had already been gained, a separate meeting of CFDT militants in a neighbouring plant resolved that they would rally their forces to retake the transmitter. Factory hooters were sounded and a loud-hailer car toured the streets to summon workers from their beds. Assuming – erroneously – that the transmitter would now be under heavy police guard, the militants 'requisitioned' a bulldozer and a truck full of quicklime was overturned in the access road to the transmitter to prevent the police bringing up reinforcements. The crowd then surged towards the transmitter and only at this stage did they discover that it had been retaken by their own forces some hours before. In order to avoid this comic-opera anticlimax the crowd now decided upon an assault on the local Police Commissariat.

The attack began at 6 a.m. in the freezing wintry dawn – it had been delayed in order to strengthen the force with workers coming off the night shift. Many of these now streamed straight from the plants to the town centre, steel-helmeted and armed with steel bars. The surrounding streets and the road to Metz were blocked with trucks to prevent the return of the gendarmerie and the bulldozer was rigged up with a battering ram with which to break down the steel doors of the Commissariat, inside which were some twenty nervous policemen. These latter were in steady radio and telephone contact with reinforcements which, however, the authorities held back, hoping the Commissariat could hold out without them and knowing that the arrival of several hundred gendarmes on the scene would provoke a pitched battle from which casualties, even fatalities, might well result.

Their luck held. The bulldozer could not break down the door and from the broken windows of the Commissariat the police kept up a barrage of tear-gas and smoke grenades against their attackers. For over two hours the police fired away at the steady rate of six or seven grenades a minute, so that the light of morning found the whole centre of town wreathed in swirling gas and smoke. A crowd of about 1,000 people milled around in some confusion, watching, more or less passively, the determined efforts of the assault force of some 200 or so. These latter made repeated charges, hurling steel pins, bolts, ball-bearings and ingots at the Commissariat, only to be repeatedly repulsed by the wall of smoke and gas. Several of the attackers – local journalists claimed never to have seen them around the town before – seemed to have almost professional skills in street-fighting and began to hurl Molotov cocktails (bottles and beer-cans of flaming petrol) through the broken windows of the Commissariat. Three of them actually had guns – two held hunting rifles and one a .22 long carbine. When local CFDT militants saw this latter figure purposefully loading his gun all three were hurriedly disarmed. For by now the local trade union leadership, both CGT and CFDT, was thoroughly alarmed, and tried strenuously to bring the attack to an end. Indeed, it seems fairly certain that the union leadership had, during the early hours of the morning, made a deal with the police whereby they would try to restore order if the police would hold back from provocative shows of force.

By 8.15 a.m. the attack on the Commissariat petered out – the police inside later said they could not have held out more than another hour, having already expended some 800 grenades. The CGT and CFDT leaders finally managed to convince the crowd that further action was futile and that the best thing to do was to set up barricades on the edge of Longwy to prevent the arrival of police reinforcements. While this tactic succeeded in getting a number of militants out of the town centre, a considerable crowd continued to mill around there. There was a lull while many retired to cafés or homes for breakfast, but at 10 a.m. enough were refreshed and ready for further action to attack the offices of the local employers' association. The offices were completely sacked and the furniture pulled out on the street and set alight. The town fire brigade arrived but was prevented from putting the fire out.

Until this point most of the running had been made by CFDT militants, although the CGT was the predominant union in the steel plants. The CGT leaders now decided they must act strongly to take the situation in hand. It was, by now, mid-Saturday morning and with a steadily growing crowd of over 2,000 milling around in the town centre, almost anything might happen. Accordingly CGT militants now swept the streets and shops clear of people, ordering the shops to shut and the crowds to go home. The plan, they said, was to make Longwy 'a dead town' as a symbolic gesture of protest. No sooner was the centre clear than, as if by prearranged signal, seven truckloads of gendarmes burst, with suspicious ease, through the barricades intended to stop them and stationed themselves in front of the Commissariat. At this stage the local Communist deputy for Longwy, M. Antoine Porcu, materialised for the first time and told the remaining crowd that 'uncontrolled groups', were 'trying to embitter public opinion. We won't let them do it'.[15] He appealed to them all to return home now prior to giving their support to a large peaceful demonstration organised by the PCF for that afternoon. The demonstration passed off without incident and Sunday, blessedly, intervened . . . much to the relief, no doubt, of the local Communists.

Passion was, however, by no means spent. The Longwy chief police commissioner, M. Albert Michel, surveying the near-ruin of his Commissariat (with repair work now providing employment for twenty men), claimed to have found ten bullet marks on the building. This was no mean feat amidst the general shambles – the windows were all smashed, the roof was in tatters, furniture inside had been burnt and fourteen cars belonging to the besieged policemen had been heavily damaged. In particular it must have taken great expertise in detection on M. Michel's part to distinguish between the marks made by ten bullets amidst the thousands of marks left by the steel ball-bearings hurled in such profusion against the building. M. Michel warned, moreover, that another such attack was to be expected. This pronouncement drew the ire of Longwy's Communist Mayor, M. Jules Jean, who immediately demanded of the Prefect that he suspend M. Michel for remarks of such gross provocation. This request, as M. Jean doubtless anticipated, was ignored. The shadow-boxing of local politics, like the old programmes from the television transmitter, had been resumed.

Meanwhile the workers continued to display their anger. On 28 February the court rooms at Longwy were occupied by workers again (for the third time) and occupations of banks, building societies and other symbols of capital continued quite routinely, as did the blockage of roads and railways throughout the area to prevent the movement of all 'foreign products necessary to steel production'. But such activities now showed signs of spreading away from Longwy proper. At near-by Homécourt the factory manager of the Sacilor steel plant unwisely announced a number of 'technical redundancies' on 28 February. His office was immediately occupied by workers, who held him prisoner until the early hours of the next morning when he was freed on the intercession of the CGT and local PCF representatives. On the same day hundreds of workers in Valenciennes attacked the offices of the director of the steel employers' association, completely sacking them before setting them alight. Only the speedy intervention of the fire service prevented the whole block from going up in flames.

Throughout the Lorraine region occupations, road- and railblocks, and sequestration of personnel had now become a widely generalised phenomenon. Almost any government building was a potential target – at Cambrai the local tax offices were sacked and, doubtless to the pleasure of many citizens beyond the proletariat, a large bonfire of tax records and files was lit. Longwy, indeed, began to seem an oasis of relative calm, particularly once it was announced that the plan for the 'restructuring' of the main Usinor plants had been indefinitely suspended. The unions cautioned that a battle, not the war, had been won but it was, clearly, a major victory. Less cautiously, M. Giraud, the Industry Minister, announced that a 'dramatic situation' no longer existed in Longwy. The very next day, however, witnessed a bizarre and literally theatrical event when 100 CFDT militants from Longwy descended on Metz, where the rock singer, Johnny Hallyday, was giving a concert and hauled him back for a tour of the Usinor plant at Longwy lasting until 3.30 a.m. the next morning. The gesture, they said, was intended to show the public that 'they could do other things besides fight the forces of law and order'.[16] Hallyday, understandably, professed himself 'surprised' but took it in good part and declared he would be 'delighted' if his presence was of any help to the workers. More significant, however, were the events which had begun to unfold in the steel town of Denain at the very moment that M. Giraud was welcoming the returning calm at Longwy.

Denain, which perches on the Belgian border not far south of Lille, is very much a film producer's idea of what a steel company town might look like. The main street, the Avenue de Villars, has a statue of Marshal Villars at one end and, at the other, the Usinor plant: a series of enormous grey buildings topped by eight prodigious chimneys. One does not leave the town centre to get to the factories – the factory site *is* the town centre. All around are row upon row of prim little red-brick workers' cottages with tiny vegetable gardens struggling for life amidst the industrial haze. The roads in which these houses lie all bear the same designation, 'Chemin particulier de la Compagnie des mines d'Anzin'. Behind lie slagheaps, untidily half-covered with straggling urban vegetation. It is difficult to believe that this sad, grey little place ever had a pre-industrial existence, despite the statue of Villars, hammer of the Huguenots, Commander of the Rhine, conqueror of all southern Germany. But there is no mistaking the inscription – it was here, at the battle of Denain in 1712, that Villars defeated the Austrian host under Prince Eugène. It seems as distant as Julius Caesar: a time before the factories were born and when the chimneys had not grown so tall.

On the evening of 6 March workers from Usinor-Denain set out, as they had for weeks past, 'on operation' – that is, to block the transit of foreign steel or associated products by road or rail. That day, however, turned out to be different, for the authorities had decided abruptly (Giraud's declaration may have been a sign of it) that this sort of thing must stop. When one group of workers reached Saint-Amand-les-Eaux they found the usual detachments of police and CRS (*Compagnies Républicaines de Securité* – the riot police) with whom, over the weeks, they had enjoyed a friendly joking relationship. This time, however, the Denain police Commissioner, M. Pastorini, ordered the police to break the demonstration up right away. After a number of charges by the tough CRS the rather battered workers beat a retreat to Denain, where about 100 of them vented their anger in a brief assault on the Commissariat de Police.

Meanwhile two other busloads of Denain workers were returning from similar operations at the frontier when, as they passed through the forest of Hasnon, they were overtaken by two CRS motor-cyclists who signalled the buses to halt. As they did so further detachments of CRS hove into view. The driver of the first bus was told to get out. 'Why should I get out? I'm doing my job.' 'So much the worse for you', he was told. The CRS then surrounded the bus, smashed its windows with rifle butts and hurled tear-gas grenades inside, simultaneously preventing any of its fifty passengers from getting out. At length the retching and gasping passengers (who included several trade union officials and a Denain municipal councillor) were allowed out one by one, to be roughed up by the police and made to stand hands against the side of the bus in true hold-up style as they were subjected to rigorous body-searches. Finally they were allowed to remount their now badly damaged buses and reel back to Denain to tell their story.

The authorities' strategy appears to have been based on the assumption that, now that the suspension of redundancies (applying to Denain as well as Longwy) had been announced, the workers had no further cause for grievance and that, accordingly, their 'operations' must be brought to a sharp and, indeed, brutal halt. If so (and it is the best sense one can make of their actions) they betrayed a woeful ignorance of the depth of the workers' resentment. A great groundswell of anger and bitterness had gained strength over a period of several months, a mood which was not to be instantly or easily dissipated by a mere suspension of execution. Left alone, this mood would doubtless have subsided gradually, burning itself low, if not out. Instead, the authorities had provocatively attacked the workers, treating even their trade union and political representatives as suspected criminals. The workers could turn the other cheek – accept their humiliation – or have a cathartic showdown with the CRS, who now stood several deep around Denain's Commissariat de Police.

Next day some 1,600 workers from Usinor-Denain walked out of the morning shift to 'decide on how to hit back'. Their union leaders, doubtless mindful of the recent fracas at Longwy, managed to push through a resolution to cut the Paris-Brussels autoroute. It was no use: incidents had already begun around the police Commissariat and it was to this scene that the militants were irresistibly drawn. By mid-morning a full battle was in progress between around 2,000 workers, armed with steel bars, bolts and pins, and the CRS, who used tear-gas and chlorine grenades. Towards midday the (PCF) Mayor of Denain, Henri Fièvres, phoned the Commissariat to suggest a truce on account of the 1,200 children due to leave their high school, close by the Commissariat, at 12.30. According to the Mayor, agreement was reached on his plan to prevent the children emerging on to the field of battle. The union leaders managed to pull back the line of workers and the police and CRS were ordered to retire inside their trucks. As the children emerged, however, the CRS were ordered out of their vehicles again and then launched them in a charge against the retreating line of workers, with whom hundreds of children now mingled. Pandemonium ensued, with the CRS actually shooting grenades inside the school buildings (forty grenade cases were later picked up there). The effect was, of course, a violent renewal of hostilities as the workers returned to the assault on the Commissariat in a mood of utter fury.

The Mayor held hurried council with local CGT and Communist leaders. There was now little chance that they could restrain the workers and the only hope of preventing further escalation lay in a deal with the authorities. They phoned the commissariat again, announcing that they were sending a delegation led by the Deputy Mayor to negotiate a truce. The delegation set forth, bearing a tricolor, only to be met with a shower of tear-gas grenades, and when they reached the Commissariat, subjected to a body search. In the street the battle raged on. By 4 o'clock the workers, far from slackening after six hours of fighting, had requisitioned a bulldozer to aid their charges.

At 6 o'clock the Mayor, flanked by three PCF deputies for the area and representatives of all the trade union organisations, held a press conference. After denouncing the CRS and the police, the Mayor (who was invited to 'change his job and domicile as rapidly as possible') admitted that he and the PCF were at their wit's end. They had effectively lost control of the workers – they spoke of a completely recalcitrant hard-core group of about 1,000 – and feared the loss of lives if the fighting continued much longer. The Mayor and his deputies then set out to leaflet the streets and homes with tracts calling on workers to return to their factories and occupy them, calling on them to support a peaceful demonstration the next day and reminding them that the government had, after all, agreed to suspend the 'restructuring' of Usinor-Denain. Nothing more vividly revealed the weakness of the elected authorities than that, though Communists, they were now reduced to pleading the government's case to the workers. It was no use. Many workers tore up the leaflets as they received them and others refused to accept them at all. The fighting continued. The Deputy Mayor and local trade union leaders retired gloomily to a near-by café, Le Point Central, to wait upon events.

By evening the street combatants had dwindled to the hard-core 1,000 or so, including a clearly discernible group of about 100 *gauchistes*. As at Longwy this group showed considerable street-fighting skills and had manufactured a supply of Molotov cocktails to hurl at the CRS as well as slings and catapults with which to fire ball-bearings. An ominous new weapon made its appearance: camping-gas canisters wrapped in bundles of flaming straw. Several score of these impressive home-made bombs were manufactured and hurled at the CRS.

With midnight approaching, the police, who after more than thirteen hours of battle must have been nearing exhaustion, seem to have decided to bring things to a summary halt. They were, after all, heavily armed and had refrained from using their simplest weapon up to this point. But if guns were now to be used, spectators would be a nuisance. Such, at least, was the popular interpretation of the sudden CRS raid now made on Le Point Central. According to the trade union and municipal officials who had been sitting gloomily over their beers in the café, the CRS suddenly burst in, searched all present and warned them to stay inside whatever happened. They then retired to the street, smashed the café windows and fired seven tear-gas grenades inside. As the occupants reeled desperately about trying to escape the fumes, they heard firing break out in the street. In the end some thirty demonstrators were seriously injured, including one whose foot was shredded by bullets and another whose hand had to be amputated. The police sustained fifteen casualties, including seven with bullet wounds from a .22 rifle. Hostilities now ceased, leaving the statue of Marshal Villars gazing down on the debris of this second battle of Denain.

The next day the trade union leaders reached a truce agreement with the Deputy Prefect (the Prefect himself waved away protests, saying he had come to regard himself as a 'permanent accused'). The union leaders agreed to pull back their men and the authorities agreed to pull the 700 CRS and *gendarmes mobiles* out of the town. Despite this, however, three truckloads of CRS remained stationed in front of the Commissariat and there was much angry discussion among the large crowd (of around 6,000) in the streets about what to do. Around 5 o'clock about 150 teenagers attempted to recommence the assault on the Commissariat but were easily dispersed. Two air-rifles were confiscated. By now, however, the PCF and CGT had reasserted their control over a populace which in any case evinced a sense of emotional disarray and shock.

On Saturday (10 March) some 25,000 people assembled for the peaceful demonstration promised by the PCF. Sympathisers had come from far and wide to show solidarity. The local PCF and CGT headed the procession but there was also a contingent from Longwy and, at the back, a Socialist contingent led by Mauroy and his partisans from Lille. The Communists, eager to parade their 'national' face, carried the tricolour, sang 'La Marseillaise', and shouted slogans against the EEC; the Socialists, anxious to show they were left-wing (and not necessarily against the EEC), sang 'L'Internationale'; the Longwyites, keen to display their recently established links with the world of popular music, sang the compositions of Johnny Hallyday . . .

This was, though, the only light note. It was a sad procession in a sad town. It rained; the rain turned to snow. Many of the children in the procession wore around their necks the empty canisters of spent tear-gas grenades – they'd been able to pick up some of them inside their own school. But the dominant mood was sombre rather than angry. There was, this time, no trouble – for there was not a policeman in sight. The demonstration had, in any case, a meaning which ran deeper than simply a protest against police tactics, government policy or the immediate sorrows of Longwy, Denain and the other steel towns. Few of those who marched now could fail to remember other great demonstrations of Left unity in which they had participated in recent years. They had been joyous, exultant affairs. For, in the mid-1970s, after the long night of conservative rule, a great hope had been born on the French Left. The Right, no longer shored up by the awesome figure of De Gaulle, had fallen into an apparently irreversible decline and the Left had felt sure its time had come at last. Moreover, the whole Left – Communists, Socialists and even Left Radicals – had put their old quarrels behind them. It had been a crusade of brothers and it had gone from strength to strength.

All that had been shattered by the events of 1977–8 and the pieces still lay everywhere on the ground. The parties of the Left had quarrelled and gone down to crushing defeat. All the old hopelessness had come flooding back: perhaps the Left could *never* win. To walk in procession now was to feel a deep and painful nostalgia for the brave and hopeful days before that fall. The demonstration became a procession, a cortège at the funeral of the Left's hopes. But there was something more, too. What had brought all these people together, many of them from far beyond the steel towns, was the need to assert that the Left would not lie down under defeat. They could not accept that the Left should be disarmed by its own demoralisation. They had counted for too much, they had felt their strength and they were determined that others should acknowledge it, too. Perhaps – and the wish was father to the thought – the Left might rise again, might yet have its day.

But why and how had it all happened? The Right had seemed virtually invulnerable ever since De Gaulle's foundation of the Fifth Republic in 1958 and had gone on winning quite comfortably even after the General's demise. Why, then, had its strength ebbed away with such apparent suddenness in the mid-1970s? Equally, the Communists and Socialists had behind them a long history of weakness and fratricidal conflict, referring to one another as the *frères-ennemis*. How had it happened that the apparently dying Socialist Party had, in the space of a few years, doubled in size to become the largest party in France? And how had the Left managed so dramatically to rediscover a unity it had not known for forty years? And why, then, did the Left squander all it had gained, throwing that hard-won unity overboard just as victory loomed in sight? Was it, as some said, because the Communists did not, in their hearts, want the Left to win? Or was Left unity really so crucial – could the Left have won the 1978 elections even it *had* remained united? Rocard, for one, was behaving now as if he thought the Left might have a better chance if Socialists and Communists were quite open about their differences. But, above all, did it *need* to be like this? In just under two years the Left had gone all the way from the euphoria of electoral triumph to the scenes of bitter and almost hopeless protest we have described above; from winning three-quarters of the towns of France in March 1977 to shooting in the streets of Denain in March 1979. But the road was much longer than that – it had not begun in 1977. It had been a long, long march. The journey had been too bitter and too miserable for the questions not to be asked. Was victory for the Left truly impossible? Even after the débâcle of 1978, could not the Left somehow rise again?

# 2 The Last Left Government

## i THE REVOLUTION THAT NEVER WAS

On his swing through the South of France on the eve of the Socialist Congress of April 1979, François Mitterrand, anxious to leave no stone unturned in his battle to retain the party's leadership, stopped at the little town of Bandol to address the local PS section. Some 300 people (more than twice the section's membership) packed into the tiny village hall to hear him. The Mayor, literally moved to tears by the folk-memory of a previous political visit, explained his emotion to the Socialist leader: 'The last great personality who stopped at Bandol was Clemenceau. In 1908. And the mayor, a Socialist, refused to shake his hand.' Cheers, as well as laughter, prevented the Mayor from getting much further with his welcome...[1]

As the French Left contemplates its own history in this century the foreground is usually occupied by such memories of brave refusals and heroic gestures, for its concrete achievements have been few. In part it is a question – as Tom Lehrer used to sing of the Spanish Civil War – of 'They won all the battles, but we had all the best songs'. But the theme runs deeper than that. Resistance is remembered better than victory, gallantry in defeat better than pleasure in winning. It is part of this trait that gives the Popular Front government of 1936 so hallowed a place in the folk-memory of the Left. True, thanks to that government's institution of paid vacations many working-class families enjoyed their first ever holidays in the glorious summer weather of that never-to-be-forgotten year. But the fact remains that the Blum government – the *only* truly left-wing government of the Third Republic – was a dismal failure. The Communists refused to join it (though they supported it). It faced crippling waves of sit-down strikes; failed ignominiously to support the Spanish Republic and: had virtually no real programme; was rent by dissension; devalued the franc; and lasted only a year.

Yet, without any doubt, the Blum government is remembered with greater romantic affection than the only other left-wing government France has known to date, the tripartite coalition of Communists, Socialists and Christian Democrats (the MRP – *Mouvement Républicain Populaire*) which ruled France from September 1944 to May 1947.[2] This is true despite the vastly more impressive record of the tripartite government. It was, for a start, enormously strong – its three constituent parties had three-quarters of the popular vote and of the parliamentary seats between them – and it lasted much longer. Despite the utter chaos of the post-war crisis, it pushed through a series of fundamental reforms. It nationalised coal, gas, electricity, Renault, the Bank of France and four of the great deposit banks – Crédit Lyonnais, BNCI, the

Société Générale, and the Comptoir d'Escompte – as well as part of the aviation industry; it set up Air France, Agence France Presse (AFP) and various other state agencies; it created a vastly improved social security system (nationalising thirty-four assurance companies), reformed the labour laws, raised pensions, instituted generous family allowances, launched an immense hydro-electric construction programme, and created an Atomic Energy Commissariat (directed by the Communist scientist Frédéric Joliot-Curie). Moreover, thanks largely to the strong restraining influence of its Communist Ministers on the trade unions, it was able to hold a wage-freeze for several years in the teeth of an inflationary gale. The result was hardly appreciated by the working-class – by October 1946 real wages had fallen 50 per cent from their 1937 level and the PCF came down hard against workers who wanted to strike to improve things. But the fact was that these measures, together with the workers' sacrifices, played an indispensable role in the great effort of national reconstruction on which all later French economic success was to depend. In 1919, after the First World War, the index of general production had stood at 57 per cent of its 1913 level, climbing slowly to only 78 per cent in 1922 and 88 per cent in 1923. In 1944 the position was much worse – the index was only 35 per cent of the 1938 figure – but two years later it had already recovered to 90 per cent. In the two years after the Liberation France achieved what she had not managed in five after the First World War.[3]

Moreover, the tripartite government did not merely seek to redress the social balance by the extension of State control; it was, too, in the fullest sense a government of emancipation. It repealed the whole body of repressive Vichy legislation – but was remarkably restrained in reprisals against collaborators, for all the Right's hysterical claims to the contrary.[4] It instituted elected factory committees throughout French industry. It extended full citizenship rights – including the vote – to the feminine majority of the population (who rewarded the Left by voting against it). It carried through sweeping colonial reforms, creating elected assemblies in all the colonies and welcoming into the Paris National Assembly seventy-five colonial deputies, including several scores of Arabs, Africans and Asians. If anything, the government had to be faulted not for excessive *étatisme*, but for sometimes ill-judged libertarianism. Far too many Vichyites escaped scot-free. Food rationing was abolished too soon and had to be reimposed as the free market ran wild, with disastrous results. Even the system of publicly licensed brothels was abolished. Amidst much ribald comment private enterprise rose magnificently to *that* challenge, however . . .

For all its problems, and despite the chaos of post-Liberation France (where, for example, black market motor licences were being sold by the Prefecture of Police),[5] the record of *tripartisme* remains impressive. Yet the memory of this, the last Left government, is not particularly cherished on the Left; it evokes respect, sometimes a certain pride; but not, on the whole, affection. There are two main reasons for this. First, there is the solid fact that the government presented the anomalous spectacle of a united Left presiding over a steep deterioration in working-class incomes and, probably, a corresponding redistribution towards the better off. The passage of time, later affluence and the assimilation of the hardships of those years into a generalised 'wartime experience' have, however, all tended to blur and soften this reproach.

A far more powerful argument – one whose force has increased, not diminished with time – has also tended to reduce the stature of *tripartisme*: the notion that *tripartisme* was the shabby compromise forced upon the workers in place of a full-blooded revolution. According to this view the PCF should never have accepted the disarmament of its Resistance *maquis* but should, instead, have carried through the armed struggle to final revolutionary triumph in much the same way as occurred in Yugoslavia and Albania. The PCF and, more particularly, its leader, Maurice Thorez, are the major villains of such an account, for they stand accused of simply throwing away perhaps the greatest revolutionary opportunity the French Left has ever had, opting instead for a sort of Stalinist reformism whose main victim was the French working-class. In such accounts[6] Thorez's reiterated condemnation of strikes and his appeals for national production are generally set against his entire subservience to Stalinist directives, in particular Stalin's deal with the West at Yalta whereby France was to remain within the Anglo-American sphere of influence. This is further taken to 'prove' that neither Stalin nor the PCF had any interest in the propagation of Socialist revolution in the West; if they had, it is implied, Thorez would have behaved more like a French Tito or (preferably) Mao.

Such a view, espoused by a minority within the PCF at the Liberation, has gradually become almost the conventional wisdom within a wide circle of Left opinion. In the wake of the 1968 May Events the conviction hardened among many intellectuals that the PCF was constitutionally incapable of exploiting *any* revolutionary situation. In such an atmosphere the myth of the 'lost revolution' of 1944–5 naturally flourished. It is, accordingly, necessary to confront this view head-on. For, as revisionist history, it reflects at best a staggering degree of intellectual confusion, at worst a wilful, almost childish, naïveté born of disappointed romanticism.

One may certainly concede that the decisive pivot of the situation lay in the Yalta agreement. But Stalin made the best deal he could get at Yalta. In October 1944 he had won Churchill's consent to Russian primacy in Bulgaria and Roumania and 50 per cent control in Yugoslavia and Hungary, in return for Western primacy in Greece.[7] Later, thanks to the fact that the West was only too happy to leave the bloody job of driving the Nazis out of Eastern Europe to the Red Army, Stalin was able to add Poland, Czechoslovakia and East Germany to the Communist camp as well. There was never any question of Communist frontiers stretching further than that. (Indeed, the continuing myth of expansionist Soviet intentions in Western Europe has never come to terms with the fact that the Red Army actually honoured its commitment to evacuate Austria, Finland and northern Iran at the end of the war. The myth survives, as myths tend to do on both Right and Left, largely as a result of wilful historical amnesia.)

As far as France, Italy and the Low Countries were concerned, Stalin was well aware that the Western Allies would brook no compromise; indeed, that they would hold Moscow directly responsible for any attempt at revolution in those countries. In practice, of course, the presence of their armies in Western Europe gave the British and Americans the same *de facto* ability to dictate that region's future political complexion as the presence of the Red Army in Eastern Europe gave to the Russians there. Stalin was only too keen that this modern extension of *cuius regio, eius religio* should be recognised, for it gave the USSR a better deal than it could have achieved any other way. Where the Red Army was not in a position to control events – not just in France or Italy, but in Greece, Yugoslavia, Albania and China – Stalin cautioned the local Communist leaderships against any hope of revolutionary victory. When such hopes were, none the less, realised in the latter three cases, Stalin was, of course, gratified – but quite publicly surprised. The Red Army, with little help from the Allies, had destroyed the hitherto invincible Wehrmacht – until then the mightiest land army ever seen – and Stalin saw it, quite rightly, as by far the most powerful weapon of the international Communist movement. Bolshevik soldiers and sailors had made the 1917 Revolution and nobody, anywhere in the world, had made one without them since. The discovery – in China, Yugoslavia and Albania – that the Red Army was not entirely indispensable was something of a shock. The crucial condition, of course, was that the Western armies were absent from these countries, too. This was not the case in France . . .

What Stalin knew, Thorez knew too. (The point was axiomatic – though more under the heading 'Lessons of History' than as a matter of Comintern discipline.) Quite simply, the British and American armies had not shed their blood on the beaches of Normandy and in the forests of Ardennes in order to see the hammer and sickle run up over Paris as the swastika was run down. Apart even from that insuperable fact, any attempt to carry the Resistance through to armed revolution would have encountered grave intrinsic difficulties. No more than 2 per cent of the population – a poorly armed 2 per cent at that – were actively involved in the Resistance[8] and only 60 per cent of them were Communists. The movement's immense moral stature within the country depended in part upon the feelings of guilt and relief amongst the passive majority that at least someone had kept the flag flying; upon a confused identification between the movement and the quite separate figure of De Gaulle; and on a spirit of renascent national unity which the Resistance was taken to symbolise. Revolutionary insurrection, had it occurred, would quickly have lessened the moral sway of the Resistance as it pitted one faction against others, would have deeply affronted the popular longing – felt perhaps most deeply within the working-class itself – for peace, unity and national regeneration. But even had an insurrectionary movement managed, miraculously, to surmount all these obstacles, the presence of the Allied armies would still have doomed it to swift and ignominious defeat. At worst, of course, the terrible carnage which attended just such a Communist insurrection in Greece might have been visited upon France. More likely, however (for the Allied armies were already in France, as they were not in Greece), the event would have been far briefer, less bloody and more purely farcical. Such outcomes were, after all, seen close to home in Holland and, more particularly, Belgium, where the disarmament of the Resistance took place only under the threat of armed force by the Allies against the *maquis*. In the end only thirty-five Resistants were shot and wounded by the Brussels police – though with British tanks standing by should they be needed.[9]

Thus the theory of a 'lost' revolutionary opportunity in the France of 1944–5 must be discarded. It is true that there was support for an insurrectionary struggle amongst significant elements of the PCF at the time.[10] It is true, too, that one may trace a fairly consistent 'reformist' line between Thorez's utterances in support of the Popular Front in 1936[11] and his 'national reconstruction' speeches of 1944–7. It is true, finally, that Thorez was a most faithful servitor of Soviet policy (though, it should be noted, while serving in the tripartite government he picked a quite open quarrel with Stalin over the Saar question).[12] But all this is beside the point. For, quite equally, there was no doubt as to Anglo-American concern over the possibility of a revolutionary insurrection in France,[13] nor any real doubt as to what the Allied response to such an eventuality would have been. When Thorez declared that 'With the Americans in France the revolution would have been annihilated'[14] he was merely facing facts in a way some of his critics have refused to do.

Accordingly – and this is the point of our excursus – *tripartisme*, for all its weaknesses and faults, represented the best alternative available to the Left, even the revolutionary Left, in the situation as it was. This is a cardinal point for, more than thirty years later, *tripartisme* remains the high-water mark reached by the French Left in modern times. Never again was the Left to be so strong, never again was the Right to be so discredited and demobilised. As such it constitutes a key point of reference and departure for any survey of the French Left. *Tripartisme* represents, moreover, a record of achievement which, utopian hopes aside, the Left would do well to equal should it reconquer power at any future date. In just thirty-two months a programme of reforms was pushed through which compared favourably with what, for example, a post-war Labour government was, under far easier circumstances, able to achieve in Britain in six years. It was, undeniably (no one attempted to deny it), a 'reformist' government, but the onus is on those who would affix such an adjective in order to juxtapose some imaginary alternative to show how that alternative could conceivably have taken shape in the real world.

What of the fall in working-class living standards under *tripartisme* with which Claudin and others have so bitterly reproached the Left? French workers certainly made the greatest sacrifices in making the achievements of *tripartisme* possible. It is difficult, though, to see how this could have been otherwise. Similar or greater sacrifices were, after all, being contemporaneously extracted from the working classes of the Soviet Union and Eastern Europe in very much the same 'war' of national reconstruction. It is hard to avoid the inference that in economic wars, as in real ones, the plight of the 'poor bloody infantry' is hardly to be envied. Had revolution somehow occurred in the France of of 1944–5 the lot of the French proletariat in 1945–7 could hardly have been better and, would, far more likely, have been worse.[15] Moreover, such relief as that proletariat was ultimately to gain was to derive in no small part from the effects of Marshall Aid, of which, doubtless, there would have been little hope in a post-revolutionary France . . .

Finally, it may be objected that the arguments marshalled above derive much of their force from the fact that *tripartisme* existed under a historically very special set of external constraints. This is, of course, true – though it is also the case that the Left derived certain special advantages from the post-war international environment which, to put it mildly, it has not enjoyed since: the vast international prestige of the Soviet Union, the general dénouement of the European Right, the not inconsiderable popularity of Stalin, and so on. None the less, the point is not to be dismissed. Indeed, *tripartisme* casts so long a shadow over the French Left precisely *because* it stands as a testament to the significance of international constraints in determining the fate of the European Left. The nature of these constraints has certainly changed since 1947 but it is a moot point whether they have diminished. It was only after 1947 that France joined NATO, whose Charter speaks of its members' commitment to defend one another not only against external attack but against 'internal subversion' – a clause which sprang sharply to mind in 1958 and 1968. Despite the (largely nominal) French departure from NATO such fears were strongly reawakened on the French Left after the 1973 coup against Allende in Chile – and kept awake by Henry Kissinger's reiterated public warnings to the Italians not to allow Communists into their government. Moreover, Germany had, by the 1970s, re-emerged as a powerful conservative force in Western Europe. The funds to prop up right-wing European Socialists which were so generously supplied by the CIA and the Congress for Cultural Freedom in the 1940s and 1950s were, in the 1970s, more likely to come from the ample coffers of German Social Democracy and the Friedrich Ebert *Stiftung*. Moreover, the integration of the world economy has proceeded far and fast since 1947, with France very much at the centre of developments. A Left government now would have to confront the awkward dilemma of the EEC and the fact that the prosperity of the French working-class has come to depend no little on the status of France as the fourth greatest capitalist power in the world. France, in a word, is no more an island now than it was in 1945, and in many ways the possibilities of insularity have diminished since then . . .

## ii THE FALL OF *TRIPARTISME*

In Williams's words, 5 May 1947 was 'the most important date in the history of the Fourth Republic',[16] for it was on that day that *tripartisme* ended. With its ending, all progress towards the radical social democracy the Left had begun to build was halted, and the Left itself was permanently exiled from power. After May 1947 the Fourth Republic became locked in perpetual stalemate. Reform all but ceased and even many of the *tripartiste* reforms were diluted or negated. The Right came increasingly into its own and gradually consolidated its hold on French life – a hold which, after 1958, was to become almost absolute. The consequences of the end of *tripartisme* were so fundamental and lasting that it remains of some moment, even today, to understand how and why this, the last Left government, fell.

*Tripartisme* had, from the beginning, lived under the normal stresses and party rivalries of any coalition government. Thorez had taken the view that the Popular Front government of 1936–7 had failed in the end because the PCF, with only 15 per cent of the popular vote and no Ministers in the government, had been unable to control events and had simply been towed along behind Blum. Now, with the PCF's vastly greater strength and full participation in the government, he hoped to push the government along. After all, the PCF's membership was now near the 1 million mark; in votes, too, it was the biggest party in France; it controlled the trade unions and it alone could hold down the immense upward pressure on wages. In the last analysis, surely, the government simply couldn't do without the Communists, let alone govern *against* them?

Socialist fears were the mirror opposite of these confident hopes. The SFIO (*Section Française de l'Internationale Ouvrière*) was appalled and alarmed to find itself suddenly and for the first time in a junior position to the Communists. The PCF, moreover, was urging on it the idea of organic Left unity which, it was sure, would simply involve the PCF swallowing the SFIO. All over Eastern Europe Social Democrats were being gobbled up into 'Socialist Unity' parties which quickly became mere Communist fronts. The SFIO had no wish to go that way. Instead, the SFIO thankfully reflected that the new system of proportional representation had made electoral alliances with the PCF unnecessary. The Socialists, accordingly, took every opportunity to limit the influence of their over-mighty partners and to mark their distance from them.

The Christian Democrats (MRP), the third leg of the tripartite alliance, stood rather to one side of this quarrel and, at first at least, tended to feel with rather naïve goodwill that the spirit of Resistance unity would tide the coalition through. Their attitude began to change rather sharply after General De Gaulle's resignation from the government in January 1946 led to a growing rightward shift amongst their own (always rather conservative) electorate. It hardened even further when their leader, the Foreign Minister, Georges Bidault, returned from the abortive Four Power Moscow Conference in April 1947, utterly convinced that it was impossible to work with the Communists.

Beyond such predictable tensions, however, a single fundamental question stood out. For all the heroic achievements of economic reconstruction, France was a ruined country. Holding down wages for a year or two was all very well. In Russia, doubtless, the Communists could, by suitably totalitarian means, hold such a wage-freeze almost indefinitely; but France was not Russia. Here the wage-freeze could only be a stop-gap – the dam would burst sooner or later – and only a very large infusion of new financial resources could save the day. The only possible source of such assistance was the USA – already Blum had been sent off to plead for loans in Washington and although he had not returned empty-handed far, far more would be needed. It speedily became clear – it was made clear enough to Blum[17] – that the presence of Communists in the French government was a major barrier to such aid. US policy was to weld Western Europe into a homogeneous anti-communist alliance: once such a NATO bloc could be achieved the credits would doubtless flow. But not before . . . (Those who tend to see the hand of Moscow in all the actions of Western Communist Parties have sometimes suggested that the PCF left the government in May 1947 at Moscow's behest. A moment's reflection – let alone the historical facts – shows just how foolish is this view: while Communists remained in the French (and Italian and Belgian) governments NATO remained an American pipe-dream.

The Russians had every interest in maintaining this situation as long as possible.)

No particular subtlety,[18] let alone conspiracy, on the part of the Americans was necessary for their pressure to be felt – doing nothing was pressure enough. The US attitude was made perfectly clear by President Truman in August 1945 when he urged De Gaulle to disembarrass himself of the PCF. It was made clearer still during the passage of the Atomic Energy Act in July 1946 when, in amending the Act to prevent the communication of nuclear secrets to America's allies, Senator MacMahon openly cited the composition of the French government as his reason. American fears increased greatly when a Communist, François Billoux, was appointed as Minister of National Defence in Paris – and gave way to what Elgey calls 'a paroxysm'[19] when Billoux selected as his *directeur de cabinet* Vice-Admiral Le Moullec, the French naval attaché in Washington whose departure the State Department had just requested on account of his 'communist activities'. American fears were, morcover, assiduously exploited by General Billotte, the Gaullist then serving as head of the French UN delegation, who drew the attention of hawks such as Senator MacMahon to the gravity of Billoux's takeover of the Defence Ministry. Already, however, the same point was being made strongly in the White House by Dean Acheson, Truman's principal foreign policy adviser. On 11 March 1947 these pressures found issue in Truman's famous speech resolving to stop Soviet expansionism in Europe. In effect Truman identified Communism anywhere as the principal enemy of the United States. The implications for *tripartisme* escaped no one and the cracks in the coalition's unity grew visibly wider, with an increasing number of SFIO and MRP leaders taking the view that they must, somehow, get rid of the Communists.

At the same time Thorez was coming under increasing intra-Party pressure to go into opposition. Within the Politburo a group led by Léon Mauvais, Laurent Casanova and André Marty all took the view that the Party was becoming seriously compromised. During the debate on the government's Indochina policy the PCF Ministers had voted with the government while, anomalously, PCF deputies abstained. This was no way to carry on. In any case, discontent within the trade unions was daily more visible and Party membership was falling. Against such opposition Thorez argued strongly for the PCF's continuation in government, pointing out that they still enjoyed the support of the (Socialist) Prime Minister, Paul Ramadier, who continually insisted that France could not be governed without the PCF. It was essential, argued Thorez, that such a view be established for future reference. As always he carried the day.

Thorez had been wrong about Ramadier. Ever since January 1947 the Premier had been swinging towards the anti-Communist hard line espoused by increasing numbers of Socialists. In the week following Truman's speech he took the decision to evict the PCF from the government and began to work secretly with General Revers, the new army chief of staff (appointed, significantly, on the very day of Truman's speech), to set up a secret transport and communications network connecting all military regions with Paris. This network – kept scrupulously secret from Billoux, the Communist Minister of Defence – was to provide a safeguard against the revolutionary *putsch* which it was (ludicrously) thought possible the PCF might attempt if evicted from the government.[20] By April 1947 everything was in place. In effect – and strongly urged on by Jefferson Caffery, the US Ambassador – [21] a sort of secret, anti-Communist, government-within-the-government had been formed. By this stage some SFIO Ministers were near hysteria. Jules Moch, the Minister for Public Works, for example, insisted that he had 'certain information' that the PCF would attempt a coup on 1 May. With Billoux again kept carefully in the dark, General Revers was called in. Throughout France the commanders of the military regions were discretely put on alert, as were French troops in Germany. Emergency mass transport was organised and carefully camouflaged armoured vehicles were brought quietly into Paris at dead of night.[22] Everything was ready.

Thorez knew nothing of all this. His attention was concentrated instead on the wildcat strike which had broken out at Renault on 25 April, led by a young Trotskyite, Pierre Bois. For several days the PCF and CGT railed furiously against the 'Hitlero-Trotskyites' and 'Gaullist-Trotskyite-Anarchists' which it saw behind the strike. But it was no good. Even the Socialist and MRP press supported the workers and the strike spread day by day. On 30 April the PCF Politburo caved in and accepted the equity of the workers' wage demands. The wage-freeze had broken – for faced with this sort of rank and file revolt the PCF felt it had no choice but to side with its own. Ramadier seized his chance and made the maintenance of the government's incomes policy a matter of confidence. On 4 May the PCF – deputies and Ministers – voted against the government. On 5 May Ramadier summoned the Cabinet and demanded to know if the Communists were resigning from the government. Thorez, who had no intention of doing anything of the sort, smilingly replied, 'I've never resigned from anything in my life.'[23]

Thorez felt fairly certain of his ground. A premier who found his Cabinet unable to agree, by well-established republican precedent, tendered his resignation to the President, who then had the job of appointing a premier to form a new government. If Ramadier wanted to resign, he could. Any other Socialist would, Thorez knew, have a difficult job forming a government without asking the PCF back in. After all, the SFIO was already split down the middle on the mere hypothesis of whether it would consent to govern without the PCF. The young Turks of the SFIO Left, led by Guy Mollet,[24] the new General Secretary of the party, were already in open revolt on the question of principle alone. Anyway, had not Ramadier himself repeatedly asserted that France could not be governed without the Communists?

Ramadier had, however, prepared his ground carefully. He announced that he was empowered to retract the grant of responsibilities he had made to Ministers in asking them to join his Cabinet, and that he was now doing so. The Communists were thus dismissed. Not only they but many of the other Ministers (including the thirty-year-old 'baby' of the government, François Mitterrand) were thunderstruck at this turn of events. Thorez recalled the scene with some bitterness later:

All my colleagues were full of praises and kindnesses for us – they were prodigal with their declarations of appeasement. Ramadier told us: 'I have no reproaches to make of you. You have always been loyal.' And Teitgen came forward to say 'We shall miss you a lot!' They all threw flowers on us, the better to bury us. I knew that Ramadier was cooking up something bad, but never did I think he'd go that far . . .[25]

The Communists departed quietly. Despite all the wild-eyed preparations set afoot by Ramadier and Revers, nothing at all happened. A few days later Jacques Duclos,[26] Thorez's chief lieutenant, announced angrily that 'People who talk about a general strike in France are imbeciles'.[27] Partly the Communists were simply at a loss – they had not expected this; and partly they continued to hope that the government would prove unable to do without them. It could – and did.

## iii THE COMING OF THE ICE AGE, 1947–8

Within days of the Communists' eviction from government commentators such as Raymond Aron had picked up the rumour of greatly increased US aid,[28] a rumour which took flesh with Marshall's Harvard speech on June 5 laying down the main lines of the Marshall Plan. Stalin, naturally enough, viewed this development as the prelude to the consolidation of an anti-Communist Western bloc. To the State Department's immense relief, he angrily rejected the idea that either the USSR or the Eastern European states might accept such aid. Instead, the world's Communist Parties were summoned to a secret destination in Poland in September 1947 to found the Comintern's successor, the Cominform. The meeting was dominated by the Russian representative, Zhdanov, who laid down the new line: American imperialism was bent on the enslavement of Europe via the Marshall Plan, using right-wing Socialists like Blum, Bevin and Attlee for cover; the US military presence in Europe was ever more clearly directed against the Soviet Union and German militarism was being revived; a Third World War was now more probable than not. The duty of Communists was clear: 'Particularly in France and Italy,' Zhdanov underlined, 'the Communist Parties must resist the plans of imperialist expansion and aggression all along the line – politically, economically and ideologically . . .'[29]

This call to arms undoubtedly depressed Duclos and Fajon, the PCF delegates. The PCF already faced a tidal wave of hysterical anti-Communism at home, led by De Gaulle's newly formed *Rassemblement du Peuple Français* (RPF). The RPF was stampeding all the other parties before it – the SFIO Congress in August, for example, had become a virtual festival of anti-Communism, with even Mollet joining in for all he was worth. The working-class was near starvation – the bread ration had been cut from 300 grams to 250 in May and to 200 in July. Food riots had already become a commonplace and prices were running away from wages faster than ever (in the second half of 1947 wages rose 19 per cent, prices 51 per cent).[30] In this context the announcement of Marshall Aid had come as the first piece of good news French workers had had for a long time. But now, apparently, the PCF had to persuade the workers that Marshall Aid meant 'enslavement', that it had to be refused; and, just as the anti-Communist wave was breaking over it, the PCF must take a new, tough line and seek battle with the vastly stronger forces arrayed against it. Not surprisingly, Duclos 'sounded uneasy, gloomy, and apologetic . . . He was clearly out of his element at the Cominform meeting, and seemed to feel singularly uneasy at the thought of all the hard days lying ahead . . .'[31] He stated his case fairly frankly, accepting Zhdanov's criticism that the PCF had not denounced American imperialism strongly enough, but arguing powerfully that the PCF had achieved a record in government of which it could feel proud. It stood ready to resume its role in government again. He could not accept the furious accusations of reformism hurled at him by the Yugoslav delegates (Milovan Djilas and Edward Kardelj). At this not only Zhdanov but the Czech delegate, Anna Pauker, and Stalin's protégé, Gyorgy Malenkov, attacked Duclos: the PCF was too keen to present itself as a party of government – it ought to be a party of revolutionary opposition. Duclos continued to defend himself but ended, of course, by accepting the new line.[32]

In one sense Zhdanov and his henchmen were right. Duclos, still hankering for the old Resistance alliance, had attempted to draw a distinction between left-wing Socialists like Mollet, with whom the PCF might be able to work, and the SFIO right-wingers. To Zhdanov all Socialists were enemies, for they had 'objectively' become part of the American camp. For the question of American aid and influence did indeed lie at the heart of the Socialist collapse from their radical, even revolutionary commitments. Ramadier had lent himself quite straightforwardly to the American line in evicting the PCF from government and the SFIO's centre of gravity had moved with him. While the PCF denounced the RPF as 'the American party' (and De Gaulle's movement was certainly a beneficiary of CIA funds at this time), there was an important sense in which the title more truly belonged to the SFIO. Subsidies to the RPF helped strengthen the general tide of anti-Communism in France and were an insurance policy in case De Gaulle managed to return to power. But the SFIO was *actually* in power and provided the main counterweight to the PCF within the labour movement as a whole. French Socialism was, inevitably, the anvil on which the strategy of containment and consolidation of the Western Alliance would be beaten into sharpest definition.

The SFIO's dilemma had been apparent from the early days of Liberation. It was, perhaps, seen at its clearest in Blum's famous mission to Washington to plead for US aid in June 1946. Blum, the old comrade in arms of Jaurés and Guèsde, was formally asked by Fred Vinson, the US Treasury Secretary, to oust the PCF from government and form an anti-Communist coalition.[33] Returning from this encounter, he was interviewed by Jean Davidson, the Washington correspondent of the Agence France Presse (AFP):

Looking at this ghost of European Socialism . . . I could not restrain myself: 'Are you still a convinced Marxist, *Monsieur le Président*?'

Léon Blum could not conceal his surprise. Suddenly leaning back, and then doubling up, as though he had been kicked in the stomach, and taking my arm, he said: 'Now, *mon ami*, this is strictly between ourselves – our American friends might take this very badly, for they are still a bit muddled about Socialism,

Marxism, and Communism, of which they are afraid . . . But of course, *mon ami*, I remain a convinced Marxist. Besides, paragraph 2 of the latest Declaration of Principles of the French Socialist Party says . . .' and he rattled off from memory the paragraph in question . . .

'You realise, of course, *Monsieur le Président*', I said, 'that the Americans who talk of Socialism as a rampart against Communism in Europe, hope in reality that Socialists like you will, above all, form a rampart against Marxism as such – don't you think so?'[34]

At this point, Davidson recalls, Blum had a coughing fit and asked him to come back some other time . . .[35]

Not that the Socialists were mere passive victims of a cruel situation. The fact that they had so decisively lost ground to the Communists in the labour movement and the electorate not merely made them less able to refuse American support (open or covert) when it was offered, but also bred a sort of desperate opportunism amongst them in general. Their displacement as the premier party of the working-class deprived them of their traditional *raison d' être* and threatened them deeply. In the early post-war years they had hoped against hope that they might reverse this situation by emerging as the indispensable party of government and using the power this gave them to crush their Communist rivals. Almost any weapon would have been good enough if it had helped toward this end, (an attitude which the Cold War tended to legitimate in both camps). The SFIO, for example, never tired of accusing the PCF of being paid by Moscow. When this accusation was repeated by the SFIO Minister, Jules Moch, in 1948 Duclos immediately demanded a parliamentary committee of enquiry to investigate the funding of the PCF *and* the SFIO. The Socialists were deeply embarrassed, for it was widely known that their main party newspaper, *Le Populaire*, was being subsidised by AFL (American Federation of Labour) (in fact, CIA) funds. Amidst much derisive cheering from the Communist benches the SFIO deputies hurriedly voted down the proposal . . .[36]

The battle lines between the two Left parties were clearly drawn up once the PCF was evicted from government in May 1947. The summer passed in a state of phoney war, but the autumn brought a clear hardening of attitudes. The government parties were appalled by the news of the Cominform resolutions, which they saw as a virtual call to insurrection. Their minds were concentrated further by the RPF's phenomenal sweep of 38 per cent of the vote in the October municipal elections. Given the strength of the anti-Communist hysteria sweeping France the choice before the government seemed only whether to put itself at the head of this movement or be submerged by it. The PCF, on the other hand, had actually been told to go on to the offensive by Stalin and anyway wished to show the government how uncomfortable life could be without Communists in the coalition. But the most important factor was that neither the PCF nor anyone else could now hold back the pent-up torrent of long-suppressed wage demands. For by now large sections of the French working-class were in a state of angry despair. They were well aware that all the brave hopes of the Resistance were now in danger. The middle and lower middle classes were gripped by an unreasoning panic which saw as the enemy not the looming threat of starvation but the Communists – 'their' party. Real wages had now plummeted so far below their pre-war level[37] that piecemeal strike action to gain a few more francs seemed beside the point. The sentiment grew that only a general strike aimed at changing government policy itself could reverse the trend. Such, at least, was the view urged by the Communist majority within the CGT, led by its Secretary-General, Benoit Frachon. It was opposed with equal force by the Socialist minority led by Léon Jouhaux, whom Frachon had displaced.[38] These latter were by no means reconciled to the PCF's domination of the CGT and utterly refused to countenance the idea of a political general strike, particularly one aimed at a Socialist-led government.

On 12 November the CGT gave the order for a general strike in Marseilles. Thousands of dockers occupied the city's public buildings, demanding the resignation of the RPF Mayor just elected. Large-scale violence and rioting followed both there and at Valence. For several weeks Marseilles remained a centre of violent confrontation (the future SFIO leader, Gaston Defferre, then a young Marseilles deputy, went about armed with revolver and machine-gun:[39] such precautions were not unusual). This was followed by a miners' strike in Nord and Pas-de-Calais, sparked by the beginning of a purge of Communists from the boards of nationalised industries by the SFIO Minister of Industry, Robert Lacoste. In Paris the strike wave surprised even the PCF by its vehemence. The Renault and Citroen plants were occupied and soon a quarter of a million men were on strike in the Paris region. Across France as a whole 3 million came out on strike, effectively paralysing the country.

The Socialist-led government now came under unbearable pressure. The USA rushed to help. On 10 November (before the strikes) it had announced a grant of $140 million aid to France; on 17 November, as the strikes spread, it suddenly discovered the previous week's grant to be insufficient and announced another aid package of $597 million.[40] On 18 November Jouhaux's faction formally walked out of the CGT, constituting themselves as the CGT-*Force Ouvrière*, and called on the strikers to return to work. It was no good: on 19 November Ramadier resigned. For five days France had no government and the country appeared to tremble on the brink. A Gaullist coup was one distinct possibility, the return of the PCF to government another. Both solutions were repugnant to the 'Third Force' politicians (as those sandwiched between Gaullism and Communism referred to themselves). They were also quite unacceptable to the US State Department . . . On 24 November a new MRP-SFIO government was formed, led by Robert Schuman (MRP), who moved ruthlessly to break the strikes. Quite clearly, the SFIO had paled at the idea of leading a government whose main objective was to wage war upon the organised working-class. Instead – as their opponents were quick to point out – they had surrendered the national interest to a Catholic from Alsace-Lorraine, a man born and brought up a German, who had even fought for Germany in the First World War . . .

Schuman, in common with several of his SFIO Ministers, was obsessed with the idea that the Communists would use the strike to launch the armed insurrection they had renounced in 1944. Rumours flew wildly of old *maquisard* arms caches being opened up and one Ministry of the Interior report spoke of 15,000 Spanish

Communists, Civil War guerrilla veterans to a man, waiting the call for action at the PCF's side in the frontier regions.[41] Accordingly, the government announced a military and policy mobilisation unprecedented in peacetime. Thousands of police and CRS were drafted into the strike areas; 80,000 army reservists were called up; several extra divisions were pulled back from Germany; and a law was rushed through parliament providing for sentences of up to five years for anyone interfering with 'the freedom to work' (i.e. pickets). Scenes of great violence flared throughout the strike regions – particularly in the mining areas of Nord and Pas-de-Calais – as the police and soldiers moved in. Slowly the strikes began to crumble, though feeling was still running at fever-pitch when, on 1 December, to the disbelief and consternation of many strikers, the CGT called off the strikes and admitted defeat. By no means all the strikers were willing to accept this and, since many of them *were* former *masquisards*, some began to deploy the same weapons against the government which they had used to such effect against the Germans – dynamite and train derailments. The next fortnight saw a wave of violent sabotage, including the derailment of the Paris-Lille express, with sixteen dead and thirty injured. Besides this the strike had produced ninety-six other acts of sabotage, over 23 million work-days lost, 1,375 arrests and unknown numbers of casualties in the violent clashes between the strikers, soldiers and police.[42]

With the strike wave of November 1947 France plunged irrevocably into the ice age of Cold War politics. A wide section of the working-class now stood ranged in bitterness and frustration against a government which had shifted decisively to the Right. The PCF, only six months after leaving the government, had again become the lepers and untouchables of French political life. A minority amongst them, the veterans of the Communist ghetto-culture of the inter-war years, seemed almost to exult in this return to the politics of revolutionary defiance. A much larger number – for one Frenchman in four was now a Communist, as against one in twelve in the early 1930s – came to live the experience with a new, deep, and original bitterness.

The split within the Left seemed equally irrevocable, for the PCF and SFIO now stood ranged against one another with an animosity unparalleled since the days before the Popular Front. SFIO Ministers like Jules Moch and Robert Lacoste had put themselves in the van of the government's strike-breaking campaign; Socialists had voted through the anti-strike law, depicting the furious strikers as mere Cominform agents; and Socialists had celebrated the strikers' defeat as a triumph. In order to win this battle the SFIO had wholeheartedly thrown in its lot with the American side in the Cold War. The government was being propped up with American aid; so was the SFIO; and so, it seemed clear, was Jouhaux's new *Force Ouvrière* (FO), which gave enduring organisational expression to the split within the labour movement. Only days before leading the walk-out Jouhaux had returned from a trip to America where his consultations with the AFL President, George Meany, had clearly provided him with the support he needed to launch the breakaway union. (Later, Meany was to crow openly of his funding of the FO.)[43] Beyond any real doubt the US State Department had played a critical strategic role throughout the affair. Apart from US financial aid to the government, the SFIO, and the FO, the USA had stiffened the resolve of the

Third Force parties, had helped the Schuman government to bring back troops from Germany, and had maintained daily contact in support of the French military authorities.[44] Probably only the most crass of American politicians would have gone so far as to visit France at this time to boast of this major victory in the Cold War. In John Foster Dulles, however, the State Department had such a man. Arriving in Paris as the strike ended Dulles announced that 'The French Communist Party is not a French party', adding, with visible satisfaction, that 'what was happening in France was far more important for the future of Europe than what was happening in London'.[45]

The US role in the events of 1947 was enacted too far backstage to detract seriously from the favourable regard in which the Americans – the liberators of Paris and donors of Marshall Aid – were held, even by French workers. None the less, the US attitude was clear enough for the working-class audience of the PCF and CGT to take the point that the USA was not wholly on their 'side'. Given the overwhelming strength of the US colossus, it was a feeling which could only increase their sense of embattled isolation. Going along with the PCF's ritual denunciations of Marshall Aid did not, however, answer to the need thus generated to be able to look to someone, somewhere, for recourse, protection and solidarity. Thus Thorez's confident and repeated assertion that they could indeed look to the USSR for succour and comfort was greeted with a real warmth and relief. This is a fact of no small importance if one is to understand the real emotional chords Thorez was able to touch within the French working-class by his endless eulogies of Stalin. Thus, by a quite straightforward dialectical process, the Cold War worked to produce a popular Communist glorification of Stalin and Stalinism whose grassroots emotional reality later (anti-Stalinist) Marxists have found it surprisingly difficult to concede.

1948 saw the consolidation of these trends on every front. In March France signed the Brussels Treaty, the prelude to full NATO membership in 1949. In April the first tranches of Marshall Aid began to flow. The PCF reacted by hinting strongly that *its* first loyalty in any future war would lie with the Soviet side. Within every level of French society a major purge of Communists from responsible positions was launched, starting with a major press campaign to dislodge Joliot-Curie from the Atomic Energy Commissariat and spreading throughout the armed forces, the civil administration and industry. At factory level PCF and CGT militants found themselves systematically victimised – to the advantage of the FO and CFTC (the Catholic trade union federation). Suddenly the cause of Vichy again became respectable and a flood of books appeared justifying collaboration with the Germans against 'the Communist menace'. Even ex-Vichy Ministers and extreme *'collabos'* emerged to announce their own self-righteous vindication.[46] Many ex-Vichyite magistrates and police joined enthusiastically in the anti-Communist purge which quickly became an anti-Resistance purge. As (the anti-Communist) *Combat* put it:

Not a day passes without the papers announcing sentences passed on members of the Francs-Tireurs-Partisans or of the FFI [*Forces Françaises de l'Intérieur*] for reprisals which they carried out against traitors during the Resistance or during the national Insurrection in 1944. Not only excesses and crimes, but even many inevitable acts of war are now being punished . . . And the most abominable thing is that many of these lads of the FTP and FFI should now be charged on the strength of forms they had themselves filled in in perfectly good faith after the Liberation, recording what they had done. From all sides we hear of charges being brought against members of the Maquis, of arrests and sentences . . .[47]

Most dramatic of all, however, was the deliberate pitched battle the government provoked with the miners in October–November 1948, a fairly clear 'revenge' for the events of 1947 against the most powerful and heavily unionised section of the working-class – for no less than 200,000 miners were CGT members, making them the central bastion of Communist strength in the labour movement. The operation – masterminded by two Socialist Ministers, Moch (Interior) and Lacoste (Industry) – began with a series of decrees by Lacoste in September, issued with no semblance of prior consultation with the unions. A whole 10 per cent of the workforce was to be fired; strick disciplinary rules were instituted (in flat contravention of all previous agreements), including automatic dismissal for absenteeism; and a further purge of PCF and CGT personnel was announced. A general strike throughout the northern mining areas followed almost automatically.

The government and the inevitable General Revers reacted with a large and pre-planned military operation (in the months before the strike a military radio-communications network had been carefully put into place in the mining areas).[48] Some 5,000 police and CRS were drafted in and a helicopter fleet brought in 40,000 troops from Germany. The FO and CFTC quickly dissociated themselves from the strike and opened a register to recruit blacklegs. Violent confrontations flared throughout the region, with troops opening fire and wounding strikers on at least one occasion. Moch justified this virtual reign of terror by claiming that the miners were acting on the direct instructions of the Cominform. Challenged for evidence for this assertion, however, he confessed it was a mere 'hypothesis'. J. M. Domenach of (the Left Catholic) *Esprit* recorded the scene as the strike, inevitably, collapsed:

> The leaders or those alleged to be the leaders were systematically hounded by the police – trade union delegates, town councillors, former Resistance members. This vast system of repression and blackmail was directly aimed at the miners' trade union. Several 'ringleaders' were dismissed the day the strike ended: 'you'll be sent for when wanted'. In some mines an attempt was made to replace a CGT delegate with an FO man. Under the double pressure of poverty and fear the strike gradually collapsed . . .[49]

It was, literally, workers against tanks. At the strike's end 4 miners were dead and an uncounted number injured; 2,000 more were in prison and 6,000 had been fired.[50] The employers, after some consideration, decided to allow 700 of those dismissed to continue to live in their company-owned houses. As one member of the (nationalised) board later put it, with evident satisfaction:

Living in the midst of their comrades who saw their difficulties, [these unemployed] became permanent and living witnesses for the whole mining basin of the consequences of a strike and the misery it brings. It was a very salutary lesson which still bears fruits today. Now things go better for these strike-abusers. Their children have grown up and can earn their own living. The ostracism does not extend to the whole family. And, in any case, they've grown old – they've reached retirement age . . .[51]

In the wake of the strike many miners came to resent the CGT, which had led them into two disastrous strikes in two years. Even many who didn't blame the union tended, not unnaturally, to regard continuing membership of it as a liability, and the CGT's strength in the area plummeted. It was not until the great miners' strike of 1963 that the CGT was able fully to re-establish its old influence amongst the miners of the Nord.[52] This was a not inaccurate measure of the scale of the defeat suffered. For the miners, the Communists and, indeed, the Left as a whole, a new Ice Age had descended.

# 3 The Ice Age of the Left, 1947–58

## i THE SOCIALISTS AND THIRD FORCE POLITICS

The demise of *tripartisme* and the brutal confrontations of 1947–8 gave definitive shape to the French party and political system for the next fifteen years. The renewed stigmatisation of the Communists as political untouchables was, of course, a major structural feature in its own right and the PCF, it seems clear, will remain haunted by this bitter heritage well into the 1980s. More immediately, the fratricidal war between Communists and Socialists had a rippling, domino effect across the entire political system. With the Left so badly split all possibility of a coherent left-wing government was simply removed from the political agenda, tipping the whole system to the Right. The SFIO now became the outer edge of the politically possible and even for it anti-Communism became a principal *raison d'être*. In many areas its electoral position came to depend on its being not the radical Marxist party it claimed to be, but the main locally available form of anti-Communism. Moreover, both locally and nationally the party was in coalition or at least alliance with the centre and Right – in the new political universe, with both Communists and Gaullists ruled out as potential partners, it simply had no alternative. The party had, perforce, to attune itself to the political sensibilities of its partners and, indeed, often sought to outdo them in order to prove that it was not 'soft' on Communism or lax in its regard for French colonial interests. In any case, its more conservative partners were well able to head off whatever feeble reformist momentum the SFIO still retained. It was hardly surprising under such circumstances that the reforming heart went out of French Socialism. This was not just a development affecting the likes of Moch and Lacoste: the party leader, the once-radical Mollet, far from resisting the trend, came increasingly to personify it.

In turning their backs on a united Left the SFIO had made much of the so-called Third Force strategy, envisaging a steady coalition of a moderate social democratic cast between itself, the MRP, the Radicals, and the *Union Démocratique et Socialiste de la Résistance* (UDSR). In the event the strategy proved viable only in the negative sense that it blocked the ambitions of the PCF and the Gaullist RPF. As a coherent programmatic force it simply lacked substance. The UDSR, which had once contemplated fusion with the SFIO, drifted steadily rightwards and by 1948–9 'was behaving almost as a Conservative group'.[1] The Radicals were split down the middle, frequently opposed to the Third Force idea even in principle, and proved equally poor partners. Most important, the MRP, once its first flush of Resistance radicalism had faded, settled down to being merely the conservative clerical party its voters had, in the main, always wanted it to be. The fact was – and all the heated talk of a genuine reformist alternative could hardly disguise it – that the Third Force was a very typical construct of Cold War liberalism in which anti-Communism came first and everything else a pretty distant last. Probably the most significant domestic achievement of the Third Force parties was flatly anti-democratic – the last-minute rigging of the electoral system to head off the RPF and PCF in the 1951 elections. The new electoral law was, indeed, such a marvel of ingenuity that although the SFIO and MRP together only narrowly exceeded the popular vote of the PCF, they received twice as many seats as the Communists. Some of the results almost staggered belief. In the department of Herault (with six seats), for example, the MRP received one seat for its 20,766 votes while the rival RPF, with 21,256 votes, went empty-handed. This seemed almost fair compared to the situation on the Left, though, for the SFIO's 39,028 votes earned it three seats while the PCF, with 69,433, got none at all.[2]

Despite this elegant statecraft, the 1951 elections effectively killed the Third Force. It had hardly proved popular with the voters: the SFIO had lost one-sixth and the MRP over half of their respective electorates. Shocked by this result, and taking advantage of the fact that the electoral law had helped give the new Assembly a conservative majority, the MRP hurried to give its clerical supporters what they wanted – the *Loi Barangé*, with provision for state aid to church schools. A greater affront to the SFIO's anti-clerical susceptibilities was scarcely imaginable. The two pivotal parties of the Third Force parted company in the clouds of furious acrimony which this time-honoured issue was always guaranteed to raise. Within eight months the frankly reactionary government of Antoine Pinay was in power. The SFIO, having turned its back on a government of the united Left in 1947 and striven mightily to prove the viability of a Centre-Left alternative, had taken only four and a half years to bring to birth the most conservative government seen in peacetime France for twenty years. Having accomplished this remarkable feat the SFIO left the government, participating in no further ministries for the next five years. They were not wholly reluctant to embrace a period in opposition, the better to compete with the PCF, whose popular vote in 1951 had come close to doubling their own. This soon became a matter of making a virtue out of necessity as RPF defectors swelled the ranks of the Assembly's conservative majority: for De Gaulle's bid for power had clearly failed and it did not take long for the 120 RPF deputies to draw the appropriate conclusions and begin tip-toeing across the floor to support (and enter) the government. De Gaulle raged impotently at such treachery until 1953 when, accepting the *fait accompli*, he dissolved the RPF and retired to Colombey-Les-deux-Eglises. With government in the hands of the likes of Pinay and René Coty (President of the Republic, 1954–8), both of whom had voted for Pétain in 1940 (Pinay actually serving on the Vichy national council), there was hardly much further need for conservative 'saviours' or strongmen.[3]

Oddly, one effect of the SFIO's refusal to serve in the governments of 1951–6 was to focus a not unfavourable light on those men of the Left who *did* serve in them, notably Pierre Mendès-France (whose resolution and courage in bringing the Indo-China War to a speedy end earned him a permanent place in the heart of the Left) and François Mitterrand. Mitterrand's achievement was the more mysterious for he was, almost classically, a 'man of the system', serving almost continuously in a great variety of posts in governments of every complexion. In particular, it was something of a minor miracle that he was able to serve through the Fourth Republic's incessant colonial wars, repression and bloodshed[4] and emerge with the reputation of a leading colonial reformer. True, as Minister of Colonies in 1950–1, he broadened the franchise in French Africa and halted the repression of the nationalist RDA [*Ressemblement Démocratique Africaine*]; but the price of the deal was that the RDA should adopt a strong anti-Communist stance and support the French war in Indo-China.[5] As Minister for Algeria and North Africa in 1952–3, he gained much later credit for his resignation over the deposition of the Sultan of Morocco in 1953. By then, however, he had already presided over one of the bloodiest periods of repression in Tunisia, as well as the smashing of the Moroccan trade unions in the Casablanca riots of December 1952 which had left hundreds dead.[6] As Minister of the Interior he delighted the Left by sacking the reactionary Paris Prefect of Police. It was, however, also in this capacity that he presided over the key period of escalation of the Algerian conflict into a full-scale war and he was personally responsible for the forcible dissolution of the main Algerian Nationalist Party. In part his reputation as a liberal survived because he was the Left's (forlorn) best hope in otherwise reactionary governments. What guaranteed it, however, was that – as with his British contemporary, Iain Macleod, whose career in many respects ran parallel with his – he did enough to earn the undying enmity of the colonialist Right.

For the 1956 elections Mitterrand banded together with Mollet, Mendès-France and Chaban-Delmas in the 'Republican Front', a broad alliance of the anti-Communist Left committed, *inter alia*, to a more liberal Algerian policy (the issue which dominated the election).[7] The Front succeeded beyond its wildest dreams – by a complete fluke: the far-Right Poujadists ate heavily into the conservative vote, thus helping the PCF win 50 per cent more seats than in 1951. The result was an Assembly tilted strongly toward the Left. The Front parties took office with Mollet as premier, Mendès as his deputy and Mitterrand as Minister of Justice. After a promising start (pensions were increased, paid holidays extended and sweeping reforms introduced in black Africa) the government slid into ignominious reaction.[8] With the ferocious Lacoste in charge of Algeria the government actually stepped up the savage war of repression. With only Mendès dissenting, the government launched enthusiastically into the Suez expedition; within France minorities were harrassed and press freedom interfered with; Ben Bella and the FLN [*Front de Libération Nationale*] leaders were invited to talks and then kidnapped by the French Army while on their way; and Lacoste handed over complete power in Algiers to General Massu's dreaded *paras*, who instituted a regime of indiscriminate mass torture to break the urban guerrillas. By the time the Mollet government was overthrown in May 1957 it had more than thrown away whatever reputation for radical principle the SFIO had regained in five years in opposition. The failure of Blum's Popular Front government twenty years before had attested the exhaustion of the political possibilities of the Third Republic, providing, in the end a mere prelude to Vichy. Now Mollet's government had performed a similar role in the Fourth Republic, revealing the utter bankruptcy of the non-Communist Left and paving the way for a further return to authoritarian conservatism – this time under De Gaulle.

## ii THE COMMUNISTS AND GHETTO POLITICS

Isolated from the public politics of governmental coalitions – the great game of who was in and who was out – the PCF lived instead the unhappy but intense inner life of the ghetto. The Party was guided by several fixed stars: an unconditional loyalty to the USSR, the great solace to the workers (as their true fatherland) whatever woes they had to endure in France; a corresponding loyalty to every twist and turn of Cominform policy; and an intense personal devotion to Stalin. These currents met and found their highest expression in the figure of Maurice Thorez, who dominated his Party in a way no other Western Communist leader has ever done.

Thorez, a miner's son who had started work in the mines himself at the age of twelve, had become a full-time Party official at the age of twenty-three. Thereafter the Party was his life.[9] At twenty-eight he was on the Comintern executive and at thirty (in 1930) became leader of the PCF. The rapidity of his ascent was due in large part to the fact that temperamentally he was ideally equipped to carry through the 'Bolshevisation' of the Party ordained by Moscow: a cool, phlegmatic, and cautious organisation man rather than a revolutionary firebrand. Above all, he met and gained the confidence of Stalin even before the latter's rise to total power. Thorez, whose first pilgrimage to Moscow in 1925 was followed by frequent and often lengthy visits thereafter, probably appealed to Stalin as a man after his own heart and of his own ilk. Both men had emerged from childhoods of grinding poverty (Stalin's father had been a cobbler) to become rather remarkable working-class intellectuals, self-taught vulgar Marxists whose careers had depended on their worsting the men of greater advantages, brilliance and sophistication who had stood in their path. In any event, there was no doubting that the relationship between the two men gradually matured into a significant and exclusive friendship, one which lasted for more than quarter of a century and placed Thorez in a position probably unique within the whole of the world Communist movement. While other foreign Communist leaders – not to mention Stalin's Soviet comrades – had much just cause for reproach against Stalin, the reverse was true of Thorez. Stalin had helped him into the PCF leadership and sustained him in that position. Through the purges of the 1930s Thorez went to and fro to Moscow – quite unscathed. In 1940 Stalin ordered Thorez to desert the French Army for the safety of Moscow where, during the war years, Stalin frequently sought his advise and counsel on French and European problems. To Thorez Stalin was patron, protector, friend and model – and Thorez rewarded him with an intense and emotional loyalty. Indeed, Stalin's only known criticism of Thorez (voiced to Tito in 1946) should probably be read as a reflection on this excessive deference. Thorez, he said, had only one major fault: 'Even a dog that doesn't bite shows its teeth if it wants to frighten someone. Thorez isn't capable of it.'[10] Undeniably, Thorez was no hot-head; and, doubtless, his doglike affection for Stalin encouraged the Soviet leader to this flight of canine imagery; but Stalin might, perhaps, have considered that he was the very last person in the world at whom it was at all advisable to bare one's teeth . . .

At war's end Thorez returned to lead the PCF very much in the spirit of his master. He allowed his own personality cult to flourish in imitation of Stalin's own – after 1945 the PCF happily called itself 'the party of Thorez'. His birthday, like Stalin's, was publicly feted. He was allowed to place his venomous wife, Jeannette Vermeersch, on the central committee (1945) and then on to the Politburo (1954), a fateful step, for this bitter, authoritarian woman had – as Thorez had not – a vindictive cast of mind and many scores to settle. Thorez publicly rejoiced in the appellation of being 'the best Stalinist in France'. And he attempted, with some success, to project his view of Stalin on to the PCF as a whole. 'We Communists,' he declared,

> whom the class enemy and their agents think they can outrage by calling us Stalinists, we say again with all our might – as we have for twenty years – that we are proud of this honourable and glorious title and that we shall try our best to deserve it. With all our hearts we proclaim our ardent love for Stalin and assure him of our unshakable trust in him.[11]

The same note of devotional mysticism was reflected in the Party's prayerful approach to its own leader. Thus the PCF national conference of 1953, held whilst Thorez was ill, addressed its absent Secretary-General in the following tones:

> Hundreds of eyes imagine you present at this Gennevilliers conference as you were three years ago; the calm gesture of your hand when you explain . . . It seems to us that your voice resounds under the immense canopy of the great hall . . . your voice which has built our party . . . Your presence gives an aspect of hope to us all. And we feel you present in each of us . . . There are hundreds of us here who are this moment aware that you have given our personal lives their meaning and our party its style and grandeur . . . Following your example we have learnt to love the Soviet Union, to love Stalin, and from that love, to love the future as it appears in its most radiant guise . . . Under your leadership we shall fulfil our task with honour, for we want to be able to say, on the wonderful day when you return: thanks to your teachings and your example we were able to build a party and a France worthy of you . . .[12]

It is easy – and by no means unfair – to respond to such utterances with derision. Simply and only to do this, however, is to miss a major historical and sociological point. For sociologists of religion who have studied the behavioural characteristics of militant sects under state of threat will find many familiar strands here: the exaggerated piety and devotionalism which often bespeaks an impulse towards quietist retreat from the harsh world outside where the blows rain down; the strange co-existence of such sentiments with a sense of militant resistance and out-and-out defiance; the millenarian longings attached to distant figures; the sublime assertion of confidence in the future salvation they will bring; and the urge to combine all these elements within the absolute certainties and huddled security of the all-protective (because self-encapsulating) association, Church – or Party. For the PCF was, after 1947, a suffering church militant. It *was* persecuted. It had its martyrs, its devils, its saints and it had its holy faith. In the circumstances its chief saint was bound to be Stalin and Stalinism its holy faith. But had neither the Cominform nor Stalin ever existed the Party would have undergone much the same pattern of pressure and response that it in fact experienced. What was of some moment was that Stalinism was so powerfully and pervasively inserted into the Party's life at this juncture. For Stalinism thus fused with the larger ghetto experience. The PCF's Stalinism helped legitimate, in their own eyes, the efforts of those who wished to fight and suppress it, but it also legitimated certain codes of conduct and behaviour within the PCF and became the major ideological grid through which the Party lived and expressed its ghetto experience. In a word, Stalinism was, in the end, no mere excrescence but had real popular roots in the PCF in a way it did not in, for example, the Italian Communist Party (PCI). Thus while the PCI was able to toss Stalinism aside with relative ease when the period of de-stalinisation arrived, the PCF had, instead, to contemplate the painful problem of amputating a still living organ.

In 1947, we have seen, the PCF was made to take the brunt of the Cominform's retrospective criticism of the *tripartiste* period. The Yugoslavs had, on that occasion, been Duclos's chief tormentors[13] and it was not long before the PCI and PCF were being patted on the head in the Cominform press for having 'honestly acknowledged their errors and accepted as Marxists the severe criticisms levelled against them – errors which they afterwards conscientiously corrected'.[14] There was, accordingly, considerable *Schadenfreude* within the PCF leadership in mid-1948 when they were called on by Stalin to denounce the Yugoslavs. They responded enthusiastically, reviling the Tito regime as 'neo-Fascist' and full of 'spies and murderers'.[15] Thereafter the Party joined, in the approved manner, in the condemnation of Gomulka in 1948, in applauding the Sofia and Budapest trials, the Slansky trial – and, indeed, in providing the 'right' response to every new twist and turn of Stalinist policy. These *pro forma* stands on foreign events over which the PCF had, in any case, not the slightest influence were hideously expensive of the Party's domestic credit. Most Frenchmen were naturally revolted by the PCF's behaviour and the pressures on the Party increased commensurately. By 1949–50 the Party had begun to live in an Eastern European atmosphere itself and there was much threatening talk about the need to expel a long list of enemies from its own ranks – sectarians, policespies, *agents provocateurs*, Titoists, Trotskyites, enemy agents, and *petit bourgeois* nationalists. One PCF deputy from the Somme who quarrelled with his constituency party was, ludicrously, labelled 'the French Tito' and expelled . . .

It was with some relief that the Party turned to the major task ordained by Stalin, the great 'peace campaign' aimed at neutralising the threat to the USSR posed by the formation of the NATO bloc. It was, in principle, not an unpopular cause and the PCF was able to make some headway at least in so far as the business of organising peace congresses and mass petitions was concerned. But what undermined the campaign quite fatally – as also the PCF's agitation against the incessant French colonial wars – was that the PCF could not disguise the fact that it was, in the end, on the side of those who were actually killing French soldiers (the Vietnamese, the Chinese and North Koreans, and, later, the Algerians) or might soon be doing so (the Russians). Inevitably, in domestic political terms this was a ruinous position but the Cominform's post-1947 hard line did not allow the PCF to skirt the question. When the NATO pact was signed in September 1948 Thorez boldly declared that 'The people of France will not make – will never make – war against the Soviet Union.'[16] Not until February 1949 did a journalist follow this up with the obvious question, 'What would you do if the Red Army occupied Paris?' 'Would the workers of France behave any differently than those of Poland, Roumania and Yugoslavia?' was Thorez's reply.[17] There was a huge and immediate explosion in the press, media and parliament, where Thorez was summoned before the Foreign Affairs Commission, accused of being, in effect, the leader of the Red Army's fifth column. Thorez treated his interrogators with icy contempt but, for the first time, furious and quite serious demands were heard for the outright suppression of the PCF. The Vatican led the way, announcing the mass excommunication (in July 1949) of all Communists – a weapon not used in this collective sense since the days of the Albigensian crusade. (In terms of Catholic law Christians may, without fear of sin, kill all those whom the Church has excommunicated; under certain circumstances it may even become their duty to do so.) The PCF stood its ground, calling defiantly on the workers to step up the campaign of sabotage of war matériel intended for Indo-China and, soon thereafter, for Korea.

In November 1950 Thorez suffered a stroke and partial paralysis. The news quickly leaked out (*Le Populaire*, the SFIO paper, reported that Thorez had been attacked by enraged PCF militants).[18] Stalin, solicitous as ever, sent a special plane to Paris to bear Thorez off to Moscow for specialist medical attention. He recovered slowly and Stalin would not hear of his returning until his recuperation was complete: 'You're not sufficiently recovered. You must be patient – it's an important quality in a revolutionary. France won't disappear,' he told him.[19] By the time Thorez was well, Stalin was himself dying, so Thorez naturally stayed on to be at his patron's bedside. Only with Stalin's death in March 1953 did the heartbroken Thorez return to France – after an absence of two and a half years.

With Thorez away Duclos became the *de facto* Party leader, with the almost immediate task of leading the PCF in the 1951 election. Temperamentally always inclined towards Popular Front tactics, Duclos placed a lesser emphasis on the PCF's habitual hostility towards the SFIO, calling instead for a wide 'national front' of all pro-peace and anti-imperialist forces. Duclos lacked Thorez's authority, however, and almost immediately the factional tendencies within the PCF, hitherto held in check by its overwhelming leader, began to manifest themselves. The Politburo was reshuffled, with Auguste Lecoeur, a tough young miner, promoted to the No. 4

position (after Thorez, Duclos and Marty) and Jeannette Vermeersch accorded Politburo alternate status. Both moves were disastrous. Lecoeur had served in the International Brigade in the Spanish Civil War and ever thereafter nursed a bitter hatred of Marty, the Brigade's organiser. Mme Vermeersch was also determined on revenge against Marty and Tillon, the former Resistance leader, for previous slights against her.[20] Almost immediately a secret Party enquiry was opened against the two men. Worse still, Mme Vermeersch flitted continually back and forth to Moscow to see her husband, each time returning with the claim that she alone could speak for Thorez, and always insisting on the hardest of hard lines. Thus while Duclos was calling for a common front with Frenchmen of all parties and creeds to maintain French independence against American imperialism – Catholics and Gaullists as well as Socialists – Mme Vermeersch issued bitter denunciations of even the most Left Catholics, the worker priests.

Ironically, with its leadership absent, under investigation, or fighting one another, the PCF's peace campaign had begun to gather popular momentum. In part this was due to simple weariness with the stalemate in Korea and the endless war in Indo-China; in part it was fuelled by De Gaulle's angry denunciation of 'American imperialism' (after the CIA had cut off its subsidies to the RPF); in part the running out of the $2.5 billion Marshall Aid programme in 1951 caused not a few Frenchmen to look with at a fresh eye at the price they had paid for this assistance. Even such moderate voices as that of Mendès-France pointed out the absurdity of France fighting apparently endless Asian wars on America's behalf while industrial production in the France of 1951 was still no higher than it had been in 1929. Politicians who defended such positions were increasingly likely to be accused of a shameful servility towards the new American overlords.

But the PCF also made headway with its assertions that France – which would be in the front line of any Third World War – was being pulled by the USA towards an aggressive confrontation with the USSR. In this the Party was greatly helped by the often incautious remarks of American politicians and generals, which lent a certain credibility to the PCF claim that they were considering a pre-emptive strike eastwards. Others behaved with a degree of swaggering presumption which helped push even moderate voices – most notably *Le Monde* – towards a neutralist position.[21] Eisenhower, who tended to use his position as Supreme Allied Commander in Paris as the base from which to campaign for the US presidency, was particularly prone to shock French sensibilities. His utterances, aimed in practice at preventing the right-wing of the Republican Party from delivering the nomination to Taft before he could return from Paris, were seldom understood as such by his French listeners. When Eisenhower, on his first arrival at SHAPE headquarters, faced a PCF demonstration against him, he commented – in the more-in-sorrow-than-in-anger tone typical of most American appraisals of their French ally, 'It doesn't matter about 3,000 Communists demonstrating *against* me; what *is* serious is that there shouldn't have been 3,000 or even 300 Frenchmen to demonstrate *for* me.'[22] That the foreign general now in control of France's destiny should have been expecting the natives of Paris to demonstrate in favour of him, like South Sea islanders welcoming

MacArthur, was a novel idea for Frenchmen of any persuasion . . . Later in 1951 Eisenhower told *Paris-Match* that he would like to see France rediscover the 'spirit of Verdun' (where 300,000 Frenchmen lost their lives in 1916 – since when the French have used the word as shorthand for 'pointless slaughter'). For, he cheerfully added, a showdown with the Russians might be imminent. Before long Western armies might be fighting in the Ukraine or 'in the neighbourhood of Leningrad'; the Russians' 'noses would bleed' alright . . . [23]

With assistance of this calibre it was hardly surprising that the PCF was able to awaken strong pacifist and neutralist sentiments amidst a growing wave of anti-American French nationalism. But at leadership level the PCF was deadlocked, with a hard-line faction, led by Mme Vermeersch and the Party's ideologist, Billoux, vehemently opposing Duclos's wish to renegotiate an alliance with the SFIO, now again, like the PCF, an opposition party. In early 1952 Billoux and Mme Vermeersch went to Moscow and returned, predictably, with Thorez's blessing for an ultra-hard line. Thorez had strongly criticised the PCF's representatives in the peace movement for countenancing neutralism; dismissed all ideas of a popular front with the assertion that the French bourgeoisie had sold itself out beyond redemption to the US; insisted that the PCF must not entertain any further ideas of parliamentary alliances (i.e. with the SFIO); and instructed the PCF that the time was ripe to launch the masses in (extra-parliamentary) motion against US imperialism. The wavering Party leadership fell into line: the PCF representatives in the peace movement were disciplined; their journal, *Action*, was abruptly closed down; co-operation with the SFIO was rejected as an alliance between 'the traitors and the betrayed'; and a large mass demonstration was called against the new head of SHAPE, General Ridgeway,[24] who arrived in Paris in May 1952.

The result was disaster. The Pinay government, perhaps frightened by the PCF's new hard line, decided to crush the Party and any opposition to Ridgeway. An anti-American play was first broken up by police-organised rioting and then summarily prohibited. André Stil, the editor of *L'Humanité*, was imprisoned for publishing a call to demonstrate. Finally, on the day of the demonstration, the protestors were met by the concerted fury of thousands of police and *gardes mobiles*, producing the famous 'Ridgeway riots'. Duclos was imprisoned on a ludicrous, trumped-up charge (he was accused of sending messages to the Russians by carrier pigeon) and throughout France the police raided PCF offices, arrested thousands of militants, seized Party newspapers and announced the uncovering of a 'gigantic Communist espionage organisation'.[25] Many Communists went into hiding, for it seemed the government was bent on the Party's complete suppression.

With Duclos in jail and Thorez still away, the leadership devolved to the Party's No. 3, Marty. Lecoeur, the No. 4, knowing that Marty was under investigation, attempted to seize the leadership himself. Mme Vermeersch, for her part, now regarded herself as the natural leader and it was on her urging that a political general strike was now called. It was, inevitably, a complete fiasco. The PCF's sudden hard line had brought it close to ruin – at a time when its chances of leading the burgeoning wave of French nationalism had seemed distinctly bright. In September 1952 Marty and Tillon were expelled – a major blow to Party morale, for both were regarded as heroic figures by many militants.[26] In October the government launched a further wave of repression, arresting more militants and trade unionists and attempting to lift the parliamentary immunity of PCF deputies in order to try them for sedition (for opposing the war in Indo-China). The Slansky trial and then the affair of the 'Jewish doctors' who, allegedly, had hastened Stalin to his death further deepened the gloom and the PCF's isolation. In the end the Party was saved from complete suppression not by its own efforts, but by the government's growing unpopularity and the growing liberal outcry against 'French McCarthyism'.

With Stalin's death Thorez returned, energetically taking in hand the near-wreck of the PCF. Lecoeur was quickly purged and expelled (he, too, had fallen out with Mme Vermeersch, whose version of events Thorez naturally accepted: 'Lecoeur wanted to bury me before I was dead,' was his explanation).[27] He was replaced with Marcel Servin, a young railway worker who had earned his spurs as one of the Party 'judges' against Marty and Tillon. (Georges Marchais and Roland Leroy, the PCF's future Nos. 1 and 2, were to earn *their* spurs by playing a similar role in 1960–1 when it was Servin's turn to be expelled.)

Ironically Thorez, in effect, now accepted Duclos's more moderate line. The Korean armistice, the execution of Beria and the emergence of a new Soviet leadership bent on peaceful co-existence with the West all contributed to a notable softening of the climate. Before long the PCF began to multiply its appeals to the SFIO for a new popular front, claiming that only this could achieve a satisfactory settlement of the mounting war in Algeria. Mollet spurned all such offers with contempt – indeed, he entered the 1956 elections proclaiming that he would rather lose twenty seats than accept the PCF's embrace. This was a shade disingenuous, for the fact was that the 1951 electoral system meant that, anyway, the SFIO stood to fare much better in alliance with the Centre. Nonetheless, the PCF voted for the investiture of the Mollet government issuing from the elections and tried by every means to coax the SFIO into alliance with them. Mollet's first move was to ask the Assembly for special powers over Algeria. The PCF, conscious that these would be used to send more troops to intensify the repression in Algeria, pleaded with Mollet against such a step but, when he went ahead, the PCF voted for the measure. With the PCF deputies quite vocal in their abhorrence of such a move, only the most brutal exertion of discipline by the Party leadership was able to secure such a result. (The deputies' fears were quickly borne out, with Lacoste displaying the same ferocity in Algeria he had earlier revealed in dealing with the miners of the Nord.) When the Mollet government was overthrown in May 1957 the PCF redoubled its attempts to secure an alliance, even promising Mollet a compromise over Algerian policy to that end. It was no good.

Meanwhile the PCF had to confront the awesome crisis posed by Khrushchev's anti-Stalin speech at the 20th CPSU Congress (February 1956). There was no sign that Thorez was in any way prepared for this onslaught on all he held most dear. Indeed, shortly before the Congress Pierre Hervé, a leading PCF intellectual, had been expelled for criticising 'dogmatism' (i.e. Stalinism). Thorez (a delegate in

Moscow, with Duclos and Servin) greeted the Soviet delegates with a speech hailing the CPSU for 'ceaselessly providing a model of tenacity, of unfailing fidelity to the noble ideas of Marx, Engels and Stalin'.[28] Then came the epochal speeches of Mikoyan and Khrushchev . . . Although they were only published in full four months later (by the US State Department), the general drift of the speeches leaked out almost immediately – with electrifying effect.

The PCF delegates returned home. Neither they nor the PCF as a whole said anything about Khrushchev's speech. A month later the central committee met. Thorez was absent, pleading ill-health – though he was well enough to leave for Italy with his entire family, there to consult with Togliatti.[29] In his absence Waldeck-Rochet[30] argued for the speedy de-stalinisation of the PCF, Mme Vermeersch for a slow and partial process. Thorez's own view was almost certainly more conservative still. All else apart, he knew Khrushchev well, had, indeed, lived in Khrushchev's house with him during the war[31] and almost certainly regarded himself as his senior in the international Communist movement. Finally, Thorez broke his silence: 'the mistake of Comrade Stalin was, during the latter period of his leadership, to ignore certain rules for the life and conduct of the party which he had himself taught to Communists the world over . . .' This hardly constituted a ringing condemnation of Stalin's crimes (the word 'crimes' was never used by the PCF), particularly since Thorez continued:

> As if the CPSU's general line has not led the Soviet Union from triumph to triumph on the path to prosperity, cultural progress and national greatness . . . As if the necessary criticism of certain errors could take away anything from the historic merits of Stalin! Stalin deepened and advanced the theoretical and practical heritage of Lenin. He was the driving force behind the fulfilment of the Five Year plans and the construction of socialism over a sixth of the planet. He played a decisive role in defeating the party's enemies – Trotskyites and Rightists who would have led the October Revolution to defeat and connived with the plots of international imperialism against Soviet power . . .[32]

Even Ulbricht was more forthright than this in condemning Stalin – while Togliatti warmly welcomed the move and set course right away for a policy of complete independence for the PCI. Surely, Togliatti argued, the fault lay not with Stalin but with the Soviet system – and the other Soviet leaders who had cultivated the Stalin cult? The fact was that the Soviet system could no longer be accepted as a model – there was no 'unique guide', merely Communist polycentrism.[33] This speech drove Thorez close to apoplexy and a PCF delegation, led by Waldeck-Rochet, was immediately despatched to Moscow for talks with Khrushchev. They returned with the predictable message that Togliatti was speaking out of turn and that the source of Stalin's crimes must not be sought in the nature of the Soviet system.[34] For the PCF that was the end of the debate. Thorez quickly condemned his own personality cult – there must be no more talk of 'the party of Maurice Thorez' or 'the exaggerated celebration of certain birthdays'.[35] But that was all. Although Thorez criticised the notion of an 'unconditional attachment to the USSR' he swiftly fell back towards his old stance, strongly supporting Soviet intervention in Poland and Hungary. Inevitably, these events, together with Khrushchev's speech, led to great confusion and despair within the PCF – and open disaffection amongst large numbers of the party's intellectuals. Ten of these, including Pablo Picasso, were bold enough to sign an open letter of criticism to the Party. They were – of course – brought sharply to heel.[36]

One can only guess at the moral and emotional anguish Thorez suffered as a result of these events. And not just Thorez – for almost the whole Party was in the same condition. When news of Stalin's death had first reached France, a hardened cadre like Lecoeur had been so overcome that he had lost the power of speech for a while[37] – and such reactions had been not atypical. In the end, of course, the PCF's cadres and leaders were too well trained at hiding their feelings and in following every twist and turn of Moscow's policies not to be able to cope. But they coped, in large part, by refusing to assimilate the full import of Khrushchev's speech. One can gauge something of Thorez's true feelings by his behaviour in 1958 when Suslov, a Kremlin hard-liner, alerted European Communist leaders that Khrushchev was on the point of rehabilitating Bukharin, Rykov, Zinoviev and other victims of the Moscow Trials of the 1930s. Only Togliatti supported the move fully. Thorez flew to Moscow to plead with Khrushchev: 'After the 20th Congress and the Hungarian events we lost almost half of our Party. If you were formally to rehabilitate these who were tried in the open trials, we could lose the rest . . . You can rehabilitate them later, not all at the same time, but one after another, slowly.' Khrushchev, to his undying regret, had to give way.[38]

By 1958, however, the PCF – and the whole French Left – faced an even greater crisis in France itself. For, under the terrible stress of the Algerian war, the Fourth Republican system was finally disintegrating. In the wings, waiting to usher in a new period of authoritarian conservative rule, was De Gaulle. Even faced with this overwhelming threat the Left proved incapable of unity. The PCF vehemently opposed De Gaulle's return but the SFIO split down the middle – with Mollet, Defferre and Lacoste voting for De Gaulle. Mollet – inevitably – joined De Gaulle's first Cabinet. There was no trace now of the Left unity with which the Fourth Republic had begun. The Fifth Republic – the joint child of Massu's *paras* and the old Gaullist network – had been born amidst the ruins of the Left.

# 4 Towards Left Unity, 1958–72

The Fifth Republic came to birth as a result of the bitter and terrible conflict over Algeria. While the conflict continued at anything like peak intensity – which it did for another three years – the Left, like the rest of France, was mainly conscious of the sheer fact of crisis and the terrifying possibility of civil war which lurked behind it. This in turn produced a certain ambivalence on the Left towards De Gaulle's new regime.

The PCF had been thunderstruck by the events of 1958. A revolutionary situation along classically Leninist lines had existed – the ruling class had been unable 'to live and rule in the old way'[1] – and the revolution had duly taken place. But it had been De Gaulle's revolution, not theirs – indeed, everything had taken place almost as if the Party had not existed. For a few months the PCF tried to rally the masses in defence of the fallen Fourth Republic, but quickly gave up as it realised that that cause was now for ever lost. The PCF was then utterly humiliated by De Gaulle in the 1958 elections, losing at least a third of its vote. Traumatised by this result, the PCF railed so hysterically against De Gaulle that even when the General pronounced for Algerian self-determination in September 1959, the Party immediately attacked the plan as a clever demagogic device for prolonging the war. Two months later the PCF reversed itself entirely, considerably embarrassed that it had so lost its grip as to compromise its position on the central issue where, alone among French parties, it had shown a creditable consistency. Its embarrassment was compounded a few months later when Khrushchev visited Paris. Already De Gaulle had recognised Germany's Oder-Neisse frontier, halted the integration into NATO of the Armée de l'Air, withdrawn the French Mediterranean fleet from NATO's wartime command and challenged US control over all nuclear weapons and missiles stationed in France. It was hardly surprising that Khrushchev took pleasure in showing that he, at least, took seriously these growing signs of an independent Gaullist foreign policy.

Within the PCF Politburo this produced a major crisis for Thorez, whose stern insistence that De Gaulle was no more than the counter-revolutionary lackey of US imperialism had attracted increasing criticism from a younger group, led by Servin and Laurent Casanova.[2] These young Turks had argued that both Gaullism's clear mass appeal and its alignment with 'national bourgeois' interests against US imperialism merited an entirely fresh (i.e. softer) approach by the PCF. The wave of anti-American French nationalism (which the PCF had led a decade before and which, under a Duclos, it might still have been leading) had grown steadily in depth and intensity through the 1950s: now, at last, it had found issue in De Gaulle. The PCF, they argued, needed comprehensively to reappraise its objectives in this new political world.[3] Thorez replied (truthfully enough, but at deliberate cross-purposes) that the new regime was more infeodated than ever to monopoly capital. The issue was never in doubt: Servin, Casanova, and their friends were expelled from the Politburo and other party offices in January 1961. Thorez then proceeded – in classic style – to adopt most of the dissidents' views, expressing his satisfaction that the Gaullist regime, 'pushed by the pressure of the masses', had taken many positive steps – the recognition of China, opposition to the USA in South Asia and Latin America, and withdrawal from NATO. In one foreign affairs debate after another in the Assembly PCF deputies joined with the Gaullists against the other parties, competing in reviling them as American lackeys.[4] What was good for the Kremlin was good enough to put the PCF in two minds . . .

Socialist ambivalence towards the new regime sprang from different causes. The non-Communist Left had been badly split by the advent of De Gaulle. Mendès-France had refused utterly to compromise with this regime of 'personal power'; Mitterrand put himself forward immediately as a potential leader of a popular front against Gaullism; and a substantial minority broke away from the SFIO in disgust when Mollet decided to support the General's new constitution in 1958. This group, the *Parti Socialiste Autonome*, merged with other dissident left groups to form the *Parti Socialiste Unifié* (PSU) in 1960. Mitterrand submerged himself in the new world of the political clubs which blossomed in the otherwise sterile, apolitical desert of the early 1960s, when the chief opposition parties were clearly at a loss and the endless Algerian crisis had numbed all but the bravest spirits. The clubs ultimately federated into the *Convention des Institutions Républicains* (CIR) under Mitterrand's leadership.

All these new groupings shared several characteristics: numerous and enthusiastic activists; miniscule popular support; a feeling of outraged republicanism against the new Bonapartism of De Gaulle; and a consequent desire for the broadest possible unity of the Left – including the PCF. The Radicals were, as always, divided but were too much of a rag-bag party actually to split. Most, though, felt an instinctive sympathy with this republican current.

Mollet's SFIO stood apart from these newcomers and was far slower to adopt a clear-cut attitude. At the 1958 elections the SFIO's state of mind was revealed by its posters declaring 'De Gaulle and Mollet saved the Republic' and by one of its candidates who switched between ballots from telling voters that he had demonstrated against De Gaulle in May 1958 to reminding them that he had written a book praising him in 1945.[5] Such tactics had not, though, prevented electoral disaster. SFIO pessimists had feared the party might win as few as eighty seats. It won forty. After this Mollet could stay in the government only at the cost of presiding over policies not of his choosing. In December 1958 the government, secure in its huge conservative majority, launched a heavily deflationary economic policy. Mollet decided it was time to go and the SFIO left the government in January 1959, though promising that the SFIO would be only a 'constructive opposition' – a stance the party maintained for over two years. In Mollet's case, however, no smoke-signals from Moscow were necessary to reinforce such ambivalence. The Socialists were terrified of the sheer electoral power of the Gaullists, whose party, the UNR,[6] had been formed only a few weeks before the election but had still managed to win five times as many seats as the SFIO and twenty times as many as the PCF, hitherto the largest single party. In Mollet's considerable political repertoire the role of David against Goliath was perhaps the least favoured part. And, above all, the SFIO knew it had no alternative to offer to the new regime. It shrank from the dread possibility of having to manage the Algerian crisis and was entirely happy to surrender the task to De Gaulle instead. Meanwhile it turned a deaf ear to the reiterated Communist appeals for a popular front. Like the PCF – though much sooner – the SFIO came to feel that the alternatives to Gaullism might be worse.

By 1977 a united coalition of Communists, Socialists and Radicals, basing itself on a programme jointly agreed by all three parties and fired by the élan of its *dynamique unitaire*, was sweeping to power in three-quarters of urban France. The idea that such a thing could happen would, in the unpromising situation of the early 1960s, have seemed miraculous – perhaps even preposterous. That the miracle was achieved was due, essentially, to De Gaulle's very success in fashioning not just a makeshift Roman dictatorship to tide France over the Algerian crisis but a new political system – in French terms, indeed, a whole new world.

For many facets of this new environment worked – over time – to force the Left together. The most central factor was the simple and overwhelming strength of Gaullism, not just the General's ability to bring off one plebiscitary triumph after another, but the institutionalised power of the Gaullist party. In 1962, 1967, 1968 and 1973 it repeatedly swept in overall majorities to parliament; something never achieved before in French political history was now performed four times in a row. This success was based on Gaullist ability to attract the Centre as well as the Right behind a stable, modern, business-minded conservatism – integrated and crowned, of course, by the towering and charismatic figure of De Gaulle. Their position was consolidated by, on the one hand, a return to the old two-ballot system of the Third Republic for legislative elections, and, on the other, the creation of a directly elected presidency.[7] The two ballot system favoured those parties with a solid block of support on Left or Right *and* an ability to win over the Centre. In the Fifth Republic it at first almost wiped the PCF out of parliament (as it was designed to do); gradually annihilated the pure Centrists; and consistently favoured the Gaullists and their allies. The (similarly two ballot) presidential system – an obvious vehicle for De Gaulle's enormous personal appeal – consolidated the whole system by making effectively impossible any return to rule by Assembly.

The sheer strength of the Gaullist bloc and these institutional changes which gave it a stable and enduring form impacted upon the Left at many points. The Socialists lost the pivotal position they had enjoyed under the Fourth Republic when their votes had been decisive to the life or death of every government. The Gaullists were now easily strong enough on their own to set about giving their conservative supporters what they wanted, and simply ignore the SFIO. This was made brutally apparent to Mollet as early as 1959 (when he was still practising 'constructive opposition'); for the government not only adopted classically conservative economic policies, but also dealt the staggering affront of a new Act to increase subsidies to church schools – described by Debré, the Prime Minister, perhaps unfortunately, as 'the final solution' to the issue. Even the Catholic hierarchy gave the measure no support, fearing the ultimate results of such a gross provocation to the anti-clerical Left. Mollet tried at first to show 'understanding' for the government – but was quickly swept away by the intransigent fury of his followers, who awoke suddenly from their apolitical apathy to turn out in droves at angry meetings across the country.[8] The moral was obvious: there was now a strong conservative government whose friends were the clericals, the bankers and the upper classes. It *would* do things like this: there was nothing to stop it. For a time Mollet continued to resist this moral, for the obvious implication was that the SFIO had nowhere else to go but towards a united Left. In January 1962, with OAS terrorism at its height, Mollet acknowledged for the first time that the SFIO might need to ally itself with the PCF to oppose a fascist putsch. It was bad enough that the Left's disunity had opened the way to Gaullism; at least they must never repeat the errors of the German Communists and Social Democrats in 1933 and let in something even worse. The idea of a united Left fighting the good fight for republican democracy was, as Mollet knew, still an extremely potent one at the grassroots – and it did no harm to such hopes that Thorez had at last, in 1961, brought himself to condemn Stalin's crimes (though not Stalin) . . .[9]

In the end, of course, Mollet was not a politician to be swayed by general ideas such as these. He remained convinced that in any alliance with the PCF the SFIO would risk being eaten alive by its more powerful partner, and simultaneously lose valuable centrist support. To remove that reservation only the fear of electoral annihilation would suffice. And, in the shape of the all-conquering Gaullists, that too had now arrived . . . At the 1959 municipal elections, to the enormous satisfaction of the PCF, Mollet had accepted joint lists with the PCF in fifty cities (elsewhere remaining in coalition with Centrists) after the Gaullists had changed the municipal electoral law to their own advantage. Then, in September 1962, De Gaulle (illegally) rammed through a referendum on direct presidential election. Mollet was appalled and abandoned 'constructive opposition' for total opposition – and lost. In the general election which followed Mollet found himself backed up against the wall. The Gaullists were clearly set for another big win, would take the centre ground, and might annihilate the SFIO. Just before the poll Mollet accepted the inevitable and told his voters that in seats where the run-off was between 'an unconditional follower of De Gaulle and an unconditional follower of Khrushchev', it was better to vote PCF. In any case, he added, the PCF would be too weak to have any real influence, so no harm could come of the move.[10] It was hardly a ringing endorsement, but it was enough. A delighted Thorez quickly reached agreement for a series of local deals for mutual withdrawal at the second ballot – even (and to a grim silence from PCF militants) throwing in a number of *'cadeaux'*: that is, withdrawing PCF candidates who had run *ahead* of the SFIO in seats where the latter had a better chance of ultimate victory. The Radicals hastily followed Mollet's example and reached a similar deal.

In parliamentary terms the deal was a resounding success, with the three Left parties advancing from 75 to 147 seats. The PCF, hugely gratified, immediately announced that 'Communists have *no higher duty* than to extend and consolidate the rapprochement affected with the Socialists and other republicans'.[11] The Party's aims in this alliance were, of course, very much what Mollet feared they were: to bind the Socialists to them and colonise their support. Now, with nearly half the Radical and perhaps five-sixths of the SFIO deputies owing their seats to PCF votes,[12] a large step had been taken in that direction.

Within a few months this shaky rapprochement had taken on a substantial new dimension with the great miners' strike of March–April 1963. De Gaulle decided to break the strike by simply decreeing the requisitioning of the workers. The miners, supported by the whole Left and sympathetic liberal and Catholic opinion, simply ignored the order. De Gaulle had to make a humiliating climbdown and his popularity fell to a record low.[13] The strike had seen all the major trade unions united in a common front. Henceforth the CGT, CFTC and FO worked increasingly towards a co-ordinated unity of action, a development which undoubtedly increased the groundswell towards unity at grassroots level as the Left parties began to revive after the long dark night of the Algerian crisis. A new generation of militants was beginning to emerge on the Left (notably the Left Catholics of the PSU) for whom Left unity seemed the more, rather than the less obvious course. Such younger voices had an influence greater than their small numbers or organisational strength. For the old leaders of the Left had failed and were visibly in eclipse and the emasculation of parliament after 1962[14] diminished their ability to use their old national forum as a route back.

In July 1964 Thorez died. Had he lived he would, doubtless, have led a second popular front with the same enthusiasm he had brought to the first one thirty years before; that is, PCF tactics would not have been different. But his passing marked the end of an epoch none the less. He belonged to that pivotal generation who have largely made the history of the twentieth-century, those caught up by the First World War, scarred beyond recovery, then cast loose as jetsam (like Hitler, Thorez had a brief period as a housepainter and odd-job man) – until they fixed their loyalties on a new vision of the world. In Thorez's case the Soviet Union had been the unconditional, the unalterable centre of that vision – something which was less true of the new (and more collective) PCF leadership under Waldeck-Rochet. Thorez was mourned by the greatest proletarian funeral ever seen in France (only De Gaulle's was to be a greater national occasion). But nothing seemed more fitting than that he had died while on holiday in his beloved Soviet Union . . .

The old guard of the SFIO had, however, by no means committed themselves to a united Left alliance. Moreover, with the party out of government, effectively redundant in the Assembly, and organisationally weaker than ever, the party rested ever more solidly on its remaining municipal bastions. (By 1971 some three-fifths of its party members were local councillors and over two-thirds of its deputies were also mayors.)[15] Many of the SFIO mayors retained power thanks only to Third Force coalitions with the Centre and were deeply threatened by the possibility of having to compromise their traditional anti-Communist stance. The PCF's dearest wish was, they knew, to force them to drop their Centrist partners and bind themselves to the PCF alliance right down to the local grassroots, for then there would be no going back. Mollet – of course – favoured a policy of local opportunism, with no overall national agreement: he himself was elected as a deputy thanks to PCF votes and as a mayor thanks to Catholic votes . . .[16]

Gaston Defferre, the millionaire lawyer and newspaper-owner who was the boss of the greatest SFIO bastion, Marseilles, was of a rather different view. His Third Force coalition depended on a visceral anti-Communism – every municipal election in Marseilles was virtually a pitched battle with the PCF – and the recipe had brought him repeated success. In 1964–5, attempting to apply the same formula at national level, Defferre launched an ambitious bid for presidential nomination. A Communist could never win the presidency, or, probably, even poll the PCF's normal vote in such a hopeless cause; nor could a Socialist who was dependent on a Communist alliance; but a Socialist with Centre support might beat the PCF at the first ballot and then win by taking their votes anyway (as the Left's best hope) at the second ballot: thus the Defferre strategy. Had the Defferre strategy succeeded all prospects of Left unity would have been dashed for years to come. It was, however, defeated by a strange and unholy alliance of Gaullists (who saw Defferre as a formidable opponent), the PCF (who were deeply threatened by his strategy and preferred De Gaulle as president on foreign policy grounds), and the SFIO Establishment (which disliked the idea of an alliance with the clerical MRP and feared Defferre would found a new Centre-Left presidential party to take over the SFIO). The showdown came with the 1965 municipal elections which saw a furious and concerted attempt by the Gaullists and the PCF to dislodge Defferre in Marseilles. The Gaullists, disappointed by the results of their gerrymandering of the electoral system in the 1959 elections, now changed the law again: in a way that was strongly unfavourable to Defferre. The PCF's all-out assault in Marseilles succeeded in splitting the SFIO there but Defferre managed to hold on – though only by moving so strongly to the Right as to damage his presidential chances. Elsewhere the PCF and SFIO ran popular fronts in sixty of the 159 large towns, obtaining a number of notable victories.[17] Defferre's bid collapsed a few weeks later.

With time running short – just two months before the presidential election – the Left parties settled on François Mitterrand as their joint candidate. The speed and easy unanimity of this choice (Waldeck-Rochet announcing the PCF's support apparently on his sole personal initiative)[18] were somewhat surprising. Mitterrand's political credit had seemed irretrievably damaged by the peculiar 'Mitterrand Affair' of 1959. (His car had been followed and shot up by OAS terrorists, but later evidence showed that Mitterrand had had advance knowledge of the attempt, knowledge he had concealed from the magistracy when he filed charges. He had, his enemies claimed, merely been seeking heroic publicity.)[19] Moreover Mitterrand was running on a pro-EEC, pro-NATO ticket indistinguishable from Defferre's, save for a harder line against church schools. But the Left had to have *a* candidate – and time was short. Moreover, Mitterrand *was* willing to accept an informal alliance with the PCF. And, given that victory for De Gaulle was a foregone conclusion anyway (the Left were delighted merely to force him to a second ballot), it was not worth disrupting the nascent Left alliance (and thus threatening SFIO deputies elected on PCF votes) to no obvious purpose. In a very real sense the Left turned to Mitterrand out of relief that they did not, after all, need to cope with Defferre's problematic candidacy. Instead, all sections of the Left were able to campaign enthusiastically in the accustomed, and therefore comfortable, style of vague popular republicanism. It was a fateful decision, lightly entered into. The PCF's eagerness for a popular front had led it implicitly to accept its own absence from the crucial presidential arena; Mitterrand emerged with enormously enhanced stature – the 'Mitterrand phenomenon' was born; and first the SFIO and then the PCF were to find they had created a new leader of the Left able to threaten them both. For what neither had fully recognised was that the new instrument of direct presidential election was to be an extremely potent agent of a simple Left-Right polarisation. In the supreme political arena there could, in effect, now be only two parties: and the candidates who led them would develop their own supra-party personal followings. Such a process made Left unity almost inevitable, but it also greatly weakened the ability of the established Left parties to dictate the terms of that unity.

Mollet was the first to feel the pressure. Mitterrand hastened to consolidate his non-Communist electorate in the *Fédération de la Gauche Démocratique et Socialiste* (FGDS), consisting of the SFIO, Mitterrand's own CIR, and the bulk of the Radicals (the PSU refused to join). The intent, clear from the first, was to build a large new party of the non-Communist Left, one in which the SFIO would be invited to merge and dissolve itself and from which the discredited old leaders of the Fourth Republic (meaning, remarkably, Mollet and Defferre, but not Mitterrand!) would be dropped. The resultant party would accept the popular front logic of the presidential election but, presenting the newly presidential figure of Mitterrand as leader and grouping together the major fragments of the non-Communist Left, would achieve a new strength and credibility as at least a fully equal partner of the mighty PCF. For in the end, Mitterrand knew, only a party able to deal with the PCF from a position of strength would be able to escape the accusation of being a mere tool of the Communists. Given the horror in which the PCF was held by centrist voters whose support would always be crucial to electoral success, any hope of eventual victory must depend on a 're-equilibration' of the forces of the Left. Thus Mitterrand's strategic answer to Defferre.

The popular impetus provided by Mitterrand's relative success against De Gaulle gave Mollet little choice about accepting SFIO membership of the FGDS, but he stubbornly refused all proposals for a real merger. He had, however, accepted the logic of the popular front strategy and in 1967 the FGDS and PCF actually drew up a national electoral agreement providing for mutual withdrawal across the board in favour of the best-placed Left candidate at the second ballot. The PCF, delighted by this further step (and the FGDS kept its word, sternly expelling the – rare – local rebels against the pact), again rewarded the FGDS with second round *'cadeaux'*, standing down fifteen PCF candidates in favour of less well-placed Left rivals. The agreement worked smoothly. The Left gained votes and seats, and, after the election, managed to draw up a common policy declaration which, while full of agreements to disagree and pregnant silences over foreign policy, represented a new high point of Left unity.

From the PCF's point of view all was not entirely well and good, however. They recognised that the stability and economic success achieved by the Gaullists meant that, if they were to be taken seriously, opposition parties had to operate more and more as an Opposition in the British sense – offering the voters a coherent governmental alternative. But this was not the reason why they had wanted a popular front. The SFIO had backed so reluctantly (and only in desperation) into such an alliance, with the PCF coaxing and encouraging them at every point, because they both held the same underlying assumption that a popular front would principally benefit the PCF. Mollet and Thorez were nothing if not shrewd tacticians of long experience. They 'knew' that when their parties formed an alliance – as in 1936 or 1944–7 – the PCF came off best in terms of votes.[20] The trouble was that their experience was *too* long that they were men of the Fourth (in Thorez's case the Third) Republic. They had, quite understandably, failed wholly to grasp that they were living in a new political universe, where the old rules did not apply. For the fact was – the 1967 results made it clear – that the major benefits of unity were going to the FGDS, which had nearly drawn level with the PCF. Mitterrand's strategy was working. For the moment the PCF could brush aside these worrying signs. The new, post-Thorez leadership was determined to clamber out of the ghetto. Indeed, after years of not daring to think such thoughts, they had begun to consider the possibility of the Party achieving some real governmental power. And, after all, the PCF had gained *some* votes in 1967. The signs were noted – in the 1968 elections the PCF gave the FGDS only three *'cadeaux'* – but this was not time for faint-heartedness. Almost all the FGDS deputies were now dependent on PCF votes. Their strategy was working too. The Party would press on.

All mere electoral calculations were, in any case, quickly swept aside by the epochal events of 1968. There is no need to retell here the story of either the Czechoslovakian drama or the Paris May Events. What concerns us more is to detail their results.

This is much easier to do in the former case. Waldeck-Rochet, on the eve of the Soviet invasion of Prague, flew to Moscow to attempt, desperately, to dissuade the Soviet leadership from this course; he failed; the PCF made a historic declaration of independence by condemning the USSR for its action; and Mme Vermeersch departed in high dudgeon from the Politburo in order to affirm her continuing and unconditional support for the Soviet Union. Externally this stand did the PCF little good: the wave of public anger against the Russians inevitably hurt the Party all the same. Internally, however, the Party began a major process of reorientation. For the first time the PCF had taken its distance from the USSR, embarking on the same independent road the PCI had taken under Togliatti twelve years before. Traumatically for many members, the question of by which star the Party was to set its course was now an open one. Mme Vermeersch remained an isolated figure but she undoubtedly represented many older militants who felt uncomfortable deprived of this rudder, and who were too marked by the long ghetto experience not to nurse deep reservations about the Party's cordial relations with the SFIO as well. Such militants were, by definition, last-ditch Party loyalists: there was no question of their breaking ranks into public visibility. But the PCF leadership was nervously aware that it now had within the Party a grumbling potential opposition, whose sensitivities it would have to respect.[21] Thus the PCF leadership left open the question of how it now regarded the Soviet model in general: there was no ideological follow-through to the Party's new posture. The true significance of the move was, rather, that the PCF, conscious of the horror felt by the rest of the Left at the Prague events, had done the indispensable minimum to maintain popular front unity in France, giving this domestic consideration higher priority than Soviet foreign policy for the first time.

Even today it is far harder to gauge the real results of the 1968 May Events – the student riots, the general strike of 10 million workers, and the enormous electoral landslide to the Right which brought down the curtain on eight extraordinary weeks of theatre. At the time the claim was widely made that the Events had proved both the possibility of revolution in advanced capitalist societies and the PCF's firm rejection of such a possibility. It is, however, difficult to accord much sense to the first proposition or, in consequence, to the second. The student riots produced a large number of bruised, bewildered and angry policemen and CRS cadres in Paris, but made no greater dent in the State's defences than that. The general strike posed a far greater threat to the regime, but only at one remove. The country was brought to a halt (though by year's end the strike was a mere statistical hiccup in the economy's smooth, continuing ascent). But the strikers were, in the end, happy enough to accept the extremely handsome wage deal ultimately wrung from the *patronat* by the trade unions – they had no alternative programme. True, an intransigent minority demanded a revolutionary coup in Paris and the creation of a new Commune. But the PCF saw, quite rightly, that this would, if attempted, produce only a bloody disaster. The students had managed to set in motion a syndicalist wave over which neither they nor, to its fury, the PCF had any control: then – with tanks ringing Paris, the forces of law and order still entirely intact, and troops actually on the move – the *gauchistes*, in effect, turned to the PCF and demanded that it lead the way into the valley of death. The PCF, well aware that it would be blamed for any such attempt no matter how much it opposed it, recoiled in furious horror from a venture in which the working-class suburbs of Paris, *not* the university area, would be likely to play the main sacrificial role. At worst the 1871 massacre of the Communards might be re-enacted with modern weaponry: Budapest 1956 would be the nearest model. Its base, its militants, its industrial strength – not the students, already swanning off on vacation – would be smashed. The Party, the unity of the Left, and the labour movement as a whole would be broken, perhaps for a generation, by such an adventure. In the event the PCF could feel only relief that this was avoided, that wage increases and the extension of union rights were achieved, and that the Left got away with only an electoral hiding.

For this was the paradox of May. There was, undeniably, an unprecedented mood of revolt against all notions of hierarchy, authority and *dirigisme*, one which shook the parties of the Left almost as much as the Establishment. So great, indeed, was this shock that the regime wavered and trembled. For the first time the general popular assumption that De Gaulle was invincible, that his regime was invulnerable, came under decisive challenge. This much was comprehended by all, with lasting effect. But there was no popular majority – as the elections were to show – who actually wished to push this challenge to a conclusion. Indeed, the Left suffered most precisely when its leaders attempted to exploit the regime's sudden, new vulnerability. In the anti-Communist crusade which the June 1968 election campaign quickly became, few things were more sharply remembered than the badly misjudged remarks by Waldeck-Rochet and Mitterrand calling on De Gaulle to resign and declaring their willingness to take his place. Waldeck-Rochet had announced that 'we are ready to assume, within a people's government of democratic union, all the responsibility that devolves on a great workers' party such as ours'.[22] Mitterrand had gone even further, proposing the immediate formation of a provisional government including the PCF, FGDS and Centre under either himself or Mendès-France, and had simultaneously announced himself a candidate for the presidency.[23] As the Gaullists were quick to point out, both proposals smacked of opportunistic compromise with a *coup d'état*. The two great (self-proclaimed) defenders of 'republican legality' were suggesting the replacement of a recently and democratically elected government ... by themselves.

The trouble was, as Régis Debray succinctly pointed out ten years later,

People did not want a right wing government; they were ferociously against it. They did not want a left wing government either; they were not at all in favour. Mendès-France, Mitterrand, Waldeck: still the Old World, the incarnation of the system. Left and Right, same fight. Well, how about no government at all. Every time the shadow of some alternative or provisional plan was erected in a corner, there were storms of facetious abuse. Unhappily, a society, any society, abhors a vacuum, like nature; it has to have a government, any government. Then we'll have one. The old one, that is; no hassle, it's there already.[24]

The June election reduced the Left's painfully constructed popular front almost to ruins. The FGDS and PCF respected the same second ballot discipline as before, but the old spirit of unity was gone. FGDS candidates frequently wilted under the heat of the anti-Communist campaign and some – Defferre, most notably – tried hard to distance themselves from the PCF and woo the Centre.[25] Mitterrand's stock had fallen so low that he was now a positive liability to his party. His new-born FGDS began to disintegrate before his eyes. The PCF watched the process with dismay, but saved its real fury for its enemies on its Left – the Trotskyites and the PSU (the only party to support the students). In the event the PCF and FGDS both lost more than half their seats and the PSU was wiped out. Even its leader, Mendès-France, lost his seat and, soon afterwards, left the PSU. He was succeeded by Michel Rocard, who signalled his emergence as a new star on the Left by restoring the PSU to parliament, almost immediately winning a sensational by-election against the Gaullist premier, Couve de Murville.

The PCF had lost votes – votes it was never afterwards to regain – but it had survived. It was not long before it began to win its bitter defensive battle against *gauchiste* influence in the factories and, with the CGT sharing in the general boom in trade union membership after the May Events, the Party could even claim greater industrial strength than before. (The major gainer was, though, the CFDT, which had been far more in tune with the workers' mood and which now drew closer to parity with the CGT.)

Mitterrand and the FGDS were far harder hit. So great was Mitterrand's public discredit that the first act of the savagely reduced FGDS parliamentary group was to vote to send a delegation to its leader demanding that he resign. Mitterrand was saved from this dénouement only by the almost equal humiliation of being saved by Mollet.[26] But both the Radicals and the freshly ascendant Mollet used their position to break with Mitterrand's strategy and steer sharply away from the PCF (finding its stand over Czechoslovakia insufficiently anti-Russian). Criticism of Mitterrand continued to mount and in November 1968 he resigned his presidency of the FGDS, calling for a new party with new leaders (a parting shot at Mollet).[27] Mitterrand's own CIR took up the call, announcing that the FGDS was dead. The idea of a new party was gradually and hesitantly taken up by the remnants of the FGDS but De Gaulle's resignation after his April 1969 referendum defeat found the non-Communist Left still at sixes and sevens.

The ensuing presidential election saw the contradictions of the Left glaringly exposed. The FGDS remnant met hurriedly, decided to form a new *Parti Socialiste,* and then transformed itself into a nominating convention. Mollet fought desperately for the nomination of a mere cipher – for he had already decided to back the Centrist, Poher, at the second ballot. He was defeated and instead the PS nominated Defferre, attempting belatedly to revive his bid of five years before. The PCF saw this as tantamount to a declaration of war and nominated Duclos. The PSU angrily dissociated itself from both the major Left parties and nominated Rocard, while the Trotskyites nominated the former student leader, Alain Krivine. Mendès, in an act of hideous unwisdom which was to signal the effective end of his career, agreed to be Defferre's running mate. Mitterrand, the hero of 1965, was not considered and had the good sense to maintain a low profile. He was, as it turned out, well out of it all. Pompidou was an always certain winner and the real battle on the Left quickly resolved itself into a trial by ordeal of the old Defferre strategy.

The first IFOP poll[28] confirmed the worst fears of the PCF: Duclos and Defferre were running equal at 10 per cent each (Rocard taking 3 per cent) with the bulk of the Left's vote sliding to Poher. Defferre, in other words, seemed on the verge of being proved right: the PCF could not poll its full strength in a presidential election and Left voters would move to the Centre if that was the best hope of winning. The PCF instructed its organisers to concentrate their attentions merely on ensuring that the hard-core faithful were pulled into line. A week later this process saw Duclos creep up to 12 per cent, then 14 per cent – while Defferre drifted down to 8 per cent. This was enough to establish Duclos as the Left's best hope and support continued to crystallise around him. With a week to go he reached 16 per cent, with two days left 18 per cent. On election day he won 21.5 per cent against Defferre's derisory 5.1 per cent. Duclos had, indeed, almost caught Poher (23.4 per cent). PCF leaders I spoke to after the election believed they could have done this had the campaign been only another forty-eight hours longer. Had this happened the polls suggested, interestingly, that Pompidou would have beaten Duclos by a 69 per cent: 31 per cent margin – probably a fairly accurate measure of the outer limits of PCF support. the PCF rounded off this virtual triumph by calling for 'revolutionary abstention' on the second (Pompidou *v*. Poher) ballot, a move which reduced the *gauchistes* (with their slogan of 'Elections – trahison') to muttering silence.

The problem which the PCF faced was, ironically, that the Socialists, their old *frère-ennemi*, were too weak. Defferre, and the Defferre strategy, had been crushed once and for all but the non-Communist Left was in ruins as a result. Straight after the election the new PS had selected a virtual unknown, Alain Savary, as its leader, thus ending Mollet's twenty-three-year reign. It was a brave attempt to revitalise the party by turning to a new, younger generation. In the wake of Defferre's crushing defeat – his 5.1 per cent of the vote had almost been equalled by Rocard (3.7 per cent) and Krivine (1.1 per cent) – what the PS lacked, however, was substance and credibility: something which Savary and his team of young enthusiasts simply had insufficient stature to provide. And for the PCF's popular front strategy to work it was essential that it should have a credible non-Communist partner which was strong enough not to be a mere Communist front, however committed to the PCF alliance it might be. The idea that the PCF had anything to fear from the resurgence of such a party (which, on the 1967 results, had seemed plausible) was now buried. Instead, the PCF returned to its former strategy of attempting to breathe life into its flagging partner.

This was no easy job, despite the wholesale rejuvenation of the PS launched by Savary. By 1971 he had replaced 70 per cent of the Party's Federal Secretaries and the average age of Party office-holders had fallen by 20 years.[29] The ease with which this new generation took over the party was, however, more a sign of organisational morbidity than of growth, for party membership continued to decline steeply.[30] Moreover, while the old SFIO initials had disappeared (after sixty-four years) and Mollet's old SFIO gang had been largely displaced from the PS national organisation, the party relied more heavily than ever on the old SFIO municipal redoubts.

In the wake of the dramatic events of 1968–9, however, the problems of the Left did not seem to be primarily or even very importantly about questions of party strength or organisation. For several years the echoes of May 1968 continued to drown all such concerns. To stroll through Paris in this period was to experience the lingering power of the Events. The new battlegrounds were the *lycées*, where hordes of latter-day Cohn-Bendits flourished briefly in a welter of sit-ins, strikes, protests and, above all, graffiti. One passed street corners where little knots of concierges stood gazing with bleak fear and hatred at the antics of twelve- and thirteen-year-olds as they emerged from their schools through menacing cordons of police. The ferocious air of gentility's panic was never far away. Authority – headmasters, employers, parents, police – experienced fresh twinges of the *crises nerveuses* they had known in May and, almost invariably, overreacted, to the point of self-parody. Pompidolian Paris lived with the continuing question of whether 'it' might somehow start all over again. The Events had been so sudden and shaking and yet, in a sense, so causeless that it was feared they could return as quickly, rather as the plague had paid recurrent, fearsome visits to medieval cities. The far Left was equally committed to this fantasy and confidently predicted that the process begun by May would produce the revolution, so long and patiently awaited, by '''70 or '72''.[31] Nothing happened, of course, to lend the slightest credence to these fears and hopes, but while they lingered the Left was in no mood to undertake the slow and painful work of reconstruction.

There was, moreover, an understandable reluctance to allow the spirit of May to die. For many, especially the young, it had indeed been bliss to be alive through that utopian spring. Everything, suddenly, had seemed possible. A handful of laughing radicals had created a sort of joyous anarchy and lo! the system had trembled. The radicals had outflanked everyone and undermined everything. How to be a political leader after May, when all politicians and all authority had been so decisively challenged, so hilariously mocked? How could any mere party programme compare with dreamworld slogans such as *'L' imagination au pouvoir'*? How could one go back to the mundane tedium of electoral politics? 'Run, comrade, the old world is behind you . . . ' May, surely, had changed all that? It had changed France, the world, one's private life, one's consciousness. May had been an earthquake which had made the 'old world' seem unreal. When, after May, France returned to the old world – the real world – that too seemed unreal.

The mood ebbed, slowly. On the Left, beneath a continuing cloud of verbiage about revolution and the 'quality of life' – the detritus of May – a process of fundamental reassessment began. Its conclusions were the polar opposite of those espoused by the *enragés* of May and its result was the almost magical rebirth of the 'Mitterrand phenomenon' which had, in May, seemed a part of ancient history. *'Non à De Gaulle. Non à Mitterrand. Oui au pouvoir populaire'*, the posters around the Sorbonne had read. Despised by the spirit of May, disliked by the bourgeoisie, and a source of embarrassment to the Left, Mitterrand had seemed lost beyond recall. True, many Frenchmen besides him had talked and behaved in May 1968 in ways they later found it discomforting to recall, but Mitterrand's opportunism then was only the most recent mark against him. If a fresh beginning was to be made, surely his games of Fourth Republic ministerial musical chairs made him at least as much a relic as Mollet? And then there was the still unsolved, still mysterious 'Mitterrand Affair' of 1959 . . . How could he make yet a third comeback? But he could – and did.

For the 'old world' had not gone away. Slowly and painfully the realisation grew that it was May that had been the dream, not all the time before and since. And as the dream cleared the Left faced the same procrustean facts it had confronted before. The Left lacked the industrial strength to win change that way. In 1968 the workers had rebelled, had come closer than ever before to fulfilling the old anarcho-syndicalist myth of the general strike. But the system had survived – and gone from strength to strength. Even the wage increases were quickly wiped out by inflation and the employers' counter-offensive neutralised most of the newly won union rights. Within a year or two the jungle had grown over and was in full flower where the monuments of May had stood; it was a tale of Ozymandias.[32] Oddly, perhaps, the Events redounded ultimately in favour of the pursuit of power by orthodox electoral and parliamentary means.

If one believed that May 1968 had not, in fact, been a revolutionary situation, it became difficult to believe in the arrival of such a situation at all, for no greater challenge to the existing order than that posed by the Events could easily be envisaged. Alternatively, if one believed that 1968 *had* presented the Left with a revolutionary opportunity, then it became all the clearer that the Left, particularly the PCF, were not prepared or able to grasp such opportunities. Either way the electoral road to power remained as the only alternative. For all save revolutionary utopians it was again clear that the only way to get rid of the Gaullist party-state was to vote it out. In which case, Mitterrand's way had, surely, been the right one . . .

For, as the disasters of 1968–9 were slowly absorbed, the Left looked back with increasing regard to the 1965–7 period when under Mitterrand's leadership, it had known unity, growth and progress. Surely the Left's best hope lay in getting back on the track from which 1968 had derailed it? The 1969 election had proven the bankruptcy of the only available alternative strategies: on the one hand Defferre had been humiliated; on the other, Duclos had shown, despite his relative success, the conclusive impossibility of a Communist winning a presidential election. In 1965 Mitterrand had taken over 45 per cent of the second ballot vote against De Gaulle. In 1969, against the much lesser figure of Pompidou, the Left hadn't even made it to the second ballot. The choice was stark: Mitterrand's strategy or irrelevance.

This logic was accepted without much question by most of Savary's young Turks now running the PS, particularly by the party's left wing organised in the *Centre d'Etudes, de Récherches et d'Education Socialistes* (CERES) run by Jean-Pierre Chevènement. CERES, though it included many Left Catholics, and felt itself close to the burgeoning 'new politics' of women's rights, ecology and workers' self-management, often merely illustrated how ideologically dominant on the Left the PCF was. For CERES's real guiding principle was that the new PS must be really a new party, a truly Marxist Party which would turn its back for ever on the shabby compromises and opportunism of the Mollet era, a party which, above all, would have no enemies on the Left. In practice this meant that CERES was unconditionally favourable towards whatever proposals the PCF put forward to advance the popular front. The PCF, from 1970 effectively under Marchais's leadership (Waldeck-Rochet having fallen incurably ill), continued to push for maximum unity, including the binding of the PS to a common programme with the PCF: very well, CERES too would support a common programme . . .

This view was, inevitably, not shared by the PS's only real source of strength, its bevy of ex-SFIO mayors. However, in the March 1971 municipal elections the current in favour of a renewed popular front was strong enough to produce a sweeping extension of PCF/PS alliances at city level. In 1971 there were such alliances in nearly two-thirds of the large towns, compared with not much over one-third in 1965.[33] PS leaders remained carefully insistent, however, that such co-operation was only a technical matter. Thus Pierre Mauroy, the mayor of Lille, thanked the PCF for withdrawing in his favour at the second ballot with a statement that 'There is no question of collaboration with the Communist Party. Withdrawal is an electoral tactic. Nothing more.'[34] This was, in fact, disingenuous: with the bulk of PS mayors as well as deputies now dependent on PCF votes the PS had taken a huge step towards the effective consolidation of the popular front. If some mayors wished to make the movement while walking backwards or on tiptoe, the PCF's satisfaction was hardly diminished – for the direction of advance remained unmistakable.

The stage was now set for Mitterrand's comeback. Mollet no longer stood in his path. Defferre could never be a rival again. The memory of his ill-judged speech in 1968 had begun to fade. The young PS had accepted his strategy implicitly at the municipal elections and was now bound almost irrevocably to it, whatever its reservations in principle. And weak though the PS was organisationally, it was clearly still a prize worth capturing. At the municipal elections the Left's combined score had been around 47 per cent,[35] suggesting a potential of as much as 25 per cent for the non-Communist Left. If the PS could be invigorated – and there was no alternative vehicle, it was the PS or nothing – perhaps it could organise and incorporate that support to make itself as strong as the old FGDS had been at its height. Mitterrand accordingly mustered his CIR loyalists to battle and launched a campaign to dispossess Savary of the PS leadership. Savary, whose position had been continuously contested by both the right and left wings of the party, resisted with a fury born of long insecurity. Mitterrand, he pointed out, had been most things in his life but never before a Socialist. His sudden conversion in middle age not only to Socialism but even to Marxism was merely a cynical cover for carpetbagging. He had a point . . .

It was no good: at the PS Congress at Epinay-sur-Seine in June 1971 Mitterrand was elected as the new first secretary. It was an epochal victory – and a curious one. Mitterrand had controlled only 14 per cent of the delegate vote (mainly his old *Conventionnels*, whose Secretary-General, Claude Estier, now moved into the PS secretariat), but had struck a deal with Gaston Defferre for his crucial bloc vote – the largest in the party, and, on the extreme opposite wing, with CERES, whose support he won by promising to negotiate a common programme with the PCF, an initiative Savary strongly opposed. Even with these deals and the power of his name with the middle ground, Mitterrand scraped home by only 1 per cent of the vote. It was all in the best SFIO tradition.

The CERES deal moved the PS sharply to the Left, for the PS was now committed to the closest possible collaboration with the PCF. Chevènement and his henchman, Georges Sarre, moved into the PS leadership; CERES crowed in triumph – and its membership soared. In 1971 it had elected only one delegate in twelve to the PS Congress; by 1975, despite a greatly swollen PS membership, over a quarter of the delegates belonged to it.[36] The PS now had a dynamic left wing which made much of the running in the party's advance from Epinay – and which identified its success with the new ascendancy of Mitterrand.

The PCF, now in sight of the goal it had so long sought, reacted with suspicion. It had embraced Mitterrand in 1965 not because it thought him different in kind from Defferre, but because he had not presented himself as a principled anti-Communist. He was, in their eyes, merely a more subtle and supple opportunist, a horse-trader one could bargain with, but never trust. Mitterrand offering a common programme was a Greek bearing gifts and the PCF was not having a Trojan Horse at any price. It stepped up its pressure on the new PS leadership, abruptly publishing a new PCF programme in October 1971 while the PS was still considering its approach to a common programme.

Mitterrand pressed on, unruffled. On 11–12 March 1972 the PS national convention drew up its own programme and invited the PCF, PSU and the Radicals to join it in hammering out a common programme. Pompidou, eager to strangle this baby at birth, immediately announced a referendum on British entry to the EEC, knowing the PCF would be against and the PS in favour. The Left, he hoped, would split down the middle on this issue of principle before they could consolidate their new, and potentially threatening, popular front. Mitterrand was equal to the challenge. He first pleaded with the PCF to adopt a united appeal for electoral abstention as a compromise, a position which then enabled him, when Marchais announced, inevitably, in favour of a flat No, to campaign as part of a united Left against a Yes vote. In the event abstentions reached 40 per cent, spoiled ballots a record level of 7.1 per cent, and nearly one-third of the electorate voted No. Pompidou's ruse had backfired badly and the Left was able to draw considerable comfort from the President's evident reverse.

Negotiations on the common programme now proceeded speedily. Mitterrand's determination that the negotiations should succeed was clearly sincere and Marchais overcame the lingering reservations of the Politburo by throwing his weight strongly onto the same side. He had little real choice: it would, after all, have made a nonsense of the PCF's strategy ever since 1962 to reject this culminating success of the popular front. In the early hours of 27 June 1972 Marchais and Mitterrand reached final agreement and signed the common programme which became, overnight the Common Programme. The long march towards Left unity had ended in complete success. Pompidou, who understood better than most how threatening this achievement might be for the Right, responded immediately by firing his liberal Prime Minister, Chaban-Delmas, and replacing him with Pierre Messmer, a conservative traditionalist. If the Left could achieve such unprecedented unity, Chaban's conciliatory wooing of the Centre-Left had clearly failed. From now on it would be a hard, tough fight . . .

With the achievement of the Common Programme the Left stood poised for an historic advance, a renaissance whose nature and magnitude were to confound all conventional opinion – and the parties of the Left themselves. Within months the PS had, astonishingly, though only fleetingly, showed ahead of the PCF in the opinion polls. In 1973 it all but drew level with the PCF in actual votes. In 1974 Mitterrand, again the Left's candidate, came within an ace of winning the presidential election, an election in which the 'invincible' Gaullists were humiliated. Thereafter the PS surged far ahead of all other parties, including the PCF, in every variety of by-election, local election and opinion poll. In 1976 the Left swept to victory in the cantonal elections, in 1977 to an even greater victory in the municipal elections. In the space of a few years an electorally unstoppable popular front had emerged, a triumphant Mitterrand leading it at the head of a jubilant PS, now easily the largest party in France. A miracle – perhaps several miracles – had apparently occurred. To understand how this transformation came to pass no account centring merely on personalities and party strategies will suffice. We must, rather, seek to understand the sociology of this Left renaissance.

# PART TWO

# The Sociology of the Left's Renaissance

# 5 Gaullism and the Right: the Sociology of Political Decline

The more violent the crisis of revolution or war, the more the 'little man' suffers while (the) wealthy man gets by. If the nation's humblest class have one overriding interest, it is the maintenance of peace and order, the time-honoured handing down of its meagre possessions.

> Charles Maurras,
> *The Politics of Nature* in J. S. McClelland (ed.)
> *The French Right from de Maistre to Maurras*,
> London, 1971, p. 293.

The rising strength of the Left's challenge in the 1970s derived only in part from its new-found unity. This unity enabled it, for the first time since 1947, to mount a coherent governmental alternative to the Right and to develop a deep-rooted popular élan, its so-called *'dynamique unitaire'*. But, on its own, this would not have been enough, for the Right had owed its long hegemony not merely to the Left's disunity, but to its own independent sources of strength. Chief among these was Gaullism, the dominating – almost the domineering – force in French life for so much of the post-war period. Even the Left acknowledged, implicitly, that it was doomed to remain in the wilderness, united or not, while Gaullism retained its full strength. Accordingly, as the end neared to De Gaulle's long reign excited speculation grew – in anxious tones on the Right, in hopeful ones on the Left – as to the nature of a political future without De Gaulle.

The Gaullist parliamentary landslide of 1968, De Gaulle's departure, and then Pompidou's smooth succession to the presidency (he beat Poher 57.6 per cent to 42.4 per cent)[1] ended this speculation. Indeed, it was all so clear-cut and easy that it seemed rather as if the long debate about *l'après Gaullisme* had been empty and pointless. The threat from the Left, so vivid and dramatic only a year before, seemed light years away. De Gaulle had gone but Gaullism lived on – effortlessly. It had a new leader who had matched, even surpassed, De Gaulle's vote-winning power. It had control of the presidency for the next seven years at least and it had the biggest parliamentary majority ever in a country where any sort of majority was almost a historical miracle. Gaullism hadn't just survived – it was prospering as never before. A new era had, apparently, begun. France had a stable, dominant, conservative party of government which, for the first time, no longer depended on a charismatic leader. The Pompidolian succession had simply settled all the outstanding questions.

71

This expectation perhaps accounts for the mood and tone of Jean Charlot's *The Gaullist Phenomenon*, written and published in 1970, which remains by far the most influential work on Gaullism as a mass movement. Charlot frankly eulogised Pompidou: 'It would have been underestimating this grandson of country peasants, this son of primary school teachers, this intellectual, to have thought that he would be content with a minor role, without regard for conscience and self-respect.'[2] And Charlot had no doubts that the Gaullist achievement was a permanent one:

> For some who dreamed of bringing together workers and executives, left and right alike, it will be a disappointment that Gaullism has in the end only managed to unite the right. But this in itself is no mean achievement . . . The creation of a large party of the right, with no great weakness in any particular region or any one social category, capable of assuming power alone, was not easy nor was it of little import.[3]

Less than four years after these words were written the Gaullist candidate for the presidency trailed in, a distant third, with under 15 per cent of the vote. Four years after that the Gaullist RPR ran second behind the Socialists in the 1978 elections. Even this performance was heavily dependent upon the wasting asset of large numbers of locally entrenched notables within Gaullist ranks.[4] Without the aid of these personal followings in the June 1979 European elections (conducted on a PR list system) the RPR fell back to 16.2 per cent,[5] leaving it far behind the Giscardians, the PS and the PCF.

The decline – almost the collapse – of Gaullism not merely confounded the confident expressions of Charlot, the movement's most expert analyst. It profoundly modified the balance within the Right – and more. For the erosion of Gaullism, hitherto the central pivot of the Right, destabilised the Right as a whole so that many formerly conservative voters strayed not just to new homes on the Right, but became available, instead, to the burgeoning forces of the Left. The fact that the newborn PS, rather than the PCF, was able to reap the lion's share of this harvest produced, in turn, the 're-equilibration of the Left' for which Mitterrand had long prayed, pulling the PS comfortably ahead of the PCF for the first time since 1936: which in turn created an entirely new set of tensions and animosities within the so recently united Left . . .

The decline of Gaullism as a mass force had a fair claim to being the central political process in the France of the 1970s. Thus any attempt to understand the Left's renaissance in this same period can hardly afford to ignore the nature of this fundamental shift within the fold of French conservatism. Such an attempt is best begun by situating the peculiar mass phenomenon of Gaullism within the general evolution of French conservatism since the Liberation: that is, within the same timescale we have employed in our examination of the Left.

# i GAULLISM: THE FIRST WAVE

Despite De Gaulle's heroic wartime role and his overwhelming personal stature at the Liberation, Gaullism did not emerge as an organised mass movement until after the wide ground of the Centre-Right had already been occupied by other parties. The resumption of party politics at war's end had found the forces of conservatism in a confused and demoralised state, discredited and split by the disaster of Vichy. The only coherent force to emerge from this morass was the *Mouvement Républicain Populaire* (MRP), which gained 23.9 per cent of the vote in October 1945 and 28.2 per cent in June 1946, thus becoming the largest party in France in only its second year of corporate existence. At this point it seemed not implausible to imagine that the MRP might become the same hegemonic force on the French Centre-Right that its Christian Democrat counterparts were fast becoming in both Italy and Germany. All three parties were new elements within their respective political traditions – Weimar, pre-Fascist Italy, and the Third Republic had all been equally prone to fissiparous multi-partyism; and all were part of a European-wide Christian Democratic phenomenon which sought, amidst the ruins of defeat and Fascism, to give conservatism a new and morally sounder base. The MRP was not immediately much weaker than its confrères – its 28.2 per cent of June 1946 ranked it not far behind the German Christian Democrats' 31 per cent vote of 1949 and the Italian Christian Democrats' 35.2 per cent of 1946.[6] One of the great might-have-beens of French post-war history was the possible emergence of a majoritarian MRP had it been able to sustain its position into the late 1940s (when it would surely have benefited from the same Cold War polarisation which so assisted its German and Italian counterparts) – particularly if De Gaulle had consented to take the party's leadership.

But there was the rub. For the MRP's hopes were dashed beyond recovery through De Gaulle's formation of a competing force on the Right, the *Rassemblement du Peuple Français* (RPF). Indeed, the consequence for the MRP of finding itself opposed to De Gaulle's awesome electoral power was evident as early as October 1946 when the MRP campaigned in favour of the new constitution and De Gaulle against it. In the subsequent election of November 1946 the MRP fell back to 26 per cent, while the newly organised *Union Gaulliste*, though unblessed by De Gaulle, stole 3 per cent of the vote. The MRP's momentum had been checked and henceforth it had to compete quite openly with the RPF. In the June 1951 elections the MRP fell back to only 12.6 per cent (the RPF taking 21.6 per cent). By then any prospect of the emergence in France of the united, hegemonic Christian Democracy seen in Italy and Germany, was well and truly over – ruined by De Gaulle.

The great revelation of the 1946 referenda had been the unique electoral strength of De Gaulle. When, together with the MRP, he opposed the constitutional draft at the May referendum, the constitution lost. When, virtually alone, with even the MRP joining the PCF and SFIO against him, he repeated his stand at the October referendum, the constitution scraped through on a low poll, with 46.4 per cent of voters supporting De Gaulle's position. A key element in De Gaulle's strength was, from the start, an ability to appeal beyond the normal confines of conservative opinion to those who saw him as a non-party figure. Thus an early poll of February 1946, taken immediately after De Gaulle's resignation as Prime Minister, showed that 49 per cent saw him as a man of the Right, 1 per cent a man of the Left and 39 per cent as having no party. More than a year later, at the foundation of the RPF, an essentially similar (52 per cent – 1 per cent – 37 per cent) distribution of views was held and his own followers were particularly prone to take a non-party view of their leader.[7]

Nothing is more striking, in fact, than the speed with which the essential contours of Gaullist support took shape in these early years, foreshadowing a configuration of electoral support which was indelibly to mark French conservatism for years to come. In particular, it was possible, almost from the outset, to discern four distinct levels of Gaullist support:

1 a *faithful hard core* of around 21 per cent of voters on which the movement could rely in conditions of open, competitive politics even when not reinforced either by strong Right-Left polarisation or by the movement's tenure of governmental authority;

2 the *complete* Gaullist electorate, consisting of around 35 per cent of the electorate (i.e. including the 21 per cent hard core), which could be mobilised only under conditions more favourable to the movement, notably when it was a matter of supporting De Gaulle personally (and not just his party), when Right-Left polarisation was greater, or when the Gaullist movement was armed with the extra legitimacy accruing from the possession of governmental authority;

3 an *enlarged* Gaullist electorate of 40–46 per cent (each increment beyond the hard core naturally containing larger and larger numbers of weak partisans, the instability and 'spread' of the groups increased steadily with size); this level of support (first seen in the October 1946 referendum) could be mobilised only under conditions of extreme polarisation (e.g. in the 1968 election) or for De Gaulle personally as president (as in the 1965 election where he polled 43.7 per cent at the first ballot);

4 finally, a *maximal* electorate of around 55 per cent could be assembled where Gaullism was the only alternative to the Left in a straight fight. This level of support was attained by De Gaulle (54.5 per cent) in his 1965 run-off against Mitterrand and by the Gaullist-led Majority at the second ballot of the legislative elections of the 1960s.

These levels of support – as also some of the characteristic social components of Gaullist support – began to emerge immediately after De Gaulle's departure from the government on 20 January 1946 signalled to the electorate that there was potentially a choice to be made not only between De Gaulle and the Left, but between Gaullism and more traditional forms of conservatism. Despite the initial confusion of public opinion, the first polls of February 1946 already found 32 per cent saying they would support a political party if De Gaulle assumed its leadership. By October 1946 the choice had been clarified and 35 per cent were willing to support such a party.[8] That is, within the space of a few months, and well before there *was* such a party to support, the *complete* Gaullist electorate had taken shape. And, already, it displayed many of the social hallmarks which were to distinguish the UNR electorate in the 1960s. In part De Gaulle derived his support from traditionally conservative voters: the old and the bourgeois were, from the first, the most likely to support him and there was a heavy feminine predominance among his following. Of those polled in October 1946 men declared themselves unwilling to support a Gaullist party by a 2:1 margin (56 per cent: 28 per cent), but a clear plurality of women (41 per cent: 38 per cent) favoured such a party.[9] But, equally – and again this fact was to distinguish the 1960s Gaullists as well – De Gaulle's support already departed quite distinctively in other ways from the classic profile of mass conservatism. His peasant support was only average (i.e. peasants were no more numerous amongst his followers than they were within the electorate as a whole) but he was favoured by a strikingly large bloc of working-class voters. Thus while traditional conservatism was essentially rural, the Gaullist electorate actually had a clear urban bias. In the polls of 1946–7 support for a Gaullist party was, indeed, at its weakest in the countryside and the smallest towns, reaching a plurality (40 per cent: 38 per cent) only in the largest conurbations.[10]

When the RPF was founded in April 1947 it was, then, in the unusual position of inheriting an already formed and stable electoral bloc: the first poll of April 1947 found support steady at 34 per cent.[11] At this point support for De Gaulle and the RPF were identical (the RPF's declared objective was, after all, simply to reinstall De Gaulle in power). There was no hint of the later emergence of two separate electorates – those supporting a Gaullist party and those supporting De Gaulle personally.[12] Nonetheless, the formation of the RPF and its entry into the party arena inevitably sharpened the partisan image of Gaullism as a movement of the Centre-Right. Equally, the incursus into the political arena of this powerful new force cut deep into the electorates of other parties, sharply altering the configuration of the party system. By the end of 1947 the RPF had pulled over to it more than 70 per cent of the supporters of the Rightist *Parti Republicain de la Liberté* (PRL), over 50 per cent of the MRP,[13] 25 per cent of both Radical and SFIO voters, and 10 per cent of the PCF vote. Thus the overall result was the creation in embryo of something very like the party system of the Fifth Republic, with a dominant Gaullist party at around 35 per cent; a residual group of conservatives (those staying loyal to the PRL) who were not anti-Gaullist and who would rally to the General in a crisis; a strong Centrist remnant (12–13 per cent) of the MRP which was positively anti-Gaullist; a diminished SFIO – down to 12–13 per cent; and a PCF which had had its wings sharply clipped. Inevitably, though, the RPF did most damage to the conservative parties. It stole most of their support – and split the Right's two fractions into three.

The RPF's strategic hope was that the Cold War climate would polarise the whole of the anti-Communist Centre-Right behind it. The October 1947 municipal elections suggested that this was no vain ambition, for the RPF won thirteen of the largest cities, taking an astonishing 38 per cent of the vote (against 25 per cent for the SFIO and MRP together).[14] But it could not maintain this momentum. In Italy and Germany the Cold War worked in favour of the dominant conservative parties precisely because, as parties of government, they were natural rallying points. The RPF was in the opposite position – it was trying to overthrow governmental authority, not consolidate it. For a while it might benefit from the mantle of authority which De Gaulle had worn until January 1946, but as time elapsed and tensions eased, the General and his movement became merely clamant voices in the wilderness. The opinion polls of the period graphically reveal both the initial steadiness and the subsequent erosion of Gaullist support. On eighteen separate occasions between June 1946 and October 1948 IFOP asked voters whether they would like to see De Gaulle return to power and found a very steady average of 33.3 per cent saying they would.[15] Only in early 1949 did this body of affirmative opinion begin to slip under 30 per cent, gradually falling back to its hard-core 21 per cent. When the test of the 1951 election finally came the RPF won just 21.6 per cent of the vote. De Gaulle soon found himself unable to prevent his deputies from crossing the floor to support or join governments. Rather than wait for his movement to break up entirely he summarily dissolved it in May 1953 and retired to Colombey-les-deux-Eglises.

With this Gaullism effectively died as an electoral force. Those Gaullists who ran without official blessing as Social Republicans in 1956 won only 3.9 per cent of the vote. They were back, effectively, to the position of the *Union Gaulliste* with its 3 per cent of the vote in November 1946. The damage the RPF had wrought to conservative unity lived on, however, with the Centre-Right fragmented between Radicals, Social Republicans, Poujadists, MRP, *Modérés* and others. Significantly, the MRP had been too badly hurt by the RPF onslaught to stage any recovery and its vote actually fell again to 11.1 per cent. Forced to fall back on a bedrock of support which was frankly Catholic and right-wing,[16] the MRP had lost all chance of becoming a broad party of the conservative Centre. The first Gaullist wave was over. It left no monuments, only debris.

## ii THE SECOND COMING OF GAULLISM

De Gaulle returned to power in May 1958 but it was not until October of that year that the new Gaullist party, the UNR, was founded in preparation for the November 1958 elections. The UNR, though plentifully endowed with funds, was a hurriedly organised piece of political makeshift and failed, for example, even to field candidates as widely as the RPF had in 1951. It had to operate, moreover, in the context of considerable political turmoil and a confused public opinion. Its capture of 20.5 per cent of the first ballot vote was, accordingly, generally regarded as a remarkable achievement. This success was, however, entirely dwarfed by a far greater landslide to the UNR at the second ballot a week later. Williams observes that

> For those anxious to vote Gaullist but also worried about wasting their votes, the first ballot had shown that the UNR was a 'serious' party. Thus it emerged triumphant from the second round. Before the first poll it had been expected to win

80 or 90 seats at most. In the next week the shrewdest commentators gave it 120 or 130. When the second ballot votes were counted it had 188 . . .[17]

The UNR's organisational achievement seemed little less than astonishing – it had, on the instant, reconstituted and even expanded the Gaullist electorate which had collapsed and vanished in the five years since 1953.[18]

The truth of the matter reflected less credit on the UNR but was more astonishing still, for when in September 1958 – a month before the UNR had been born – IFOP had asked voters 'If De Gaulle took the leadership of a political party, would you vote for it?' they had found 21 per cent answering 'Certainly yes'. Thus the hard core of Gaullist support, the faithful 21 per cent, had already been conjured back into existence by September (if not before) and were thus 'available' to the slower-moving politicians as soon as they were provided with a suitable receptacle for their preferences. If one allows for the fact that there was not a Gaullist candidate for whom to vote in every seat, the party's first-ballot score of 20.5 per cent represented an almost uncannily accurate reflection of the faithful 21 per cent discerned by IFOP two months before.

The September 1958 IFOP poll also provides us with a fascinating picture of the wider Gaullist potential in the electorate at this key point when opinion was being recrystallised between the polarities of Gaullism versus the Left. In addition to the 21 per cent who told IFOP they would certainly vote for a Gaullist party, there were a further 25 per cent who said they 'probably' would. Fairly certainly it was from among this group that the UNR received its fresh wave of support on the second ballot. Together, it will be seen, the two groups constituted the *enlargened* Gaullist electorate of around 46 per cent which we have posited as typical of periods of high polarisation.[19] By contrasting the two groups it is possible to see that although the 1958 hard core (the 21 per cent) was more evenly distributed across social class groupings than the Gaullist electorate of 1946–7 had been, it was none the less a socially more concentrated group than the *enlargened* Gaullist electorate of 46 per cent. That is to say, as Gaullism extended its appeal beyond its core group it did not merely recruit 'more of the same', but tended to 'top up' its support in various social groups, so that the larger Gaullist electorate was less socially differentiated at almost every point. Thus only 18 per cent of workers were found in the hard-core group, but 40 per cent in the *enlargened* group, while businessmen gave 29 per cent support to the former and 54 per cent to the latter group. Thus as Gaullism expanded it became somewhat more proletarian and more secular. On three points the large and small electorates were much the same. They both exhibited a very even spread across age groups; both revealed the existence of a strong 'generation of '58' (the 21–4 age group being more favourable to Gaullism in both electorates than any other group save the over-65s); and both exhibited the same feminine predominance. Of those who said in September 1958 that they would certainly vote for a Gaullist party, 57 per cent were women; of those who said they would probably vote Gaullist, 57 per cent were women . . . Thus, whether one was considering the small or large Gaullist electorate, it remained true that it was a movement with four feminine supporters for every three men.[20]

The striking Gaullist success of 1958, which was more than sustained in the General's crushing referendum victories of 1961–2, left unanswered the question of what level of support the Gaullist party could stabilise behind it. In 1958 its gains had been made as part of a general conservative swing. Overall the parties of the Left (PCF, SFIO and Radicals) had lost 12.6 per cent of the vote and these gains had been shared between the MRP (+0.1 per cent), the Gaullists (+16.6 per cent) and other conservatives (+6.8 per cent) at the same time that the Poujadists and extreme Right collapsed (−10.8 per cent). As the November 1962 elections approached there was considerable uncertainty as to whether these gains from the Left could be held and whether the 1.5 million votes gained between ballots by the UNR in 1958 was not an unrepeatable freak. Indeed, the UNR entered the election campaign with the press speculating as to whether it could hold even 100 of its seats.[21]

In the event the UNR and its allies took 35.7 per cent of the vote and won an overall parliamentary majority. In one sense this was not as striking as it seemed. The pre-election commentators would have done better to have studied the IFOP poll of September 1962 which had forecast the result with great accuracy a month before the October referendum and two months before the election. IFOP had asked voters whether 'you want as your deputy a candidate who supports De Gaulle, who opposes him – or is it important to you?' Only 31 per cent had believed the question unimportant and 35 per cent had said they wanted a deputy who would support De Gaulle.[22] Thus what we have termed the *complete* (35 per cent) Gaullist electorate which the RPF had quite routinely assembled over a two and a half year period in 1946–8 had long since crystallised. Indeed, the 1962 first ballot result merely recorded the same level of Gaullist support which had already crystallised at the 1958 second ballot.

What was striking was the effect of this development on the other conservative parties. While the parties of the Left recovered very slightly (gaining 0.8 per cent between them), the extreme Right lost a further 1.7 per cent, the MRP 3.2 per cent and other conservatives (*Modérés* and Peasant Independents) a huge 11.1 per cent. The UNR's success in polarising opinion between itself and the Left meant that it had become, in Charlot's term, the great 'federator of the Right, the centre-right and a part of the centre-left'.[23] Henceforth conservative politicians – and, ultimately, whole parties – must creep beneath the Gaullist umbrella or risk annihilation. Already in 1962 the UNR had allowed within its camp candidates describing themselves as '*Indépendants–Ve*', '*MRP–Ve*' and even '*Divers gauche–Ve*', the most notable of which were the first group, led by Giscard d'Estaing.

### iii THE GAULLIST ZENITH

With the 1962 result the Gaullists had visibly entered on their high period of dominance. In the largest sense this period extends from the first crystallisation of their electoral bloc around the 35 per cent mark at the 1958 second ballot through the consecutive victories of 1962 (35.7 per cent), 1967 (38.5 per cent), 1968 (46.4 per cent) and 1973 (36.7 per cent) to its final dissolution as a united bloc in 1978. More narrowly, it was in the 1962–7 period that the Party found its classical definition: a stable, dominant and united party in an era of prosperous calm. The essential secret of the Party's strength lay, of course, in the fact that De Gaulle was able to transfer to it the major part of his own enormous electoral support. It was, at least in the first instance, a quite classical example of the institutionalisation and routinisation of charisma, with the party only gradually achieving an autonomous life of its own. When the electorate perceived a clear connection between its vote and the General's national purpose (as in legislative elections) the Gaullist coalition regularly reaped its 35 per cent share. When, however, this connection was less clearly made – in both the 1959 and 1965 municipal elections – the Gaullists were quickly back with their (roughly) 21 per cent hard core.

Routinisation worked both ways. That is, while the UNR drew strength from its association with De Gaulle, his acceptance as a national leader above party was inevitably weakened by his association with it. His image was gradually 'partified', as it were. That this process was under way was most clearly signalled, of course, by the 1965 presidential election, in which he took 43.7 per cent of the first and 54.5 per cent of the second ballot vote. His failure to win outright on the first ballot was acclaimed as a victory by the Left and received as something of an affront by the General, for both they and he tended to draw implicit comparisons with the magnitude of his referendum victories (79.3 per cent, 75.3 per cent, 90.7 per cent and 61.8 per cent) of 1958–62. Such comparisons were quite misleading, however, neglecting as they did both the party base of support and opposition in those referenda (the 90.7 per cent Yes vote to the Evian Agreements in April 1962 had been achieved with only the extreme Right in open opposition, for example) and the substantive content and circumstances of the referenda themselves. As we have seen,[24] when pollsters *had* attempted to give voters a simplified choice between De Gaulle and anti-Gaullists in 1947–8 (when the choice seemed real enough) their results had effectively simulated a first-round Gaullist vote of 40–43 per cent and, on a straight Gaullist-Left fight, a maximal (second round) Gaullist vote of around 55 per cent. Nearly twenty years later these prognostications were exactly vindicated.

There were other straws in the wind to suggest that, while there might be a maximal 55 per cent bloc willing to support De Gaulle when all alternatives save the Left were eliminated, there was never much prospect of this majority being attracted to him in a more openly competitive situation. On the only occasion prior to 1965 that he had been opposed by centrists and the Left – during the miners' strike of March 1963 – his popularity had immediately plummeted to 42 per cent.[25] Moreover, the polls conducted during the presidential campaign clearly revealed the existence of several layers of Gaullist support. A poll just before the 1965 first round found that 26 per cent were real loyalists, wanting the General to win easily on the first ballot. A further 10 per cent (making up the remainder of the standard 35 per cent Gaullist bloc we have observed) wanted him to win on the first ballot, but narrowly. A final 10 per cent wanted him to win only on the second ballot (38 per cent wanted him to lose and 16 per cent didn't know or refused to answer). Again, an outer Gaullist bloc of 46 per cent emerges. If one eliminated the non-respondents (in order to simulate a second-round elimination effect) Gaullist support rose to 54.8 per cent[26] – a perfect prediction of the actual result.

Thus the notion that De Gaulle could somehow defy the ordinary dynamics of political partisanship was always rather wishful. Commentators were perhaps too impressed by the large numbers of voters generally willing to say that they were 'satisfied' with De Gaulle as President. But, as Charlot points out, the leader of the executive in France benefits from the fact that he is not being compared, as in the British case, for example, with a strong alternative leader of a united opposition.[27] Even so, one may point out that 'satisfaction' poll ratings in the 60–70 per cent range were unique to De Gaulle's tenure of office during the Algerian crisis. On just three occasions the 70 per cent line was crossed – when the barricades went up in Algiers in 1960, during the attempted Algiers *putsch* of 1961, and when the Algerian ceasefire was reached in 1962. After this the ratings oscillated around the predictable 55 per cent mark for the next seven years.[28]

De Gaulle did, however, profoundly modify the French party system and with these figures we are now in a position to estimate the overall effects of his two irruptions (1947–53 and 1958–69) into the political arena:

1  In the 1945 and 1946 elections the three Left parties (PCF, SFIO and Radicals) reached their zenith, taking 60.1 per cent and 58.7 per cent of the vote, leaving the combined forces of the Right with 39.9 per cent and 41.3 per cent. In 1951 the Right included the RPF for the first time and its combined poll soared to 48.5 per cent. With De Gaulle's departure the Right sagged to 46.5 per cent in 1956[29] but did not fall back to its level of the Liberation period. Thus De Gaulle's effect in this period was to pull across a full 7 per cent of the electorate from Left to Right, damage which was relatively lasting. In the same period he demonstrated his ability to marshal a minimum of 21 per cent and often 35 per cent of the electorate behind his movement – that is, to unite between half and three-quarters of the Centre-Right behind him.

2  De Gaulle's re-emergence in 1958 produced a further large shift from Left to Right. Having achieved 46.5 per cent in 1956 the Right won 56.4 per cent in 1958, 55.6 per cent in 1962, 56.4 per cent in 1967, and 58.9 per cent in 1968. Thus De Gaulle not merely recovered for the Right the increased margin of support he had won for it in 1947–53 (and which had begun to slip away again in 1956), but added to it a further increment of 9–10 per cent. Again, the damage to the Left was relatively lasting. And, again, De Gaulle demonstrated his ability to unite between two-thirds and three-quarters of this bloc behind his own movement.

3  Finally, De Gaulle himself was able to unite no less than four-fifths of this conservative bloc behind him even in the electoral free market of the 1965 presidential first ballot. On the second ballot he united the entire bloc – the

coincidence between both his average 'satisfaction rating' of 58–59 per cent and his second ballot vote of 54.5 per cent with the steady new high-water mark of the Right of 55–58 per cent should not be missed.

Such was the problem, as well as the opportunity, of the Gaullist party. It possessed a leader of unique electoral power upon whose coat-tails it rode with great success. But could he channel to it institutionally all the support he enjoyed personally? If so, how far would the Gaullist party be able to develop an autonomous 'hold' upon that electorate? If not, was it fated to remain in a situation where there were essentially two different conservative electorates, the General's and its own?

For there were two Gaullist electorates and they differed not merely in size but in social composition. This becomes strikingly clear if one compares De Gaulle's 1965 electorate with the 'mature' Majority electorate of 1967.[30] While the two electorates are identical in their heavy feminine predominance (57 per cent of the General's voters and 58 per cent of the Majority's) and are not dissimilar in their degree of white-collar support (35 per cent of whom voted for De Gaulle, 39 per cent for the Majority ), they contrast strongly in other respects. Despite the fact that there was a 5.2 per cent gap between the General's electorate and the Majority's, the latter actually received 45 per cent of the votes of both farmers and peasants and the business and professional classes against De Gaulle's 37 per cent and 41 per cent respectively. But De Gaulle more than made up for this with his greater strength among the retired and non-employed (receiving 57 per cent of their vote against the Majority's 44 per cent) and among the industrial working-class (winning 42 per cent of their votes against the Majority's 30 per cent). What gave De Gaulle his decisive electoral advantage over the Majority was that he was strongest where it counted most – among these, the two largest groups in the electorate – the workers making up 31 per cent and the retired and non-working 22 per cent of the whole.[31]

Gaullist politicians boasted of their party's broad, inter-class following, of having captured the 'rush-hour crowd'. There was some truth to this – relative to other French parties the UNR *was* broadly based – but the statement applied with much greater force to the General's electorate. For his was a truly popular, big city following. He received above average support from business and white-collar groups as well as from housewives and pensioners – at the same time that he pulled more working-class support than either the PCF or SFIO. He was weak in only three areas: he attracted considerable peasant support but, none the less, polled far below his big city level in the small towns and the countryside; second, his early support in the 20–34 age group quickly withered and from 1963 on this group became more and more marked in its anti-Gaullism; and, third,

Among the constants of relative anti-Gaullism, the most striking development is incontestably that of the French intellectual elite – those with post-secondary education. Their anti-Gaullism – existing, it seems, largely indifferent to circumstance, continually reinforced itself . . . culminating in 1968.[32]

In 1958 the UNR inherited a fairly straightforward cross-section of the General's electorate. But with the great sweep of 1962, when it trounced the old Right in its traditional rural strongholds, it increasingly developed the classic profile of French conservatism. Through the 1960s its urban support moved steadily in the direction of the professional and business classes, while its white-collar and working-class following stagnated. Overall its centre of gravity came to rest increasingly in its peasant, rural and small town vote. Finally – and rather oddly for a conservative party – it was less obnoxious than the General in the eyes of the young but never remotely approached his level of support among the old. It was this deficiency, together with the party's persistent failure to match De Gaulle's proletarian support, which kept it lagging well behind its leader's overall popularity.

iv THE TURNING POINT: 1968–9

It is essential to bear in mind the fact of these divergent electorates as one examines the great watershed of 1968–9, for the great electoral confrontations of this period – the June 1968 election, De Gaulle's defeat in the April 1969 referendum, and Pompidou's subsequent presidential victory – saw both the culminating triumph of Gaullism and the first seeds of its decline.

For the bare electoral statistics[33] suggested strongly that the dialectic of the two Gaullisms – De Gaulle's and his party's – had at last been resolved. In 1968 the Majority won 46.4 per cent of the vote, surpassing De Gaulle's 1965 level of support (43.7 per cent). In 1969 De Gaulle went down to referendum defeat with 46.8 per cent and Pompidou then won 44 per cent on the presidential first ballot. Gaullism, in other words, seemed to have coalesced at the level of its 'enlargened' electorate, producing a steady, homogeneous bloc of around 46 per cent . The process whereby De Gaulle transferred his support to the Majority had, apparently, reached its culmination even as De Gaulle fell.

The sociological reality was, however, more complex than this statistical coincidence suggests. For the Majority's high tide of 1968 was reached with an electorate which, while equalling De Gaulle's following in size, diverged from it more widely than ever in its social composition. Compared to its 1967 showing the Majority received large extra margins of support from the professional and business classes (+6 per cent) and white-collar workers (+5 per cent). Simultaneously it heavily surpassed its previous best performance in the countryside, among the peasantry, and in small town France. But its support in the larger cities actually *fell*. Perhaps most striking of all was its performance amongst the two groups where De Gaulle was distinctively stronger: in an election where it gained 7.9 per cent overall the Majority received only 1 per cent extra support from workers and actually lost 2 per cent among the retired and non-working population. That is, the Majority achieved its triumph by becoming more like itself, not more like De Gaulle.

Second, De Gaulle's defeat in the April 1969 referendum was due to a complex shift of social groups within the electorate which left him with a following approximating rather more closely than hitherto to the normal Majority electorate. This is best seen by comparing the composition of the 46.8 per cent group who supported him in 1969 with the 54.5 per cent who had supported him at the 1965 second ballot – the previous occasion on which the electorate had had to decide whether or not to disembarrass themselves of De Gaulle. What emerges clearly is that De Gaulle owed his defeat to defections in his big city following, which had hitherto provided him with his distinctive extra margin of personal support. Thus while he lost only 2 per cent of his rural support and 6 per cent of his small town support, he lost 8 per cent in cities of over 100,000 population and a huge 14 per cent in the Paris region. His support fell only 1 per cent among pensioners – the most loyal group – but 6 per cent among white-collar workers and 7 per cent among industrial workers. But above all the General lost the big cities because the professional and commercial classes – who had always preferred his party to him – withdrew no less than 19 per cent of their support. This striking exception apart, his support held up best where the Majority was relatively stronger than he was: among the peasantry (down only 2 per cent), in the medium-sized towns (down 4 per cent), and even among the 20–34 age group, where his 6 per cent decline compared favourably with his 10 per cent drop among the 35–49 age group. Finally, his 5 per cent decline among men was far outstripped by his 9 per cent loss among the hitherto faithful women voters.[34]

Perhaps the best way of comprehending the changes in De Gaulle's electorate at the end is to say that it stood midway between his own 1965 support and the bloc which supported Pompidou in 1969. For the Pompidou electorate – which now included a margin of Centrist support, the *Progrès et Démocratie Moderne* (PDM)[35] group having been wooed over – was in many ways the quintessence of the Majority. Just how radically the presidential electorate had changed is evident from Table 5.1.

Thus the 'culmination' of Gaullism in 1968–9 was a more ambiguous process than

TABLE 5.1 First-ballot electorates of De Gaulle (1965) and Pompidou (1969) compared

| | *De Gaulle* % support | *Pompidou* % support | *Difference* |
|---|---|---|---|
| All | 43.7 | 44.0 | + 0.3 |
| Retired, non-active | 57 | 47 | − 10 |
| Industrial workers | 42 | 29 | − 13 |
| Professions, business | 41 | 46 | + 5 |
| White collar workers | 39 | 48 | + 9 |
| Peasants | 37 | 50 | + 13 |
| Men | 40 | 35 | − 5 |
| Women | 46 | 46 | 0 |
| 21–34 years | 36 | 38 | + 2 |
| 35–49 years | 36 | 38 | + 2 |
| 50–64 years | 48 | 41 | − 7 |
| 65 and over | 61 | 54 | − 7 |

*Source*: IFOP, *Les Français et De Gaulle* (Paris: 1971), p. 73 and J. Charlot, *The Gaullest Phenomenon* (London: 1971), p. 74.

it first appeared. The greater irony is that it is in the snap election of June 1968 – the hour of greatest Gaullist triumph – that one also perceives the first seeds of Gaullist decline. For while the election provided the thunderous response necessary to quell the Left's challenge and the disorders of May, it also provoked a fundamental crisis within the Gaullist movement.

The whole Gaullist phenomenon, it must never be forgotten, depended in the last analysis on a fairly inflexible relationship between party and leader, with De Gaulle always the dominant partner. De Gaulle's superordinate position rested in turn on his ability as *le grand indispensable* to command an allegiance wider than his party's. This dominance, however much it might rankle with the party's leaders, making of them all *inconditionnels*, provided the party with the leadership, discipline, cohesion – and following – to unite the Centre-Right behind it. The movement simply could not work in any other way. If the party's deputies and notables could call the tune things would fall apart – just as the RPF had done after 1951.

This critical relationship was undermined in 1968. De Gaulle's prestige was badly, perhaps irreparably, damaged. Simultaneously the party achieved a prodigious electoral triumph, one it did not owe to him – indeed, it had actually overtaken him in public support. Moreover, in Pompidou it had a potential new leader: De Gaulle was indispensable no longer. In the 1968 election the Right had been united as never before – and it did not, this time, owe its unity to De Gaulle. Now, with its legions of new and often clamantly right-wing deputies pouring into the National Assembly, many of them endowed with an independence which only the certainty of future defeat can bring, the party and its notables stood in a different position from their stricken leader. Only a large new personal mandate could re-establish the old equilibrium. The alternative was a growing dependence on the party's notables and, ultimately, a probable split in the Majority as some went their own way. De Gaulle had no desire to relive the painful experience of 1951–3 – and settled instead on the double-or-quits gamble of the 1969 referendum on the (lifeless) question of regional and Senate reform. He lost – and quit.

It is difficult to see how De Gaulle *could* have secured the mandate he required. His previous referenda triumphs had been achieved by demanding answers to important questions and posing as the alternative to a Yes vote the alarming possibilities of the unknown. But in the wake of 1968 this could hardly be done. The most important questions had just been settled – the Right would rule France for the foreseeable future. There was no alarming unknown in that sense. That had been despatched when the strikers went back to work and the students went off on holiday, the revolution having been indefinitely postponed. And in Pompidou there was a known, safe and likely alternative. Perhaps if De Gaulle had simply resigned without more ado in 1969 Gaullism might have prospered longer. For there was no doubt that De Gaulle's defeat was a fateful step towards the decline of Gaullism. This was not merely because the referendum made it clear that the heroic leader was not invincible, but because it allowed the mobilisation of a moderate majority in favour of a known *status quo* AND against Gaullism. This new majority, moreover, resulted from the defection of electors who in many cases were never to return to the Gaullist cause. Giscard's treachery in counselling a No vote was to live in infamy for true Gaullist believers. While in the event only 25 per cent of his small band of RI voters heeded his call, so did 16 per cent of the UDR electorate of 1968, a much larger group.[36] It was enough.

## v POMPIDOU AND THE INCORPORATION OF THE CENTRE

The referendum result in turn threatened Pompidou. If a moderate majority could be assembled against Gaullism in April 1969, why not in June? For several alarming weeks it appeared possible that Poher might achieve just this: only two weeks before election day the polls showed Poher trailing Pompidou only 41:37 per cent and 40:36 per cent.[37] This in turn forced Pompidou to bid for centrist support – at the price of having formally to enlarge the Majority to allow in a PDM/CDP wing alongside the now provenly pivotal *Républicains Indépendants* (RI). Pompidou, to maintain his position, had begun a fateful process. Gaullism, he hoped, would bolster itself by progressively swallowing the Centre into the Majority. The process was to end with the Centre swallowing the Majority, to the discomfiture of the Gaullists ...

It was not accidental that this incorporation of the Centre began immediately upon De Gaulle's departure. While he had been at the helm there had been a genuine incompatibility. He was, after all, the man who had done most to wreck the MRP (the mother organisation of the *Centre Démocrate* (CD) and later PDM/CDP) and Bidault, the former MRP leader, had conspired against him. There was a genuine and deep difference over policies, particularly in foreign affairs. De Gaulle's following (as opposed to the UNR's) differed sharply from the Centre's – his was more urban and secular, theirs rural and clerical. And, finally, De Gaulle's electoral appeal was too great for him to need to bid for the Centre institutionally. He simply did not need to allow the Centre to become an autonomous faction within the Majority (as Pompidou did) because in the last analysis he could either win over its supporters piecemeal or be strong enough to do without them.

Pompidou's position was quite different. He had needed to bid for Centrist support to get elected at all and had won with a classically conservative electorate (virtually indistinguishable from the Centre's). He was, essentially, a business conservative who neither wanted nor could afford enemies on the Right – almost his first move as president was to allow Pétain's remains to be brought back to France for a state funeral, something De Gaulle would never have done. He did so advisedly, for there was never any prospect that he could equal De Gaulle's popular nationalist appeal. De Gaulle's unique strength as a conservative leader had been his large proletarian following – even against Mitterrand in 1965 De Gaulle had been supported by 45 per cent of the working-class in the run-off.[38] Pompidou could clearly never hope to equal that, nor to recapture the proletarian votes De Gaulle had lost in 1969. He would do well even to hold the 30 per cent of the working-class vote the UNR had – helped by De Gaulle's coat-tails – polled through the 1960s. Policy and personal predilection may have pushed Pompidou towards the Centrist alliance, but so did electoral exigency. Faced with the virtual certainty of large defections from the old Gaullist following, he was going to need all the new friends he could make.

Immediately, the alliance appeared to strengthen the Gaullists, but over time it gravely weakened them. This was for three reasons. First, the consolidation of a rural-business social bloc helped further to repel working-class support away from Gaullist ranks towards the Left. Second, the process of incorporation destabilised the Centre. Many of its 12–13 per cent of the electorate had voted for it because they were anti-Gaullists. If their leaders were incorporated into the Majority some were bound not to follow but to break away towards the Left. This was to provide the main dynamic of Socialist growth through the 1970s. Third, allowing the Centre in on its own terms (and the CDP and RI were overrepresented in the Cabinet) meant allowing the proliferation of autonomous factions within the Majority where they could gradually build up their followings to the detriment of the Gaullists proper. This was what Giscard had stealthily achieved for his RI party through the 1960s, taking 2.7 per cent of the vote in 1962, 5.5 per cent in 1967 and 8.4 per cent in 1968. Pompidou's invitation of the CDP into the governing coalition meant allowing other leaders to play Giscard's game or, as it turned out, providing a fresh source of recruits for Giscard. While De Gaulle was in power Giscard had never been imprudent enough to compete openly with him, but having played Brutus to De Gaulle's Caesar in 1969 Giscard was now positioned to prepare his takeover bid for the Majority. He cultivated his new CDP partners, urged the incorporation into the Majority of further centrist elements, notably the *Réformateurs*,[39] and worked to give the RI (hitherto regarded as the Majority's right wing) a more centrist image.

What suited Giscard best of all was the gradual blurring of the distinction between Gaullists and non-Gaullists within the single catch-all definition, 'the Majority'. The term had been employed with deliberate arrogance by the Gaullists in the 1960s to mean, essentially, the Gaullist bloc and those hangers-on (i.e. the RI) willing to acknowledge their supremacy and unique legitimacy. Now, however, it came to denote simply the governing coalition in which the Gaullists figured merely as one of three constituent parties. Gaullist distinctiveness was thus progressively dissolved within this more amorphous 'Majority' and the junior coalition partners became increasingly unwilling to acknowledge any overall Gaullist supremacy.

The 1973 elections represented a further important stage in this process, with this new conception of the Majority taking on institutional form in the creation of the *Union des Républicains de Progrès Pour le Soutien au Président de la République* (URP) as an umbrella organisation for all fractions of the Majority. Candidates thus stood as URP-UDR, URP-RI, URP-CDP, or even URP-*non-inscrit*. The non-Gaullists were able to insist, moreover, on holding official 'primaries' in thirty-four seats (and could not be prevented from staging unofficial ones in thirty-six more) between the various fractions of the URP.[40] The entry of the RI and CDP into open political conflict with the UDR, on however limited a scale, was the decisive step by which these factions became 'real' parties. Hitherto it had been legitimate to count (as we have done) RI votes, for example, as part of the Gaullist bloc, for no one doubted that RI deputies could be elected thanks only to the grace and favour of the Gaullists. Had the UNR, then closely in De Gaulle's shadow, put up rival candidates to the

Giscardians in 1962, few of the latter would have survived such internecine strife. But by 1973 the situation was different – the non-Gaullists of the Majority were positively keen to contest the hegemony of the UDR.

The behaviour of conservative electors showed that Giscard's strategy was working, for they clearly drew no fine distinctions about which fraction of the Majority they were voting for, simply transferring their allegiance to candidates with the URP label and witholding it from those who lacked it. Competition between the UDR, RI and CDP was still too restricted for their electoral tallies to be fully revealing but it was notable, none the less, that the final URP vote of 36.7 per cent split 6 per cent to the CDP, 6.9 per cent to the RI and 23.8 per cent to the UDR[41]. The Gaullist party proper was, in the absence of De Gaulle, heading back down to its familiar 21 per cent mark. Indeed, the safe return of a still Gaullist-led Majority in 1973 tended to mask the fact not merely that the Right had slipped back, but that the Gaullists had suffered far greater losses than the other components of the Majority. The Right overall had lost 4.6 per cent from its record 1968 level (despite the addition of the CDP faction which, locally, at least, brought some new votes),[42] but the UDR was down no less than 13.5 per cent. In 1968 it alone had constituted over 80 per cent of the Majority electorate, in 1973 under 65 per cent of it. Thus the effect of 1973 was greatly to improve the relative standing of non-Gaullists – above all Giscard – within the Majority. The Majority electorate was consolidating around the clerical and rural milieux where they were strongest; they had advanced from being a subordinate fifth of the Majority to an autonomous third and more; and they knew that the first loyalty even of most UDR voters was to the Majority, not the UDR, so that they were regarded as legitimate leaders even by many who had not voted for them.

## vi THE CENTRE'S REVENGE: GISCARD TAKES OVER

The full implications of the 1973 results were not widely realised, a fact which lent a nightmarish quality to the events of 1974 for Gaullist true-believers. Pompidou, who had long been mortally ill, retreated more and more into the Elysée, a heavy, glowering presence who played only a fitful role in government. On his (rare) public appearances comment fastened mainly on the puffy, mask-like countenance he presented behind the ever-drooping Gauloise, his heavy jowls now entirely suffused with cortisone. None the less, the Elysée assiduously, even angrily, denied all rumours of ill health until 2 March 1974, when it announced that Pompidou was dead.

The succession had not been prepared. There was a confused mêlée within Gaullist ranks, with first one and then another Pretender throwing his hat into the ring, all the while insisting on the necessity for Gaullist unity. Giscard waited carefully – even announcing, loftily, that his true ambition lay in the field of literature, not politics. In fact his time was spent encouraging the split in Gaullist ranks, winning to his side the quite crucial figure of Jacques Chirac, the tough and ambitious young Minister of the Interior. Only then did Giscard allow his candidacy to 'emerge'. His main Majority rival, it was now clear, would be Jacques Chaban-Delmas, the liberal-minded Gaullist mayor of Bordeaux and former Prime Minister.

Chaban (his Resistance *nom-de-guerre*) was an attractive candidate – young, handsome and a former rugby international (in the film *Is Paris Burning?* it had seemed natural to cast the dashing young screen idol, Alain Delon, to play Chaban). But Chaban had been badly scarred by a scandal over his failure to pay any income tax while premier and even more by the clearly reluctant and grudging support lent him by older Gaullist notables. For them there was something slightly raffish and lightweight about Chaban: he was too handsome, he was on his third wife, he lacked the *gravitas* for them to accept him, above themselves, in the line of De Gaulle and Pompidou. Gaullism had, as it dissolved into the Majority, grown ponderous and stodgy. To the electorate it seemed, suddenly, to have become mainly an affair of querulous and self-important old notables. Chaban was hurt quite as badly by the general demeanour of those who, in the end, supported him as by their evident reservations about him.

Most of all, though, Chaban was hurt by Jacques Chirac. There was no love lost between the two. Chaban was a member of the original Gaullist generation – he had been with De Gaulle in London during the war, an RPF deputy after it, and had played a major role in helping De Gaulle return to power in 1958. Chirac was, by comparison, a parvenu. He had been only thirty when he had joined Pompidou's *cabinet* in 1962, becoming the future president's all-purpose fixer, troubleshooter and hatchet-man. Elected as a deputy for the first time in 1967 he had, aged thirty-five, been immediately given major Cabinet rank as Secretary of State for Social Affairs. The next year he rose to the commanding height of Minister of Economics and Finance. This breathtaking career had suddenly slumped in January 1971 when Chaban became premier. Chirac was immediately demoted to being Minister in charge of relations with parliament; a Ministry without power or patronage; indeed, given the Assembly's impotence, hardly a job at all. Chirac was left to gnash his teeth over the thankless task of explaining Chaban's liberal policies to the great phalanx of diehard UDR reactionaries elected in the 1968 sweep. Chaban's fall in July 1972 was for Chirac a blessed relief. Under the new premier, Messmer, he immediately gained the substantial Ministry of Agriculture, then, just a month before Pompidou's death, Messmer reshuffled the Cabinet and Chirac took over the Ministry of the Interior – a fateful move. Within days Chirac had begun a series of changes within the prefecture with a clear eye to future political advantage. Pompidou's death thus found his principal protégé strategically placed. He was too young (forty-two) to be a presidential candidate himself, but he could probably settle who was to win if he played his cards right. And he knew that he had everything to lose from a victory for Chaban . . .

In all previous elections the Ministry of the Interior had, through the prefecture, played a crucial role in organising election campaigns to suit Gaullist purposes.[43] Now that Chirac had made his deal with Giscard – thus catapulting himself right through the bevy of older Gaullist notables above him to become, after the election, Giscard's first prime minister – the Ministry of the Interior, the prefects and the police were suddenly withdrawn from their subtle but important roles in the political arena. Without the habitual messages, prodding and information flow from above, the Gaullist party in the country was at sixes and sevens. Suddenly, there was no 'right' candidate – even Gaullists were left to make up their own minds between Chaban and Giscard. Many UDR deputies, knowing that their voters favoured Giscard and their militants Chaban, simply fled from their constituencies rather than be forced to face up to such an invidious choice. Thus Chaban was deprived of his greatest advantage: the well-oiled UDR machine which had, over the previous decade, perfected itself in the business of winning elections, never really got into gear behind him.

While Chaban's campaign took on an increasingly bedraggled look Giscard was gathering in endorsements from renegade Gaullists, Lecanuet, and – in the end – from JJSS too. For a week the two men were neck and neck in the polls. Chaban was reduced to arguing that he was the only man who could keep out Mitterrand and the Left. Unfortunately for him this merely focused public attention on the polls, which predicted precisely the opposite: against Chaban Mitterrand would win at the second ballot, against Giscard he would lose. As this perception sank in, Chaban's campaign simply fell to pieces. In the end Giscard took 32.9 per cent to Chaban's 14.5 per cent (and Mitterrand's 43.4 per cent). On the second ballot the whole Majority swung behind Giscard, who scraped in with 50.7 per cent to Mitterrand's 49.3 per cent. The erosion of the Right's old lead to this wafer-thin margin was clear evidence of a large and subterranean shift within the electorate which boded difficult days ahead for French conservatism. But for the moment the decline of the Right took second place to the revenge of the Centre. A triumphant Giscard set up house in the Elysée – and an equally satisfied Chirac moved into the prime ministerial residence at the Hôtel Matignon. France had a new leader – or rather, and as it turned out, very much to the point – it had two of them.

The Gaullists' loss of the Elysée after sixteen continuous years in possession was a greater blow to the movement than even De Gaulle's death had been. The Fifth Republic was no longer unequivocally theirs – and it was quite certain that Giscard would move just as fast and far to dismantle the 'UDR state' as the still predominant UDR deputies in the Assembly would allow him. For Giscard could not feel entirely secure until he had broken the power of the UDR, preferably by attaching its remnants to some new umbrella movement of his own. A large and ominous question mark now hung over the survival of Gaullism as a united, let alone a dominant, political movement.

Most commentators were simply unprepared for this earthquake within the Right. Charlot, for example, reacted by stressing the continuing strength of Gaullism institutionally: 'Giscard's victory in no way threatens the institutions set up by the Gaullists . . . One might almost say that this victory of a non-Gaullist is a guarantee of the continuation of the system'[44] – and by again eulogising the victor:

The fundamental liberalism of the new president, his firm desire to reduce the tensions in French political life and to bring the state, the presidency, and the other institutions nearer to the people . . . will contribute to the strengthening of the political system he has democratically inherited from the Gaullists.[45]

Charlot claimed indeed that Gaullists had no need to worry that they were doomed to decline in the manner of the RPF:

> Today the Gaullists have no necessity for such heart-searching. They are within a political system they themselves erected; they are part of the majority; and in the very first days of Giscard's presidency, Chirac, the UDR prime minister, and Jacques Soufflet, the Gaullist minister of defence, clearly showed their capacity to defend what they considered the essence of Gaullism . . . It seems as if the Gaullist party has decided to win over its brilliant adversary rather that confront him.[46]

Such wishful thinking could hardly disguise the fact that 1974 was an utter disaster for the Gaullists, depriving them at a stroke of the power, patronage and authority which had provided the bricks and mortar for their leadership of a cohesive Majority.


## vii THE GAULLIST COLLAPSE

Giscard's sensational presidential victory had the effect of making it seem that the virtual collapse of Gaullism – a phenomenon fraught with consequence for the Left as well as the Right – had taken place, virtually overnight, in 1974. It is of some moment to understand that this was not the case. Rather, 1974 merely revealed a state of affairs which dated back, in all probability, to 1972, with the emergence of a Left united around the Common Programme and Pompidou's disastrous referendum on Britain's EEC membership (see above, p. 67). The collapse of Gaullism, particularly the loss of its large working-class following, and the rise of the Left, particularly the PS, from 1972 on were thus not merely contemporaneous but integrally connected phenomena. Thus the first (brief) surge of the PS past the PCF in the polls of late 1972 coincided exactly with the falling back of the Gaullists towards their 'hard-core' 21 per cent level. The 1973 pre-election polls gave the UDR a consistent 22 per cent and the final election result gave it 23.8 per cent. At the same time the Socialists bounded from their 1968 level of 16.5 per cent to 20.8 per cent. The writing was on the wall for Chaban at least as early as March 1973 – and rather earlier than that for anyone who subjected the opinion polls to close scrutiny.

The first IFOP polls taken once all the candidates had emerged in the 1974 presidential election (showing Chaban and Giscard virtually neck-and-neck) were thus less surprising than most commentators thought. On 16 April IFOP showed Chaban at 25 per cent and on 18 April and again on 22 April at 23 per cent.[47] Only after this point did Chaban's vote begin to crumble away to its eventual 14.5 per cent of 5 May, as conservative voters plumped heavily for Giscard as the best-placed candidate of the Right. This last-minute tactical switching, dramatic though its effects were, should not disguise the fact that for most of the campaign Chaban's support was exactly what the evidence of 1972–3 had long before suggested might be available to a Gaullist candidate.

The extensive survey data gathered during the 1974 election is of considerable

TABLE 5.2 Percentage of each social group supporting Chaban-Delmas in mid-campaign and on first ballot, 1974, compared with first-ballot support for De Gaulle (1965) and Pompidou (1969)

| | (1) De Gaulle | (2) Pompidou | (3)* Chaban-Delmas 16–22 April | (4) 5 May | Col. 3 as % of Col. 1 | Col. 4 as % of Col. 1 |
|---|---|---|---|---|---|---|
| All | 43.7 | 44.0 | 24 | 14.5 | 55 | 33 |
| Retired, non-employed | 57 | 47 | 32 | 14 | 56 | 25 |
| Workers | 42 | 29 | 19 | 13 | 45 | 31 |
| White-collar | 39 | 48 | 18 | 17 | 46 | 44 |
| Professions, business | 41 | 46 | 21 | 16 | 51 | 39 |
| Peasants | 37 | 50 | 32 | 19 | 86 | 51 |

* This column averages the results of three IFOP surveys of 16, 18 and 22 April.

*Sources*: IFOP, op. cit., p. 73; J. Charlot, 'The End of Gaullism?', in H. Penniman (ed.), *France at the Polls: The Presidential Election of 1974* (Washington: 1975) p. 83; A. Lancelot, 'Opinion Polls and the Presidential Election of May 1974' in Penniman, op. cit., p. 192.

interest, for it enables us to chart the stages of the hapless Chaban's dénouement. We may thus evaluate the relative strength of the loyalties which had bound various social groups to Gaullism. Table 5.2 compares the social composition of De Gaulle's and Pompidou's first ballot electorates with those of Chaban both in mid-campaign (when he was still at a 23–25 per cent level) and on the actual first ballot, and then expresses Chaban's support at these two points as a proportion of De Gaulle's in 1965. It will be seen that, apart from the sheer fact of decline, the major theme visible in Chaban's support was the continuation of the trends marking the transition from De Gaulle's electorate to Pompidou's. Thus where Pompidou's working-class support had fallen sharply from De Gaulle's level, Chaban's support, even at its peak, was marked by particularly heavy losses amongst this group. But where Pompidou had fared better than De Gaulle – amongst white-collar workers and, especially, among peasants – Chaban's support held up relatively well. Perhaps the most striking case was provided by the group among whom De Gaulle had enjoyed his highest level of support, the old faithfuls of the Gaullist movement among the retired. Pompidou's downward trend was continued here too, but while this still left Chaban with a very substantial bloc of older voters at the mid-campaign point, the collapse in this group's support thereafter was particularly dramatic. The same was true of that other preternaturally Gaullist group, women. At mid-campaign women had stayed so faithful to Chaban that they actually made up a greater proportion (60 per cent) of his electorate than they had of De Gaulle's (57 per cent). Thereafter women defected more heavily than men, so that only 55 per cent of Chaban's first ballot vote was feminine.

Given Giscard's extension of his Centrist alliance beyond the Majority to the Reformers (57 per cent of whose voters supported him, against only 18 per cent for Chaban), Chaban's main hope lay in wooing to his banner those groups who had provided the backbone of the General's 'popular Gaullism': workers, the retired and women. Despite Chaban's best efforts these were the very groups among whom his losses were greatest: the impression is of Canute appealing against an electoral tide – one which was going out. For the groups whose support had given De Gaulle his distinctive political 'edge' were also those whose allegiance to Gaullism proved to be weakest.

The narrowness of Giscard's victory on the second ballot was, moreover, due to the fact that as this Gaullist hard core fell away from Chaban it sometimes escaped the Right altogether. This was true even on the first ballot, when at least some defectors from Chaban clearly went to Mitterrand. One might have imagined that those who stayed with Chaban to the bitter (and rather hopeless) end were thus nothing if not diehards of the Right. But it was not so. On the second ballot more than 20 per cent of Chaban's supporters did not vote for Giscard and of these defectors over half (11 per cent) voted for Mitterrand.[48] Most of these defectors – the polls leave no doubt[49] – were white-collar and industrial workers who, it seems clear, were willing to vote against their 'natural' class party when it was a matter of supporting De Gaulle or even, *in extremis*, the fraying remnant of Gaullism represented by Chaban, but were not willing to vote for Giscard's Majority of rural clericals[50] and businessmen. The changing nature of Giscard's Majority emerges clearly from Table 5.3, which compares it with De Gaulle's 1965 electorate. Table 5.3 reveals that the erosion of support for the Majority among the three distinctive groups of 'popular Gaullism' – workers, the retired, and women – had proceeded very unevenly. Most dramatic, clearly, was the erosion of working-class (including white-collar) support, a trend which, over this period, moved the French political system a long way towards bipolarisation along class lines. The fall in conservative support among women was of almost equal moment when one considers that women regularly constitute some 52 per cent of the overall electorate. On the other hand Giscard's support amongst the retired held up surprisingly well. The group that was best able to remember De Gaulle in his finest hours, in 1940 and at the Liberation, was, in the event, the most willing of his real loyalists to rally to a non-Gaullist who had 'betrayed' the General in 1969. This is paralleled by the other striking trend revealed in Table 5.3, the dramatic further erosion of support for the Majority amongst the youngest age-group, a majority of whom had opposed even De Gaulle in 1965. Thus the only generation to have come of age exclusively during the Fifth Republic was also the most opposed to those who had built and inherited it. The losses in these categories were less than compensated for by the consolidation of business and professional support and the gains among peasants. The Majority – what Giscard henceforth always referred to as 'the presidential Majority' – had settled more comfortably than ever into the classic profile of French conservatism. But by the same token its hold on power was now less comfortable and more vulnerable than for decades.

## viii  GAULLISM REBORN? JACQUES CHIRAC AND THE RPR

In the wake of the shattering defeat of May 1974 it seemed to some of the older

TABLE 5.3 Social changes in the presidential Majority: social composition of presidential electorates (second ballot): De Gaulle (1965) and Giscard (1974)

|  | *De Gaulle* % | *Giscard* % | *Difference* |
|---|---|---|---|
| All | 54.5 | 50.3 | − 4.2 |
| Men | 48 | 47 | − 1 |
| Women | 62 | 54 | − 8 |
| 21–34 years | 49 | 41 | − 8 |
| 35–49 years | 54 | 51 | − 3 |
| 50–64 years | 55 | 54 | − 1 |
| 65 and over | 64 | 60 | − 4 |
| Peasants | 60 | 69 | + 9 |
| Professions, business | 65 | 66 | + 1 |
| White collar | 53 | 47 | − 6 |
| Industrial workers | 45 | 27 | − 18 |
| Retired, non-employed | 60 | 55 | − 5 |

*Source*: IFOP, op. cit., p. 245 and Lancelot, op. cit., p. 202.

Gaullist diehards that France was now ruled by two traitors: Giscard, who had stabbed De Gaulle himself in the back; and Jacques Chirac, who had performed much the same bloody act upon Chaban and thus on the UDR. This was not Chirac's view of things. Whatever other UDR deputies might feel, the fact remained that he, Chirac, was now easily the most prominent and powerful Gaullist in France. The UDR, moreover, still had 183 of the Majority's 281 deputies (in an Assembly of 490 seats). Provided the party held firm and united (i.e. behind him) it was in a position to dictate its will to the new man in the Elysée. The simple facts of Chirac's power of patronage as prime minister and the lack of any real alternative vision on Chaban's (or anyone else's) part made this a more compelling argument than it looked at first sight.

There were only two problems. First, it was already quite clear that the Hôtel Matignon did not represent the summit of the restlessly energetic Chirac's ambitions. Chirac had scythed his way quite ruthlessly through Gaullist ranks. In no sense was he a man who stood still. Journalists who followed him round the country on his later election tours found themselves utterly exhausted by their attempts to keep up with him. Even after four or five speeches in a sixteen- or eighteen-hour day Chirac's fingers drummed nervously on the table while his feet tapped under it – though, of course, he seldom sat down at all. He was a ball of compulsive energy, throwing out orders, instructions and an interminable stream of suggestions, shot from the hip. He both devoured and spewed out ideas as a fruit machine swallows and throws out pennies. The ideas were frequently half-baked but that didn't matter – Chirac was no intellectual. But his ambition was as great as his energy. He was, quite clearly, a workaholic and an egomaniac. Rallying round Chirac could mean only one thing: the complete subordination of the UDR, even its leading lights such as Chaban, to the goal of placing Chirac in the Elysée in Giscard's place in 1981.

Hence the second problem: Chirac's ambition was as plain to Giscard as to anyone else. This was a serpent he must strangle at birth. To be sure, he needed the UDR's support in the Assembly but he had no intention of allowing the Matignon to dictate to the Elysée, nor of allowing Chirac to build up his strength there. The Gaullists themselves had fashioned the Fifth Republic to enable presidents to lead and to force ministers, including prime ministers, to follow – Giscard knew this bitterly enough from his own long ministerial experience. Very well, he would turn the Gaullists' weapons back on them and call Chirac's bluff. The Elysée would simply dictate to the Matignon and Chirac would have to accept it (and be crushed), resign (and lose his base), or bring down the government – and take the blame for letting in the Left.

Thus began a long guerrilla battle. In December 1974 Chirac won a major round by staging a coup to make himself Secretary-General of the UDR. A handful of Gaullist deputies walked out and Chaban announced that he would henceforth boycott UDR parliamentary meetings, but to most UDR militants in the country it was a joyful sign that their period of painful disorientation was over: they had, once again, a forceful and charismatic leader. Chirac set about welding the UDR group into a cohesive bloc with which to threaten Giscard. Giscard furiously insisted that he could not have a premier who was also a party leader. So, in June 1975, Chirac handed over the leadership to one of his yes-men and proceeded to pick fights with Giscard on one policy issue after another. Giscard stood his ground and in August 1976, after a long series of bitter altercations with the President, Chirac resigned as premier. Thus freed, he began to wage conventional war against Giscard's policies in the Assembly, forcing the President into a series of humiliating retreats. Giscard, for his part, hinted ever more openly at his wish for a broadening of the Centrist alliance to include the Socialists. It was not a threat he could make good (Mitterrand, too, had his eyes on the Elysée – and his hopes depended on maintaining the PS alliance with the PCF) – but the President's wish to rid himself of dependence on the Gaullists was lost on no one. To this end Giscard talked airily of his 'social democratic' hopes of making France a somewhat less unequal country and even introduced a (toothless) proposal for a wealth tax. Chirac led the UDR in righteous attack against it: what was the point of having a conservative government if it introduced socialistic measures? The UDR was on safe ground with all Majority supporters here and rammed through scores of crippling amendments. Giscard had no option save humiliating retreat and the tax bill was finally allowed to pass only in grotesquely emasculated form and with a solemn promise that it would not, in any case, be applied.

By the time of Chirac's resignation in August 1976 the UDR had climbed painfully back to 17 per cent in the polls.[51] This modest recovery from Chaban's 1974 performance was, it was realised, largely due to the growing threat from the Left – signalled by all the polls, by-elections and the Left's sweeping victories in the March 1976 cantonal elections. Alarmed by this threat, conservative voters tended to view Giscard's airy discussions of the need to start building a new, technologically advanced France to face the third millenium as so much lofty dithering. The threat from Mitterrand and Marchais was here and now – and the President's self-absorbed playing with 'social democratic' formulae simply meant building one's own Trojan Horse inside the Majority's gates. Chirac's visceral anti-Communism and the old war-horse of the UDR gradually began to seem a safer last recourse.

Chirac determined to capitalise on this mood by launching a new Gaullist mass movement. In November 1976 he won back his old parliamentary seat in Corrèze in sensational style and, having thus shown that he, at least, could win elections for the Right, launched the *Rassemblement pour la République* (RPR) the next month. The RPR was to be modelled on the RPF (the near identity of name was not accidental). In 1976, as in 1947, Gaullism would define itself as an oppositional mass movement, would centre itself slavishly round a single, charismatic leader, and would derive its essential strength from a Great Fear of the Left (*'les socialo-communistes'*, as Chirac always called them). And the RPR's essential goal – like the RPF's – would be to place its leader in the Elysée. De Gaulle had been President of the RPF. The UNR and UDR had only had secretaries-general. Chirac unhesitatingly took the title of President of the RPR (he was elected on a 97 per cent vote) . . .

Gaullist mass membership had always been inversely related to the movement's security in power. The RPF, baying in the wilderness, had claimed no less than 800,000 members in May 1947 and, in April 1948, 1.5 million membership applications. The wave was brief: by 1949 it claimed only 450,000 members and thereafter never more than 500,000.[52] Once De Gaulle had regained power in 1958 Gaullism had little need for a mass membership and very little appetite for one. A large, clamantly Rightist membership threatened trouble, might alienate the Centre, and would in any case disrupt a movement based on deference to the General's *hauteur*. In 1959 the UNR had barely 25,000 members; in 1960, 35,000; in 1963 still only 86,000. It was only with De Gaulle's eclipse and the launching of the UDR in 1968 that a mass membership drive began, carrying membership up to a claimed 180,000 (and real 160,000) by 1970.[53] Pompidou was too shrewdly aware of the forces eroding the movement to allow things to stand still and under him the party's membership continued to grow – as its popular support began to shrink. Thanks to Pompidou – and to Chirac's energetic 'taking in hand' from December 1974 on – the UDR, on the eve of its transformation into the RPR, was able to claim 285,000 members. It was not enough for Chirac. In the next two years he tirelessly criss-crossed the country, setting afoot the most powerful mass organisation of the Right the Fifth Republic has seen. By February 1978 the RPR boasted a powerful hierarchical structure flowing down from a Political Council to a Central Committee to 22 regional councils, 108 departmental federations and local organisations in every one of the 491 French metropolitan and Overseas constituencies. All told, it boasted 620,000 members – 70 per cent of them men.[54] In organisation, discipline and size it was unrivalled on the Right – Giscard's *Parti Républicain* (the rechristened RI), as also his UDF coalition put together for the 1978 elections, were awash with (government) funds but could not otherwise begin to compete with the RPR.[55] Its only real rival was the PCF – indeed, the image of the RPR as the PCF of the Right was the movement's gravest handicap amongst centrist voters.[56]

In part, at least, this image was relished by RPR militants. Chirac and the RPR had allowed them to rediscover – when they had feared it lost for good – the old excitement, dynamism and élan, the same feeling of belonging to a truly formidable movement, one which stood fast when others wilted, which was a definitive repository of patriotism. At RPR meetings, bedecked with the cross of Lorraine, portraits of De Gaulle and vast posters of Chirac against a *tricolore* background, crowds of comfortable bourgeois could roar out the chorus of *'La Marseillaise'* and feel they were asserting themselves as part of a higher struggle, the crusade to save France from Georges Marchais. Their problem, and thus Chirac's too, was that they could neither understand nor, in the last analysis, tolerate RPR attempts to undermine and harass Giscard. Whatever the government's faults, it *was* still the Majority in power. Chirac was admired as a bonny fighter but also as something of an *enfant terrible*, even by the RPR faithful (and certainly by RPR deputies). It was good to have him on one's side. It was even admissable that he should criticise Giscard and the government. But even Chirac's keenest admirers doubted whether he had the *gravitas* befitting a president and were entirely unwilling to be dragged into anti-government activities merely to further his personal ambitions. In the end RPR voters were just Majority voters and, in the end, Jacques Chirac was not De Gaulle . . .

Such reservations were of little moment while the Union of the Left was sweeping to one victory after another in 1976–7. It was extremely noticeable in local and by-elections that while Giscard's motley band of Centre-conservatives were going down like ninepins, the RPR, with its disciplined battalions, was holding up much better. While the Left was carrying three-quarters of the major cities of France in the March 1977 municipal elections, Chirac alone brought cheer to the Majority by scoring a decisive victory in Paris, becoming the capital's first elected mayor in a century. There seemed little alternative, even for Giscard, to accepting Chirac's demand that the Right rally behind him as the only man who could stop the Left. In practice this was a demand that Giscard should organise no alternative challenge to the RPR. Conservative voters had already begun to accept Chirac's logic. In January 1976 Giscard's PR had led the Gaullists 24 per cent: 15 per cent in the polls and in October still by 22 per cent: 18 per cent. With the RPR's foundation in December the Gaullists moved up to 20 per cent. In early 1977 they overtook the PR and by September 1977 were moving sharply ahead, 23 per cent: 19 per cent.[57] There was no escape for Giscard. He would have to come to Canossa.

At this point, the negotiations on the Common Programme broke down and the Left split. Chirac tried to look pleased – had he not always predicted the Left would never win? In fact, of course, a Left victory would have served Chirac perfectly. Giscard would be gravely weakened. He would have to compromise with the Left or, more likely, be forced out. Either way the RPR and Chirac would become the sole real hope of the Right. Even a narrow win for the Majority, with the Left threatening to win all the way to the finishing post, would have served the RPR well enough. The one thing Chirac had never bargained for was that the Left might publicly throw its chances away six months beforehand. The RPR's ascent in the polls stopped abruptly and went into reverse, moving it back to 20–21 per cent. Giscard was off the hook. He hurriedly threw together what Chirac had always feared, a coalition of centrists and conservatives (the UDF) to fight for the President's cause against the Left – and the RPR. UDF candidacies now blossomed in one RPR-held seat after another and

Raymond Barre, Giscard's replacement for Chirac as Premier, doled out plentiful funds to such hopefuls. Chirac, seeing his nightmare coming true, blustered vainly about treachery – and then tried to grin and bear it.

In the event Chirac was saved from the worst. While Giscard and Barre used all the old (Gaullist) tricks to put the State's and the media's support behind the UDF, the coalition had been put together too late and too hurriedly to reap the full benefit. Moreover, the dislike of conservative voters for squabbling within the Majority at this crisis hour restrained the UDF from attacking the RPR as well as vice versa. The RPR finally won 22.6 per cent of the vote and held on to 153 of its seats (losing 30). The UDF won 20.6 per cent and claimed all the remaining 137 Majority deputies as its own.[58] The RPR was still the largest party, but its lead had been sharply cut back. Moreover, those of its deputies who had crossed the floor to Giscard almost invariably held their seats, a clear encouragement to others to do the same. The RPR had held on as well as it had mainly thanks to its large number of well-entrenched *députés-maires*: the RPR, like the RPF after 1951, was effectively at the mercy of its notables. Moreover, the RPR was easily the oldest party in parliament (over two-thirds of its deputies were aged fifty-one and over).[59] Replacing them as they died, retired or deserted to Giscard would be difficult, to say the least.

Within a few weeks of the election the size of Chirac's future problems became clear as the RPR parliamentary party announced that they would not necessarily feel bound by the decisions of Chirac's party executive. There was, moreover, no shortage of RPR deputies willing to accept Giscard's invitation to serve in his Cabinet and, even more dramatically, to flaunt Chirac's public and vehement wishes by helping elect Chaban as the new President of the Assembly. This emergence of a new Giscard-Chaban alliance boded nothing but ill for Chirac. It came as no surprise, a little later, when Giscard changed the rules of diplomatic protocol so that visiting heads of state were no longer to be officially welcomed by the Mayor of Paris – or that Chirac should find himself having to fight desperate battles for government funds suddenly unavailable to pay the Paris police . . . Nor was it surprising that the UDF now began to soar ahead of the RPR in the polls. In the June 1979 European elections the RPR won only 16.2 per cent of the vote, while the Giscardians[60] took 27.5 per cent. True, the elections were, in a sense, a 'free vote': the question of who held power in France was not at stake and thus there was no threat from the Left to rally conservatives to the RPR. Even so, it was the last full-scale electoral rehearsal before the 1981 presidential election. The results showed yet again how desperately important it would be to the survival of Gaullism that Chirac should run in and win that contest – and also just how difficult that would be.

## ix THE IMPACT OF GAULLISM

Winding up his campaign in 1978 Chirac declared that 'In the hardest times the RPR has shown that it can be relied upon. Whatever happens it is going to have to be reckoned with.'[61] The RPR's relative success prompted many besides Chirac to assume an indefinite continuation of the Gaullist movement and its line of inheritance. If this should transpire to be the case it would be the most remarkable of all De Gaulle's legacies. No other European state, indeed, no other developed state, can exhibit such a personalist movement maintaining itself long after its author's demise. It is possible to speak of political traits and traditions in these terms – Maoism, Jacksonian Democracy, Marxism-Leninism, and so on – but in all cases a more or less coherent system of beliefs is denoted by the accident of name. Even in the highly personalist French system there is no parallel – Bonapartism and Boulangism survived their creators but neither bequeathed a highly organised mass movement. For a comparable example of such a movement, so strongly stamped by a purely personal style and precepts, one can appeal uniquely and remotely to the case of Peronism in Argentina.

That it should still be an open question whether Gaullism can defy these apparent historical laws provides a rough measure of the movement's unique and extraordinary impact on French politics since the Liberation. A survey of the Left – or any other aspect of French political life – ignores Gaullism only at its peril. It is hardly accidental that what we have termed the 'ice age' of the Left began just as the RPF was founded in 1947, or that the Left's renaissance in the 1970s has coincided so precisely with Gaullism's decline.

We have already seen how profound was the impact of De Gaulle's two irruptions into the political arena in 1947 and 1958. On both occasions he not merely created a mass movement of great strength, but brought across two large waves of support to the Right, consisting largely of working- and lower-middle-class support he alone could command. In assessing Gaullism a decade after De Gaulle, however, what we need to gauge is the significance of his *departure from* the political system. In one sense, of course, the continuation of a powerful Gaullist movement years after the General's death might be taken to imply that his importance had been exaggerated, that his going made little difference. That this was not the case emerges very clearly from Table 5.4.

It seems clear from Table 5.4 that just as De Gaulle's departure from the scene in 1953 led to a slippage of support away from the Right (a process probably not complete as early as the 1956 elections), his resignation in 1969 had a similar effect. In the subsequent 1973 election the Right slipped back under the 55 per cent level it had maintained quite comfortably ever since 1958 and the Gaullist party suffered a particularly dramatic contraction, losing at a stroke the easy dominance of the conservative electorate it had enjoyed since 1962. Essentially, 1973 seems to have constituted an intermediary stage in which Gaullist support ebbed not to the Left so much as to the other fractions of the Right and Centre from whom it had been expropriated in 1962. The full extent of these losses was masked by Pompidou's continuing tenure of the Elysée and the still predominant position of the Gaullists within the parliamentary Majority, both of which allowed Gaullist supremacy to persist in a somewhat artificial way.

It was only with their dispossession by Giscard in 1974 that the true measure of the

TABLE 5.4 Gaullism and the Right in post-war France

| General Elections | Gaullist parties* % vote | | Total Right** % vote | Gaullist support as % age of total Right |
|---|---|---|---|---|
| 1945 |  | – | 39.9 | – |
| 1946 |  | – | 41.3 | – |
| 1951 | RPF | 21.6 | 48.5 | 44.5 |
| 1956 |  | – | 46.5 | – |
| 1958 | UNR | 20.5 | 56.4 | 36.3 |
| 1962 | UNR | 31.9 | 55.6 | 57.4 |
| 1967 | Ve Rep. | 31.4 | 56.4 | 55.7 |
| 1968 | UDR | 37.3 | 58.9 | 63.3 |
| 1973 | UDR | 23.8 | 54.3 | 43.8 |
| 1978 | RPR | 22.6 | 48.6 | 46.5 |

* I.e. strictly Gaullist parties, not including RI. CDP or other fractions of the Majority.
** The basis of calculation has been to total the votes of the Left Parties (counting the Radicals with the Left, save in 1956 and from 1967 on when only Left Radicals were thus counted), and to term the remainder as the total Right. The 1978 Ecologists I have counted as neither Left nor Right.

Gaullists' decline became apparent and with it an acceleration of the haemorrhage from the Right, whose score fell to only 50.7 per cent. The trend continued in 1978 with the Right falling back all the way to its 1951 level, now actually behind the Left's 49.3 per cent. This virtual landslide occurred as Gaullist support, which had mainly stopped at the halfway house of non-Gaullist conservatism, now moved all the way across into the Left column. At this point the Right had lost the whole of the second wave of support brought to it by De Gaulle in 1951 and the question remained open as to whether it could prevent further erosion from carrying it back all the way to its 1946 level. At the time of the 1977 municipal elections this seemed to be a real enough prospect and even the early polls of 1978 showed the Right trailing along at a 43–44 per cent level prior to its last-minute recovery in March.[62] It was, of course, to be expected that it would take some time for the full effects of the General's departure to be visible – such large-scale shifts in opinion as those we have seen take time to 'feed through'. But it is clear enough now that this departure, which both the Gaullists and the Right appeared to have survived with ease in 1969, has been a long-run disaster for them both.

Such a finding, it may be noted, helps to 'solve' the riddle of the 1968 May Events: how such a profound political earthquake could, apparently, be entirely devoid of consequence. With the benefit of a decade's hindsight it is possible to see that the Events did indeed have issue, that they were the first step in a long and complex process through which first De Gaulle and then the Gaullists were progressively dislodged from power. 1968 saw the apotheosis of Gaullism: its greatest triumph and, simultaneously, its decisive transformation into being 'just' the Majority; a victory without precedent which humbled De Gaulle and forced him into the ill-fated referendum of 1969 – and hence out. In the end, we have seen, the Gaullists could not afford this loss. Cohn-Bendit and the students had their revenge in the end – but their beneficiaries were, in the first place, a rag-bag of centrists and conservatives led by an aristocrat descended from the Bourbons; and, second the old parties of the Left led by a permanent minister of the Fourth Republic. It was not quite what the students had had in mind . . .

The decline of Gaullism, we have argued, was a fundamental factor in the Renaissance of the Left in 1970s, with large numbers of lower-class voters released towards the Left, particularly the PS, as the old bonds tethering them to the Right withered away. The formation of the RPR – a new, highly organised and disciplined mass movement under another 'strong man' leader – may be seen as an attempt to stop this 'rot' by solidifying the remains of Gaullism into a tight, coherent bloc. Hence Chirac's defensive stress on the party's ability to 'endure' and 'hold' even 'in the hardest times'. The days of a 35 per cent Gaullist bloc were tacitly admitted to be over for good. In effect in 1976–8 Chirac sought, instead, to consolidate Gaullism at its familiar 21 per cent 'hard-core' level. With a 22.6 per cent vote in 1978 this was, indeed, roughly what he achieved.[63] The question remains whether the RPR will be merely a pause in the continuing decline of Gaullism – and whether the slippage to the Left can carry the latter all the way back to its 1945–6 peak.

There are, in fact, considerable grounds for scepticism about Chirac's ability to halt the Gaullist decline. The lesson of the RPF's post-1951 decline was, after all, that there is simply no substitute for power and the patronage it brings. Without it De Gaulle was unable either to control his deputies or to maintain the momentum of his mass movement. In these respects Chirac's position is no stronger than De Gaulle's was, and he lacks the latter's unique stature. Moreover, the RPR's apparent consolidation at its 21 per cent 'hard-core' level may prove a mere mirage. The party owed this level of support in 1978 to its entrenched notables and the feverish atmosphere created by the expectation of Left victory. Lacking such assistance in the 1979 European elections, it lost over a quarter of its vote – a dire augury for 1981, when these factors will again be unlikely to play a major role.

In the post-De Gaulle era there is also simply less reason to believe in the existence of a hard-core Gaullist bloc. To argue, as we have, for the existence of such a hard core is historically and politically convincing, but it is difficult to provide a sociological explanation for this phenomenon beyond De Gaulle's special appeal to lower-class voters. This the RPR lacks – there is no real sociological distinction to be made between its electorate and the rest of the Majority. It is, in any case, not very meaningful to compare the hard-core 21 per cent of 1951 or 1958 with the 1978 RPR electorate. Demographic turnover has been too great for the electorates of these years to have much in common with one another – and, indeed, it was precisely the older voters who *could* have formed part of all three electorates who were most easily seduced by Giscard in 1974. Finally, it is simply misleading to speak of a 'hard core' in the conditions of great electoral fluidity seen in the 1970s. Lindon and Weill have shown[64] that in 1973 no more than 26 per cent of all Majority voters could be regarded as truly hard core. In 1975 Charlot put the figure at only a little over 30 per cent.[65] Indeed, the experience of 1973–4, when the Gaullist vote collapsed from 23.8 per cent to 14.5 per cent in just fourteen months, or 1978–9, when it fell from 22.6 per cent to 16.2 per cent in fifteen months, suggests both that the RPR vote is the very opposite of shock-resistant and that if there is a hard-core level it is now nearer 15 per cent than 21 per cent.

The Gaullist decline, then, may well continue. But it seems unlikely that the Left stands to reap any further benefits from the process. The lower-class electors whose defection from Gaullism so dramatically swelled the ranks of the Left from 1972 on had already virtually all departed by 1978, leaving the Gaullists an electorate almost indistinguishable from that of the overall Majority. This emerges clearly from a comparison of the 1978 RPR and UDF electorates.[66] There was almost no trace of the old Gaullist superiority amongst workers, women and the retired; indeed, the UDF actually took a larger (16 per cent) share of the working-class vote than the RPR (14 per cent). The only significant differences lay in the RPR's superiority amongst white-collar workers (20 per cent to the UDF's 14 per cent) and the latter's advantage amongst regularly practising Catholics (39 per cent to the RPR's 31 per cent). The conclusion appears inescapable that as a potential reservoir of defecting recruits to the Left, Gaullism has already been drained dry.

This conclusion is reinforced by two further facts. First, the pivotal group of centrists wavering between Right and Left in 1978 were almost exclusively composed of those moving between the PS and the UDF:[67] there was little sign of any traffic in either direction between the RPR and the Left. Second, the sharp drop in the RPR's vote in 1979, visible first in the cantonal and then in the European elections, was not paralleled by any accompanying rise in the Left's vote. Between March 1978 and June 1979 the RPR lost 6.4 per cent of the vote but the Left simultaneously fell back 2 per cent, with only the Ecologists and the UDF gaining clearly. The previous Gaullist collapse of 1974 had produced major gains for the Left; in 1979 it could not even help the Left hold its ground.

Thus by the late 1970s the decline of Gaullism had become a parochial concern of the Right. It was, for the Right, none too soon, for the large-scale movement to the Left of erstwhile Gaullist supporters had gravely endangered its continuing security in power. It was, moreover, not the only form of electoral attrition operating against the Right for, as we have noted, a not inconsiderable number of centrists were simultaneously being repelled towards the Left in reaction to the Centre's incorporation into the Majority. Taken together these two processes produced an effect which, in the context of the almost glacial stability of French voting behaviour, constituted something akin to a long drawn-out landslide.

The explanation for this momentous shift within the French body politic cannot, however, be sought only in the behaviour of parties and politicians, nor even in the peculiar electoral power of a De Gaulle. Such purely political factors cannot be dismissed as merely epiphenomal – but nor are they the whole story. Further beneath the political surface, deeper – and less overtly political – forces were at work, in part causing this attrition of the Right, in part resulting from and interacting with changes at the political surface. Two of these subterranean forces merit our particular attention: first, the declining strength of the Right's major traditional base, the solid Catholic bloc vote; and second, in part resulting from the diminishing significance of this religious cleavage, the emergence (perhaps, more exactly, the re-emergence) into greater prominence of the old politics of social class and social inequality. It is to these concerns that we now turn.

# 6 The Changing Politics of Faith and Infidelity

## i SET IN A TIMELESS MOULD...

In the wake of the 1965 presidential election the French political scientist Michel Brulé analysed the electorates of De Gaulle and Mitterrand to see how far the traditionally powerful variable of religious practice had played any role in this climactic battle between Right and Left. His conclusions came as a considerable shock:

> the best sociological explanation of French people's electoral choice last December 5 is provided by their religious situation – defined both in terms of their beliefs and their degree of religious practice – rather than by their membership of an age or occupational group or by their sex. In a society which takes pleasure in emphasising everything that differentiates it from its own past, the persistence of such a deep and traditional cleavage as this at the political level deserves to be thrown into sharp relief.[1]

No one was unaware, of course, that the bitter clerical/anti-clerical divide had provided the central cleavage of French political history since the Revolution, and the pioneering voting studies of André Siegfried had long ago revealed how these divisions had continued to determine the electoral geography of France well into the 1920s. But Brulé's finding was a rude surprise to many Frenchmen (and perhaps particularly political scientists) who had confidently assumed that the modern, prosperous and secular France of the 1960s had long since left behind these 'primitive' traits. That religion might play the central role in political choice seemed redolent alternatively of the Dreyfus era or of a 'backward' country such as Italy. Moreover, although opinion polling in France had achieved a considerable sophistication, it remained strongly marked by its origins in market research. Political sociologists who analysed poll data were used enough to dealing in correlations between voting behaviour and income, sex, age, class, region, urbanisation and consumption patterns – but not religion, a variable of little interest to the commercial companies who were the principal clients of the main polling agencies, IFOP and SOFRES.

But there was no doubt that Brulé's findings were very striking. Only 8 per cent of the regularly practising (about a quarter of the electorate in 1965) had voted for

Mitterrand at the first ballot, against 86 per cent for De Gaulle and Lecanuet together. Even amongst the irregularly practising (some 40 per cent of the electorate), nearly 70 per cent had voted for the Right – which less than 30 per cent of non-Catholics and the irreligious had done.[2] It was clear that the enthusiasm for the Left of agnostics and atheists (a smaller, 10 per cent group) lost nothing in comparison with the zeal of devout Catholics for the Right – 59 per cent of them voted for the PCF and another 24 per cent for the Socialists.[3] While the contrast was greatest at the extremes of atheism and devoutness, there was no doubt that the religious variable exercised a powerful influence right across the spectrum in between.[4] It was far more powerful than social class: an atheist businessman was more likely to vote Communist than for the Right – and the reverse was true of a devoutly Catholic worker. The influence of religion was, indeed, so overwhelming that Brulé was led to ask 'what influence remains to other factors of analysis – sex, age, occupation or region – once the weight of the religious variable is cancelled out?'[5]

Brulé's findings had a dual impact. In part, of course, he suffered the fate of any sociologist who produces a striking set of irrefutable conclusions: that is, to be immediately told that everyone had known these facts perfectly well already. But the opposite reaction – one of shock – was more common among professional political analysts and commentators. Indeed, the possibility that the large body of voting studies which had neglected this variable might now be declared virtually irrelevant naturally created a degree of consternation.[6]

Some surprise was pardonable, though. After all, political Catholicism had accepted the Republic at least from the Liberation on, so there was now no longer an issue, as for so long before, over the nature of the regime. There was no great Catholic party in France akin to the Italian or German Christian Democrats – by the mid-1960s the only more or less Catholic party was Lecanuet's CD – and that was small. In any case, the bitter clerical *v.* anti-clerical disputes which had for so long dominated the political stage had now largely disappeared. Such controversies had emerged only sporadically under the Fourth Republic. Under the Fifth – once the great excitements of 1959 had subsided[7] – such disputes simply failed to surface at all. The steam had gone right out of the old church schools issue (and, despite De Gaulle's increased State aid for them, so had many pupils out of the church schools). [8] The French clergy had all but ceased to offer political advice to the faithful. In 1958 the hierarchy had suggested that a No vote in the constitutional referendum would be 'inopportune'.[9] In 1962 it had counselled a Yes vote over Algerian independence. And its opposition to Communism was well enough known to need only occasional and general reiteration. But that was really all – the Church was no longer a monolithic, interventionist force for the Right. Indeed, all the public running had for some time been made by younger Catholic militants and clergy of distinctly leftish hue – worker-priests, Jocistes[10], and supporters of the PSU and the now left-wing CFDT, which had actually thrown off its old 'Christian' label in 1964 in its eagerness to take up a secular, humanist struggle based on class, not faith.[11]

All this was real enough. Yet there was no doubting Brulé's findings: religion (and religious practice) was still the great dividing line between Left and Right. Indeed, there seemed reason to doubt that the old religious cleavage had eroded at all. If one looked back to one of the very few earlier surveys of religious voting, conducted by IFOP in September 1952, one found that regular churchgoers then were voting 54 per cent MRP, 20 per cent for other conservatives, 18 per cent for the RPF, 5 per cent Socialist, 2 per cent Radical and 1 per cent Communist.[12] In a sense the 1956 data were even more impressive. It was generally agreed[13] that the victory of the Republican Front at that election had been due to the leftward movement of around half a million Catholic voters. None the less Lijphart, analysing the 1956 data, found that the index of religious voting in France was no less than four times as great as that for class voting.[14] Yet the implication of Brulé's 1965 data was that the religious cleavage was back to its even higher 1952 level, for in both years just 8 per cent of regular churchgoers were supporting the parties of the Left. French politics seemed to be set in a timeless mould. And, if that was true, what hope could there be for the Left?

Ironically, Brulé had focused attention on the enduring importance of the religious factor on the eve of a period of dramatic change. In a sense the picture he provided was one of the hillside just before the avalanche. His findings had come as a shock because the prosperous modernity had given birth to a confident secular consciousness which, it was now easy to show, did not reflect social reality. But this consciousness was not meaningless either. Rooted as it was in the most 'advanced' and metropolitan sectors of society, it merely ran ahead of social change in the rest of France: it was, at least, predictively valid. (Much the same phenomenon was contemporaneously visible in Britain, where the 1960s ideology of 'classlessness' was rudely brought up short by works of political sociology attesting the enduring power of the class cleavage. A few years later class voting had diminished so drastically as to vindicate most of the prophets of 'classlessness'.)[15]

The reasons for this change were complex. It seems probable that the decline of Gaullism was a partial cause – as well as a partial result – of the diminution of the electoral solidarity of the Catholic bloc. Certainly, the strong leftward drift of Catholic voters from 1952 (when the RPF was still a force) to 1956 (when it was not) suspiciously foreshadowed the tendency of a significant fringe of Catholic voters towards the Left in the decade after De Gaulle's second departure from the political scene, in 1969. To be sure, Gaullism was never primarily or even largely a Catholic movement; but at its peak, at least, it united and gave coherence to French conservatism in a way which made the political choices of the conservatively-inclined – Catholics above all – both easy and simple. For such voters the final option was never in any real doubt: *of course* they preferred De Gaulle to chaos or to the Left. With this settled in advance – apolitically, as it were – all other political concerns were second-order questions. To this extent Gaullism may have helped 'freeze' and solidify traditional conservative support in its old and comfortable patterns of behaviour. With Gaullism's decline and the emergence of competing factions within the Majority the choices to be made became harder and more real. Just as the process was to produce a 'fall-out' effect among other, particularly lower-class, voters, so it had at least some marginal effect amongst Catholics too.

There is less doubt about other forces for change. The Church and Catholic militants were themselves undergoing a major period of turmoil and reappraisal even as Brulé wrote. To some extent this actually brought change in the political meaning of Catholicism itself, so that it became altogether less axiomatic that a devout Catholic was a man of the Right. Such change was, however, often exaggerated and, as we shall see, touched the small elite of Catholic militants far more than it did the wider flock of the faithful.

Finally, and most importantly, the secularisation of French society took a giant stride in the 1970s in the most direct way of all – in steeply falling rates of religious practice. All these changes combined to produce a considerable erosion in the significance of the religious cleavage which had been so fundamental to French society ever since the Revolution. It was a development of epochal importance, one which still continues. And for the Left it presented a major opportunity.

## ii THE CHURCH, THE MILITANTS AND THE FAITHFUL

The Church, in France as elsewhere, had entered a period of questioning and turmoil in the wake of the changes of the Second Vatican Council of 1962–5. John XXIII had effectively sought to bring about the rapprochement of the Church with European social democracy and with the concerns of the Third World. This meant that the Church had to depart from the genteel paths of traditional piety towards an altogether more adventurous and uncertain course – from which there was no going back. In 1966 the French episcopate took up the new themes with the publication of a social and economic charter clearly, if gently, critical of the capitalist order.[16] This was followed in 1967 by the papal encyclical *Populorum Progressio* – which caused even the PCF Politburo to describe the Church's evolution as 'interesting'. Many of the younger clergy and lay militants of the Church were profoundly influenced by the 1968 May Events and the stage was set for an unprecedented and open dialogue between the Church and the Communists on the general theme of 'Marxism and Christianity'. The PCF's spokesman, Roger Garaudy, was engaged in debate in 1970 first by Fr Girardi and then by Cardinal Daniélou. Even Garaudy's subsequent expulsion from the Party could not diminish the psychological effect upon the faithful of seeing a prince of the Church enter into equal and friendly discourse with a member of the Politburo. Moreover, this more liberal stand received fairly clear papal acknowledgement in Paul VI's letter to Cardinal Roy in 1971 in which he agreed that 'the same Christian faith may lead to different political commitments'. In 1972 the French episcopate, meeting at Lourdes, translated this into the document 'For a Christian Political Practice'. Henceforth the official attitude of the Church towards politics was to be enshrined in a doctrine of 'pluralism', which in effect gave equal legitimacy to political action within the old anti-clerical parties, the Socialists and Radicals. The line was drawn, implicitly, but quite firmly and clearly, at anything left of that.

In the political context of traditional Catholicism these cautious steps seemed almost revolutionary. For, quite apart from the impulsion of the Second Vatican Council, the Church was well aware of the changing tenor of the times, and was determined not to allow itself to be boxed in within a diminishing circle of pious rural conservatism. The mood of the young Catholic elites of the JOC, the JAC and the JEC[17] had become increasingly clear from the late 1950s on. If the Church was not to lose all touch with urban workers, with the young and now even with important elements within its traditional rural bastions, it had to invest for the future, for one or two generations hence. It needed to show itself more open, more willing to change and it had to abstract itself from its implicit political context which, truth to tell, had little profit left in it in the new France. The Church had not, of course, ever seriously envisaged a reconciliation with the Communists. The Marxism-Christianity debate was useful to both the Church and the Party hierarchies as a lever with which to extract themselves from their respective political ghettoes – but that was all. The point of the debate lay not in its possible philosophical interest but in the fact that it took place at all. For the PCF the debate also offered possibilities of proselytisation which could not be ignored given the Party's desperate struggle with the Socialists for supremacy on the Left. Accordingly the Party sought to keep the debate going, while the Church hierarchy lost interest once the original symbolic point had been made.

For the Church the debate had been a chance to show its new liberalism – and to define its limits. The faithful might now extend all the way across the political spectrum to the very fringes of the PCF – but no further. Having achieved this much the Church had arrived at its objective – and stopped. There was no further leftward movement by the hierarchy after 1972. Indeed the Episcopate's 1975 declaration on 'The Liberation of Man and Salvation in Christ' was roundly condemned as a conservative document by Catholic radicals. As the 1978 elections approached, and perhaps in case the point had become confused, M. Francois Marty, the Archbishop of Paris, reiterated the Church's stand. The Church was now entirely tolerant of the widest political pluralism – except that 'One cannot be both a good Christian and a good Communist at the same time.'

If these limited aims were understood by the lay militants of the Church, they were seldom accepted. The younger generation of Catholic radicals (including some of the younger clergy) had embarked with great verve but without official blessing on their new course. They were little inclined to heed the hierarchy's attempts to put on the brakes and not infrequently came into head-on conflict with it. All things seemed possible in the effervescent world of the young radicals. A small nexus of PSU militants and Jocists had, after all, virtually taken over the CFTC, won the battle of deconfessionalisation, led the resultant CFDT into a series of advanced positions (especially in 1968), and made their goal of *autogestion* a central objective of the movement. Their rural counterparts had achieved similar successes within the main farmers' union, the *Fédération Nationale de Syndicats des Exploitants Agricoles* (FNSEA). There was no conference, seminar or convention of the Catholic laity where the voice of the young radicals was not heard, often succeeding in drowning out the more conservative tones of the hierarchy and the country ladies who had hitherto enjoyed an easy predominance in such milieux. The militants looked for inspiration not to their own hierarchy but to the episcopal radicals of the Third World, Camillo Torres and Dom Helder Camara (whose great public meeting in Paris in 1970 was, for them, a landmark quite of its own). Perhaps above all the militants had lived through the experience of May 1968. They had seen the walls of Jericho tumble before them. Naturally, they took the debates on Marxism and Christianity deadly seriously; 'naturally' they supported the workers' occupation at the Lip watch factory; 'naturally' they were attracted by the new vogue for ecology and communal living; 'naturally' it was the Left Catholic journal, *Esprit*, which was the first to introduce the writings of Ivan Illich into France. And so on. In 1974 the JOC Congress invited the Communist leader, Marchais, to participate at one of its sessions and later that year a group of 'Christian Marxists' was officially founded.

In the early 1960s the question of political affiliation had been something of a problem for the Catholic militants of this 'new Left'. However impatient they were of the staid conservatism of their elders and the hierarchy, few were willing to make the total and violent break with their own background that joining the PCF, the main working-class party, would entail. And if the still Stalinist PCF held few attractions, the dying remnant of Mollet's SFIO held fewer still. Accordingly, the militants tended to take refuge in the tiny PSU ('the MRP of the Left', as its detractors called it) and in the deliberately apolitical syndicalism of the CFDT. The situation was transformed, however, by the creation of the new Socialist Party, the PS, and then by the formation of the Union of the Left in 1972. With a credible alternative now available, the militants lost much of their political reserve and moved strongly towards the united Left, mainly towards the PS (and within that to the leftish CERES[18] faction) but a few towards the PCF as well. The CFDT, which had given only its implicit support to the Left at the 1973 elections, publicly endorsed Mitterrand's presidential bid in 1974.

By the early 1970s there had thus come into existence a recognisable category of Catholic militants whose support for the Left went far beyond the derisory 8 per cent of the devout (regularly practising) Catholics who had supported Mitterrand in 1965. On the eve of the 1973 elections IFOP carried out a special poll on the voting intentions of Catholic militants and found no less than 44 per cent of them favouring the Left.[19] At the same time the Left-Catholic *Témoignage Chrétien* carried out a survey of its readers which showed no less than 94 per cent of them supporting the Left (53 per cent PS, 31.5 per cent PSU, 8 per cent PCF, 1.5 per cent Trotskyite).[20] Even the conservative and mainstream *La Vie Catholique*, conducting a similar survey in 1974, found 27 per cent of its readers supporting Mitterrand even on the first round against Giscard.[21]

The existence of this new group had a greatly distorting effect on the political image of French Catholicism. The young radicals tended to be the most literate, articulate and – being young – most photogenic of the faithful. The press and the media were tireless in their fascination with the new phenomenon and no programme, survey or, indeed, Catholic conference was complete without the obligatory declarations from a Marxist curé or lay militant who seemed to be moving in favour of proletarian dictatorship just as the PCF was deciding to abandon it. It was known, of course, that such views were not shared by the hierarchy, if only because the militants were recurrently involved in well-publicised clashes with it. But a good deal of commentary neglected to notice just how atypical and politically unrepresentative of the faithful as a whole the young radicals were.

For while the Catholic 'new Left' was not without influence, political change amongst Catholics generally was slow and uncertain. The Left's (in practice, the PS's) first noticeable gains in Catholic areas were not visible until 1973. In that year's election 13 per cent of regularly practising Catholics voted for the Left at the first ballot (10 per cent PS, 2 per cent PSU, 1 per cent PCF), as did 17 per cent at the second ballot, when the elimination of Centrists in most seats forced a straighter choice.[22] Polls also showed that 62 per cent of CFDT members had voted for the Left, not far behind the level of FO members (66 per cent) even if still lagging well in the rear of the almost monolithically left-voting CGT membership (88 per cent).[23]

Interestingly, the early polls of the 1974 presidential election showed something of a 'relapse' of the Catholic Left, with only 8 per cent of the regularly practising favouring Mitterrand – the very same proportion that had favoured him on the first round in 1965. After the first-round vote 11 per cent of this group admitted to having voted for him – still a lower level than the 13 per cent who had given the Left first-round support in 1973. In the showdown of the 1974 second ballot, however, no less than 23 per cent of this devout group voted for Mitterrand.[24]

This trend continued in the 1976 cantonal elections when no less than 32 per cent of regularly practising Catholics voted for the Left.[25] By this stage it had become clear that a large bloc of devout Catholics (and an even larger one of the less devout) was hovering gingerly on the edge of the Left's camp. They were, however, the least certain of the Left's new recruits and, as the 'crunch' of the 1978 elections neared, the fragility of their attachment became, from the Left's point of view, distressingly evident. The high-water mark of 1976 (when little was really at stake) was not reached again. At the 1977 municipal elections only 26 per cent of the regularly practising voted Left, with many of those who had voted Left in 1976 defecting to the Ecologists.

New-found Catholic loyalties to the Left were particularly sensitive to the breakdown of the negotiations on the Common Programme in September 1977. Polls showed that while many Catholics were enthusiastic for a greater degree of (vaguely defined) social justice, they were particularly prone to view politics as a 'dirty game'. To such voters the embittered and prolonged wrangling between the PS and PCF was an unpleasant reminder that social justice was a matter of politics too. By January 1978 IFOP showed *pratiquants* dividing 72 per cent for the Right, 5 per cent for the Ecologists and only 23 per cent for the Left (18 per cent for the PS and MRG, 3 per cent for the PCF, and 2 per cent PSU).[26] As election eve neared the polarisation of Right and Left increased and there was an increasing tendency for the Catholics who had defected from the Right in 1976–7 to 'home' back whence they had come. A SOFRES study after the 1978 second round showed that, at the last, the devout had voted 80 per cent for the Right and only 20 per cent for the Left.[27] Had the Left held its 1976 level of support among this group it might well have won the election.

The 1970s thus saw a significant erosion of the conservative electoral solidarity of devout Catholics. At the peak (1976) almost one-third of this group were voting Left and even at the 'crunch' (March 1978) the Left still had two and half times the support it had enjoyed in 1965 from this group. None the less, it is also clear how exaggerated have been some of the claims made of a wholesale *'virage à gauche'* by French Catholics. It remains true that no group in French society (no matter how defined) is more hostile to the Left than devout Catholics. The Catholic 'new Left' have made considerable sound and fury – but they haven't changed that.

## iii THE EMPTY CHURCHES

A far more powerful factor which has acted to erode the importance of the religious cleavage has been the process of secularisation within French society as a whole. It is, however, difficult to chart this process owing to the dearth of reliable statistics collected before the 1960s. Thus Bosworth quotes a 1952 poll showing that 37 per cent of the population were then regularly practising Catholics, but provides no figure for the occasionally practising.[28] Bosworth also cites a 1958 survey which found that 34 per cent of young adults were regular churchgoers,[29] a figure which probably tallies with his earlier one, given the lesser propensity of the young to religious practice. Dogan cites an apparently exhaustive study for 1956 which, however, classifies the irregularly practising and the non-practising together as 'non-active'. His 'active' (regularly practising?) figures are somewhat higher than Bosworth's 32 per cent for men and 47 per cent for women, giving a probable overall figure of 40 per cent.[30] It seems safe to conclude only that the proportion of the French population in the mid-1950s who were regularly practising Catholics was somewhere between 35–40 per cent.

This figure should be set against those in Table 6.1. Whatever basis of classification

TABLE 6.1 Religious practice in France, 1966, 1974, 1977

|  | *1966* | *1974* | *1977* | *Change 1966–77* |
|---|---|---|---|---|
|  | % | % | % | % |
| Catholics (self-identified) | (87.3) | 86.5 | 81.0 | − 6.3 |
| Of whom: Regularly practising | 24.3 | 21 | 17 | − 7.3 |
| Irregularly practising | 40.7 | 18 | 14 | − 26.7 |
| Non-practising | 23.3 | 47.5 | 50 | + 26.7 |
| Other religions | (3) | 3.5 | 4 | + 1 |
| No religion | 9.7 | 10 | 15 | + 6.3 |

*Source*: E. Aver *et al.*, 'Pratique Réligiouse et Comportement Electoral', *Archives de la Sociologie des Réligions*, 29 (1970) p. 33; and C. Peyrefitte, 'Réligion et Politique', in SOFRES, *L'Opinion Française en 1977* (Paris: 1978) Table I. Aver *et al.* excluded 'Other religions' entirely from their study. I have added in the 3 per cent normal for this category in surveys of that period (the figures in brackets) and recalculated the other percentages accordingly.

is used the overall trend revealed in Table 6.1 unmistakable. Even by 1966 the regularly practising had fallen from at least a third of the population to a quarter – and by 1977 had fallen to a sixth. Initially this fall merely swelled the numbers of the occasionally practising but by the 1970s their numbers, too, were dropping sharply as the numbers of the non-practising and those declaring themselves to have no religion at all began to rise abruptly. (The 1977 SOFRES study actually found 25 per cent of those in the Paris area declaring themselves to have no religion.)[31] Thus in little more than a decade the proportion of the population classifiable as (regularly *or* irregularly) practising Catholics has fallen from almost two-thirds to less than a third. To be sure, the phenomenon of secularisation is an international one.[32] None the less, its incidence on French society in recent years has been striking. Moreover, while the 'secular revolution' can proceed elsewhere unencumbered by political significance, in France the process is fraught with major political implications. It is, for example, worth asking what *political* meaning should be attached to the fact that between 1974 and 1977 some 2 million French people ceased to identify themselves as even nominal Catholics. It seems suspiciously coincidental that this period of record attrition should have also have been one in which the Left surged ahead as never before . . .

As Table 6.2 shows, the process of secularisation over the last two decades has been visible amongst all social groups in French society, but has touched some far more heavily than others. In particular, industrial and lower white-collar workers – the most secular groups twenty years ago – have continued to abandon religious practice more rapidly than others. This development has undoubtedly increased the salience of the class cleavage in French society by releasing to the Left large numbers of those hitherto influenced away from their 'natural' class party. In particular, of course, the PS was the great beneficiary of this trend. One has, indeed, only to glance at the figures for the most proletarian groups to understand the desperation with which the Catholic Left argued for urgent steps by the Church to preserve its position in the *monde ouvrier* – and also to see how inadequate (or pointless?) such steps have been. Indeed, while radical Catholics may be unrepresentative of (still) practising Catholics as a whole, it may be that their own leftward gravitation has merely seen them follow formerly *pratiquant* workers in that direction.

The religious cleavage has weakened in another way, too. As Table 6.2 shows, the decline in religious practice has been least steep precisely amongst those groups (peasants, the retired, the professions and business) which tended to be part of the conservative voting bloc anyway. Even there, doubtless the phenomenon of secularisation has not been without its political effect. Nevertheless, it is clear that the religious cleavage cross-cuts the class cleavage less and less. More and more it tends merely to reinforce a social alignment which might well have existed without it.

The gradual erosion of the religious cleavage does the Left some harm as well as much good. For just as it is no longer outlandish to be both Catholic and left wing, so it has also become somewhat more common to find agnostics, atheists and anti-clericals who are political conservatives. This becomes very clear if we examine electoral change amongst those 'without religion' in the 1966–73 period (when the Left was gaining overall). During that time the proportion of this group voting Communist fell

TABLE 6.2 Religious practice in France by class and sex, 1956, 1977

| | CATHOLICS | | | | OTHER RELIGIONS | | NO RELIGION | |
| | Active/Regularly Practising | | Inactive/Non- and Irregularly Practising | | | | | |
| | 1956 % | 1977 % | 1956 % | 1977 % | 1956 % | 1977 % | 1956 % | 1977 % |
|---|---|---|---|---|---|---|---|---|
| Men | 32 | 13 | 51 | 65 | 3 | 4 | 14 | 18 |
| Women | 47 | 21 | 42 | 62 | 3 | 4 | 8 | 13 |
| Farm workers | 38 ⎱ | ⎱ 31 | 50 ⎱ | ⎱ 59 | 2 ⎱ | ⎱ 4 | 9 ⎱ | ⎱ 6 |
| Farmers, Peasants | 58 ⎰ | | 34 ⎰ | | 4 ⎰ | | 4 ⎰ | |
| Industrial workers | 28 | 9 | 54 | 72 | 3 | 4 | 15 | 15 |
| Shopkeepers, artisans | 36 | 15 | 49 | 67 | 6 | 5 | 10 | 12 |
| White collar (lower) | 34 ⎱ | 9 ⎱ | 49 ⎱ | 70 ⎱ | 3 ⎱ | 3 ⎱ | 14 ⎱ | 18 |
| White collar (middle) | ⎰ | 14 ⎰ | ⎰ | 65 ⎰ | ⎰ | 3 ⎰ | ⎰ | 18 |
| Upper white collar, business, professions | 41 | 23 | 37 | 50 | 5 | 6 | 17 | 21 |
| Retired, non-employed | 43 | 24 | 44 | 59 | 3 | 5 | 9 | 12 |
| ALL | 40 | 17 | 46 | 63 | 3 | 4 | 10 | 16 |

*Note:* Comparable statistical bases were obtained by (a) collapsing the 1977 categories of 'Irregularly practising' and 'Non-practising' into a single 'Inactive' category to match Dogan's 1956 classification, and (b) averaging the male and female figures given for each group by Dogan, allowing feminine predominance to round figures up or down to avoid half percentage points.

*Source:* M. Dogan, 'Political Cleavage and Social Stratification in France and Italy', in S. M. Lipset and S. Rokkan (eds), *Party Systems and Voter Alignments: Cross-National Perspectives* (New York: 1967); and SOFRES, *L'Opinion Française in 1977* (Paris: 1978) Annexe I.

from 59 per cent to 44 per cent, while those voting Socialist rose from 23 per cent to 27 per cent – a net loss of 11 per cent for the Left combined.[33] Here too the net effect is an increase in class-based voting as middle-class anti-clericals gradually decide that their dislike of the priests is no longer a good argument against them joining the bulk of their class already voting for the Right. The smaller size of this group means, however, that the Left has still potentially far more to gain amongst recruits moving in the opposite direction. Anti-clericalism is becoming 'secularised', too – but it pales in significance along side the changes occurring within the Catholic fold.

Secularisation is unlikely to be a reversible phenomenon. The signs are clear of a decline in ecclesiastical institutions which can only lead to a further secularisation of social life as time goes on. The proportion of the population receiving Catholic baptism is on a falling curve (91.7 per cent in 1958, 82.7 per cent in 1968), as is that of those having Church weddings – more than a quarter of all marriages were not being religiously celebrated by 1971.[34] The number of priests in France fell by over 22 per cent between 1965 and 1975 (from 40,994 to 31,825);[35] the male religious orders lost 31 per cent of their membership in the same period (from 19,000 to 13,031), and even the always far more numerous nuns lost 16 per cent (from 105,900 to 89,000).[36] Moreover, all these groups are increasingly top-heavy in their age-structure, so that further massive losses must be anticipated. Thus in 1950 50 per cent of all French priests were aged 25–45; in 1970 25 per cent; for 1980 the forecast figure was 10 per cent.[37] Indeed, the number of priests is forecast to fall to only 10,000 in all of France by the end of the century.[38] This rapidly aging clergy creates other sorts of problems for the Church, too, for it tends to place greater pressure on the already severe generation gap between the younger and older clergy.

The aging clergy ministers to a steadily aging congregation. For, predictably, but ominously for the Church, regular religious practice is increasingly confined to the old. While the overall proportion of regular *pratiquants* was 17 per cent for France as a whole in 1977, for the over-65s the figure was 27 per cent, for the 50–65s 21 per cent, and for the 35–49s 19 per cent. For the 18–34s the proportion of such *pratiquants* (9 per cent) was less than half that who had no religion at all (21 per cent).[39]

Intrigued by this quiet social revolution, *Le Monde* sent a special correspondent to report on changes in the formerly heavily *pratiquant* villages of Brittany and Mayenne in the summer of 1977, providing a sad but fascinating chronicle of secularisation in the heartlands of French Catholicism.[40] At Penvenan (pop. 2,600), where the rate of religious practice has fallen from 40 per cent to 10 per cent since the last war, the curé inveighed against modern society, the materialism of the young, and, above all, the mischief of the Second Vatican Council. 'Too many things', he complained to Alain Woodrow (the correspondent) 'were altered too quickly.' He was bitter:

Modernisation hasn't paid off. For the first time, this year there hasn't been an ordination in the diocese. Mind you, it's logical. If no-one practises their religion any more, what do you want priests for? We country priests have the feeling that we are the last of the race.[41]

Proceeding to the village of Port-Blanc (pop. 400) Woodrow met the Abbé, M. Camper, who 'resembled Jean Gabin, with the same pithy language'. If there was a crisis in the Church, the Abbé declared, it was because

> there are too many imbeciles amongst the clergy, trying to traumatise people with their outpourings. There are no confessions any more but instead they get people to take communion whenever they like and however they like after so-called 'collective' absolutions – which are certainly forbidden by the Pope.[42]

The Abbé had no more time for the Left than for the younger clergy. When asked about the progress of the Left locally in the recent municipal elections 'his emotion was such that he mixed his metaphors a bit':

> The victory of the Left? Unthinkable – that would be to kill the cow that lays the golden eggs! The union of the Socialists and Communists is against nature. Christians would do better to re-read the enclyclical of Pius XI, which described communism as intrinsically wicked.[43]

Moving down to Mayenne in the West, Woodrow came upon a team of four young priests operating a mission, with two of their number working in full-time jobs. One, a labourer in a building factory, explained:

> At the beginning I simply wanted to share the people's life, but I very quickly realised that one had to take up the workers' struggle and I've been a trade union member for eighteen months now. I chose to work in a large commercial firm because a lot of uneducated country boys and girls are exploited there . . .[44]

Woodrow noted that more and more priests were taking full-time jobs, so that even the clergy was secularising itself as it shrank in numbers. One inevitable result was to throw an increasing share of priestly duties on to the laity, who tended to be left in charge of the church and even the organisation of the Mass, whether they liked it or not. Many of the still-practising, Woodrow noted, did not like it at all and viewed the identification of the younger priests with the Left with near-outrage. One is a long way from the world of Don Camillo.

An oddity of the changes through which the Church is passing as it declines – which emerges from polls as well as from the interviews above – is that even the still faithful have acquired an idiosyncratic political structure, far from the political monolithism they once displayed. The episcopate, at the summit, is still a fairly conservative group, though given to making declarations against nuclear weapons and taking up liberal good causes in a way which often leads to criticism from below that they are 'interfering in politics'. The older clergy in general, including the episcopate, but also those hierarchically below them, is, however, still a massively conservative group – particularly when compared to the younger clergy. In 1973, when polls showed 17 per cent of *pratiquants* favouring the Left, an IFOP poll of the clergy showed them giving the Left 22 per cent support (16 per cent PS, 5 per cent PSU, 1 per cent PCF). When this was broken down by age, however, one found that clergy under forty years of age were actually voting 51 per cent Left (34 per cent PS, 12 per cent PSU, 5 per cent PCF).[45] This was, indeed, a slightly more left-wing group than Catholic militants as a whole (44 per cent Left, according to IFOP)[46] – and, of course, it was staggeringly more radical than the mass of their active parishioners. The latter have least of all in common with the younger clergy who will constitute the main personnel of the Church in years to come and with the young Catholic militants who will tend to dominate the Catholic laity. The faithful have their reservations about their bishops, too, and are really in tune only with the older curés who feel they are 'the last of the race' . . .

The political division of society into clericals and anti-clericals, the cleavage which has been so fundamental to the last two centuries of French history, has thus at last begun to break down. This process has visibly gathered momentum in the last decade and clearly underlies the attrition of support for the Right in the same period. None the less, the period of greatest change may still lie ahead and it is important not to exaggerate the change which has already occurred. In 1978 it was still the case that 80 per cent of devout *pratiquants* voted for the Right, as did 66 per cent of occasional *pratiquants*. On the other hand 59 per cent of the non-practising voted for the Left, as did no less than 88 per cent of those professing no religious belief.[47] Almost half the Right's total vote in 1978 came from (regularly and irregularly) practising Catholics.

Of greater significance is the process of headlong secularisation through which French society is passing. Already, for example, this process has produced a working class of whom 77 per cent never practise their Catholicism, belong to other religious groups or profess no religious belief at all.[48] The institutional decay of the Church makes it seem extremely unlikely that this process can be halted – and, in any case, under these pressures the Church itself is being gradually transformed in a way which renders it less and less likely or willing to play its old role of bedrock of the Right. At present, indeed, it seems almost a race against time as to whether a left-wing clergy can take over the Church before their parishioners all vanish (in the eyes of many of the faithful these are not seen as separable evils). If the Church has become increasingly marginal to politics, so politics has become of less account to the Church: the question at stake is not so much its political future as its very survival.

The declining significance of the religious cleavage influenced the politics of the 1970s not so much by any simple mechanical process whereby Catholics hurried out of the confessional into the arms of PS and PCF organisers, but in a series of subtler changes of tone and emphasis. In particular, the recession of religious influences on political behaviour created more room for other, hitherto less powerful, lines of political cleavage to come into their own. One result was a proliferation of regionalist and separatist movements, often in formerly 'solid' Catholic areas;[49] another was the rise of the Ecologists; but most of all it led to an accentuation of the class cleavage and, accordingly, to a 'rediscovery' of the old facts of social inequality. It is to this latter concern – so crucial to the Left – that we now turn.

# 7 Class, Inequality and the Political Order

## i CLASS AND INEQUALITY

In 1965 the Left was able to mobilise only 55 per cent of the industrial working-class behind Mitterrand in his presidential run-off against De Gaulle. Nine years later no less than 73 per cent of workers supported Mitterrand on the second ballot against Giscard. The conservative working-class vote had fallen by two-fifths in less than a decade. This large and rapid shift towards more class-based political behaviour affected not merely election results but the whole tenor and content of political debate. With a quite surprising suddenness politics ceased to centre on the Algerian and constitutional crises and French *grandeur* and became, again, the old battle-ground between haves and have-nots.

No one who observed French elections in the 1970s needed statistical reminders to be aware of this change in atmosphere. Elections in France, as elsewhere, had, of course, long been chapters in a continuing 'democratic class struggle', with the politics of distribution much to the fore. But the 1973 and 1978 elections saw distributive politics reach a distinctly unusual pitch of intensity. On the Left the miseries of the poor and the satisfactions of soaking the rich were both evoked with a ferocious clarity which would have embarrassed left-wing politicians in most other European countries. One of Marchais's most popular and theatrical gambits in the 1978 election, for instance, was simply to read from the price-lists of Parisian jewellers what the bourgeoisie were able to pay for trinkets while workers stood in dole queues. Mitterrand's rhetoric was often not far behind.

On the Right there was a commensurate panic. In the last few months before the 1973 election it was impossible to buy or sell a house or apartment in Paris – the market was frozen rigid. In 1978 the situation was even more extreme. On both occasions there was a stampede into Gold Napoleons, diamonds and currencies even harder than the franc. In 1978, indeed, the franc fell heavily as the election approached and money flowed in panic across the Swiss and German borders – not merely the 'normal' hot money of the big speculators but the small-scale funds of private individuals, many of whom found pressing reasons for pre-electoral holidays in Switzerland, carrying their family assets (literally) with them in their car.[1] It was a social commonplace to find members of the middle-class talking with a steely bitterness of their determination to emigrate if the Left won.

There is a strong temptation to view the picturesque anxieties of the French bourgeoisie at the prospect of a Left victory as quaint and anachronistic; anarchically (and thus typically) Gallic. The middle classes of Britain, Germany, Austria, the Low Countries and Scandinavia, after all, have all long ago learnt to live with governments of the Left – indeed, to prosper under them. Sweden, the richest country of the Western world, advanced to that happy state under the rule of Social Democrats occasionally reliant on Communist and other far Left support. When Callaghan, the British Labour premier, announced in September 1978 that he would not risk his government in an early election, the London Stock Exchange soared. The SPD's Helmut Schmidt was held in similar regard by the Frankfurt *bourse*. But if social democracy had become the proto-typical form of government in advanced Western societies – capitalism with a human face, as it were – news of this development had not yet reached France.

The standard retort of the French bourgeoisie was, of course, that for them the Left in power meant the PCF in power. This objection it unyieldingly maintained against all contrary argument. The fact that the PCF could come to power only as a junior coalition partner in a position far weaker than it enjoyed in 1945–7; that *tripartisme* had, in any case, been clearly beneficial to French capitalism; or that the PCF had changed its spots and could no longer be seen as the advance column of the Red Army – none of this made the slightest difference. A government of the Left meant Marchais in the Cabinet and that was enough; indeed, that was far more than enough.

The uncompromising fear and hostility in which the bourgeoisie held the PCF did much to explain the hysteria aroused on the Right by the Left's advances of the mid-1970s. But the fact that this anti-communism was was so implacable, so unreasoning, so regardless of time and context, betrayed the fact that this class panic derived from more commonplace reasons as well. It was, quite simply, the necessary ideology of a bourgeoisie which had a great deal to lose, which has known success and enrichment on a scale granted to few other groups in history.

For, by the 1970s, France had become not merely a modern industrial state but the fourth largest capitalist economy on earth. In *per capita* income it lay third only to the USA and Germany among the major capitalist states, far ahead of Japan and twice as rich as Britain. Germany was richer – but then Germany had been Europe's leading economic power in 1914. For France such wealth was a newer, more original experience. The almost complete stagnation of the French economy through the twentieth-century up till 1945 made the French economic 'miracle' the most truly miraculous in Europe. Figure 7.1 handily summarises this experience and, although its semi-logarithmic scale tends to 'flatten' the curve of recent growth, it has the merit of showing the falsity of the customary view that rapid growth was attributable to Gaullist stability or the EEC. In fact growth has been rapid and continuous throughout the post-war period, being steepest of all under *tripartisme*. The French economy has never really looked back from 1945 on. Herman Kahn is only the most prominent voice to predict that from this base France will, before long, overtake even Germany.[2]

Such predictions were disseminated with some pride by the French government which entered very fully in the 1960s into the competitive gamesmanship of the 'growth league'. This spirit of joyful self-congratulation has remained the keynote of

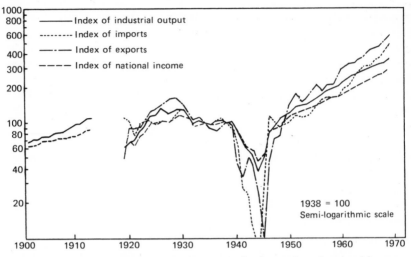

FIGURE 7.1. France 1900–70: industrial output, foreign trade and national income.

*Source*: C. Fohlen, 'France 1920–1970' in C. Cipolla (ed.), *The Fontana Economic History of Europe* (London: 1978) p. 109.

official appraisals of the economy. Study of how this wealth was actually being distributed amongst the French populace was, revealingly, not encouraged by (state-financed) academic and official research agencies. For such questions were potentially explosive; in an era of (Gaullian) national greatness to draw attention to the quite dramatically unequal distribution of the new affluence was a distinctly subversive act. Here, indeed, lay the seeds of fierce distributive battles, for the French bourgeoisie is the most privileged class in the Western world and, by the same token, the French working-class the relatively most deprived.

This, at least, was the unmistakable general conclusion of the studies on inequality in France which began to emerge in the 1970s. The initiation of such enquiries was in itself a powerful indication of the changing social climate produced by the increasing political polarisation of social classes. None the less, there was something of a political storm when the OECD in Paris (a body, it should be noted, outside direct French governmental control) published the first data on income distribution in mid-1976. The OECD study (whose main findings are summarised in Table 7.1) discovered that whatever indices it used 'France is consistently ranked as the country with the most unequal distribution'.[3]

Data of the type assembled in Table 7.1 need to be treated with some caution, given the differences in the methods and efficiency of the various national collections of data. The finding that the poorest 30 per cent in France were actually relatively poorer than their counterparts in Spain is, for example, almost certainly wrong – the Spanish data treated all peasants as self-employed and omitted them. None the less the overall conclusion to be drawn from Table 7.1 is that France was quite strikingly more

TABLE 7.1 Percentage distribution of total post-tax income in France, Spain. the USA, West Germany, the UK. Japan, Norway, Holland. and Sweden

| | Poorest 30% | | Richest 20% | | Richest 10% | |
|---|---|---|---|---|---|---|
| | Absolute | Standardised | Absolute | Standardised | Absolute | Standardised |
| France (1970) | 8.5 | 7.4 | 46.9 | 47.1 | 30.4 | 30.5 |
| Spain (1971) | 11.3 | 8.6 | 42.3 | 45.0 | 26.7 | 28.5 |
| USA (1972) | 9.0 | 9.5 | 42.9 | 42.1 | 26.6 | 26.1 |
| West Germany (1973) | 11.1 | 11.1 | 46.1 | 46.3 | 30.3 | 30.6 |
| UK (1973) | 11.8 | 11.4 | 38.7 | 39.3 | 23.5 | 23.9 |
| Japan (1969) | 14.0 | 12.8 | 41.0 | 41.9 | 27.2 | 27.8 |
| Norway (1970) | 11.9 | 12.3 | 37.3 | 36.9 | 22.2 | 21.9 |
| Holland (1967) | 11.7 | 15.9 | 42.9 | 36.3 | 27.7 | 21.8 |
| Sweden (1972) | 12.5 | 13.6 | 37.0 | 35.0 | 21.3 | 18.6 |

*Note*: Inter-country differences were occasionally explicable in terms of differing household sizes of various groups. Accordingly the data was recalculated on the basis of a 'standardised' household size – shown here in the 'standardised' column.

*Source*: M. Sawyer, 'Income Distribution in OECD countries', *OECD Economic Outlook* (Paris: July 1976) pp. 14–19.

unequal than all other comparable industrial nations surveyed. This despite the fact that these are post-tax figures which tend to mask the degree of inequality in countries particularly prone to tax-evasion, such as Spain and France. (All such data is complicated by the fact that the poor very frequently tell lies about their incomes, while the rich tell almost nothing but lies.) What is particularly notable is that the richest 10 per cent in France were better off than the richest 10 per cent in Spain (the omission of peasants makes no difference to comparisons at this end of the scale) – despite the fact that the privileges of the Spanish upper classes had been buttressed by more than a generation of totalitarian enforcement and control. On the other hand, this was not merely the inevitable difference between a corporatist and a more free market economy: inequality in France clearly exceeded that in either Germany or the USA, despite both countries being less inclined than she towards *étatiste* intervention in the economy. Inequality in France is not only not an accident of the free market but, fairly clearly, is actually increased by the operation of State policy.

This is not contradicted by the decreasing inequality of incomes since 1956 (Table 7.2) for almost the whole of the change is explicable by the movement of (poorly paid)

TABLE 7.2 Percentage pre-tax income distribution in France, 1956–70

|      | Poorest 30% | Richest 20% | Richest 10% |
| ---- | ----------- | ----------- | ----------- |
| 1956 | 3.0         | 55.0        | 36.2        |
| 1962 | 5.0         | 53.4        | 36.1        |
| 1965 | 7.0         | 50.5        | 34.0        |
| 1970 | 8.1         | 47.6        | 29.3        |

*Source*: Sawyer, op. cit., p. 26.

farmers, peasants and farm labourers into (relatively better paid) urban employment.[4] The period covered by Table 7.2 was in fact that of the most rapid contraction of the peasantry experienced in French history: between 1954 and 1968 the proportion of farmers in the active population declined from 21 per cent to 12 per cent, a drop of over two-fifths.[5] Even so, those who remained on the land still included most of the 'very poor' stratum of French society.[6] By 1970 most of this process of contraction had probably run its course, for by then more than two-thirds of the population had become urbanised.[7] The result was a once-and-for-all improvement in the equality ratio – a fact borne out by the 1975 income data, which showed no further movement towards equality from 1970 and, indeed, a sharp rise in the share of total income going to the richest 10 per cent.[8]

Table 7.2 reveals another oddity of the French income structure, for it will be noted that the income-ratio between the richest and poorest is essentially the same as that in Table 7.1, although the former refers to pre-tax and the latter to post-tax earnings respectively. This was, indeed, a further striking finding of the OECD study – that where the share in total income of the poorest 20 per cent of the population was concerned, tax effects made no difference at all: with or without tax this group received the same 4.3 per cent of total income. This staggering finding – unparalleled in any other European[9] country – was borne out when social transfer payments (i.e. income supplements, family allowances, dole payments, etc.) were examined. While in other OECD countries such payments constituted at least a mild form of countervailing redistribution towards the poor (in Britain, for example, the bottom 20 per cent received 42.4 per cent of such payments), the opposite was true in France, where the bottom 20 per cent received only 17.7 per cent of such payments – less, even, than their proportionate share.[10]

Other countries have shown that it is possible to erect social welfare systems which are little better than neutral in their overall redistributive effects, but France, starting from a position of uniquely steep inequality, has managed to erect a system which has the net effect of redistributing from the poor to the better-off – a truly startling achievement.

Studies of wealth distribution in France show a similar picture of extreme inequality. Data for 1975 show the top 10 per cent owning 50.2 per cent of all wealth, while the poorest 50 per cent owned 4.95 per cent.[11] By international standards of comparison it would seem that France, again, stands near the top of the inequality league.[12] There is, moreover, little doubt that wealth inequalities have actually increased in the period since the Liberation. This is true despite the spread of home-ownership coupled with house price inflation, which has exercised a strong countervailing pressure towards greater equality by giving substantial sections of the population a large capital asset of increasing value.[13] In effect, of course, the result of inflation is the drawing of a new inequality line between home-owners and non-owners, but the process does none-the-less produce a once-and-for-all diffusion of capital values amongst as many as half the population. Thus between 1949 and 1974 the proportion of total wealth owned by all households became more concentrated in houses (from 41 per cent to 53.7 per cent of total wealth) and less in land (from 21.2 per cent to 13.7 percent).[14]

The development of home-ownership has, in fact, played a similar role in trends in wealth inequality that the movement from the land played *vis-à-vis* the inequality of incomes – and over very much the same period. Thus Babeau found that while the distribution of wealth in France had become more unequal over the period 1949–75 as a whole (the Gini co-efficient moving from 0.516 to 0.552), the whole of the increase in inequality had occurred by 1962, since when a static situation has prevailed.[15] Babeau explains this pattern essentially by the fact that until 1962 the price of both houses and shares rose steeply, with only a wealthy minority owning either asset. The period since 1962 has seen the greatest expansion in home-ownership, while share prices have performed poorly on the whole. Again, the suggestion is of a once-and-for-all gain producing a temporary countervailing effect to hold steady a more fundamental and underlying trend to greater inequality.

These findings are essentially confirmed by Lattes, who found that the poorest 60 per cent of the population held 15 per cent of the total wealth – exactly the same proportion held by the richest 0.6 per cent.[16] A later report by the *Centre de Récherche*

*Economique sur l'Epargne* (CREP) suggested, however, that inequalities had been stable only since 1968, the Gini coefficient moving from 0.45 in 1949 to 0.52 in 1962 to 0.54 in 1968 – at which level it remained in 1975.[17] CREP suggests that while the main reason for the recent stabilisation of inequality has been the growth of home-ownership, a further factor has been the striking trend towards greater wealth equality between age groups as French families become more willing to transfer pre-inheritance assets to their progeny. This too, it should be seen, is a once-and-for-all effect, which inspires no confidence that a fundamental reversal of the trend towards greater inequality is likely. The CREP researchers, indeed, calculated the ratio of wealth held by the poorest tenth of the population in 1949 and 1975 relative to that held by the richest tenth, showing a ratio moving from 1:15.6 to 1:28.3. This led them to assert bluntly that 'inequality has doubled in twenty-five years'.[18] They took the view, moreover, that the period of the 1960s and early 1970s had been exceptional in that the overall economic growth witnessed in that period had allowed historically unusual once-and-for-all gains to be made, which were unlikely to be repeated. 'The period now opening', they concluded, 'appears hardly favourable to a reduction in the inequalities of wealth.'[19]

Not surprisingly these basic inequalities of income and wealth find their analogies throughout every aspect of the social structure. Perhaps the most fundamental example lies in the field of housing. No other condition of life in modern societies bestows greater cumulative social disadvantage than poor housing.[20] Inequalities in this field are, moreover, highly visible and thus relatively quick to trigger both political resentment and political action. If only for this reason the governments of the Fifth Republic were, from the start, committed to a major programme of construction and renewal to ameliorate the housing conditions of the poor which, it was generally agreed, constituted a major national scandal. It is difficult to argue that they have achieved any great degree of success. In 1968 only 52 per cent of all houses had inside lavatories and less than half (48 per cent) had an inside bath or shower.[21] Even on official definitions 44 per cent of all manual workers and 47 per cent of farmworkers were at that point still living in overcrowded conditions. The housing conditions of the rural poor remained notably bad – in 1970 only 8 per cent of all rural dwellings were equipped with all basic amenities.[22]

Official rhetoric has tended to concentrate on the fact that there has been at least some improvement in absolute standards of housing, particularly through the large-scale construction of low-cost apartments, the HLMs (*habitations à loyer modéré*). Such claims are open to the most serious questioning, and it seems likely in practice that inequalities in housing have actually increased. Over the period 1958–72 HLM construction (completed units) increased by an impressive 85 per cent – but in the same period free-market (i.e. expensive) house construction increased by 500 per cent. Moreover, HLM construction showed no sign of catching up with the rate of private apartment building – over the 1958–72 period the latter increased at twice the rate of the former.[23] In any case the simple assumption that the HLMs are the equivalent of, for example, British council housing – an attempt to solve working-class housing problems by low-rent public housing – does not hold. Such housing was a clearly desirable commodity and it should come as no surprise to anyone familiar with the ways of the social coalition which has ruled the Fifth Republic to date to find that the middle classes were allowed to appropriate a disproportionate share of it. Parodi's findings revealed that 'the main beneficiaries of low-rent accommodation schemes are the liberal professions and middle executives, while low-income households are relegated to the slums, furnished lodgings, or the grey zones'.[24] Five years later Parodi found that there were three times fewer low-income families living in HLMs than there were in the population as a whole.[25] Perhaps the most significant statistic of all, however, is that, while between 1962 and 1968 the number of persons per household decreased for the population as a whole (as available housing space expanded), the number of persons per manual working-class household actually increased, so that the proportion of this group living in overcrowded conditions (even on official definitions) rose to 44 per cent.[26]

The social (and political) effect of these protean inequalities of income, wealth and housing might be mitigated to some extent if it were the case that French society encouraged a high degree of social mobility through its educational system. In practice the opposite is true. A study undertaken in the early 1960s showed that while 58.5 per cent of the children of higher executives and liberal professionals went to university, the same was true for only 1 per cent of the children of industrial workers and only 0.7 per cent of those of farm workers.[27] It seems possible that these inequalities have lessened slightly in the subsequent period, but they remain extreme, particularly as one mounts the educational hierarchy towards the Grandes Ecoles, whose graduates entirely dominate all the leading institutions of both the public and the private sector. The political elite is equally narrowly recruited, with only the Communists – permanently excluded from power in the Fifth Republic – consistently sending any workers at all to parliament.[28]

The achievement of French society since the Liberation has, indeed, been to combine a series of prodigious social changes – rapid urbanisation, high economic growth and considerable occupational change – with a fundamental, and underlying social immobility. Thus a 1964 study found that 71 per cent of manual workers were themselves the sons of manual workers, with a follow-up study of 1970 putting the proportion at 64 per cent[29] – astonishingly high figures when one takes into account the large intake of former peasants into the urban working-class in those years. There was, moreover, even less mobility at the other end of the scale. A 1968 study of the French business elite found that no less than 85 per cent of all chief executives came from the 'upper social class' and less than 3 per cent from the 'lower' class.[30] Comparing this finding with patterns of recruitment to the analagous business elites of Britain, Italy, Holland, Belgium and West Germany, the authors of the study concluded that 'France appears to have the most rigid society of all the countries in our study'.[31]

It would be possible to extend this brief analysis of social and economic inequalities in French society both in depth and into fields beyond those of income, wealth, housing and education. It would be difficult, though, to modify very greatly the picture we have already assembled of a rigidly stratified society in which the inequalities between social classes exceed, in almost all respects, those found in virtually any other industrial nation. It is, indeed, some measure of the French situation to say that France is more typical of the semi-developed than the developed world. A search for comparably unequal societies will take one not into the neighbouring countries of northern Europe, but into some of the more brutal and authoritarian states of Latin America.

## ii THE POLITICAL ORDER

Such findings may make our reflections at the beginning of this chapter seem rather odd. The data we have assembled may seem suggestive of a society continuously racked by fierce and open distributive struggles. Little wonder that the social tensions of elections in the 1970s have been so great: self-evidently, the French bourgeoisie has a great deal to lose and the working-class as much to resent in the present situation. But, we have seen, the movement towards a more open politics of class – both at the level of electoral behaviour and of the issues at the heart of political debate – has been relatively recent. Clearly our question of 'Why class politics?' needs to be reformulated to 'Why class politics only now?'

Much of the answer to this question lies in the fundamental fact that France has urbanised slowly, so that the polity has until recent time contained a large rural, particularly peasant segment. In 1901, when 77 per cent of the British population was already living in towns,[32] only 40.9 per cent of the French population was doing so. A French urban majority did not appear until the time of the Liberation and even by 1968 more than one-third of the population was still living in the countryside and in towns of less than 10,000 inhabitants. Only by 1985 will France be as urbanised as Britain was at the turn of the twentieth-century.[33] This long-persistent rural and peasant bias has been the determinant force in French political and social life and, in a multiplicity of ways, has hindered the emergence of a clear-cut opposition between workers and bourgeoisie.

First, it has meant that industrial workers have never been – and will now never be – in the same majority position in France that they have, for example, occupied in Britain (see Table 7.3).[34] Moreover, this has not meant merely that politics could not

TABLE 7.3 The employed population of France by sector, 1936–68 (%)

|                      | *1936* | *1954* | *1962* | *1968* |
|----------------------|--------|--------|--------|--------|
| Mining, Agriculture  | 37     | 28     | 21     | 16     |
| Manufacturing        | 30     | 36     | 38     | 39     |
| Services             | 33     | 36     | 41     | 45     |
|                      | 100    | 100    | 100    | 100    |

*Source*: Marceau, *Class and Status in France: Economic Change and Social Immobility 1945–1975* (Oxford: 1977) p. 23.

be reduced easily to the simple two-class model long typical of Britain.[35] From its inauguration in 1870 French mass democracy was accommodated not to a homogenised, national and urban setting but to a host of particularist local arenas. Indeed, the typical features of 'peasant politics' – the prominence of the local notable and of local issues, the weakness of national parties and the disaggregated nature of political life in general – were found not merely in rural and small-town France but, to a remarkable degree, were transposed even on to the urban and national levels of the polity. Even in the most industrial constituencies deputies were often 'notables' with considerable personal followings which enabled them, particularly if they acquired a strong municipal base, to ignore wider party loyalties.[36] The parliaments of the Third and Fourth Republics reflected the same realities, providing not for strong and cohesive party rule, but for weak, coalition governments constantly harried by a host of quasi-ambassadorial deputies and a virtual free market of particularist pressure groups. Such conditions were hardly favourable to the rise of strong, disciplined, class-based parties on the British model, or, indeed, to the decisive exertion of executive power which policies of meaningful redistribution would require. Finally, as we have seen, the strong and continuing rural 'presence' in the French polity helped maintain the religious cleavage as the main source of electoral alignment. This, by definition, tended to pre-empt and suppress a politics based on class.

The result of this configuration of forces was that although France has long possessed a large and often militant working-class, this group has been unable to impose its terms of debate or to make its interests the critical dividing line around which political actors and parties had to range themselves. The working-class movement was, in any case, as much prey to the traits of particularism and disaggregation as any other segment of French society. It was weakly organised and divided on both the political and the trade union fronts. It was ideologically torn not merely between reformism and revolution, but between quietist Christianity and syndicalist utopianism, both the heritage of its own peasant and small town artisanal roots. The most it could manage was brief explosive outbursts, as in 1919–20 and 1936, but it was quite incapable of a sustained breakthrough against the whole series of institutional obstacles and sociological handicaps which it confronted. Inevitably, large sections of the working-class retreated, frustrated and alienated, into a cultural and psychological ghetto. There was, in a real sense, nowhere else to go.

By the same token, and if only by default, the French bourgeoisie was able to preserve an almost nineteenth-century level of privilege and inequality. Despite this, it was never able to enjoy the same serene confidence and psychological security of its British analogue. It was understandably nervous about the fact that since the Liberation one Frenchman in every four or five has voted for a party (the PCF) which would like to expropriate it utterly. It had, moreover, to endure revolutions and wars, defeats and Occupation, Resistance, rebellion and military coups. But in the whole of this century it has had to endure only two truly left-wing governments, in 1936–7 and 1945–7. Even these both depended on Centrist support and, in any case, neither lasted long. Accordingly, the French bourgeoisie never had to make its peace with social democracy in the way that its counterparts in non-Latin Europe did. Indeed, the

French middle classes escaped not only the harsh possibility of income and wealth redistributions away from them, but pretty much the whole ethos of modern welfare state egalitarianism; not merely from governments which might have introduced them to the horror of genuinely progressive taxation, but even from governments truly committed to stopping gross evasions of the existing tax system. Thus the anomaly of a bourgeoisie at once hyper-privileged *and* insecure: for, while the dramatic twists and turns of modern French history prevented the bourgeoisie from feeling that its position was other than precarious, its luck held through it all.

For a while it seemed that the Fourth Republic might threaten this 'unreconstructed' character of French society. There was now a mass Communist Party, the largest party in the country. Voting was more on class lines than ever before, with two-thirds of the working-class supporting the Left.[37] All three of the Fourth Republic's general elections were won by the Left – the Radicals, PCF and SFIO together won 58.7 per cent of the vote in 1946, 51.5 per cent in 1951, and 53.5 per cent in 1956. Redistributive demands were posed as never before and, while *tripartisme* lasted, it seemed that an era of Reconstruction might be about to begin.

It was not to be. After 1947 the Left was too split for a left-wing government to be a practical possibility. The Left's theoretical electoral majorities produced Assemblies which slid ineluctably to the Right. Even when the Socialists led the government their energies were invariably directed away from the home front towards the Cold War and the crises of decolonisation. And, in any case, the Fourth Republican system militated against strong government of *any* kind. Even the most imposing electoral majorities soon dissolved in a morass of party and personal rivalries and in the brutal free market of pressure-group politics. Governments after 1947 were sometimes conservative, sometimes Centrist – but always weak. The practical result, in either case, was *laissez-faire*.

De Gaulle's return to power and the installation of the Fifth Republic in 1958 decisively broke this *immobilisme* – to the advantage of the 'haves' rather than the 'have-nots'. A strong, authoritative and conservative regime was now in place. It could win election after election with almost effortless ease. It was officered by bankers and businessmen and the friends of bankers and businessmen. Capitalists could invest with a long time-horizon, confident that their efforts would receive the State's sympathetic support and that political stability was now indefinitely guaranteed. Given the French economy's running start and its favourable conjuncture with the international (and particularly the European) economy, it was always likely that the 1960s would see a rapid and sustained period of growth. But in addition De Gaulle was able to bestow upon French capitalism relief from the drain on resources exercised by the Algerian war, a sense of renewed national confidence, and the security of a conservative political future. For French capitalists the result was euphoria. Whatever his intent De Gaulle was in practice a modern Guizot and the doctrine of enrichissez-vous, with its predictable consequences for social and economic inequality, was avidly and successfully pursued.

What was good for the capitalists was good for the workers, too. The 1960s saw the nation recover from the dramas of the Algerian war amidst a balmy and quite general prosperity. There was a continuous improvement in the absolute standard of living of *all* sectors of the population. Not surprisingly, this exercised a soporific effect on the tenor of distributive demands. What was immediately obvious was that there were no more plastic bombs going off in the Paris Metro, that there was no further prospect of military insurrection, and that everyone was materially better off with every passing year. It seemed almost too good to be true. The fact that the fruits of economic growth were very unequally distributed was less visible – indeed opinion surveys showed that the least well-off tended grossly to underestimate the high incomes earned by the upper groups. The incomes of business chief executives were generally underestimated by 50 per cent and the actual range of incomes was also twice as great as was commonly supposed.[38]

The regime largely succeeded in identifying itself not just with economic progress but with the spirit of a new age. A dynamic 'new France' was ushered into being, born of technological progress and sweeping social changes which would have alarmed all but the most confident conservatives. A buoyant industry pulled further waves of rural migrants into the great conurbations, giving a sustained and final push to the long process whereby France ceased to be a peasant nation. White-collar employment expanded rapidly – bringing *promotion sociale* for some urban workers, if not the majority. A whole category of unpleasant jobs were conferred on the burgeoning population of foreign migrant workers, thus allowing the native-born working class to move further 'up' the labour market. Such changes engendered not merely a general sense of well-being, but a diffuse aura of social progress and expanding opportunity. In such a climate it was hardly surprising that class politics, once submerged, stayed submerged.

De Gaulle's impact on class politics went deeper than this, however. In the first years of the Fifth Republic the new regime launched a frontal assault on the 'old politics' – which, very largely, meant class politics. The parties – all parties – were castigated as selfish, sectional, and anti-national. De Gaulle lost no opportunity to advertise his contempt for all those who pretended to the role of intermediaries between the French nation and its providential president (i.e. himself). This assault was at its height in the 1958–62 period, when the parties were repeatedly crushed in De Gaulle's sweeping referendum victories, each of them a triumphant exercise in the new 'direct democracy'. The aim – the wholesale 'de-politicisation' of public life – was little less than fantastical. None the less, the assault achieved considerable success. The opposition parties were trounced over and over again. They were excluded from any positive role of influence and, in a very real sense, had nothing to do. They all lost members and voters. Party leaders and militants were disorientated and demoralised. Almost as much as their voters they were numbed and anaesthetised by fear of civil war on the one hand and De Gaulle's stunning success on the other.

Class politics were simply rolled back. Under the new regime political debate was very purposefully towed away from the old 'who gets what' issues to loftier concerns about the nature of the new constitutional order, Algeria, foreign policy, national prestige and the magnetism of De Gaulle's own personality. The General's preoccupations descended into the social and economic realm only as far as still fairly ethereal notions of *participation* with which, significantly, he got nowhere at all. This last exception apart, he was allowed, to a remarkable degree, to make his preoccupations those of the nation. And there was no room for the vulgar calculations of distributive politics on the Olympian slopes inhabited by the General. The most striking index of his success was the clear political demobilisation of the working-class. If the workers had supported the Left in 1956 by a 2:1 margin, by 1965 they were dividing their votes almost equally (55 per cent: 45 per cent) between Mitterrand and De Gaulle. The class alignment was withering away. The unintended and unexpected effect, as we have seen, was to throw into sharper, if temporary, relief the even older configurations of political behaviour rooted in religious difference.

For the whole of the first decade of the new Republic the politics of class and redistribution were firmly relegated from the centre of the stage. The new mood, it could hardly be doubted, was a profound reality. But it was also fragile. It was, in a sense, a vast political conjuring trick, a collective suspension of disbelief in the (old, unequal) facts of political life. A happily credulous audience (the electorate) was invited by the conjuror (De Gaulle) to believe that if they trusted to his enduring magic the good times could last for ever. He, in return, would be licensed to perform various extraordinary antics on the international stage and, at home, to maintain an icy *hauteur* towards the whole normal range of parties, trade unions and pressure groups. While the conjuror could give his audience what they liked, who needed or wanted these raddled old actors on the set anyway?

It could not, of course, last. In particular the de-mobilisation of the working-class was unlikely to continue for long, given the sheer facts of inequality and the long-rooted strength of the left, especially the PCF, in the labour movement. Even the 1965 figure of 45 per cent of working-class electors voting for De Gaulle represented some slippage back to the Left from the General's heyday of 1958–62. For, as the 1960s wore on, De Gaulle was increasingly perceived simply for what he was – an aging, erratic, and entirely mortal conservative politician. The very achievement of Gaullist stability left less and less room for the role or the image of the providential superman. Instead, political debate dwelt increasingly on the subject of '*l'après-Gaullisme*'. And, as politicans and voters alike readied themselves for the day when the conjuror would have left the stage, the suspension of belief demanded by his act became a steadily harder exercise.

More importantly, it began to seem less certain that the good times could go on for ever. In 1967 there was a definite (though, by later standards, shallow) recession, largely as a deliberate result of the government's 'stabilisation' plan. Unemployment, particularly amongst the young, rose sharply. At the same time workers had to swallow a steep rise in their social security contributions – essentially to pay for the inclusion of the peasantry in the social security scheme. At the same time the government held down public sector wages with an iron hand.[39] The effects were not particularly severe – economic growth continued at a slower rate – but both Left parties sharply increased their vote in the 1967 elections. A clear ripple of unease continued through the labour movement, for what the downturn had emphasised most of all was just how thoroughly excluded it was from any real influence over its own fate. There had not been even a show of consultation with the unions over the new measures. The government had deliberately increased unemployment as a matter of conscious policy. It had held down wages by fiat – not by law. The extra social security contributions had been levied on the workers by simple administrative decree, without even any discussion in parliament.[40] The regime had been able to get away with this sort of arrogance routinely enough while high growth and full employment were assured. It was so far out of touch with feelings on the factory floor that it failed entirely to realise that to behave in the same way during a deliberately induced recession was to play with fire.

## iii THE RE-EMERGENCE OF CLASS POLITICS

A year later these subterranean resentments and frustrations erupted into the great strike wave of May–June 1968. The mood of 'de-politicisation' had lasted just ten years but now came to an end not with a whimper, but with a very large bang. Stimulated, in a sense goaded, by the students' example, the industrial working-class – and its white-collar brothers – emerged sharply from their long decade of somnolence.

They were quickly followed by the representatives of all the other groups which had felt excluded from the system (those who had been well within it – businessmen and the administrative elite – kept their heads well down). If Gaullist intransigence was at last to be overthrown then Pandora's Box would be open – and nobody wished to be left out. Everyone had their secret or not so secret wishes all ready for magical fulfilment. The result was an extraordinary domino effect. First the students, then one section of the working-class after another, then the farmers, then even the bourgeoisie (demanding Pandora's Box be kept safely shut), and finally just about everyone staked out their position and their grievances in a great cacophony of demands and assertion. The very general awakening – or reawakening – of class and group consciousness thus occasioned was not the least significant aspect of the Events.

The workers remained the heart of the matter though, for it was their action alone which could threaten the government badly enough for it to make concessions to anyone. The student riots were a sensation, a 'happening', but the true phenomenon was the strike wave – the greatest in recent European or even world history. As we have seen[41] it stirred high hopes on the far Left which saw in the Events and the great Italian strike wave of 1969 – the so-called 'hot autumn' – the dawning of a new era of revolutionary militancy for the European working-class.

In fact the opposite was true. The sequel to these mighty explosions was, in both cases, a prolonged period of industrial calm accompanied by the sharp progression of the *reformist* political wing of the labour movement. The inheritors and beneficiaries of the great strike waves of 1968–9 were not the far Left groups in either Italy or France, but the PS on the one hand and an Italian Communist Party dedicated to the 'historic compromise' (i.e. coalition with the Right) on the other.

Ironically, the linking of the French and Italian cases made with such hope by the revolutionary Left provides the best perspective from which to see why these hopes were so exactly confounded. The French and, *a fortiori*, the Italian working-class, it must never be forgotten, are a whole century closer to their peasant, craft and rural small town roots than, for example, British workers are (a handy bench-mark, since the latter, by dint of Britain's earlier industrialisation, constitute the oldest proletariat in the world). They are, by the same token, several generations nearer to the anarchist and syndicalist forms of response to the industrial setting which spring most readily from such roots.[42] Both the French and Italian proletariats have continued to exhibit the patterns of behaviour typical of this anarcho-syndicalist tradition – long periods of docile submission punctuated by violent outbursts and demonstrations; self-encapsulation within an *ouvrieriste* myth of resentful pride and self-assertion; the protest strike and the occupation strike; the at least nominal attachment to non-political unionism; and, most important of all, a fissiparous trade union movement whose very structure attests a preference for principled purism over the real unity and real compromise necessary for greater industrial strength.

The anarcho-syndicalist tradition has more in common with Luddism than it has with the modern practice of the British or, indeed, any northern European working-class. Its mark is, none the less, still strong on both the French and Italian labour movements, partly still at a formal level but far more profoundly in the characteristic behavioural traits of the movements themselves. The anomalous survival of this pre-industrial or, at most, early industrial tradition in the age of the French and Italian 'economic miracles' is due to many factors. The lateness and rapidity of industrialisation in these countries has meant that it is a tradition rooted in a still recent past. Then, too, the continuing weakness of the trade unions (due, in part, to their own division) has meant that they have been little able to win results by mere withdrawal of labour and, *faute de mieux*, have been forced back on to the older tradition of violent protest born of industrial impotence. This weakness and these tactics have in turn undermined the possibilities of the workers' fuller integration into civil society via a renegotiated social contract. Instead the labour movement has faced strong and unyielding bourgeois opponents who have felt no necessity to reach any sort of compromise with it. This, too, has helped prevent the progression of the labour movement very far from its syndicalist roots.

Most of all, though, syndicalism – the archetypal response of a first generation working-class to industrial conditions – survived because it remained contemporary. Throughout the century the labour movements of France and Italy have been continuously replenished (and weakened) by the fresh arrival of great waves of rural migrants into the industrial labour force – each having to undergo, *ab initio*, the harsh and primal experience of adaptation to industrial life.

The profound effect of both the Italian and French 'economic miracles' was that, at long last, the rural reservoirs of surplus labour began to run dry. This was particularly clear in the French case where, from the late 1950s on,[43] the indigenous labour force had to be supplemented by an accelerating flow of migrant foreign workers – producing a new sub-proletariat which the French countryside could no longer provide. While there had been only 1.5 million immigrants in France in 1945 and much the same number still in 1956, by 1970 the number had risen to 3.4 million [44] and, by the late 1970s, to an estimated 4.5 million.[45] As this vast influx proceeded French workers moved steadily up the labour market into more secure, skilled and better-paid jobs.

The long period of prosperous 'de-politicisation' tended to dull from sight this gradual transformation of the indigenous working-class. Social commentary tended to fasten, in a predictable but somewhat banal fashion, on the unmistakable affluence of this 'new working class', visible in its motor cars, its homes, and its changing leisure habits. But the change went deeper than that. With each passing year the labour movement's centre of gravity moved further away from the first-generation migrants from the native countryside, from those grateful to have a factory job at all, and further towards those who accepted even the new affluence as routine, who were beginning to acquire notions of consumer sovereignty along with their consumer goods, and who were beginning to chafe against the constraints of the traditional proletarian ghetto.

Viewed from this perspective both the great French strike wave of 1968 and the Italian 'hot autumn' of 1969 were more of an end than a beginning. Both signified the belated but explosive 'coming of age' of a mature working-class. To be sure, the explosion, when it came, expressed itself in the old, classic, syndicalist form, the 'revolutionary' occupation strike. (It is difficult to see how it could have been otherwise – syndicalism was still the main vocabulary of action available to the workers.) But the parallels which were widely drawn between the 1968 strike wave and the occupation strikes of 1936 (or between the 'hot autumn' and the Turin factory occupations of 1919–20) were misleading, and not merely because the working-class of the late 1960s was a far stronger, more experienced and more thoroughly urban group than its predecessors. The occupation wave of 1936 had a far better (if perhaps still insufficient) claim to having been a revolutionary movement. It had been contemporaneous with large PCF gains among the working-class and, for all its spirit of confused euphoria, had represented a genuine feeling that, with the victory of the Popular Front, the proletariat was taking power at last. The 1968 strikes, on the other hand, took place not long after an election which had returned the Right comfortably to power and in which the balance within the Left had moved sharply rightwards – towards the Socialists, not the Communists. The strikes were the expression of extremely strong but diffuse working-class discontent only *within* that context – the perspective of a workers' takeover of power was never really raised in 1968.[46]

In retrospect, at least, it seems clear that 1968 marked not a stage on the route-march to revolution, but precisely the opposite; not a step towards the workers' overthrow of bourgeois society but towards a new phase of assertion aimed at gaining their fuller integration *within* it. The failure of the revolutionary Left to maintain their leadership of the strikes after the first few days; the diffuseness and confusion of the workers' demands once the strikes had begun; the failure to elaborate any overall political or social objectives at a strategic level beyond the factory floor; the ease with which the strike action was translated into mere bargaining over pay and conditions;

and the contextual fact that the previous three years had seen a strong working -class swing towards Mitterrand and the Federation of the Left (rather than towards the PCF) – all suggest such a conclusion.

The claims made for the 'revolutionary' nature of the Events rest, by contrast, on the single slender fact that for a few days – a fortnight at most – the workers were willing to be influenced by the *gauchiste* militants and by the students' example. The fact was, however, that these were the only independent voices speaking to the workers at all. And they were emulated or listened to only in so far as they were of assistance in helping the workers disregard the labour movement's established revolutionary leadership, the PCF and CGT. This was achieved immediately the strike wave was launched – thereafter the *gauchistes* lost their position and control quite utterly. Like all other groups on the Left they attempted to expropriate the significance of the strikes to bolster their own claims, but neither they, nor the PCF, nor the Socialists were doing more than attempting to ride on the back of the tiger.

In the end the workers' assertion was quite their own. Immediately, its meaning was lost from view as the various factions of the Left closed in a furious political dog-fight over the (again quickly supine) body of the labour movement. But its significance could not be prevented from emerging, from 'filling out', as it were, in the following decade. The workers were fully conscious of the benefits capitalism had brought them and of such benefits they only wanted more. They were, moreover, increasingly dissatisfied with the ghetto posture of intransigent – but routinised and quite futile – protest against a system they could not, in any case, overthrow. Their discontent with the system was that they were treated within it as social outcasts, almost as disadvantaged children. Neither they nor their representatives, they were well aware, were really listened to or respected. An arrogant government and bourgeoisie made little attempt to hide their view of the workers as a mere factor or production, as so many dehumanised robots. The new affluence of the 1960s made acceptance of such a definition of themselves harder and harder to accept. Now they wanted nothing less than full citizenship.

Accordingly, they demanded *autogestion* – greater participation in and control over their world of work; and greater access to real influence beyond that. Above all, they demanded simply to be heard and to be taken into real account. What made the Events so general a phenomenon was that these demands could easily serve as a model for a wide variety of other groups. What gave them their distinctive note of utopian humanism was that these demands amounted to nothing less than the full recognition of even the lowliest worker as a moral entity. What made them so explosive – not just for the government, but even for the established institutions of the Left – was that such demands implied the end, or at least the self-effacement, of the authoritarian hierarchies the Fifth Republic had nurtured in every field of economic and social life. But what made the Events in the end so relatively harmless was that the unions and the Left, as well as the government, boggled at the prospect of trying to give institutional expression to so diffuse and general a demand. Hence the conspiracy on all sides to divert the Events into a routine struggle over money wages. The workers wavered, and then accepted this redefinition of their struggle – for the time being.

The prodigal upheaval of May–June 1968 had, however, shattered 'de-politicisation' beyond repair. A mature proletariat had, in the most direct way possible, posed its demands at the centre of the stage. In the short term these demands could be bought off with large wage increases, but the speedy erosion of these gains by inflation and the overall change of mood meant that the pressures now unleashed would not go away. The genie was out of the bottle and the era of Gaullist tranquillity was over. De Gaulle's departure in 1969 symbolised the change rather than causing it. This time, when De Gaulle attempted to lift politics back on to a loftier, constitutional plane, he failed – and left.

De Gaulle's departure was, as we have seen, followed by a major landslide of working-class voters towards the Left. While only 55 per cent of this class had voted for the Left in 1965, by 1974 the proportion had not merely recaptured its old 1956 height (of 66 per cent) but gone well beyond it, to 73 per cent. In the 1977 municipal elections – the apogee of the Left – the figure edged higher still. Inevitably, so profound a change held a significance not merely for electoral behaviour, but affected the whole mood and atmosphere of political life. The raising of the issue of fuller citizenship and integration of the working-class into society naturally focused greater attention on (hitherto neglected) questions of social and economic inequality. Prior to the 1970s France had lacked its Tawney. Thereafter there was a veritable rash of path-breaking studies of income and wealth distribution. Class issues gained a new centrality in polical debate and, as we have noted, were broached in an unwontedly frontal manner even by the Socialists, let alone the Communists.

This was the true heritage of 1968. Within four years the Left had effectively reorganised to give orthodox political form to the great spontaneous assertion of 1968. For the first time ever the Left parties were united behind a concrete programme centring on a swingeing redistribution of wealth, income and opportunity within French society. And, within a few years, around three-quarters of the working-class had coalesced in a single great bloc behind the united Left to give weight and strength to those demands. Class politics had returned with a vengeance – so much so that by the mid-1970s the class alignment was more pronounced in France than anywhere else in Europe.[47]

The Right seems to have sensed this shift in the political and social climate even before the Left. Despite its crushing electoral victories of 1968 and 1969 and despite the easy resumption of order, prosperity and 'business as usual' under Pompidou, the Majority seemed racked by a strange malaise as the 1970s began, by a sense that after 1968 nothing could ever be quite the same again, that its own dominance had become somehow unreal. Pompidou felt this unease as keenly as anyone. His hurried attempt (via the 1972 EEC Referendum) to kill off the Common Programme at birth, his equally hasty dismissal of Chaban as premier, and his extraordinary antics in advance of the 1973 elections (furiously warning that he would refuse to appoint a government of the Left whatever the election result – and then threatening that a vote for the Left would produce a constitutional crisis – i.e. of his own contrivance) – all betrayed a degree of nervous insecurity otherwise incomprehensible in a man who had so recently won both parliamentary and presidential elections by record majorities.

Such tactics turned out to be unnecessary. The March 1973 elections, held at the very peak of a headlong world boom, saw the Majority win again with its happy boast of permanent stability and growth. Even so, the Left made considerable inroads, wiping out the whole of the Right's 1968 gains. Then at the end of the year, the boom collapsed and France, together with the Western world as a whole, entered a new economic dark age.

With the onset of recession the political order was stripped of the last great prop which had protected it from fierce distributive struggle. It took the near dead-heat of the 1974 presidential election a few months later to reveal to the Right just how dangerously exposed it now was. The great conservative bulwark of the 'backward' countryside had fallen victim to demographic change – though, of course, the government refused to alter constituency boundaries to recognise the fact. The conservative Catholic vote was shrinking and anyway less reliable. In politics the old ways had largely disappeared. The arena left to the old independent notable was now much restricted by the 'nationalisation' of political forces. The age of the charismatic conservative leader was over at local as well as at national level. De Gaulle was gone. Even Pompidou was gone. And now prosperity had departed, too.

It was not a matter of returning – as the Majority had always warned – to the bad old days of the Fourth Republic. For conservatives, at least, the situation threatened worse than that. In the Fourth Republic conservative interests had, in the last analysis, always been protected by the Left's disunity and the *immobilisme* of the political system. The supreme irony of De Gaulle's inheritance was that he had deprived the Right of this protection. He had, by the institution of direct presidential elections, created a bipolar political system. He had forced the Left into such a corner that it had emerged, perforce, united. And he had created a strong, even authoritarian, system of executive government. All this had been accepted happily enough by conservatives while it had seemed they must always win – but their unease grew apace with the realisation that, with the Left now united, there was now a real alternative to the coalition of 'haves' which had ruled France since 1958. Should this alternative come to power there would be no *immobilisme* to stop it: De Gaulle's system would provide the perfect instrument for a strong left-wing government . . .

Hence the middle-class election panics with which this chapter began. From 1968 on every election has been, in effect, a major battle in the heightening war of distributive politics. Ever since the bourgeoisie flooded out into their great motorised demonstration in the Champs-Elysées on 30 May 1968 – for 1968 saw a class-awakening of the bourgeoisie as well as of the proletariat – France has been ruled by those with much to lose and a lively fear that they might well lose it. Every election was henceforth a crisis, necessitating frantic measures to prepare a bolt-hold. This panic frequently found 'constitutional' expression in warnings that the political system could not survive with an Assembly of the Left and a president of the Right, or vice versa. The fact that the system had been designed by the Right in its own interests; that at its inception there had been no expectation of such a correspondence between Assembly and president; that the American system quite routinely survives with presidents of one party and opposition majorities in Congress – all such considerations were the merest chaff in the wind. It was taken for granted on the Right (and usually assumed on the Left) that there was effectively no possibility of compromise. In effect such warnings boiled down to the statement that, despite a twenty-year run of conservative governments since 1958, nothing less than the indefinite continuation of such governments for ever was tolerable.

It was predictable enough that the re-emergence of class politics and the rise of the Left should have induced alarm in the bosoms of the bourgeoisie. What was far less predictable was that it should have brought almost equal discomfort to the PCF. The Communists, after all, had always predicted the heightening of class politics and the consolidation of the working-class behind the Left as a sheer historical necessity. As the most unambiguously class-based party the PCF had not unreasonably anticipated that such a process would redound heavily to its own advantage. What they had not counted on was the nature of the new class consciousness, with the working-class increasingly bent on its egalitarian integration into bourgeois society. To their amazement they now found that the political profit of the new class politics was going exclusively to the Socialists, not to them. This development undermined the old equilibrium of the·Left and, with it, all their hopes and strategies. If the sociology of the Right was changing, so, too, was that of the Left. It is to a consideration of these changes that we now turn.

# 8 Communist Tribunes and Socialists Born Again

Analysis of modern French conservatism pivots inevitably around the long dominant, if now declining, force of Gaullism. Analysis of the Left's development must, similarly, proceed from an examination of the PCF, for so long the major party of the Left and arguably the key party in the political system as a whole. Since 1945 the PCF has frequently been the largest party in France in electoral terms – and in terms of organisation and membership it has always been the largest party. Its sheer strength gave a lopsided effect to the system, for it drove the Centre into the arms of a grateful Right and, by simultaneously splitting the Left, helped keep it out of power. Doubtless the historic failure of the social democratic consensus to gain the same foothold in France that it achieved elsewhere in northern Europe contributed to the Communists' relative success. But it is equally undeniable that the PCF's strength has constituted a quite insuperable obstacle to the progress of any form of social democracy in France.

## i THE COMMUNIST ZENITH

Modern French Communism, quite as much as its Gaullist twin, is a child of the Resistance. As Table 8.1 reminds us, there was nothing innate or preordained about its later strength. After its inception in 1920 the PCF languished around a 10 per cent level of support for more than a decade, far behind the SFIO. Its strength was, moreover, confined to three isolated areas: the Paris-Nord belt, the Centre, and Marseilles. Elsewhere it hardly existed and by the early 1930s seemed, in any case, to be in a state of terminal decline, with Party membership dropping year by year from its 1921 highpoint of 118,000 to 29,000 by 1931.[1] This trend was reversed, at first slowly, and then dramatically, by the success of the Party's Popular Front campaign. Its vote leapt to 15.2 per cent in 1936 (while remaining as geographically concentrated as ever) and Party membership, which had inched up to 42,000 in 1933, doubled to 82,000 in 1935, trebled again to 285,000 in 1936 and 329,00 in 1937.[2] Both the PCF and many of its non-Party analysts have erroneously accepted the picture of an apparently smooth upward curve in Communist strength between 1936 and 1945, neglecting to notice that the gains of 1935–7 were extremely shortlived. The combination of the Nazi-Soviet Pact in 1939 and the Party's ambivalent attitude to the War in 1939–41 had a catastrophic effect, with the raw recruits of 1935–7

TABLE 8.1 Communist and Socialist voting strengths compared, 1924–78

| | Communist vote (%) | Socialist* vote (%) | Communist vote as proportion of Socialist vote (%) |
|---|---|---|---|
| 1924 | 9.8 | 20.2 | 49 |
| 1928 | 11.3 | 18.0 | 63 |
| 1932 | 8.3 | 20.5 | 40 |
| 1936 | 15.2 | 20.8 | 73 |
| 1945 | 26.2 | 23.4 | 112 |
| 1946 (June) | 26.0 | 21.1 | 123 |
| 1946 (November) | 28.3 | 17.9 | 158 |
| 1951 | 26.9 | 14.6 | 184 |
| 1956 | 25.9 | 15.2 | 170 |
| 1958 | 19.2 | 15.7 | 122 |
| 1962 | 21.8 | 12.5 | 174 |
| 1967 | 22.5 | 18.9 | 119 |
| 1968 | 20.0 | 16.5 | 121 |
| 1973 | 21.4 | 20.8 | 103 |
| 1978 | 20.6 | 24.9 | 83 |

* I.e. the SFIO from 1924 to 1962; the FGDS in 1967 and 1968; the *Union de la Gauche Socialiste et Démocratique* (UGSD) in 1973, and the PS plus MRG in 1978. The MRG won 2.1 per cent in 1978 but there is little indication that it enjoyed support independent of the PS. Thus all figures for Socialist support 1967–78 reflect the incorporation of the Left Radicals into the Socialist camp. Other Left fractions – the Neo-Socialists of 1936, the PSU, Trotskyites, *Divers gauche*, etc. – are omitted throughout.

*Source*: 1924–32: J. Meyriat, 'France' in S. Rokkan and J. Meyriat (eds), *International Guide to Electoral Statistics* (The Hague: 1969); 1936–73: F. Bon, *Les Elections en France: Histoire et Sociologie* (Paris: 1978); 1978: statistics provided by Professor J. Jaffré of the Centre pour l'Etude de la Vie Politique Française (CEVIPOF), Paris.

flooding out of the Party even more rapidly than they had entered.

The Nazi-Soviet Pact not only led to the legal suppression of the PCF: it produced a degree of anger and demoralisation within its ranks which would probably have threatened it with complete organisational collapse even if the government had done nothing. Even the most loyal of Party militants resigned in droves, including, sensationally, several deputies.[3] Thorez's flight into exile and the fall of France to the victorious German armies completed the rout. Thus by 1940 – and probably by August 1939 – the Party had lost all its gains of 1934–8 and more besides, almost certainly taking it back below even its 1932 nadir. If there was again to be a strong Communist movement in France the work of reconstruction had to begin again almost from scratch.

In the course of the war, and particularly through the dominant contribution to the Resistance made by Communists, this is essentially what was achieved. By 1945 the Party had 545,000 members and more than a quarter of the popular vote. This prodigious surge of new support reached its all-time peak with the November 1946 elections, in which the PCF, now with 800,000 members, claimed 28.3 per cent of the vote.[4] Thereafter membership declined steeply, probably standing at no more than 317,000 in 1956,[5] but the PCF vote stayed virtually steady. Just as Gaullism's political clientele found its definitive shape and proportions very quickly after the Liberation, so did that of the PCF, the Party's October 1945 score being almost exactly replicated in June 1946, 1951 and 1956.

To a considerable degree it was a new party. The 15.2 per cent won by the Party in 1936 had been achieved in an all-male electorate and universal adult franchise after 1945 created a far less favourable electoral environment. In fact the Party's 26.9 per cent poll in 1951 (for example) was the combination of a 20.3 per cent level of support among women and 34.3 per cent among men: thus the proportion of men supporting the PCF had gone from less than one in six to more than one in three.[6] Moreover, for the first time Communism became a national force. The three isolated patches of PCF strength in Paris-Nord, the Centre and the Midi were now joined in one continuous sprawl as the Party suddenly emerged with great strength in areas of the South and West where previously it had hardly existed. While previously the Party had drawn support from rural pockets of radical republicanism as well as a more substantial revolutionary proletarian base, a third tradition had now to be added: that of the *maquis*. For the new areas of Communist rural strength corresponded almost exactly to the regionally varying intensity of Resistance activity. It seems clear that much of this new peasant support came not from the Socialists but the Radicals. The result was a staggering leap in PCF support in quite various and widely separated rural departments. In Aude the Party reached 8 times its 1936 level; in Côtes-du-Nord and Loire-Atlantique it rose by a multiple of 10; in Haute-Marne by a multiple of 11; and in Morbihan by one of 14.[7]

These rural gains were only partly paralleled in the towns. The PCF did, of course, gain much new urban support and became the principal party of the working-class, but there was a clear 'levelling-off' effect in its previous strongholds. In Lot-et-Garonne, for example, where the PCF had been solidly implanted ever since 1924, it hardly exceeded its 1936 level of support. In the Party's greatest stronghold of all, the Paris-Nord region, its 1945 gains were very slight and variable. Thorez himself saw the PCF vote in his constituency fall humiliatingly to 41.7 per cent from its 1936 peak of 59.2 per cent and in the whole southern *banlieu* of Paris the PCF fell noticeably from 43.9 per cent in 1936 to 40 per cent in 1945.[8] On the whole the PCF gained new urban support only where it had previously been weak.

These major trends of the critical election of 1945 were confirmed in 1946. In June the PCF made further gains but these were confined exclusively to the rural West and the Party fell back clearly in all its major strongholds – Paris, Nord, Pas-de-Calais, Landes and the South-East. These urban losses were made good in November but the PCF's real gains were again confined to rural areas – except for the Centre, its oldest area of implantation, where the 1945 peak was not exceeded. Here, too, a clear 'levelling-out' phenomenon was visible.

These changes fundamentally altered the PCF's internal balance, making it far more a party of the peasants and agricultural workers than it had been hitherto. A 1948 survey showed that these two groups constituted over 28 per cent of the PCF's electorate, ranking next behind industrial workers (over 47 per cent) in their importance.[9] Much of this support came not so much from agricultural workers as from small independent peasants. In 1951 the 'reddest' department in France (with a PCF vote of 40.4 per cent) was Corrèze, where over 80 per cent of the agricultural population were small land-holding peasants. In 1956 the reddest department was Creuse (where the PCF took 43.1 per cent of the vote), where the proportion of independent peasants (75 per cent) was almost equally high.[10] Moreover, these new rural recruits were considerably more likely to join the Party than were industrial workers. Immediately after the Liberation the PCF's ratio of members to voters was strikingly higher in the rural departments (especially the Centre and Midi) than in the towns. This in turn greatly reduced the old dominance of the Paris region within the Party. In 1937 the 115,000 adherents in the region had made up 35 per cent of the entire PCF membership, but in 1946 the region's 147,000 members constituted only 18 per cent of the Party faithful.[11] By 1947, moreover, the region's membership had fallen to 108,000 – under its 1937 level.[12]

Change was least at the top. Although the PCF regularly sent more peasants to parliament than did any other party, the political leadership of the Party remained firmly in the hands of a largely proletarian pre-war generation. The major figures on the rostrum at the 1947 Congress were very much the same 'old guard' who had directed the PCF through the 1920s and 1930s: Thorez (leader since 1930), Marty, Duclos, Cachin, Frachon, Billoux, Mauvais, Fajon, Ramette, Guyot – a veritable roll-call of a bygone era. By definition, and without exception, these men had supported every twist of Comintern policy, from 'class against class' to the Nazi-Soviet Pact. Between them they had endured every possible combination of imprisonment, maltreatment and exile and had engaged in all varieties of warfare and undercover work. With this team back in charge political continuity and the 'leading role of the proletariat' were hardly in any danger. Moreover, while the demographic ravages of two wars and the inter-war depression meant that the electorate as a whole was heavily tilted towards the older age groups, the PCF electorate was strikingly young. In 1948 39 per cent and in 1952 42 per cent of all its voters were aged 20–34.[13] The contrast between the Party's youthful base and its Third Republic top-echelons (and what was true of the Politburo was true of many federal committees, too)[14] caused even the leadership to join in the groundswell of resentment. Upward promotion within the Party was being hindered, it declared in 1949, by 'family feeling, personal friendship and the old pals' act (*copinerie*)'. Cadres were too reluctant 'on the pretext of a false sentimentality, to point out to certain comrades that they are getting old and rusty'.[15] The fact that the leadership, stuffed as it was with veterans, had the nerve to take up this theme merely showed, of course, how entirely in control it was. The Party might have changed and grown, but it was still very much *theirs*.

While the most striking features of the PCF in the Fourth Republic were its size and stability, it did show some changes and did lose some ground, falling from 28.3 per cent of the vote in November 1946 to 25.9 per cent in 1956. In 1951 the PCF lost ground (mainly to the RPF) in the Paris region and the northern rural areas, where its roots dated back only to the Liberation. In 1956 it suffered further small losses, this time mainly to the Poujadists, and exclusively in the southern half of the country.[16]

What was noticeable in both cases, however, was that the peasant support won for the Party by the *maquis* was eroding. In part, of course, this was due to the fact that the Party had captured the allegiance of many small independent peasants at just the point when they were entering their period of most rapid decline as a class. But the diminution of the share of peasants and agricultural workers in the PCF electorate was too rapid for this to be a wholly satisfactory explanation: in 1948 they had constituted over 28 per cent of the PCF electorate, in 1952 17 per cent and in 1956 14 per cent.[17] Equally, the vertiginous drop in membership through the 1950s was particularly noticeable in the countryside, allowing the Party's old bastions to regain much of their lost importance. The Party continued to draw residual benefits from the image of the rural *maquis*, but there was little doubt that it was a wasting asset. The result was that the PCF electorate gradually became more heavily proletarian. According to Dogan, in 1956 the PCF was receiving the votes of around 49 per cent of the working-class, this group making up 71 per cent of its total support.[18] Comparable figures for the 1940s are impossible to obtain, but it seems fairly clear that the Party was compensating for some of its rural losses with continuing small gains amongst the still growing industrial working-class.[19]

This was by no means an unsatisfactory situation for an avowedly proletarian party. A decade after the Liberation the PCF had held almost all of its post-war gains and was incontestably the leading party of the working-class. Membership had fallen but, ritual expressions of regret apart, the leadership seems to have made no special effort to counter the trend. The facts of electoral strength and stability seemed to allow for a certain complacency on that score, for the PCF electorate showed a wondrous solidity through the ups and downs of the Cold War. The Russian invasion of Hungary in 1956 caused an enormous haemorrhage of members from the Party,[20] but the scattered electoral results of the next eighteen months showed no fall-off in mass support.[21] The Party had been out of government since 1947 but in 1956, despite the 1951 modifications to the electoral system designed expressly to hurt it, the PCF made sweeping gains. Capitalism might continue but the Party was powerful and, it seemed, unshakeable.

## ii THE PCF AND THE DISASTER OF 1958

All this was changed by the events of 1958, which dealt the PCF a blow from which it was never wholly to recover. In September 1958 only 20.7 per cent of the electorate voted against De Gaulle's new constitution – even though the PCF (which was only one of several groups calling for a No vote) had received 25.9 per cent of the vote in 1956 on its own. For while the RPF in the 1940s had never attracted away more than 10 per cent of the PCF vote[22], the second coming of Gaullism had an altogether more profound effect. Even if all the 1958 No voters had been PCF supporters, it would still have meant that the Party had been deserted by one-fifth of its electorate – and of course not all of them were. In fact Servin (then still a Politburo member) admitted that 'almost a million and a half Communist voters voted Yes'[23] – which amounted to over a quarter of the Party's support. But IFOP surveys suggested that at a very minimum the Party had been deserted by one in three of its voters,[24] and this is backed up by Ranger, a PCF member as well as one of its leading analysts. Ranger suggests, indeed, that the proportion of the PCF electorate who stayed unswervingly loyal to the Party under the crushing Gaullist impact of 1958–62 may have been as low as 60 per cent.[25] The damage to the Party seems to have been almost wholly sustained in the single great blow of the September 1958 referendum, an effect the subsequent Gaullist referendum triumphs of 1961–2 merely consolidated.

Undoubtedly many PCF defectors were attracted by De Gaulle's personal magnetism – the September 1958 referendum was above all a plebiscite for or against De Gaulle. But nor can it be doubted that the new constitutional order progressively unveiled by De Gaulle in 1958–62 exercised an attraction to many Communist voters, making inroads on their commitment to the Party on programmatic grounds as well. Ranger, examining a large body of polling evidence, found that PCF voters were almost as critical as any others of the institutions of the Fourth Republic.[26] Up until 1958, however, most such voters had implicitly accepted the view that the malfunctioning of these institutions was the result of the 'anti-Communist exclusion tactics' practised by the other parties. In 1958 De Gaulle offered an alternative analysis of the nation's problems, one which blamed *all* the parties, and suggested that everything – including even the pressing issue of peace in Algeria – might be capable of solution via a reform of the Republic itself. It was an attractive vision which capitalised on the strong anti-party sentiments existing very widely in the electorate and undoubtedly had an appeal for a large section of PCF voters. This appeal went far beyond the ranks of the semi-floaters on the edge of the PCF electorate.[27]

The abandonment of the PCF by one-third of its electorate in September 1958 did not result in any simple or clear-cut transfer of votes to other parties.[28] Rather, the effect seems to have been that this large group, having crossed its Rubicon in September, wandered round in a somewhat rudderless fashion thereafter. In November – when it was a question of supporting one party or another rather than responding to a personal or constitutional appeal – some even drifted back to the PCF. The Party's 19.2 per cent poll, though its worst since 1936, none the less represented the loss of a quarter, not a third, of its voters. The great majority of the defectors seem, however, to have distributed themselves amongst all other parties, usually rallying to locally well-established notables irrespective of party. In general this left them supporting conservatives of one hue or another. On the whole the PCF losses were felt across the board, with a tendency for the Party to hang on best in areas where it had been longest and most deeply dug in, and to lose most where its gains had been most recent – its 1956 gains in Alsace-Lorraine, for example, were more than wiped out. True, the vote held up relatively well in some Liberation era zones – Brittany, Champagne and the South-West – but on the whole the Party did best where its strength went back to 1924.

The 1958 losses also had a major impact on the social structure of Communist support. In particular the slow erosion of peasant support for the Party, visible through

TABLE 8.2 Social composition of the PCF electorate, 1952, 1962

|  | *1952* | *1962* |
|---|---|---|
| Peasants* | 13 | 5 |
| Business, managers and professions | 9 | 6 |
| White collar workers | 13 | 13 |
| Industrial workers | 38 | 51 |
| Rentiers, retired | 3 | 7 |
| Not in employment | 24 | 18 |
|  | 100 | 100 |
| Men | 61 | 65 |
| Women | 39 | 35 |
|  | 100 | 100 |

* Agricultural workers are counted with peasants in 1952, with industrial workers in 1962. Their shrinkage as a group by then means that the distortion thus produced is small.

*Source*: J. Ranger, 'L'Evolution du Vote Communiste en France Depuis 1945', in Fondation Nationale des Sciences Politiques, *Le Communisme en France* (Paris: 1969) pp. 242–3.

the 1950s, was given a further great push, leaving the Party more reliant than ever on its urban core. This core was also more masculine than before, for the PCF's losses among women (for whom, as we have seen, De Gaulle had a particular appeal)[29] were disproportionately great. These trends are reflected directly in Table 8.2 and also indirectly in the fall-off of PCF support among those not in employment (i.e. essentially housewives). The apparent gain amongst the retired in Table 8.2 is, however, an optical illusion. While the PCF electorate of the 1960s was significantly older than before, this change merely mirrored the overall aging of the electorate and the enhanced place of the retired within it.[30]

These losses were never wholly to be made good, for the shock of 1958 had a lasting effect, permanently depriving the PCF of one-sixth of its electorate. A further one-sixth drifted back to the PCF by 1962, but with its loyalty now permanently impaired. This group was notably more prone to support the PCF in municipal, as opposed to national, elections,[31] and showed a continuing susceptibility to De Gaulle's appeal both in referenda and in moments of crisis, such as 1968, when the PCF's support fell back almost to its 1958 level. Essentially, though, the main effects of this second Gaullist impact had been assimilated by 1962. Thereafter the PCF vote showed much the same stability it had exhibited under the Fourth Republic – but now it hovered at the 20–21 per cent level, not the 25–26 per cent it had hitherto achieved.

## iii THE SOCIOLOGY OF SOCIALIST DECLINE

Until 1940 the SFIO had enjoyed an apparently unchallengeable position as the leading party of the Left. In a few short years of Occupation and Resistance, however, this legacy of generations was lost. In a sense French Socialism was to spend its next thirty years attempting to recover from the body blow dealt it by the remarkable wartime expansion of the PCF. In 1945 the SFIO made small – though in fact illusory[32] – gains. By November 1946, however, the new fact of Communist predominance on the Left had begun to tell and the fragile Socialist vote crumpled like a boxer with a glass jaw. The SFIO not only lost all its 1945 gains but sank to its lowest level of support since the pre-1914 period – when it had been struggling with the post-natal pains of being a united party at all. This was a not unfair measure of the process of disaggregation with which the party was now threatened. It had lost its influence with the CGT; it was no longer *the* great party of the Left or the working-class; its whole *raison d'être* was in doubt.

It had only two wasting assets. It still benefited from the carry-over of at least some of its Third Republic electorate, and the decline of the Radicals allowed it to emerge as the main party of *laicité*, taking over a large share of the old Radical anti-clerical vote. It was, indeed, placed in much the same position *vis-à-vis* the PCF as the Radicals had been in *vis-à-vis* the SFIO: that is, of being virtually evicted from the major urban centres (especially Paris) and having to rely increasingly on a declining base in small rural towns. It was, though, a far worse situation for a self-proclaimed proletarian party than it had been for the Radicals – and even the Radicals had found this to be a road to ruin. It was, moreover, difficult to see how the SFIO could break out of the trap, for its most striking failure lay in its inability to attract new young voters.

This pattern of support was visible right away in 1945 and was merely accentuated by the losses of 1946. Nationally the party lost a quarter of its 1945 electorate in 1946, but it lost 33 per cent in Marseilles and 37 per cent in the Paris region.[33] The result was to leave the party thinly and fairly evenly spread out across the country, with strongholds remaining only in Languedoc and the North. In 1951 its further losses came from all round the country.[34]

By this stage the SFIO resembled nothing more than an aging heavyweight fighter who has taken a prodigious blow in the first round (i.e. from the PCF at the Liberation). Thus softened up, it could only reel from round to round. If habit, experience and sheer inertia made a complete knockout implausible it was, none the less, easy prey for any youthful flyweight willing to try his luck: for, after 1945, almost anyone could, it seemed, take votes from the SFIO. Above all, as we have seen,[35] it was more vulnerable than the PCF to the onslaught of De Gaulle's RPF. But in 1946, when the RPF had not been born, it had lost heavily to the MRP and slightly to the PCF and Radicals.[36] In 1951 it lost to the RPF – but in 1956, despite the RPF's disappearance, it regained only a fraction of these losses. Its electorate had become 'soft' and fragile, liable to continuous haemorrhage in several different directions. And whatever the original shock propelling voters away from the party, once away they tended to stay away.

What remained of the SFIO electorate lacked either geographical or sociological definition. Much was made of the fact that workers still made up the largest proportion (around 40 per cent) of SFIO support, but this simply reflected the workers' numerical significance within the electorate as a whole.[37] In fact only 15–20 per cent of workers supported the SFIO – the party's average level amongst *all* voters. More striking was the fact that the SFIO was weaker than *any* other party in the big cities and that 42 per cent of its support came from those living in villages of 2,000 inhabitants or under. With a few local exceptions, such as the miners in the Nord, the sort of workers who still voted Socialist tended to be old-fashioned (and old) small-town artisans working in small enterprises – the most rustic and 'backward' members of their class. Typically, such local coalitions also included a significant peasant and farmworker vote[38] and revolved around the rural schoolteachers of anti-clerical legend.

Outside such timeless and self-encapsulated milieux the SFIO relied heavily on white-collar workers, especially civil servants. Indeed, in 1951 active and retired civil servants and their wives made up an astonishing 30 per cent of the SFIO vote,[39] a figure which rose to 33 per cent in Paris and no less than 43 per cent in Marseilles.[40]

Party membership figures told a similar story. From an official figure of 285,000 in 1936, membership had climbed to 355,000 in 1946. By 1947 it had fallen back to 279,000 and by 1948, after the split with the PCF, it had slumped to 132,000, falling to 100,000 the next year. Thereafter the figure settled, stagnant, on a low plateau – there were 88,000 members in 1954, 85,000 in 1958.[41] Even these figures underestimated the rot, for as many as one-third of the party subscriptions paid were bogus: on examination, for example, the 1954 official figure of 88,000 yielded only about 60,000 real members.[42]

Only 44 per cent of the members of this self-proclaimed workers' party were actually workers. Virtually no farmworkers and few peasants belonged to it, either, as a detailed survey of its 1951 membership reveals.[43] Instead the party was utterly dominated by middle-aged civil servants and middle-class professionals. The 16–30 age group, though the most prone to join political associations, was underrepresented by a factor of two, while the 40–50 age group was overrepresented by a margin of 50 per cent. No less than 88 per cent of the membership was male.

These trends were more exaggerated the further up the party one went. Amongst actual party militants workers were only as well represented as artisans and small businessmen and were proportionately far less well represented than white-collar workers or even the middle classes in general. Only 11 per cent of SFIO deputies in the 1956 Assembly came from the 'popular classes' (i.e. peasants, farmworkers and blue- and white-collar workers), the great bulk being school teachers (17 per cent), university lecturers (16 per cent), civil servants and lawyers (14 per cent each). Over 70 per cent of PCF deputies, by contrast, came from the 'popular classes'.[44]

Perhaps the greatest contrast between the SFIO and PCF, however, was that the latter was virtually a new, or at least a refounded, party in 1945 and it was decidedly youthful – no other party could rival its support among young voters. Precisely the opposite was true of the SFIO, which remained rooted in the Third, not the Fourth Republic. It chose more pre-war politicians as candidates than any other party.[45] Its membership was decidedly old, its voters predominantly middle-aged. At all levels its greatest failure was to make new recruits (who were, in part, repelled precisely by the sight and behaviour of these Third Republic remnants). Before 1939 new recruits had never made up less than 15 per cent of the party's membership; after 1945 the figure fell to 4 per cent.[46] In 1946 the party had fewer deputies aged thirty-five or less than any other party; by 1956 it had none at all.[47] At grassroots the most it could hope for was that the sons and daughters of SFIO voters would carry on voting Socialist as a matter of family tradition (and doubtless most did)[48] – for the party's youth section was a weak and sickly infant. The fact that the party remained an almost exclusively male preserve may have reflected sexual prejudice less than the party's sheer failure to grasp that it was not living in the Third Republic, that women now constituted well over half the electorate . . .

It remains difficult to characterise the Socialists of the Fourth Republic with any single stroke of the brush. They were a declining party – but in 1956 appeared to have stabilised around the 15 per cent level. They were top-heavy in age terms – but 30 per cent of their voters were under thirty-five.[49] They had lost much of the urban proletariat to the PCF – but workers remained the most important element among their members and voters. The most acute judgement is that of Hardouin: the SFIO of the 1950s was a decaying workers' party and the clearest sign of this was that it had ceased to be a class party pure and simple:

> It was neither the party of the salariat, nor of the workers, nor of the consumers. It was not the party of the middle classes but it was on the way to becoming one. It was in fact a true people's party, the party of the little man and the government employee.[50]

The Fourth Republican system was not particularly friendly to this type of political formation, tending rather to favour the often intransigent expression of discrete social groups. If there was a Socialist core it tended to revolve around the time-honoured (and by the 1950s, rather dated) cause of anti-clericalism. In 1952 only 5 per cent of regular churchgoers were willing to vote Socialist,[51] and a decade later more voters still associated the SFIO with the defence of the lay school' than with any other issue.[52]

On the other hand the Fourth Republic did make the SFIO something it had never been before – a regular party of government. This, however, brought rewards mainly to the individuals who became ministers. A disastrous dialectic thus commenced: the lamentable opportunism of SFIO ministers created disaffection at the party's grassroots: this in turn made it easier for those SFIO leaders with ministerial patronage to lead the party by the nose; which in turn made the party ever more a mere vehicle for political careerism; which in turn led to mass disaffection . . . As Fauvet remarked, 'If today [the SFIO] no longer has the method of Marx nor the faith of Jaurès nor the authority of Guèsde, what has it left? Power, no doubt: which is much – and nothing.'[53]

The SFIO's continued participation in government through into the Fifth Republic shielded it at first from the hostile impact of Gaullism so strongly felt by the PCF: indeed, the SFIO actually gained slightly in the 1958 elections. This merely delayed the moment of truth until 1962 when, having now left the government, the party had to face up to the full weight of the Gaullist onslaught. Its voters fled in all directions – 14 per cent to the UNR, 7 per cent to the PCF, 6 per cent to the PSU and even 3 per cent to the Radicals.[54] Overall the party had lost one-fifth of its 1958 electorate and was now at a nadir of only 12.5 per cent of the poll. Its remaining voters clung on simply from habit and were now an older group than ever – only the (now nearly extinct) Radicals had less support from the under thirty-fives.[55]

It was in order to prevent the rout of 1962 turning into a massacre that Mollet, as we have seen,[56] grasped the nettle of an alliance with the PCF. This saved – even won – the SFIO seats, but the party's deeper sickness continued. Membership continued its steady decline (85,000 in 1958; 83,000 in 1959; 79,000 in 1960; 78,000 in 1961–2; 74,000 in 1962–3; 70,000 in 1965–6),[57] while the 1965 municipal elections saw the SFIO only hold steady (while the PCF was winning nine more major towns).[58] Even Mitterrand's first-ballot showing against De Gaulle in 1965 did not suggest any real progress in the position of the non-Communist Left. In 1962 the PCF, SFIO and extreme Left had together won 36.7 per cent of the first-ballot vote. Mitterrand, the candidate of all these groups, won only 32.2 per cent. Despite the Left's jubilation at having forced De Gaulle to a second ballot it was clear that Lecanuet's success in splitting the Centre-Right vote was the real reason for this outcome.

## iv THE TURNING POINT

It was only with Mitterrand's 45.5 per cent vote on the 1965 second ballot that the potentialities of the new alliance were glimpsed. In 1962 all the Left parties together (including the Radicals) had received only 44.4 per cent – and they had achieved that only against the UNR, not against the redoubtable personal appeal of the General himself. Mitterrand had not merely united the whole of this electoral bloc in quite unprecedented fashion, but had even made some inroads beyond . . .[59] Moreover, if one credited the PCF with responsibility for 21.8 per cent of the vote (as in 1962), this left a rather larger bloc of 23.7 per cent who, under conditions of acute polarisation, had been willing to support the non-Communist Left, even when it was allied to the PCF. From this moment on the dream of the Socialists that they might one day regain their old primacy on the Left became credible.

Thereafter, Socialist progress was fairly steady. As Table 7.2 revealed,[60] during the Fourth Republic the PCF regularly obtained 1½ or 1¾ times the Socialist vote. This ratio was upset in 1958 when the PCF felt the Gaullist impact and the SFIO did not, but re-emerged quite neatly in 1962 once this condition was equalised. In 1967 the ratio dropped sharply. In the crisis election of 1968 it held steady – although previous trends might have led one to expect a disproportionate SFIO collapse. Thereafter – and despite Defferre's disastrous performance in the 1969 presidential election – the Socialists resumed their upward swing, particularly after the effective refounding of the PS at Epinay in 1971. By 1972 the PS was actually showing ahead of the PCF in the opinion polls for the first time[61] and the 1973 election saw the gap between the parties vanish almost entirely. Then, in the Autumn of 1974, in the wake of Mitterrand's strong showing in the May presidential election against Giscard, a series of by-elections confirmed what the opinion polls were already saying – that the PS had established a decisive lead over the PCF. This lead it has maintained ever since.

The PS overtook the PCF in terms not only of gross votes but in the broad extent of its national presence. In 1962 the PCF had been the leading party of the Left in 281 constituencies; in 1967 in 251; in 1968 in 244; in 1973 in 203; and in 1978 in only 169, by which time the PS was the leading Left party in two-thirds of France. The fact that this trend continued even through 1968 – when the Socialists actually lost more votes than the PCF – shows well enough that this evolution could not be explained solely in terms of the general increase in PS strength. In good part it was also the result of the already observed tendency of the PCF to lose support in rural areas.[62]

This trend, perceptible from 1951 on and sharply accelerated in 1958, continued at a fairly steady pace right through the 1960s. Even in 1967, when the PCF increased its overall vote to 22.5 per cent (its best Fifth Republic score), the Party's rural vote continued to ebb away, in a way which could not be wholly explained by the decline of the agricultural workforce.[63] True, the re-entry of the PCF into the political mainstream (via the united Left alliance) enabled it to generalise its appeal to hitherto resistant sections of the rural population, notably to working-class electors in rural towns like Le Mans, Caen and Dijon. But even these gains were fragile, collapsing badly in 1968 while the PCF's big city support was holding up relatively well.

This erosion of PCF rural support continued even despite the decay of the religious cleavage – a phenomenon of particular importance in rural France – which was simultaneously producing a new flock of recruits for the Left. Indeed, even as the PCF fell back, the Left's overall share of the vote in the French countryside was actually *rising*, for the PS gains here more than compensated for the PCF's losses. In part this was because the new recruits were generally rather timid ex-Centrists, willing to move to the PS but not right across the political spectrum to the PCF. In part the PS, in its period of dynamic expansion, simply exercised greater powers of attraction than the stagnant PCF, particularly since the PCF seemed – and was – a more proletarian party of the big conurbations only.

But the most fundamental reason for the decline of rural Communism was the gradual disappearance of the inheritance won for the Party by the *maquis* thirty years before. By the 1970s the distribution of PCF support had reverted a long way towards that of 1936. The war and the Resistance had provided the PCF with a great increment of strength and made it, for the first time, a truly national party. Now, with the gradual disappearance of the wartime generation, the PCF was shrinking back towards its pre-war size and shape and its national presence was dwindling.

The reconquest by the Socialists of their old primacy on the Left was at once the most fundamental and the most unexpected development of the post-De Gaulle era. For the PCF it was also the most threatening, and puzzling, crisis it had faced since the war. What had happened to its legendary solidity and dynamism? The answer lay even deeper than the ebbing away of its Resistance heritage, for the PCF had been a party of resistance long before it became, 'naturally', the Party of the Resistance. It was here – in the whole question of what role the Party was to play within the political system – that the PCF's true problem lay.


## v THE UNPLANNED OBSOLESCENCE OF THE TRIBUNE PARTY

The solidity of the PCF vote in the Fourth Republic was not unrelated to the fact that the Party was operating in a political system which suited it rather well. True, it could not, after 1947, hope to participate in government. But the PCF was not a 'party of government'. As Lavau notes, it was not, finally, either a pragmatic or a programmatic party, but a tribune party.[64] That is, a party

> whose function – latent, at least, if not manifest – is principally to organise and defend the plebeian social groups (that is to say, those who are excluded or feel themselves to be excluded from the process of participation in the political system, as also from the benefits of the economic and cultural system), and to give them a feeling of strength and confidence . . . The proposal of a political programme or the carrying out of a line of policy have less importance for this type of party in terms of what they are worth or by their concrete results, than in terms of what they represent in the eyes of the plebeian masses thus represented.[65]

In particular what the PCF could hope to communicate to their 'plebs' was that their anger, frustration and resentment were given real political expression; that it was officially represented by their delegates, who resembled them, came from their own ranks and spoke their language, if in articulated political form; and that this anger was powerful, that it could frighten others, perhaps even paralyse the political system. The infliction of such paralysis on the system had been the recognised last resort of the tribunes of ancient Rome: they were formally endowed with powers to block or hinder their rulers simply on the justification of protecting and defending the interests of the weak.

The exercise of this tribunitial function depends, as Lavau notes, on several preconditions. There must be a large and relatively homogeneous group to be thus represented; one which, despite its size, is poorly integrated into the political and cultural system and placed in a position of permanent inferiority. Second, the political system's norms and structures must tolerate the exercise of such a function by legitimating the right of political *defence*. This involves a general acknowledgement of the system's imperfections and thus the right of any group to take blocking action to prevent itself from being overwhelmed by the system's mal-operation. Third, the groups thus represented – and their tribunes – must be both willing and able to settle for political defence rather than for passive impotence on the one hand and open revolt on the other.

The role of the tribunes is thus far from easy. It depends on a recognition that, while the system is so ineffective as to leave large and important groups permanently 'outside' it, it is none the less too strong to be overthrown. That is, it is sufficiently effective in managing the government of a society for other groups to be willing to collaborate with the plebs in seeking its overthrow. Given this situation, the tribune party must continually threaten the system's overthrow (keeping others alive to the threat they represent), but never actually undertake revolution. Its task is to organise the plebs into a self-conscious group, overcoming their tendencies towards defeatism and anarchic revolt, and helping provide the confidence and organisation to allow for a careful, tough-minded defence. This involves the tribune party in the exercise of very considerable social control over the plebs. It must brake and restrain tendencies towards violent mass action and launch such actions itself only under the most carefully controlled and calculated conditions. The result is that 'Those who are the guardians of the functioning of the political system end up by knowing what are the habitual margins of the game of violence which the party respects. And this recognition ends up by becoming part of the norms of the system.'[66]

On the other hand, this recognition must never become explicit. If that were to happen the tribune party would cease to make its threatening posture credible – other groups would not be frightened – and such formal collaboration would threaten a collapse into reformism, with the tribunes simply taking sides with one faction or another within the ruling group from which they remained definitionally excluded. The maintenance of such a role will, on the other hand, leave the tribune party open to accusations of not really wanting to change things and of not seeking power to do so. Such accusations it must resist – it cannot share in power without sacrificing its tribune role, which is the best the system allows it – but must do so on the grounds that it is interested in taking power only on terms which will enable it so totally to transform the system that the very plebeian condition itself is abolished. This ultimate hope must be held out to the plebs as an argument against their accepting incorporation within the system in a permanently subordinate role. Thus the tribune party must arrive at an uneasy understanding with the system's rulers while denying to its own followers that co-operation with the rulers is either possible or desirable.

Such, indeed, was the role the PCF attempted to play more or less from its inception. It was hostile both to social democratic reformism and to anarcho-syndicalist dreams of revolution ('irresponsible adventurism'). It continuously used what representation it had to protest against the validity of the entire system. Its deputies consistently broke all rules of confidentiality on parliamentary committees – and were not infrequently involved in other forms of unparliamentary behaviour, including street-brawls with the police at demonstrations. In 1925 it placed women on its municipal electoral lists although this was strictly illegal, women being ineligible to vote, let alone to be elected.[67] Yet it never seriously toyed with attempts at revolution – save possibly in February 1934 when it seemed that another group (the fascists) might join with it. Even when it espoused the Popular Front in 1936 it did so explicitly as a blocking move – 'to bar the road to reaction' – and refused any actual participation in government.

Yet while the PCF strove towards the role of tribune party under the Third Republic, it could not fulfil it, for too many of the plebs still looked not to it but to the

SFIO. Accordingly the Party lacked the sheer size necessary to play any real blocking role and for most of the inter-war period governments could afford effectively to ignore the tiny band of PCF deputies and the very minor threat they posed. The Fourth Republic allowed fulfilment of the role in almost every respect, however. As in the Third Republic, the political system provided almost explicitly for the defence of particularist interests and the power-play of veto-groups. Moreover, a system of proportional representation helped the PCF maximise its representation at the same time that it removed the need for electoral alliances which might have made interest-group representation less intransigent. Above all, the Party now had the strength and size to play a major blocking role. It was the largest party in the country and usually in parliament and its control of the CGT gave it great industrial power as well, as the 1947–8 strike wave reminded the government which had had the temerity to dismiss its Communist ministers. It was assisted, moreover, by the parallel emergence of other anti-system groups, the RPF and the Poujadists, who were equally unwilling to lend reliable support to governments, whose position was accordingly the more precarious. Armed with such weapons as these the PCF was able, quite credibly, to threaten paralysis of the system – indeed the Fourth Republic lived in a state of imminent or actual paralysis.

The coming of the Fifth Republic greatly reduced the scope for the exercise of a tribunitial role. The 'system' of the Fourth Republic had not, after all, been too strong to overthrow, but it was the General, not the PCF, who had secured such an outcome. The tactic of waiting for a crisis opportunity to overthrow the system with the help of 'other democratic forces' was revealed as utterly bankrupt. Worse still, De Gaulle had been able to do this while loftily disregarding the PCF and its rearguard action in defence of the Fourth Republic as simply irrelevant. The Resistance State in which the Party had enjoyed such a secure position had gone and in its place another was erected, constructed quite deliberately to advantage the forces of conservatism and weaken the PCF. Proportional representation, which had given the Party a plurality in parliament, was replaced by the two ballot system which, in 1958, cut its representation from 150 deputies to 10. The role of parliament was in any case so reduced that even the old level of representation would not allow the Party to exercise its old influence. Instead, power flowed up to a presidency which it was certain the PCF could never win. And, perhaps most important of all, the Gaullist – or at least conservative – stranglehold over both the presidency and the legislature produced a long, unbroken period of strong, stable and authoritative government. The persistence in power of this cohesive political bloc forged a link between electoral choice and executive outcomes which had not hitherto existed.

These changes did not have an immediate effect on political behaviour. At the level of the political elites and of the mass electorate there was a large and inevitable carry-over of Fourth Republican attitudes and expectations, the more so since the permanence of the new order was in doubt at least until 1962 and because the heroic figure of De Gaulle tended for long to overshadow the more mundane facts of institutional life. Gradually, however, the electorate (rather ahead of the elites) was socialised into the new system, whose point was repeatedly hammered home in a series of great electoral confrontations. Whereas in the Fourth Republic protest voting had been 'free' – for there was effectively no possibility of voters deciding on the complexion of future governments anyway – in the Fifth Republic merely 'representational'[68] forms of political behaviour were heavily penalised.[69] This process proceded at pell-mell pace. In the first eleven years of the new Republic's life voters were called on eleven times to decide on the fate of the government.[70] It was not merely the case that voters were now able to choose how they were to be governed (and every poll showed they valued this ability) but that, willy-nilly, they *had* so to choose.

Gradually, and in a way that was by no means evident to Mollet and Thorez when they made their 1962 pact, the norms of the new system were transposed on to the parties of opposition, requiring them, if they wished to be taken seriously, to become an Opposition in the British sense. That is, they would have to provide, or seem to provide, an alternative government-in-waiting with reasonably clear plans for the conduct of national affairs and with sufficient internal cohesion to ensure that the government they might form would not endanger the political stability which was universally regarded as the Fifth Republic's principal achievement. The creation of a united Left alliance was clearly an indispensable step towards such a goal but it was by no means a sufficient one to ensure success. For the superimposition of these new political norms created painful problems of adjustment for both the Left parties, particularly the PCF.

The implicit expectations generated by the new system ran directly counter to the tribunitial style of politics, which was all the PCF knew. Indeed, it is no exaggeration to say that De Gaulle and Debré had fashioned the institutions of the new Republic in deliberate incompatibility with such a style. With hindsight it is possible to see that the PCF's best strategy for uniting the Left under its continued leadership would have been to move as radically and rapidly as possible after 1958 towards complete de-Stalinisation, and towards a liberalised national communism on the Italian model – in a word, to have embraced Eurocommunism fifteen or more years before it did. In this respect it is possible to view the Servin-Casanova affair[71] of 1960–1 as a major historical turning point where the PCF refused to turn. Had the PCF accepted Servin's counsels it might have taken the 'Italian road' a great deal earlier than it did. It is difficult, if not impossible, however, to imagine how this might have occurred in a Party still dominated by Thorez and staffed by his hand-picked lieutenants at every level. For the PCF to move as decisively as it did towards alliance with the Socialists in 1962 was about as radical a departure as could be envisaged while the spirit of the ghetto and the habits of Stalinist loyalty remained so strong.

Instead the Party continued essentially to play the part of tribune, laying stress on its merely defensive role. Indeed, as Lavau points out, the term 'defence' continued to occupy a central position in the Party's own view of itself. Thus an official summary of the Party's social objectives in 1967 listed '1) the *defence* and increase of wages, salaries and pensions; 2) the *defence* and consolidation of social security; 3) the *defence* of employment and the reduction of hours of work; 4) the *defence* and advancement of the most disfavoured groups'.[72] Not surprisingly, the view of the

Party held by the electorate – particularly by the PCF's own electorate – associated it overwhelmingly with a parochial defence of proletarian special interests and hardly at all with national policy questions. Thus a 1962 poll found that while a large plurality (32 per cent) regarded the PCF as the party most concerned with the 'defence of workers', only 9 per cent saw it as most concerned with 'the country's economic development'.[73] The electorate's image of the Gaullist party, then carrying all before it, was the mirror opposite. By 1966 this view of the PCF had strengthened, not diminished: 43 per cent of all voters (and 77 per cent of PCF voters) saw the Party as the most concerned with the 'defence of wages', while both groups rated it at a derisorily low level in its concern for France's place in the world, economic expansion, the construction of Europe, and governmental stability. The Gaullists, who were overwhelmingly rated highest on all these latter issues, were not only rated low (8 per cent) in their concern for wage-levels, but were not particularly associated with protecting the peasants, and in their concern for small businessmen were rated below any other party, including the PCF.[74] Few things better illustrate the nature of the new political environment than that a party thought to be so little concerned with any particular class or interest could achieve such success.

Perhaps most striking of all, however, were IFOP's findings in January 1968 when they asked voters which of three (specified) reasons were most important in leading people to vote Communist (see table 8.3).[75] Thus ten years into the Fifth Republic less

TABLE 8.3. Motivation of the Communist Vote, 1968

|  | *PCF* voters | *FGDS (SFIO+Left Rad.)* voters | *All* voters |
|---|---|---|---|
| Because they want the establishment of a Communist regime in France | 18 | 7 | 9 |
| Because the PCF represents a useful opposition force | 35 | 27 | 18 |
| To express a general discontent | 38 | 52 | 45 |
| No response | 9 | 14 | 28 |
|  | 100 | 100 | 100 |

than one-fifth of the Party's own voters and only one in fourteen of other Left voters associated the Party with its avowed positive goal. It was stuck – and seen to be struck – with its tribunitial role.

## vi OUT OF THE GHETTO – SLOWLY

The post-Thorez leadership of the PCF were aware of the need for change. The coming of the Fifth Republic had destroyed the real basis of the tribune role, for the PCF could not hope to paralyse *this* system. It could muster all the tribunitial fury it liked, but the rulers of the new Republic could afford to ignore them, almost serenely. The Party's impotence in the face of the 1958 Gaullist coup was now endlessly, institutionally replicated. Even Thorez had, after all, effectively accepted this lesson by his new enthusiasm for alliance with the SFIO after 1958.

The leadership could see, too, that the PCF failed to fill the new requirements of Fifth Republic Opposition. It was uneasily aware of the weakness of the Party's 'national' credentials. Its attachment to the Soviet Union meant that it was widely regarded as the client of a foreign state, while its doctrine of proletarian dictatorship and general *ouvrierisme* disqualified it from a national appeal beyond the confines of the working-class ghetto. Even its own voters hardly associated it with the 'national issues' the new regime had made centrally relevant . . . And here was the special rub: its own electorate showed every sign of accepting at least some of the norms of the new system, too. The PCF could not even feel secure in the belief that it could always fall back on its proletarian hard core, for the working-class was increasingly determined to climb out of its *own* ghetto . . .

The PCF was, from the first, deeply troubled that these weaknesses might produce a humiliating dénouement for a Communist candidate in the (archetypically 'national') contest for the presidency of the Republic. In 1965, apparently on the personal decision[76] of Waldeck-Rochet in his first year as leader, the PCF effectively acknowledged these deficiencies when it supported Mitterrand rather than put up its own presidential candidate.

In retrospect it is easy to see that this step was the greatest single tactical mistake made by the PCF since the war, for the Party had wholly failed to appreciate the dynamics of popular frontism in a presidential Republic. Faced with a contest for control of the supreme national executive office, the PCF had simply absented itself. It thereby simultaneously legitimated the giving of top priority to the achievement of the broadest possible front against Gaullism – and the notion that its own leadership was a handicap to such a front. Instead it conceded implicitly that even the pitiful rump of the non-Communist Left and a compromised politician from the bad old days had a better claim than they to lead a national opposition. The better Mitterrand did in this great national confrontation, the more the question was posed as to why analogous tactics should not be appropriate to every lesser contest. If the PCF was serious about wanting the Left to take power, why not accept Socialist leadership in every legislative constituency too? The satisfying result of the 1965 campaign suggested that the Left could mount its most effective challenge if the PCF absented itself even from the first ballot . . . Moreover, to draw back from such tactics now would be difficult. Should the PCF enter its own presidential candidate in future (other than in hopeless contests, such as that of 1969) then it would be extremely vulnerable to the charge that it did not really want to put the Left in power.

It was, however, only with the 1967 elections that the PCF began to sense its danger. Quite as alarming as the disproportionate gains then scored by Mitterrand's FGDS were the signs that voters were beginning to apply new rules to the electoral game. Young voters in particular were seen to behave at the first ballot as if it were the second, plumping indiscriminately for the Left party with the best chance in any particular seat.[77] How long could it be before the same logic was applied by voters at national rather than constituency level?

The PCF now faced an insoluble conundrum. It could not stay in the ghetto. To do that would doom it to marginality and impotence. In the long run it might even prove suicidal, for its own working-class supporters – May 1968 was a fresh reminder – were not prepared to remain members of a sunken proletarian sub-culture forever. On the other hand, where better to go? The only real alternative was for the Party so to transform itself as to be able to provide credible leadership to a national opposition; that is, to establish its credentials – valid beyond its own ranks and superior even to those of the Socialists – as a party of broad democratic appeal. This was an extremely tall order. What made it taller still was that a lightning somersault towards the 'Italian model' – even were the leadership bold, agile and united enough to perform such a feat – would lack public credibility and engender formidable resistance from hard-liners within the PCF at every level. Moreover, as the Party was forced back electorally on to its traditional proletarian redoubts, it found itself ever more reliant on precisely those sections of the Party where Stalinist conservatism was strongest. Even when the Party took an essential and major step towards National Communism by condemning the Soviet invasion of Czechoslovakia in 1968, it had to endure the public spectacle of Thorez's widow resigning with bitter éclat from the Politburo. If it tried to go faster – and there was no leadership consensus to do so – it risked major internal disruption. The only thing to do was to try to perform the somersault – slowly . . .

Hence the Party's continuous but gradual evolution towards radical social democracy. In 1967 it had accepted the idea that it might play a part in a 'bourgeois' government with the Socialists; In 1968 it not merely condemned the Soviet Union over Czechoslovakia but issued its own Champigny Manifesto, committing itself to the peaceful, parliamentary road to Socialism via a stage of 'advanced democracy' (i.e. a government of the broad Left). In 1970 Marchais, effectively replacing Waldeck-Rochet as leader, accepted the idea of democratic alternation of governments – a promise, in effect, that the PCF would leave power if voted out. Having accepted the idea of the electoral road to Socialism, the Party now accepted the notion of an electoral road away from it, too . . . From this Marchais proceeded (at the PCF 20th Congress at Nanterre in 1972) to his celebrated call for a 'Union of the French people' behind a broad democratic front led by the PCF. The Party, he averred, had an 'open door' to elements far beyond the PCF's traditional electorate: to Catholics, small businessmen, the new middle classes, the technical intelligentsia, and so on. Such groups did not need to be nervous of the PCF's intentions, which were now nothing less nor more than the wholesale democratisation of French society. Socialism remained the ultimate goal, though only after an extensive period of reform: 'we mustn't be afraid to use the word "reform" '.[78] Marchais's signature of the Common Programme in June 1972 carried the process a stage further: the PCF was now prepared to accept the PS/MRG as full and equal comrades in struggle – and to tie the Party to concrete proposals such as the nationalisation of particular industries, which previously it had always shied away from as mere 'reformism'.

In the context of the PCF's history such changes were sweeping, rapid and revolutionary (perhaps more accurately 'counter-revolutionary'), but they still left the Party a very long way short of its goal. After much effort and fanfare the Party had merely brought to birth a series of promises which, after all, a Socialist could have acceded to quite effortlessly at any time in the last fifty years. Moreover, the retention in the Party's constitution of the ultimate aim of proletarian dictatorship and its advance to its new position as a disciplined, monolithic bloc did little to enhance its democratic credentials amongst floating voters. But the Party could hardly go faster. The expulsion in 1970 of Roger Garaudy, the Politburo's main spokesman in the Marxism-Catholicism dialogue and the leading herald of revolution through the new intelligentsia, had shown how strong conservative elements still were amongst the leadership. Marchais could congratulate himself on having led a united PCF thus far thus fast, but he could be satisfied with the pace of change only while the Party's ancient rivals, the Socialists, were standing still. The problem was they weren't.

## vii THE SOCIALIST RENAISSANCE

The new conditions of the Fifth Republic had posed difficult, if lesser, problems for the Socialists. It was not hard to list the attributes necessary to a successful opposition party in the new Republic, or to see that the SFIO lacked almost all of them. Such a party would have to provide a real counterbalance to the broad appeal of Gaullism; it would have to be a party of programmatic principle, offering a clear and workable alternative government; it would have to be able to join battle with the Gaullists even on the loftiest issues of national interest; and it would need an attractive leadership to pose a fresh alternative to the General's magnetic appeal.

The SFIO of the 1960s, an aging and dwindling band tagging along behind Guy Mollet and a handful of municipal bosses left over from the Fourth Republic, was plainly not such a party. It was too small and weak to offer any real counterweight to Gaullism, it had few discoverable principles, and its leadership had an unenviable reputation for time-serving opportunism. Mollet, in particular, was a dead weight, for his government's disastrous colonial adventures in Suez and Algeria had not been forgotten. Indeed, De Gaulle's very success in decolonising Algeria meant that Mollet's unhappy period of office, far from fading into mellow memory, came to seem all the more starkly embarrassing and indefensible. Mollet failed the very first test of an opposition leader, for it was not even very clear which side he was finally on. He had vowed never to accept De Gaulle back in power in 1958, had then served in his government, and by 1960 was again voicing his undying opposition to Gaullism. His attitude to the PCF was simply the other side of this coin: principled hostility when he could afford it, tactical alliance with it when he couldn't.

The phenomenal rise to prominence of François Mitterrand was based on a shrewd recognition of this analysis – and its limits. Mitterrand's strategy was based on the assumption that while this catalogue of difficulties meant that the SFIO as such was probably beyond salvation, there was still a large potential reservoir of support for a non-Communist Left alternative to Gaullism. Disregarding the old SFIO truisms represented by Defferre, Mitterrand realised, moreover, that while it was probably impossible to mobilise such a bloc *against* the organised hostility of the PCF, it might be possible to generate – essentially by the new Bonapartism of a plebiscitary presidency – a broad Left coalition within which the PCF might be a minority and would certainly be a prisoner. In the short run such an alliance was, in any case, the only means of constructing an opposition bloc of credible size.

Mitterrand's emergence provided an answer to many of the problems of the non-Communist Left. He was not associated with the discredited SFIO, having, instead, headed the CIR. By comparison with the old SFIO leadership of Mollet and Defferre he was even a 'new man' of sorts. Second, he was able, not altogether fairly, to take the lion's share of the credit for the creation of a united Left. It was he who brought the CIR into the Left grouping in 1965; it was he who assembled the broader grouping of the Left Radicals with the SFIO in the FGDS and UGSD; it was he who insisted, against Defferre, on the inclusion of the PCF in the Left; and, above all, it was he who had symbolised the unity of the Left in his own person in the presidential campaign of 1965 and, later, 1974. Thus while the PCF in the 1930s had drawn great advantage from having provided the driving force for the Left unity of the Popular Front, in the Fifth Republic it was Mitterrand and, later, the PS which was the principal beneficiary of the *dynamique unitaire*. Third, Mitterrand was shrewd enough to realise that, having embarked on this direction, the non-Communist Left would have to follow it through in a consistent and thoroughgoing manner. Whatever the dangers of conceding to the PCF's demand for a Common Programme, it was still desirable so to concede in order that the Left might offer some semblance of an alternative government. Similarly, the temptation to 'sell out' to the Centre-Right, however tempting the terms, must be resisted. For nothing could be more disastrous in the long run than to bid for power without a platform or to make compromising 'deals'. The Left must be a principled opposition, must at all costs avoid replicating the behaviour which had so discredited the SFIO. If the logic and good faith of the unitary strategy required Socialists to evict their Centrist allies from municipal coalitions and invite the PCF in their place, it must be done (as, in 1977, it finally was), however painful the operation. Indeed, as became clear after 1974, the strategy had to extend even to turning the other cheek to PCF hostility. The alliance must be seen to be a genuine marriage, for better or worse, in sickness and in health – not a shifty, shifting backroom deal. To be sure, Mitterrand's emergence as a man of principle surprised many who had a clear memory of the Fourth Republic, but he could at least boast that, unlike Mollet and Defferre (though in company with Mendès-France), he had taken an entirely consistent line of opposition to the Fifth Republican regime. He had called for a popular front against De Gaulle's takeover in 1958 and thereafter never ceased to advocate such a strategy.

The potential of this strategy was made clear in the 1965 presidential election and even more in the 1967 legislative election. In 1965 Mitterrand received first-ballot support only from SFIO and PCF voters, with the bulk of the Radicals rallying to him only at the second ballot. In 1967, however, his FGDS clearly received majority

Radical support even at the first ballot.[79] Moreover, even by 1966 it was clear that the FGDS had achieved a broader appeal over a wider social range than the SFIO, had a more 'national' image, and was less locked in by the confines of the old anti-clerical quarrel than either the SFIO or the Radicals.[80]

The multiple disasters of 1968–9 obscured the promise of Mitterrand's strategy but did not destroy it. By 1971, having captured the leadership of the new PS from Savary at the Epinay Congress, Mitterrand was able to assume the same strategic line, now with the added advantage of a complete personal and organisational dominance within French Socialism such as he could never enjoy while Mollet's SFIO survived. His efforts were soon attended by such prodigious success that it has become customary to date the Socialist revival from Epinay (June 1971), a habit which attributes the sole credit for this development to the change of leadership.

The progress achieved by the PS under Mitterrand was indeed so rapid and so striking that one may legitimately question whether such a judgement does not concede too far to a 'Great Men of History' approach. Certainly, much of our preceding discussion – of the decline of the religious cleavage, of the yawning gap left by the departure of De Gaulle, and of the fresh working-class push towards egalitarian social integration – suggests that a moment of great opportunity had arrived for a reformist Socialist Party, a notion at least partly borne out by the 1971 municipal election results.[81] It is worth pointing out, too, that the old SFIO electorate, diminutive as it was, constituted in embryo just the sort of socially diverse following on which a new 'catch-all' party (in the conditions of the Fifth Republic, a clear recipe for success) could most easily be built. Then, too, the rejuvenation of the party apparatus which became such a striking feature of the PS under Mitterrand was in fact merely a continuation of a process for which Savary must take most credit.[82]

Luck and circumstance also played a part. From Epinay the PS could look forward with pleasurable anticipation to the virtual certainty of large gains in 1973: the Right could hardly hope to repeat its 1968 sweep. Pompidou's ill-fated decision to call the April 1972 referendum proved, in the end, an unhoped-for bonus for the Left. The successes of 1973 were followed by the further windfall of a presidential election two years before it was due. Thereafter the PS lived in a permanent state of electoral mobilisation through the 1976 cantonal, 1977 municipal and 1978 legislative elections. The party was forged in a mood of excited optimism, engendered by this long string of unbroken electoral successes.

It is, none the less, difficult to overestimate Mitterrand's contribution. Whatever the ambiguities attaching to his reputation, he was still a household name enjoying a wide measure of political acceptability across the whole spectrum of the Left. The strategy of Left unity was the only one which showed any sign of working, and it was his. Had the PS remained under Savary there would have been no Common Programme and nor could the Left have mounted such a formidable challenge to Giscard in 1974. Moreover, having taken over the PS, Mitterrand worked assiduously to unite and rebuild the party. Under Savary party membership had continued to drop – from 70,000 in the SFIO at its demise to 60,869 PS members at Epinay.[83] Under Mitterrand the trend was reversed. By June 1973 PS membership had reached at least 110,000[84]. By October 1974 it stood at 146,000,[85] by the end of 1977 164,000[86] and by 1978 approached 200,000. After Epinay the party's youth and student groups were rebuilt, and strong though still informal links established with the CFDT. Moreover, the PS began to give the PCF quite unaccustomed competition in the sphere of workplace organisation. By late 1971, 94 PS *sections d'entreprise* had been set up; by September 1973 there were 253 such *sections*; by April 1974 707; by mid-1976 1,000, with a target of 1,500 for mid-1977.[87]

The party's expansion also saw the process of rejuvenation continued down to grassroots level, for while Savary had pushed young men into leading positions within the party organisation, the mass membership had remained strikingly old. In 1970, indeed, 40 per cent of the membership had been aged over sixty and 77 per cent over forty.[88] By 1973 these figures were down to 23.9 per cent and 62.9 per cent respectively.[89] The party was thus still relatively old, but the balance had shifted. Almost certainly the continuing expansion of 1974–8 left the party reflecting fairly accurately the age structure of the electorate as a whole – and even by 1973 the 'generation of '68' was overrepresented in PS ranks.[90] The party's political centre of gravity, as also its image, were considerably younger than its age-profile suggested. In effect the PS inherited a large bloc of SFIO old-age pensioners and middle-aged men, on to which corpus it grafted a whole new generation to whom Socialism meant the PS, not the SFIO, and who furnished the party with its distinctive new tone. Thus, despite the party's still elderly profile in 1973, analysis of the delegates to the party's 1973 Grenoble Congress revealed that 31 per cent were under thirty and 58 per cent under forty.[91] Similarly, a majority of the UGSD candidates in the 1973 election had never stood before and forty-three of the eventual eighty-nine UGSD deputies were new faces in Parliament.[92] In 1978 the PS again had a higher proportion of new deputies than any other party[93] and was also the youngest party in Parliament.

The party apparatus exhibited the same characteristics. By late 1977 its full-time paid staff at PS headquarters had expanded to ninety, of whom twenty were hangovers from SFIO days (some even from Third Republic days), but with the rest recruited since Epinay.[94] The party still had at this level a heavy personalist aspect, with Mitterrand's personal *cabinet* enjoying an importance hard to imagine in a better-established party of the Left:

> It is a case of a party whose cement is still largely provided by loyalty to the line taken by its first Secretary, and the organisation of the national headquarters eloquently institutionalises his indisputable pre-eminence at every level. There is, to be sure, a double circuit of legitimacy within the socialist *apparat*. But in the day-to-day affairs of the party it is the one which is based on François Mitterrand's trust that appears to be dominant.[95]

Mitterrand sought to emancipate the PS from the dead hand of the SFIO by the adoption of a distinctive and radical slogan-cum-strategy, the *front de classe*, which served as the party's new self-definition. The party's essential aim, both of itself and via its union with the PCF, was to assemble a broad front of all those exploited by capitalism against the Fifth Republican regime (which it regarded as virtually synonymous with monopoly capitalism). The class intended was not, however, simply the industrial proletariat (the traditional PCF view), but consisted of all wage and salary-earners, artisans and small and middle peasants. Inevitably, there was an electoralist tendency for the already vague concept of class thus implied to be broadened yet further to include the middle classes and small and middle-sized business, for 'they too [are] victims of capitalist concentration'.[96] Indeed, by 1974 Mitterrand was defining the *front* negatively in terms of the two groups who 'cannot become socialists: the exploiters and all those who, despite their exploited social situation and economic position, continue, for cultural, sentimental, or traditional reasons, to preserve and maintain the structures of capitalist domination'.[97]

In case such appeals smacked too openly of the old electoral opportunism of the SFIO, Mitterrand was at pains to make it clear that small and middle businesses were not part of the class front, but could be made its defensive allies. The PS was not, he declared flatly, a 'catch-all' party.[98] Equally, while he claimed that the PS proudly exhibited all the signs of a 'great people's party', it was not to be regarded as an example of 'inter-classism', a concept which entailed 'a sort of confusion between the notion of class, to which we remain faithful, and the notion of mass, to which we are not insensitive, but which offers us nothing in terms of sociological or political explanation'.[99]

This careful squaring of the circle was essential if Mitterrand was to appeal to moderate Centrists and the old SFIO electorate and to retain the confidence of the new generation of PS militants. Many of the latter belonged to the 'class of '68'. They insisted on a *'socialisme autogestionnaire'* which would constitute a radical 'break with the system', with the 'errors of the past', and particularly with 'social democratic nostalgia'.[100] To reassure such spirits as these it was necessary continually to stress that the PS had nothing in common with the corrupt compromises of a Schmidt or Callaghan, let alone a Mollet. Such militants were instinctively hostile to the construction of the old SFIO dream, *'le rassemblement le plus large'*, and to such old SFIO habits as the *cumul des mandats*, the habit of acquiring a plurality of elected offices. Indeed, this major section of the party's membership entertained a lively distrust of all its deputies, not just the *députés-maires*. The latter, they suspected, saw the constitution of *sections d'entreprise* simply as a means for winning electoral gains among the workers from the PCF. For the militants such *sections* were intended to give concrete form to their emphasis on extra-electoral activity. For the young Turks the Union of the Left was equally of great doctrinal importance in itself – they were far more *unitaire* than their deputies, who saw the union as essentially a tactical electoral alliance.[101]

Mitterrand's disavowals notwithstanding, there was no doubt that even by 1973, and certainly by 1978, the PS had become an inter-class party *par excellence*. Indeed, the pre-election polls of 1978 showed how far the Gaullists – for twenty years *the* great inter-class party – had been overtaken in this role, with the PS showing a more even distribution of support in every category – see Table 8.4. The anomaly of a party of the Left showing a sociological profile distinctly similar to that of Gaullism in

TABLE 8.4 Structure of PS/MRG, RPR and total electorates, February 1978

|  | *All* | *PS/MRG* | *RPR* |
|---|---|---|---|
| Men | 48 | 51 | 43 |
| Women | 52 | 49 | 57 |
| 18–34 years | 35 | 43 | 28 |
| 35–49 years | 25 | 26 | 24 |
| 50–64 years | 20 | 18 | 24 |
| 65 and over | 20 | 13 | 24 |
| Professions, business and management | 14 | 12 | 22 |
| White-collar workers | 19 | 29 | 20 |
| Industrial workers | 32 | 34 | 16 |
| Peasants, farmworkers | 8 | 5 | 13 |
| Retired, not employed | 27 | 20 | 29 |
| Rural communes | 27 | 25 | 33 |
| Towns under 20,000 | 15 | 15 | 13 |
| Towns 20–100,000 | 13 | 14 | 11 |
| Towns 100,000 plus | 28 | 29 | 19 |
| Paris region | 17 | 17 | 24 |

*Source : Le Point*, no. 282, 13 February 1978.

its heyday[102] was further heightened if the composition of the PS membership itself was taken into account, for the fact was that at this level French Socialism had become a steadily more middle-class affair. See Table 8.5.

TABLE 8.5. Social composition of SFIO-PS membership, 1951–73

|  | *SFIO* 1951 | *PS* 1970 | *PS* 1973 |
|---|---|---|---|
| Business, professions, management | 3 | 16 | 20 |
| Lower-middle class | 53 | 61 | 61 |
| Workers | 44 | 23 | 19 |
|  | 100 | 100 | 100 |

*Source :* M. Kesselman, 'The Recruitment of Rival Party Activists in France', cited in P. Garraud, 'Discours, Pratique et Idéologie dans L'Evolution du Parti Socialiste', *Revue Française de Science Politique*, vol. 28, no. 2 (April 1978), p. 227. Kesselman's 'lower-middle class' includes peasants and white-collar workers. His study, though based on a small sample, is supported by all other known data.

Hardouin's detailed study of PS members in 1973 reveals that the party is even more heavily dominated by the teaching profession than was the SFIO of legend. Teachers of all kinds made up a staggering 13 per cent of the entire membership in 1973, but what sets the PS apart from the old SFIO model is that the most overrepresented group is not composed of schoolteachers but of university and other higher education teachers; noting, however, that students, technicians, liberal professionals and engineers are also heavily overrepresented, Hardouin concludes that while teachers still hold a special position, the 'principal element structuring the sociology of socialism' is membership in general of the intellectual elite.[103]

The PS in 1973, like the SFIO before it, was an overwhelmingly masculine party: 87 per cent of the members then were men, as compared to 88 per cent in the SFIO of 1951.[104] This characteristic was considerably modified during the party expansion of 1974, with feminine membership rising to around a quarter in some federations, notably in Paris.[105] Three-quarters of this new breed of socialist ladies were working women – there were hardly any housewives among the membership, in strong contradistinction to the PCF, which has successfully enrolled large numbers of working-class housewives.

The still heavy sexual imbalance within the PS must be taken into account when we note its chief departure from the old pattern of the SFIO, the weakness of its working-class membership. Hardouin's 1973 study found an industrial worker membership of only 17 per cent and a combined industrial and lower white-collar membership of less than one-third.[106] These proportions were even more striking when they were set against the overwhelmingly male bias of party membership, for the proportion of industrial workers in the male electorate as a whole is almost half. Similarly, the white-collar proportion of the male electorate is much lower than for the total electorate, making the white-collar predominance within the PS even more remarkable.[107]

These trends were more pronounced the higher up the party hierarchy one went. The *comité directeur* in 1973 was more than 96 per cent male and had not a single worker on it, while higher-education teachers were twenty-five times better represented at this level than they were within the membership as a whole.[108] Socialist deputies presented a similar picture. The PS parliamentary group elected in 1973 was notably more upper class than the old SFIO group elected in 1968. Over 40 per cent of deputies were teachers or lecturers, and this category, together with those from upper management and the liberal professions, made up 82 per cent. Among the 104 deputies of the non-Communist Left elected in 1973 there was not a single worker.[109] The same was true of the 114 PS and MRG deputies elected in 1978, whose ranks included only 1 lower and 8 middle-level white-collar workers and a solitary peasant. Of the PS-MRG deputies elected that year, 85 per cent came from the ranks of teachers, lecturers, other professions, business and upper management (primarily in the civil service).[110]

The PS was self-conscious about its deficiencies in regard to women in a way the SFIO had never been. At its Suresnes Congress in 1974 a 10 per cent minimum quota was laid down for the representation of women at every level of the party organisation, and at its Nantes Congress in 1977 this was raised to 15 per cent. The repair of the even more serious deficiency in working-class membership (something the SFIO had not needed to worry about) was left to the new initiative of the *sections d'entreprise*.

These hopes were not fulfilled. The intention that the PS should gain its equivalent of the PCF's workplace cells was not realised, for 70 per cent of the *sections* set up by 1974 were merely groups of party members in the same factory or office without any real corporate identity. Only 30 per cent were proper party *sections* with their own internal life and a vote at party congresses.[111] Cayrol's analysis of the *sections d'entreprise* (SE) in April 1976 showed that only 21 per cent of their members were industrial workers, the overwhelming majority being middle and upper white-collar and managerial workers in large enterprises in the public sector – the traditional redoubts of non-Communist trade unionism.[112] While the PCF has always enjoyed its greatest strength among the under thirties, over 70 per cent of the SE members were aged over thirty.[113] In terms of union membership, 52 per cent of the SE members belonged to the CFDT, 30 per cent to the CGT and 6 per cent to the FO: pretty clearly the SEs derived much of their vitality from a pre-existing nucleus of CFDT-PSU militants. This impression is strengthened both by the fact that 19 per cent of SE members were practising Catholics and 17 per cent former PSU members. This was by far the most important source of previous political affiliation among SE members – only 5 per cent had previously belonged to the PCF and 70 per cent had belonged to no party prior to joining the PS.[114] Perhaps most striking of all was the fact that only 14 per cent had joined the PS prior to 1970 and only 34 per cent prior to 1973.[115] Two-thirds had joined during the PS's great electoral wave of 1973–6. It seems likely that most of them came to socialism as voters first and were then assembled into workplace groups, rather than their political commitment stemming from workplace experience.

Thus perhaps the most striking characteristic of the PS, probably the leading party of the Left quite continuously from 1974 on, was its weak and shallow roots in the industrial working-class. With the electoral wind in its sails and when it enjoyed the benevolent neutrality of the PCF, the PS was able to pull in many working-class voters behind it. In 1973, for example, its share of the working-class vote, 18 per cent in 1967 and 1968, jumped in a single bound to 27 per cent.[116] But it enrolled few workers as party members and had no use for them in leadership positions when it did. Its *sections d'entreprise* allowed the PS to talk boldly of its participation in the wider social life and struggles of the classes whose *front* it claimed to be, but this was mainly a sham. The PS was, first and last, an electoralist party. Elections were what it was good at and what it was preoccupied with; what aided its rebirth, what enabled it to grow:

> Despite the progressive emergence of new forms of action, the PS seems hardly capable of true mobilisation at the moment. Compared to its adaptation to the institutional political game, the Party's participation in struggles in the workplace and over living conditions is meagre. When it exists, such participation is far more a matter of what isolated militants do than of a coherent line of action pursued by the Party. In most cases the PS is content merely to support and popularise such struggles in order to gain credit for them.
>
> Thus, despite its numerous references to popular mobilisation and to social struggles, the PS possesses a limited capacity for mobilisation. The major part of its interventions are situated at a symbolic level . . . The strategy consists most often in 'affirming the presence of the Party . . .'[117]

This weakness was hardly noticed in the upward swing of the PS in 1973–7. It was, though, to be of crucial importance in 1977–8, when the PS was forced to confront the furious hostility of the party that did have real and deep roots in the working-class, the PCF.

# PART THREE

The Ides of March – 1978

# 9 Towards the Ides of March

## i THE PCF IN THE 1970S: DEFENSIVE MOBILISATION

The rise of the PS took the PCF by surprise. In a sense the 1968 Events had led the Party off on a false track, for they created the impression that the greatest threat to the PCF on the Left came from the *gauchistes* of the PSU and the Trotskyite groups. The trauma of seeing these elements gain the initiative in the massive strike wave of that year was too deep to pass quickly. The *gauchistes* were a continuing nuisance in the factories, in their questioning of the Party's revolutionary credentials, and in their seduction of significant numbers of energetic young militants of precisely the type the Party had always relied on. Moreover, for all their disavowals of electoralism, the extreme Left groups were stealing PCF votes. In 1962 the Far Left had received 2.4 per cent, and in 1967 2.2 per cent. In 1968 it jumped to 3.9 per cent – while the PCF lost 2.5 per cent. In 1969 Rocard and Krivine between them took 4.8 per cent of the vote and almost certainly cost Duclos a place in the second ballot – with only two-fifths of the votes they took he would have led Poher. In 1973 and 1978 the far Left stuck at 3.2 per cent – ten years on from 1968 they were still 1 per cent above their 1967 level, a fact clearly not unconnected with the PCF's failure quite to return to *its* 1967 level.

Ironically, the PCF's fury at the *gauchistes*, who in the long run were to pose no real threat to it, contrasted with their manner of positive solicitude towards the PS – who were soon to pose a major threat. The first warning signs of the PS advance came in 1972, when the PCF fell behind it in the polls for the first time. It is doubtful whether the Party leadership had to wait upon the pollsters of IFOP and SOFRES to learn of these new stirrings in the Left electorate. Besides possessing a quite unrivalled grassroots organisation which provides a comprehensive net for the gathering and transmission of such intelligence, the Party had long been an adept, sophisticated and well-heeled user of polling resources. Certainly, Marchais both knew enough, and was sufficiently alarmed by what he had learnt, to present a report to the PCF Central Committee in June 1972 on the possible dangers to the Party of its collaboration with the PS.

It seems likely that Marchais, in presenting such a report just as the PCF was, at his urging, signing the Common Programme, was attempting to cover himself from the growing criticism of the Politburo hard-liners, led by Roland Leroy.[1] Leroy, though Marchais's junior by six years, had climbed the PCF hierarchy very much in tandem with him. They had both been handpicked by Thorez as leadership recruits in 1959–60 as potential replacements for the already troublesome Servin and Casanova.

They had then both earned their spurs (particularly the tough and enthusiastic Leroy) in their mission to force these recalcitrants to the alternatives of expulsion or confession and complete submission. Marchais could not but be aware of Leroy as a powerful conservative presence moving up just behind him, particularly since the succession to the (incurably) ailing Waldeck-Rochet had not yet been completely settled. Marchais had been the *de facto* PCF leader since 1969–70 but in June 1972 still only carried the title of Acting Secretary-General. Given this constraint he had made bold use of his power, carrying forward Waldeck-Rochet's more liberal policies all the way to the conclusion of the Common Programme with the PS. To do this he had had to overcome not inconsiderable conservative reservations – it is even possible that the PCF's tough line over the EEC referendum and the sudden publication of a new PCF programme in 1971[2] represented Politburo attempts to sabotage the negotiations in advance. If, after all this, the Common Programme were to work to the PCF's disadvantage Marchais's still tenuous hold on power would come under heavy pressure. Should the Politburo decide he was leading them to disaster it could simply thank him for his work as regent and elect Leroy in his place . . .

Marchais's report was thus probably intended to reassure the Politburo that it was not being led by a French Dubcek, hell-bent on liberal popular frontism whatever the consequences. If so, the gambit was successful. The Common Programme was duly signed and in December 1972 Marchais was confirmed as the new Secretary-General. (Waldeck-Rochet was kicked upstairs into the honorary presidency of the Party.) Significantly, however, Marchais's report was suppressed from publication, probably at Marchais's behest. (It was ultimately released in July 1975.) The month of the signature of the Common Programme was hardly an auspicious moment to advertise the leadership's doubts as to the correctness of its own strategy. The result was that the PCF rank and file were left to continue the work of building a popular front in an atmosphere of enthusiasm bordering on euphoria. The Politburo conservatives doubtless winced at the sight of Party militants going to great lengths to show comradeship for their PS partners (during the 1973 election campaign one actually encountered cases of PCF canvassers helping direct Socialist voters as to how best to contact the (less energetic) PS organisation in order to enrol as members!).

When the PS almost drew level with the PCF on the 1973 first ballot, Communist posters for the second ballot gave a hint of things to come, warning voters that only the PCF could actually be trusted to carry out the Common Programme. But neither this nor the actual election result resolved the Politburo's quandary. For while the PS had taken a great stride ahead, it *had* fallen back from the lead the polls had earlier given it over the PCF; and the PCF had gained *some* votes. What was clear was that the popular front was not yet working in the way the Politburo had hoped, bringing back to the PCF the great droves of voters it had lost in 1958 and 1968. (So much depended on that 'not yet'.) Instead, most such voters had in effect made a lengthy detour via the Gaullist and Centre parties en route to their new home, the PS. As a result the Left was certainly gaining – but with most of the profits going to the Socialists. True, there was no evidence that the Socialists were making any direct gains from the PCF, but even this might follow if the PS achieved a future supremacy on the Left. On the other hand, the Common Programme had only just been signed and the idea of turning back from the strategy the Party had pursued for years at the very moment of its achievement was unthinkable. What alternative was there to soldiering on in the hope that soon the popular front would begin to work 'properly'? Meanwhile the Party would have to consider very carefully its options for the next presidential election . . . If the PS continued to advance and the PCF to stagnate the Party might need to prepare some pretext for putting up its own candidate again. At the least the Party would use the threat of such a candidacy to exert crippling leverage over Mitterrand in the long run-up period.

Pompidou's sudden death in April 1974 foreshortened the run-up period to a bare month. The PCF had no option but immediate and virtually unconditional[3] support for Mitterrand. Indeed, ironically, the Party's organisational solidity and the popular front euphoria of its voters meant that the PCF gave Mitterrand much better support than his own PS did. On the first ballot 93 per cent of Communist electors voted for Mitterrand, and on the second ballot 97 per cent did. For the less-disciplined Socialist electorate the comparable figures were only 85 per cent and 90 per cent.[4] None the less, the results showed how alarmingly far the situation had slipped out of the PCF's control. In 1965 Communist votes had made up around two-thirds of Mitterrand's first-ballot support; in 1974 they made up less than half of it.[5] For the first time it seemed clear that the leader of the non-Communist Left could beat a PCF candidate on the first round if one were put up, and then 'force' Communist voters to choose him as the only Left candidate on the second round. Mitterrand, by reversing Defferre's strategy, was in sight of Defferre's objective . . .

Within a few months the PCF's nightmare began to take shape. The polls showed Mitterrand not merely holding his second-ballot support but actually leading Giscard in a (simulated) re-run of the presidential race. By July 1974 SOFRES polls were showing the PCF merely holding its 1973 level of support at 21 per cent, while the PS/MRG soared ahead to 27 per cent. Thereafter the gap steadily widened, with the PS/MRG receiving a stable 28–31 per cent bloc of support while the PCF languished at 19–21 per cent.[6] In autumn 1974 a series of six by-elections showed that this extraordinary turnaround was no mere figment of the pollsters' imagination. Everywhere the PCF vote fell while the PS vote soared. Moreover, the Politburo noted bitterly, while PCF voters were flocking out enthusiastically to vote Socialist at the second ballot, PS voters were notably less infused with the *dynamique unitaire* and many were still refusing to vote for a Communist at the run-off. It was now only too clear how disastrous Pompidou's sudden death had been to the Party, how dearly it was to pay for having vacated the presidential arena to Mitterrand on the one hand and Arlette Laguiller, the impressive young Trotskyite leader, on the other. Both their movements, the PS and *Lutte Ouvrière* (LO), now drew steady advantage from the continuing effect of the presidential coat-tails of May 1974. (LO now pulled sharply ahead of all the other far Left groups, easily displacing the PSU—*Front Autogestionnaire* from its leading position on the far Left in 1978.) By absenting itself from this supremely critical contest the PCF had risked becoming *le grand muet* of French politics. Now it was paying the price.

This situation was deeply injurious to the Party's sense of pride, so strongly developed in its long role as the defiant tribune; for the Party had acclimatised only too well to the political ghetto. It had stood isolated and outcast; self-enclosed and suspicious; bitterly hostile to the whole established order. It gave no favours and certainly expected none. It was furiously independent of all other French parties. It was not lightly brooked, knew it, and treasured the fact. Its solace was its strength. The new dynamics of the Fifth Republican system had led it to quit the ghetto – but now only to find its primacy threatened, to find itself in danger of being taken for granted, humiliatingly marginalised. It felt strong contradictory impulses. Its hard-liners, led by Leroy, felt bitterly that their criticisms of the Party's new ways had been vindicated. They had abandoned Thorez's heritage only with reluctance and were inclined to feel that, if the ship were to go down, at least it should do so under its own (old) flag and with all guns firing. They – and not only they – longed with a deep nostalgia for the unhappy security of the ghetto. The more reformist elements grouped around Marchais were increasingly demoralised, but recognised, bleakly, that the Party had had to leave the ghetto. There could be no easy road back and it would, in any case, be a road to nowhere. There was no alternative to pressing on.

But more than pride was involved. The PCF was only too well aware of the likely fate of a Western Communist Party which falls behind its Socialist competitor – it had seen the Dutch, Belgian and Scandinavian parties slide from their post-war peaks into a wasting marginality and impotence. It had seen even the German Communist Party [the KPD], for long the strongest Communist Party in Europe, gradually relegated to the status of a sect by the onward march of the Social Democrats [the SPD]. Such, it feared, might be its own fate if the gap between itself and the PS was not closed. In the long term nothing less than survival was at stake. PCF leaders always returned, as if mesmerised, to Mitterrand's frank statement (at the Socialist International) of his party's ambitions: 'Our fundamental objective is to rebuild a great socialist party on the terrain occupied by the Communist Party itself, and thus to show that of the five million Communist voters, three million can be brought to vote socialist.'[7] It was a speech the PCF never forgot. Perhaps unwisely goaded by criticisms of his alliance with the Communists made by other European socialists, Mitterrand had succinctly stated their own nightmare – a Communist party reduced to a bare rump, perhaps finally competing only on equal terms with the Trotskyite fractions.

The PCF's fear of such a fate ran deep. But even worse might follow: once Mitterrand had reduced the PCF and had its electorate in tow what was to stop him heeling sharply to the Right? He was under enormous pressure to do so from other European socialists, particularly the wealthy German SPD, with whose leaders Mitterrand was, in PCF eyes, a sight too friendly. (Across the whole spectrum of the Left there were persistent rumours of large SPD subsidies flowing into PS coffers in return for such a deal.) In any case, Mitterrand was locked in a critical battle with Giscard for the handful of Centrist votes which had been so decisive in 1974 and would doubtless be as crucial again. The PS's strongly left-wing line had served to bring the party in sight of victory. Now it had reached that point larger ambitions and different priorities came into play.

It was thus with a strong feeling of chagrin that the PCF watched Mitterrand organise with great fanfare the *Assises du Socialisme* at Nantes in October 1974, a sort of extraordinary congress of the non-Communist Left. Held in the wake of the shattering autumn by-elections, the *Assises* were a thinly disguised celebration of the historic return to Socialist supremacy on the Left – and a stage-managed consecration of the presidential Mitterrand. Amidst the general euphoria generated by the *Assises* there was also a sharp tactical point, for among those accepting invitations to attend were Michel Rocard and most of the PSU leadership, together with leading elements of the CFDT. Rocard was a *bête noire* in PCF eyes, a principled anti-Communist who used the Leftist verbiage of *'autogestion'* to cover a position effectively to the Right of the PS mainstream. Thus while PSU militants had angrily dismissed the Common Programme as mere reformism, Rocard's own rejection of the nationalisations it envisaged was tempered with a respect for liberal market forces. At the conclusion of the *Assises* Rocard and most of the PSU leadership joined the PS – to the dismay of many PSU militants (who saw it as a sell-out) and of the PCF (who noted that the *Assises* had adopted an *autogestion* plank but had had no reservation about welcoming into PS ranks a dangerous anti-Communist who continued to advertise his rejection of the Common Programme).

In PCF eyes it seemed clear that the *Assises* represented a cleverly camouflaged move to the Right by Mitterrand, who had used the occasion to show a new tone of hauteur and disdain towards his PCF partners. As threatening was the fact that the PS stood to gain yet further votes from Rocard's adhesion and that its cultivation of the CFDT might at last give it a union base to rival that provided for the PCF by the CGT. In January 1975 the full nature of the deal done at the *Assises* became clear at the PS Congress at Pau: the Leftist CERES faction were kicked out of the PS leadership and Rocard and his ex-PSU group took their place. CERES, whose support had been crucial to Mitterrand ever since his takeover of the PS at Epinay, cried foul: the *petite-bourgeoisie* was 'taking over the PS in the interests of German-American capital'. The PCF's feelings as it surveyed a PS leadership in which Mitterrand sat flanked by its bitterest foes – Rocard, Mauroy and Defferre – were similar but less printable.

Just before the Pau Congress Marchais was hospitalised by a coronary stroke. But Marchais's problems were not merely medical. To counter the *Assises* the PCF had held an extraordinary congress at Vitry in October 1974 – at which the Leroy faction was clearly dominant. Marchais now had cause to regret that he had gone out of his way to sing Mitterrand's praises during the presidential campaign, for the congress had vented considerable criticism of the PS and its leader and adopted a strong resolution accusing the PS of a rightward shift. Most significant of all was the congress's decision to dismiss the editor of *L'Humanité* (in effect for being too liberal – a clear slap at Marchais, on whom final responsibility for the Party's main mouthpiece inevitably rested). The new editor was ... Roland Leroy, who immediately used the paper to launch bitter attacks on the policies and personalities of the PS, particularly Mitterrand's main economic adviser, Jacques Attali. By December Marchais himself felt constrained to join in, authoring three *L'Humanité* articles attacking the PS. To the general incomprehension of the Left electorate at large, the PCF's anti-Socialist campaign continued strongly into 1975, culminating in July in the publication, at last, of Marchais's 1972 report on the PS 'danger'. War – of a sort – had begun.

Towards autumn 1975 there were clear signs of an abatement in the PCF campaign and a reassertion of the 'liberal' current. In May Marchais introduced a new policy document enunciating the PCF's undying attachment to the full panoply of civil liberties. While averring that Communists had always stood for freedom of religion, association, the press, and so forth, he admitted implicitly that the Party had been wrongly reticent on the subject due to a mistaken deference to the Soviet Union. This was now to be put right. In October Marchais proceeded to the acid test of such convictions, issuing a statement condemning the USSR's treatment of political dissidents. In December this was followed by a Politburo resolution condemning Soviet labour camps – an issue of great resonance in France, where it had provided the *casus belli* between the PCF and intellectuals such as Sartre almost thirty years before. The PCF attitude then had, of course, been that to admit of blemishes as great as this within the Soviet system could imply nothing less than (unthinkable) rejection of the Soviet model as a whole. Now, clearly, the PCF was nerving itself to slaughter even this sacred cow.

Finally, Marchais announced that at the 22nd PCF Congress, to be held at Saint Ouen in February 1976, he would propose the deletion from the Party constitution of the historic commitment to the 'dictatorship of the proletariat'. (His prior announcement effectively foreclosed the issue, of course.) With this the break with Soviet orthodoxy (and the PCF's own past) became explicit and irreparable, a fact which Marchais proudly championed by insisting that the PCF would construct a *'socialisme aux couleurs de la France'*. French Communists would build their own sort of socialism because they, as patriotic Frenchmen, were alone capable of judging what was appropriate to French conditions; and because they could not rely on the USSR anyway, for the Soviet Union appeared to believe that peaceful co-existence implied the maintenance in perpetuity of the existing social and economic *status quo* in Western Europe. By this point the question had become simply one of whether the abattoirs could cope with the veritable herd of consecrated beasts queueing at their doors. On the whole the PCF rank and file loved it.

Throughout this period a lively tension continued between the PCF and PS. The moderation of the PCF's anti-Socialist campaign to a level of routine condemnation of Rightist tendencies – together with these sweeping changes in PCF doctrine – led many to believe, however, that Marchais's more liberal faction[8] had regained its ascendancy in the Politburo over Leroy's hard-liners.[9] At the same time it was noted that the anti-Socialist campaign was effectively suspended during the run-up to the March 1976 cantonal elections and the March 1977 municipal elections, thus enabling the Left to present a united front whenever it was electorally necessary to do so. These two assumptions together produced a certain complacency on the Left about the quarrel between its two leading parties. The Communists were making trouble; it was perfectly natural that they should do so – they couldn't expect to enjoy being overtaken by the PS; but in the end it wasn't serious: the PCF's liberal wing was more dominant than ever and would ensure that nothing would be done to diminish the *dynamique unitaire* in the run-up to the all-important 1978 legislative elections. If the anti-PS campaign could be put in cold storage for the sake of the (relatively trifling) cantonal elections, it would certainly be suspended before a contest when real national power was at stake. The sense of false security thus engendered on the Left was a major handicap to the PCF, which found even its most vehement attacks on the PS shrugged off as mere political muzak. It also meant that the public shock at the final explosive rupture of the Left in September 1977 was all the greater, leading many to conclude either that the Politburo hard-liners must have staged some sort of last-minute coup or that the Party was only happy in opposition and had intended all along to sabotage the Left's chances of coming to power.

The truth of the matter was, almost certainly, more complicated. The political fluidity of the Politburo and the nostalgia for the ghetto felt by at least some of its members should not be denied; but nor should the reality of the appetite for power of the post-Thorez generation or the underlying consistency of PCF strategy in this period. The fear of political marginalisation was, after all, shared by liberals and conservatives alike within the Politburo. The question was simply what to do to avert it.

The first possibility was to attack Mitterrand and the PS, thus preventing any further slippage of PCF voters their way. Such a line had several problems. To criticise Mitterrand for succeeding in what the PCF had hoped to do – that is, of taking uncomradely advantage of popular front enthusiasm to steal support from his partner – risked dismissal as mere electioneering and provided a demoralising advertisement of the Party's fears of impending redundancy. Moreover, to the extent that the campaign succeeded in halting the advance of the Left as a whole, the Party would attract all the damaging old charges of *misérabilisme* – that the PCF wanted the Left to lose in order to maintain the working-class in an alienated state and thus more receptive to Communist appeals. But the greatest weakness of such a line was that it was purely defensive. If the PCF wanted to compete successfully with the PS it would have to offer something more positive. Hence the inevitable and recurrent flux of influence back to the Politburo's liberal elements who alone had a vision of a second alternative, a democratic and national Eurocommunism. The hope was that this could constitute a real pole of counter-attraction to the PS. If, however, this strategy failed too, recourse to the first, more defensive strategy was always likely. The acid test would be the progress the Party made or failed to make by the time it reached the run-up to the 1978 elections. Those who believed that the Party was 'bound' to relax its anti-Socialist campaign prior to that crucial showdown failed to realise that the PCF was always bound to regard the 1978 contest in a very different light from those of 1976 and 1977; not despite the fact that real power was at stake, but precisely *because* it was.

The nature of the PCF response to the rising challenge of the PS provided the axis on which the whole of French politics turned in 1974–8. The apparent ambivalence of this response was due more to the fact that it attempted to deploy several strategies at once than because of any real doubt as to its objectives. From 1974 on the Party was, as it saw it, fighting for its life. In the last analysis this objective was always bound to have priority over that of a Left victory, but the PCF's fervent, even desperate hope was that it would not be forced to make such an invidious choice. Only by September 1977 did it realise that choose it must.

The PCF response fell into two halves: an ideological campaign which was largely a failure, and an organisational drive which was far more successful.

## ii IDEOLOGY: NATIONAL COMMUNISM AND THE GHOST OF THE SFIO

The ideological attack on the PS was based on a shrewd perception of Socialist strengths and weaknesses. Under Mitterrand the PS had successfully projected itself as a credible, responsible alternative to the ruling Majority, a party of broad social appeal and national objectives which was not the prisoner of any sectional interest. Mitterrand's genius lay in combining this 'national' image of the PS with a more sharply partisan appeal to the classic popular front electorate of the working and lower-middle classes. To such groups the PS appeared above all as a party whose principled commitment to Left unity provided the cornerstone of all their hopes of greater social justice, protection from the miseries of the post-1973 Depression, and the delightful prospect of evicting an arrogant Right from its long monopoly of power.

The PCF attacked on several fronts. It continually questioned the sincerity of the PS commitment to the Common Programme, suggesting that the old ghost of SFIO opportunism had been by no means exorcised. The PS, it pointed out, had, under a smokescreen of Leftist verbiage, been moving steadily to the Right ever since October 1974, when it had welcomed Rocard into its leadership despite his flat rejection of the Common Programme. In 1975 it had kicked CERES out of the PS Secretariat, putting its own left wing in limbo. Through 1974–7 Mitterrand had associated himself more and more closely with the 'social traitors' of the Socialist International – Wilson, Callaghan, Brandt and Schmidt – and he had openly boasted to them of his aim of weakening the PCF. The PS had accepted the International's condemnation of popular front governments in southern Europe and had even accepted a common European programme with them. Finally, at its Nantes Congress in June 1977, the PS had flatly refused all possibility of compromise with the PCF over the reshaping of the Common Programme – and had even entrusted Rocard, of all people, with responsibility for PS policy on the key question of the nationalisation of industry.

Second, the PCF accused Mitterrand of using the Union of the Left merely to promote his own (presidentialist) personality cult and overweening ambition. Such allusions had, inevitably, to be veiled – Mitterrand would, after all, head any future Left government in which the PCF might sit. Only in June 1977 did Marchais accuse

Mitterrand of attempting to become a new Bonaparte or De Gaulle: 'Personal power, providential men: truly, in France we've had enough of them.'[10]

Nothing, the PCF suggested, was clearer than that once in power the PS would 'sell out' – to the greater glory of Mitterrand, who would quickly become indistinguishable from a Callaghan, a Schmidt – or a Mollet. The only guarantee against this would be a strong PCF, able to force the PS to keep its word.

This analysis had the merits of containing a considerable degree of truth, of echoing what many PS militants feared in their bones, and of casting the PCF as more truly committed to unity and the Common Programme than the PCF. Such criticism would, the PCF hoped, either drive the PS to the left (accepting the PCF's moral leadership – and risking the loss of centrist votes) or push it further to the right (in which case it might lose its left wing to the PCF).

None the less, the tactic failed. Voters of the Left were not particularly concerned as to who Mitterrand met at international conclaves in Strasbourg or Dublin; anyway, it couldn't be too serious if the PCF had been able to overlook such faults right up to the 1977 municipal elections. As for a PS 'sell-out' in government, well the argument was only couched in the future conditional, wasn't it? It would be good enough to win at all ... As for Mitterrand, well hadn't the PCF itself told voters what a fine man he was in 1965 and again in 1974? The attack from the left simply failed to gain public credibility – and Mitterrand was far too shrewd to respond by moving conveniently to the right. He merely affirmed his commitment to the Common Programme (which was all the Left's voters wanted to hear), suggested good-naturedly that such obvious electioneering by the PCF did not prevent the Left from remaining a fundamentally united family – and otherwise loftily ignored their criticisms. This merely goaded the PCF's fears of marginalisation – and threw responsibility for disharmony squarely back on them. Meanwhile Mitterrand's personal stature and the scent of approaching victory were quite sufficient to preserve PS unity intact.

The second line of attack lay in accelerating the PCF's own development in a more 'national' and democratic direction. This was widely (mis)understood as meaning that the PCF, in company with Berlinguer's PCI and Carrillo's PCE, had suddenly become 'Eurocommunist'. Certainly, the shadow of the PCI's electoral success fell more and more heavily upon the PCF as it struggled to avoid electoral failure, but the amalgamation of the French, Italian and Spanish parties into a single phenomenon not only mistook their still very different cast and character, but failed to reflect the fact that all three were attempting to redefine themselves in national, not European, terms. This was nowhere truer than in France, where the PCF not merely distanced itself from the USSR – rejecting *all* foreign models of socialism – but took a positive pleasure in chauvinistic demonstrations of every sort. It was not interested in an 'historic compromise' *à l' Italienne*. It disagreed sharply with Carrillo over events in Portugal and with both the PCI and PCE over the question of EEC enlargement. It proudly launched the slogan '*Ni Washington, Ni Rome, Ni Moscou*'.[11] It defended Concorde and attacked EEC supranationality as hotly as any Gaullist; it played hard on the resurgent anti-German feelings aroused by the widening economic gap between the two countries (popularly symbolised by the franc's fall against the mighty Deutschmark); it defended nationalisation on the grounds that Renault (a nationalised company) was the 'great French success story'. Most grotesquely, for a party born of the popular revulsion against the 'national defence' policies of the SFIO in the First World War, it attempted to outflank the PS on defence policy. France must not only keep a nuclear deterrent but must have its missiles targetted at both East (the USSR!) and West (Germany). Thorez had wrapped himself in the tricolour in the Popular Front period but he could almost be heard turning in his grave at the sight of the PCF accepting the possibility of a nuclear war with the Soviet Union.'

This tactic, too, was a failure, for the PCF still had to pay the price of its long years of *immobilisme* under Thorez. The torrent of change now was too sudden to be convincing and the Party's over-long attachment to all it now denounced weighed heavy upon it. The PCI had drawn large electoral benefits from its move towards a more liberal, national position because Togliatti had grasped the opportunities provided by the CPSU 20th Congress in 1956. The PCI had changed over time, of its own courageous accord and under no real electoral pressure. The PCF's position was exactly the opposite. At best its change of heart made it seem a belated and rather overheated reflection of the PS.

Moreover, the PCF's new enthusiasm for bourgeois democracy sat oddly with the fact that its ways and manners were still far from those expected in a truly democratic party. The near-unanimity of the votes to change even the most fundamental of the Party's tenets was not lost on observers. The decision to abandon the aim of proletarian dictatorship was debated by 22,705 delegates to 98 federal conferences. In the end 113 voted for the doctrine, 216 abstained and the other 98.6 per cent sided with the leadership in rejecting the doctrine which Lenin had insisted was the great dividing line between Socialists and Communists.[12] A still Stalinist party attacking the USSR was, to most French eyes, merely a curiosity. The sight of such a party marching with near-military discipline towards 'pluralism' provoked open cynicism.

Perhaps most destructive, however, was the diaphanous quality of the leadership's attempted manipulation of opinion. The cold-bloodedness of the Party's electoral motivation both in its policy liberalisation and its wrecking tactics against the PS was painfully clear to all, and seemed to suggest a quite undemocratic contempt for the intelligence of its own supporters, let alone those it was courting. Moreover, the leadership's nervousness of internal Party reaction to the plethora of changes it was introducing actually led it to ignore some of the *old* conventions of democratic centralism, with staggering policy reversals such as that over the nuclear deterrent introduced by mere *ex cathedra* pronunciamentos. While the Party had its back to the wall in electoral battle, old habits of loyal obedience were too strong for militants to complain openly about such breaches of precedent but, as the explosion which rocked the PCF in the wake of March 1978 was to show, they had not gone unnoticed. And, ironically, the Party's commitment to greater democracy had won one lot of enthusiastic converts – its own rank and file . . . Beyond that, though, the commitment cut little ice. The leadership was too well-used to getting its own autocratic way to give a passable imitation of responsive, democratic leadership – and that was what counted.

In practice, of course, the PS was run in almost as autocratic a fashion as the PCF. The fact that this did not in the slightest hinder the onward sweep of the PS emphasises the final reason why the PCF's ideological campaign failed: the PS was operating in an extremely favourable ideological environment in a way the PCF simply was not. It was not just that the PS had élan, that belonging to it was chic, nor even that it was far more open than the PCF to the fashionable new concerns for ecology or feminism (again, the PCF's far superior record for promoting women within its own ranks availed it little); it was more that the new preoccupation with social inequality, feeding easily into the mainstream liberal current, had created a political climate and public mood strongly favourable to social democratic reform. While this mood persisted the PS was swimming in a friendly sea.[13]

### iii ORGANISATIONAL REINFORCEMENT

Although the PCF had descried the PS threat by mid-1972 ideological hostilities were not commenced against it until late 1974 and were then conducted only fitfully. Organisationally, however, the Party lost no time at all. The delivery of Marchais's June 1972 report on the PS danger was the signal for the launching of a major drive to enlarge and strengthen the PCF mass organisation, a drive which continued without any let-up right through March 1978. While the war of words within the Left caught the headlines, this organisational drive, though less noticed, was hardly less significant and by 1978 had virtually transformed the Party. Here, at least, the example of the PCI was clearly influential. There was little doubt that greater electoral success (and lesser discipline) had derived from its policy of 'presence', of encapsulating whole communities within a mass membership sub-culture. The PCF had, by comparison, been a more highly disciplined vanguard party. Thus while PCF membership had peaked, briefly, in 1946 at 800,000,[14] the PCI had already enrolled 1,700,000 members in 1945, 2,250,000 by 1947 and 2,500,000 by 1954. Although membership had fallen thereafter, the PCI had settled down on a plateau of between 1.5 and 2 million members,[15] a figure which tended to edge up, not down, as it advanced towards its electoral triumphs of the 1970s.

PCF membership figures told a less happy story, falling to perhaps 317,000 in 1956 from the 1946 peak.[16] For several years thereafter the Party issued no membership figures – almost certainly in order to hide a large decline caused by the twin blows of 1956 and 1958. Until 1964, indeed, the Party claimed the same suspiciously round number of 300,000 members every year.[17] By 1966, probably as a result of the 'popular front' enthusiasm of the 1965 presidential campaign, membership was up to 350,000. By end-1969, boosted again by Duclos's campaign, it had reached 380,000, but fell back to 375,000 at the end of 1971.[18]

By the end of 1972, with the new drive only just starting, there were 390,000 members. Thereafter growth was dramatic. By end-1973 there were 410,000 members; by end-1974 450,000; by end-1975 491,000; by November 1977 611,000; and by March 1978 632,000.[19]

The mushrooming growth of the 1970s was quite different in character from the last great surge in membership at the Liberation. At its 1946 peak the Party had had 36,283 cells (up from the pre-war record level of 12,992 in 1937), but only 8,363 (23 per cent) of these were the workplace cells (*cellules d'entreprise*) on which the Party, anxious above all to root itself in the industrial labour movement, placed such heavy, Leninist emphasis. By January 1970 the 5,050 workplace cells made up an only slightly larger (26.2 per cent) proportion of the total (19,250) than they had a quarter of a century earlier. But it was quite precisely these cells which grew fastest in number in the Party's post-1972 drive. From 5,348 at the end of 1972, they rose to 5,680 in 1973, 6,575 in 1974, 8,042 in 1975, 8,824 at mid-1976, 9,558 by November 1977, and 9,922 by January 1978.[20] Thus in five years the number of such cells had virtually doubled, so that they constituted over 37 per cent of the total number of cells (26,695). Growth in the residential cells was far less dramatic. Moreover, while workplace cells continued to increase sharply in number in the critical months after September 1977, the number of residential cells actually fell, particularly in the countryside.[21]

This pattern of growth is not wholly to be explained by the Party's gradual consolidation around its proletarian core. The share of the working-class vote received by the PCF certainly rose in this period – from 31 per cent in 1967 to 33 per cent in 1973 and 36 per cent in 1978.[22] Doubtless this trend was given some assistance by the Party's extraordinarily intensive efforts on the factory floor, but the 16 per cent gain in working-class support in 1967–78 hardly matches the 89 per cent increase in workplace cells in 1970–8. More strikingly still, of course, this huge rise in membership took place during a period when the Party's electoral support was stagnant. Between March 1973 and March 1978 the PCF vote fell by 0.8 per cent (representing a loss of 3.7 per cent of the Party's electorate), while in virtually the same period (December 1972–March 1978) Party membership rose 62 per cent! These figures seem all the stranger when contrasted with those for the PS which, between June 1973 and December 1977, gained 54,000 members while going from 20 per cent to 30 per cent in the polls. In the same period the PCF, while losing electoral support, gained over 200,000 new members . . .

What these figures indicate, in fact, is a massive, perhaps desperate, PCF effort to protect itself from PS encroachment on its electorate, essentially by signing up as members large numbers of those who were anyway traditional supporters. The multiplication of workplace cells, achieved essentially by the·mobilisation of the CGT militants towards Party work, also simply reflected the fact that when the Party went searching for new members it naturally had the greatest success in its traditional working-class milieux. Almost certainly, though, the Party's special effort here stemmed from a determination to retain its leading position amongst the proletariat even if it could not stop the PS overtaking it in other sections of the electorate. This essentially defensive attitude shone forth clearly in the Party's attitude to the new PS *sections d'entreprise*. In other periods the PCF might have sought collaboration with such groups, hoping to sweep them along in its wake in the industrial environment where its dominance was anyway assured. As it was, the Party felt badly threatened by the appearance of the SEs, even though it outnumbered them by six to one with its workplace cells:

> the question is posed of the [PCF's] relationship with socialist organisations in the workplace. It is the Communist Party's right to consider their existence as neither desirable or useful and, consequently, to do nothing to encourage them. Hence, for example, the CP's refusal to undertake joint action at enterprise level which could reinforce the activities of these socialist organisations and facilitate their implantation.[23]

That the Party was recruiting amongst its traditional electorate rather than breaking new ground was evident, too, in the geographical distribution of membership. While rural cells increased in number (with one for every six villages by mid-1976)[24] the number of Communist peasants continued to decrease, leaving such cells populated by farm labourers and schoolteachers.[25] Probably no more than one-sixth of the membership was grouped in such cells[26] and the great bulk of the Party was located at least as heavily as before in the traditional great urban strongholds. In mid-1976 28 per cent of the entire membership was in the Paris region and 60 per cent was in just four regions (out of eighteen): Paris, Picardie-Nord, Provence-Côte d'Azur, and Rhône-Alpes.[27]

The only clear breakthrough was amongst women. As a result, no doubt, of general social trends the Party's feminine membership had inched up from 49,490 (21.9 per cent of membership) in 1961[28] to 90,000 (around 25 per cent) in 1966–7.[29] By January 1978, however, nearly one-third (200,000) of the Party's membership was feminine.[30] To reach this proportion women must have constituted as much as 40 per cent of the post-1972 recruitment wave.[31] This increase doubtless resulted in part from the feminist movement which had its impact in France, as elsewhere, in recent years, as well as from a concerted Party effort to retain its position as the leading party of feminine emancipation.

This breakthrough may have been more apparent than real, however, for a large proportion of the new feminine membership consisted of young working-class housewives. Of new women recruits in 1975 over 70 per cent were housewives and only 20 per cent wage-earners or self-employed.[32] In the case of many of the former – and, doubtless, not a few of the latter as well – little more may have been involved than signing up the wives of known Party supporters and members. While such enlistment might serve to deepen the Party's penetration of its traditional milieux or, at least, to consolidate what it already held, it was unlikely to lead to a real expansion of Communist influence.

This is not to say that the PCF made no new converts in its recruiting drive. It continued to be, *par excellence*, the party of the young. The PCF had always relied heavily on a prodigious through-put of young militants who pass through its ranks in large numbers, contributing a few years of zealous effort before lapsing – hence Kriegel's term, *'le parti-passoire'*.[33] It seems clear, however, that the post-1972 recruitment drive saw a further accentuation of the PCF's traditional bias in this respect. Of post-1972 male recruits 44 per cent were under thirty, as were no less than 51 per cent of the Party's new women members.[34] Of new recruits (of both sexes) in 1975 in Paris a staggering 50 per cent were aged under twenty-five.[35] A further indication that the Party was looking to youth to an even greater degree than usual was furnished by the growth of the *Mouvement de la Jeunesse Communiste Française* (MJCF). The MJCF had achieved its record membership of 92,919 in January 1945, but throughout the period 1959–67 had claimed only 50,000 members.[36] By mid-1976 membership had risen to nearly 90,000[37] and by November 1977 to 110,609.[38] Thus, while overall Party membership had increased during 1967–77 by 63 per cent, the MJCF had grown by 121 per cent.

Inevitably, recruitment on the scale attempted after 1972 involved the acceptance of an even higher fall-off rate than usual, particularly since the Party was enlisting such large numbers in the young age group notoriously prone to such wastage. In good recruitment years in the 1960s the PCF had enlisted arount 40,000 new members (43,000 in 1967, 40,000 in 1969 – both election years). In 1972 there were 48,000 new members; in 1973 62,000; in 1974 85,000; in 1975 93,780; and in the first six months of 1976 alone, over 70,000.[39] The rising tempo and extraordinary size (by 1976, apparently, an annual rate of 140,000) of these intakes underlines the Party's frenzied determination to meet a political problem with organisational means. However, in the same period that the PCF gained these 358,780 new recruits its total membership rose by only 118,500, from 375,000 to 493,500, a wastage rate of no less than two-thirds, as compared to the 'normal' rate of around 10 per cent.[40] If this two-thirds rate held steady through to March 1978, when PCF membership had reached 632,000, a further 415,500 new members must have been recruited in just twenty-one months. This implies that between 1972 and March 1978 the PCF must have signed up a total of over 750,000 new members which, together with the 375,000 it had started with, constituted well over one-fifth of its entire electorate.

The recruitment drive made the PCF (even) richer. With every recruit paying an average Fr. 95 a year in dues alone (and considerably more in other subscriptions), Party income rose to Fr. 105 million a year in 1975[41] – without taking account of the profits accruing from the sixty commercial enterprises run by the Party.[42] In turn this probably allowed the Party to expand the number of its all-important *permanents* (full-time officials), of whom, there were 860 in 1976,[43] or ten times as many as the PS possessed.

The drive led to change even at higher levels in the Party, bringing a new generation of young militants and women into prominence. Even by 1976 more than 60 per cent of the entire membership had joined the PCF since 1968, and over one-third since 1972.[44] Of the delegates to federal conferences in 1976 no less than 41.8 per cent were aged under thirty, and nearly 70 per cent were under forty, to whom the Popular Front of 1936 was something that had happened before they were born.[45] Over half the Central Committee had been elected to it since 1970 and a quarter of its members were in their thirties. Women, who had constituted only 9 per cent of the Committee's membership in 1970, made up 19 per cent in 1976. Perhaps most significantly, 85 per cent of the Committee's members had been elected during the Fifth Republic, most since 1964.[46] For the first time in over forty years the Party was run, even at the very top, by a majority that had not been handpicked by Thorez. It was no accident that the emergence of such a majority coincided exactly with the Party's abandonment of proletarian dictatorship . . .

Expansion brought problems as well as benefits. It put the PCF on a treadmill, for with such a high membership fall-off rate the Party was condemned to maintain its recruitment effort at a near-frantic level if it did not wish to see its numbers collapse as dramatically as they had risen. It also meant that the PCF machine, now swollen with large numbers of marginal and less devoted adherents, became a slower, more cumbersome instrument. In common with all other French parties the PCF has suffered from a general *crise du militantisme* as even the faithful became more absorbed in privatised domestic lives within their notably more affluent and better equipped households.[47] It became correspondingly harder, even for the PCF, to require the same long hours of utterly selfless, unpaid labour that political organisation work requires.[48]

Moreover, the new recruits often represented a different, more conditional quantity within the Party. The new middle ranks, at least, were better educated and rather more white collar in origin than hitherto.[49] Many were part of the generation of '68 which had given its first and most passionate loyalty to another cause – and, one at that, which encouraged a more disputatious, independent set of ways. Above all, they had joined the PCF enthused with the *dynamique unitaire*, their hearts set upon the achievement of the Common Programme by a united government of the Left. Many were puzzled by the gradual escalation in the PCF's criticism of the PS in 1975–7 but loyally went along with it. They shared, after all, their leaders' distrust of the Socialists – otherwise they would hardly have joined the Party in the first place. And many of them silently accepted Mitterrand's claim that the war of words within the Left was, at bottom, merely about electoral advantage and did not compromise the fundamental objective of a Left government. If, however, this objective were to be placed in jeopardy by the Party leadership, the unconditional loyalty of this new membership could hardly be taken for granted. Thus while the recruitment drive had undoubtedly strengthened the PCF organisation, it had also made it less resilient to sudden switches of the Party line. It would certainly not be easy to swing the 'new' PCF into line if the leadership found it necessary to pursue its campaign against the PS to the point of rupture. Such an operation would, at the least, take time – and might even be impossible altogether.

## iv 'FALLING TO THE LEFT'

With the successful conclusion of the municipal elections in March 1977, the PCF reached its moment of decision. On the one hand, the auguries for the Union of the Left were good. The Left had swept to an unprecedented triumph, capturing control of 155 of the 221 large (over 30,000 population) towns and cities, as well as 140 smaller towns. The elections had, moreover, been a major test of the Socialists' good faith – one they had passed with flying colours, ejecting their old centrist partners from local alliances all over France and inviting the PCF in to take their place. With this, one of the Party's major objectives had been achieved for, in a state of some euphoria, Communists now walked into literally dozens of town halls from which they had always hitherto been excluded.

By the same token, however, the Party had now got most of what it could hope for out of the alliance with the Socialists, for the prospect ahead was truly daunting. The ideological campaign against the PS had clearly and completely failed. The PCF's broadsides after the previous year's cantonal elections had, by late 1976, reduced the gap between the parties in the polls, though only to the still large margin of 7 per cent, the PS taking 28 per cent to the PCF's 21 per cent.[50] The municipal results showed that this was no fiction, for in seventeen of the large towns the PCF and PS had put up separate lists at the first ballot, allowing a straightforward comparison with the 1973 legislative results. Overall, the PCF vote in these towns had gone up less than 0.1 per cent, while the PS gained more than 7.6 per cent.[51] Moreover, in the wake of this triumph, the PS soared back up to 30 per cent in the polls, while the PCF dropped back to 20 per cent.[52] The Communists had huffed and had puffed but the Socialist house showed not the remotest sign of falling down; rather the reverse, in fact.

Only a year away loomed the 1978 parliamentary elections with, it now seemed, a Left victory a near certainty. The most careful estimates showed that, in the large towns at least, the combined Left had advanced a full 3.4 per cent (to 53.6 per cent) over its previous record level in the 1974 presidential election.[53] A computer simulation based on the municipal first-ballot results suggested a parliamentary landslide to the Left, with the Right winning only 213 seats to the Left's 277 (PCF 105, PS/MRG 172).[54] Calculations based on the municipal second-ballot results were even more favourable to the Left[55] – and the post-municipal polls showed the Left gaining further still.

Such a victory would, though, be mainly a Socialist victory. If the PS retained its 10 per cent lead over the PCF, Socialist candidates would overtake Communists in scores of seats on the first ballot, leaving the PCF isolated in a few remaining strongholds and everywhere else helping to elect PS deputies on the second ballot. If the PS, on a 7 per cent lead, could take 172 seats to the PCF's 105, on a 10 per cent lead it could easily take 210 seats to their 75.[56] Mitterrand, whose stock would rise to fresh heights, would become prime minister and would have the parliamentary strength to justify giving all the major portfolios (defence, finance, interior and foreign affairs) to the Socialists. The hopes of a euphoric Left electorate would be invested in a Socialist leader and, in effect, a Socialist government – whose patronage powers would be used to further reinforce the PS. The Communists would be shuffled off into a few, less controversial ministries: youth and culture, social security, and labour – where they would probably be given the task of holding down a wage explosion. The PCF would have very little leverage over Mitterrand, even if he did trim in a rightward direction: the government would face a hostile President and, should the PCF bring down the only Left government the Fifth Republic had ever known, it would be open to the utterly damaging accusation of having done Giscard's work for him. The PS would then be free to make an alternative deal with Giscard's Centrists, leaving the weakened PCF stranded and back in its ghetto. Alternatively, the PCF would find itself tagging along behind Mitterrand in a showdown to force Giscard out – opening the way for Mitterrand to capture the presidency as well. Whatever happened, it seemed likely that the PS would take most of the credit for any of the successes of a Left government. If, however, as was only too likely, the government ended in disaster and a snap election called by Giscard, the lion's share of the blame would be heaped on the PCF. The Socialists would blame the Communists for pushing 'unrealistic' economic demands and the Right would unleash a frenzied anti-Communist crusade. Other scenarios were possible, but all seemed to contain the same Catch-22 element for the PCF.

Thus while the Communist rank-and-file were celebrating their municipal triumphs and gleefully anticipating a Left victory in 1978, the Politburo, taking a longer view, were grimly appalled at the prospect of what such a victory might mean for the Party. Any idea that the PCF could redress the situation with further measures of liberalisation had now to be discarded. Such measures had brought the Party no votes. Indeed, it was clear, to the Politburo's fury, that the main profits of this strategy were going to the Socialists, who patronisingly took the credit for the PCF's domestication. Under their benign leadership, the PS argued, the PCF was being conducted by degrees through an elementary democratic house-training . . .

The Politburo – with Leroy's faction naturally gaining in strength – resolved instead to harden up its position. The Party's attempt to 'fall to the Left' by accusing the Socialists of an intended right-ward drift once in power had failed both because it rested on mere future conjecture and because Mitterrand had replied serenely to all such criticism that he continued to stand four-square on the Common Programme. Accordingly, the PCF now hurried to give a detailed new definition to the Programme in order to force Mitterrand off the fence. Within a fortnight of the municipal elections Marchais appealed for an immediate start to the work of updating the Programme. Mitterrand naturally wished for delay and attempted to set limits on the PCF's proposals for further nationalisations. He was as aware as Marchais that the original Common Programme had been an extremely optimistic and expansionist document even when originally drawn up in 1972 while France was enjoying the fruits of the heady world boom which had preceded the 1973 crash. Already many of its targets looked wildly wishful. To set even more ambitious targets now, with inflation and unemployment both at record levels, might fatally damage the Left's credibility as an alternative government. By mid-April Charles Fiterman, Marchais's dauphin, no less, was giving public interviews accusing the PS leader of an ambiguous and restrictive attitude and making it clear that the PCF would brook no compromise either on its ambitious plans for social expenditure (higher pensions, family benefits and minimum wage) or on its programme of nationalisations. A liaison committee of the three Left parties (PS, PCF and MRG) was set up to discuss these new Communist proposals, with its first session set for 17 May.

Meanwhile a major television debate between the prime minister, Raymond Barre, and Mitterrand was arranged for 12 May. (Marchais had repeatedly challenged Barre to such a debate but was, of course, denied such valuable air-time by the state-controlled broadcasting services.) On 10 May *L'Humanité*, pre-empting the liaison committee's session by a week, published their costing (prepared by Philippe Herzog, one of the PCF's leading economists) of the Common Programme. The aim, quite clearly, was to torpedo Mitterrand's television appearance. For the Herzog costing assumed an unimaginable 6 per cent growth rate and assessed the Programme's cost not for 1978 but for 1980, deliberately increasing the shock effect of the figures by allowing for several further years of inflation. The Programme was to cost a staggering 493 billion old francs. General economic opinion scoffed aloud at the 6 per cent growth rate (higher than the economy had achieved during the 1960s 'miracle') and reckoned that this level of extra expenditure implied an inflation rate of around 35 per cent. An embarrassed and furious Mitterrand was forced to spend most of his television 'summit' angrily denying the PCF's figures – to the ironic amusement of an easily victorious Barre. A few days later the PCF increased the discomfort of the Socialists by its startling reversal on defence policy.

On 17 May a visibly unhappy Georges Marchais met with Mitterrand and the MRG leader, Robert Fabre, volunteering unsolicited assurances that the PCF did still want to win the elections. Meanwhile, however, the common Programme must be comprehensively overhauled to bring it up to date. Fabre, perhaps naïvely, supported this call for renegotiation but Mitterrand, who seems to have grasped the PCF tactics very quickly, was adamant. There could be no question of negotiating a second Programme. He and the PS were committed to carrying out the first one – and no further. As for costing exercises, he 'couldn't see anything useful in that'.[57] There was no need for Marchais's proposal of three new working parties. A single small commission would do. Fabre he brushed aside: 'If you want to, go and work out a programme together with the Communists.'[58] Marchais fulminated that Mitterrand's unwillingness to discuss anything in detail was both dictatorial and a sign of a lack of seriousness about the Programme, but gave way. The commission began its work.

In effect the PCF (and particularly Leroy, whose editorship of *L'Humanité* gave him a strategic vantage point in the war of words) was attempting to test the good faith of the PS by pulling it toward a more Leftist redefinition of the Common Programme. Mitterrand, who had begun to direct his attentions towards the electoral middle ground which, he knew, would finally decide the issue in March, was equally determined to stand firm.

In June 1977 the PS Congress met at Nantes, the PCF watching closely. Mitterrand declared that there was no question of the PS moving closer to the PCF and that the negotiations on the Common Programme must be brought to an immediate conclusion. He spoke enthusiastically of the Swedish model of social democracy and in favour of the Portuguese Socialist leader, Soares (the PCF's *bête noire*). Rocard, the party's spokesman on nationalisations, delivered a ringing warning of the economic paralysis which could result from too sweeping an extension of the public sector. CERES (which had wanted the PS to take a more conciliatory attitude towards the PCF) denounced the Congress bitterly for its adoption of 'the Soares line'.

Fiterman, attending the Congress as the PCF observer telephoned the Politburo: 'It's war.'[59]

The PCF bitterly condemned the Nantes Congress – as also the accord reached the same month at the Brussels meeting of the Socialist International between the PS and the other European Socialist parties. What meaning could now be given to the PS slogan of a *'front de classe'*, they demanded to know, if Mitterrand could so easily find himself at one with the likes of Soares, Schmidt and Callaghan?

But the summer holidays had come and the Left, voters and leaders alike, departed on vacation and relaxed. The shock of the PCF's behaviour had been considerable; but then some skirmish had probably been inevitable and with Marchais sunning himself in Corsica there was little indication that even the PCF thought there was a real crisis. The Communists were bound to swing into line as March 1978 neared. There was still no need to worry . . .

Such expectations were shattered when Marchais returned from holiday in early August and was given television air-time to publicise the fact that 'serious differences' remained between the Left parties, notably over the minimum wage, defence and the nationalisations. Despite the fact that the inter-party commission was still sitting to resolve such differences, the PCF now developed an increasingly aggressive campaign on all these fronts and on the question of governmental reform. The demand for a large hike in the minimum wage was clearly just populist politics and the defence issue was a barely credible source of difference. (Mitterrand was later to concede on the former and the PCF came largely to overlook the second.) The other two issues were more significant, both in their substantive content and in what they revealed of Communist intentions.

On nationalisation the PCF wanted to lengthen the list of nine major industrial groups specified in the Common Programme,[60] both by including all subsidiaries in which these groups had a controlling interest and by the simple addition of the largest private companies in steel, oil and automobiles.[61] More to the point, the directors and governing boards of all nationalised industries were to be directly elected by the trade unions active within them from lists of candidates unvetted by the government. The anticipation, quite clearly, was that the CGT's dominant position in many heavy industries would effectively allow the PCF to honeycomb the nationalised sector with its own appointees. The Party would thus gain a prodigious new domain of patronage while simultaneously carrying out a sort of vertical integration of its industrial strength, from governing board to shopfloor. Whatever cold electoral winds might then blow, the Party could dig in for the duration behind the walls of these new fortresses. The PS, naturally, insisted that the lists of candidates for such boards and directorships would have to be vetted by the Cabinet, where the non-Communist majority would kill such schemes (and, doubtless, use the same patronage to its own purposes).

The PCF also proposed a variety of governmental reforms. The future Left government must reflect the electoral strengths of the constituent parties, not their parliamentary strengths. (On the former presumption the PCF might have two-fifths of the Ministers, on the latter probably less than one-third.) Parliament must be automatically dissolved if the political complexion of the government changed (i.e. as and when the PCF decided to leave it, or if the PS attempted to make a deal with the Right). Third, the Economic and Finance Ministries must be dismantled in order to create a new super-Ministry of Planning, and similar surgery on the Ministry of the Interior would produce a new Ministry of Local Government. In return for these two Ministries, the PCF intimated, it might be willing to accept the non-appointment of Communists to such 'sensitive' ministries as defence, foreign affairs or the remainders of the finance and interior ministries (controlling taxation and the police). It took little imagination to see how a Communist Minister of Local Government might assist the Party in entrenching itself in the one-third of major towns (72 out of 221) it now controlled and possibly advancing its cause further in the scores of towns where the PCF was now the junior partner in PS-led administrations. As for the new Planning Minister, he would have the whole of the vastly enlarged nationalised sector under his control . . .

On several of these points – such as the exact composition of a future government – Mitterrand refused to be drawn. On the extension of the nationalisations list he was, at the last, willing to concede. But on the PCF proposals to entrench the Party more or less permanently within the government and the whole structure of the State machine, he gave no ground at all. As the long-awaited 'summit' between the three leaders of the Left approached, the mounting Communist campaign against the PS led not a few Socialists to urge Mitterrand to stop turning the other cheek to such attacks. This he refused to do: 'I have no intention of participating – as I am asked to do on every side – in verbal escalation.'[62] It was a masterful tactic. Nothing would have suited the PCF better (or more alarmed the Left electorate) than had Mitterrand allowed himself to be provoked to intemperate counter-attack. Instead, he maintained the serenely presidential image of being rather above such slanging matches. If the Communists were intent on disrupting the Union of the Left, they must be seen to bear the whole of the responsibility. And, he counselled his followers privately, if this was the case then 'every new concession would be wood thrown on a fire'.[63] Moreover, the Communist campaign was making no headway at all with the voters. The PS maintained a quite unruffled 30 per cent: 20 per cent lead over the PCF in the polls and by early September had begun to gain even further.[64] Almost certainly this was the determinant factor in the PCF's decision to push its campaign to the very point of rupture at the Left 'summit' in September.

The three leaders met at PS headquarters on September 14 with the task of resolving all remaining differences on the Common Programme. Mitterrand – never a man eager to share his confidence – gave Fabre no clue as to his own estimate of PCF intentions. Indeed, the only concertation between the two occurred when Fabre, arriving early, was alarmed to see that he and Mitterrand were wearing identical ties. He didn't have a spare one with him but surely, he asked, it would be better if Mitterrand changed his so that when Marchais arrived it didn't look as if they were plotting together, right down to wearing the same uniform. Mitterrand changed.[65]

Mitterrand might have done better to take Fabre into his confidence, for the MRG leader grew increasingly heated as the day dragged on without the slightest progress on the vital question of the nationalisations. Mitterrand was endlessly patient, knowing that the crucial issue now might be only who was to take responsibility for the breakdown of negotiations. Fabre reacted more straightforwardly and, when evening came with still no progress made, angrily stormed out declaring that the Communists were impossible. This suited the PCF well and Marchais obligingly made himself available for a television debate with Fabre. The task of throwing responsibility on to the other side for the failure of the talks was not going to be too difficult if its leaders could be induced to stage bad-tempered walkouts ...

But Mitterrand hadn't walked out and, almost certainly, it was he who secured the return of a somewhat subdued Fabre for the resumption of talks on 21 September, this time in the Politburo council-chamber at PCF headquarters. The day before the meeting Leroy launched a further well-aimed torpedo in *L'Humanité* by publishing a list of concessions representing the furthest limits to which the PCF was prepared to go. This adroitly gave a conciliatory impression while in fact issuing a public ultimatum to pre-empt the confidential talks: Mitterrand could now choose only between alienating centrist support by kow-towing to the full list of public PCF demands – or take the responsibility for rejecting this 'compromise'.

The whole session of 21 September produced no progress. Tension rose: in breaks between the talks Marchais and Mitterrand desperately sought neutral common ground in long and inconsequential discussions about the problems of baldness (from which both suffered).[66] Neither wished to broach the dread questions of the other's true motivation or the awful prospect of failure which now yawned ahead. Talks resumed the next day. There was still no progress. By evening total deadlock had been reached and Mitterrand asked for a short break to confer with the PS high command. It was nearly midnight when he returned with a new (extended) list of nationalisations which the PS was willing, reluctantly, to concede. These were dismissed almost out of hand by the PCF. The meeting dragged on for another hour, essentially because neither side wished to take responsibility for the final breakdown. Finally Mitterrand summed up his position: 'Well, either we are going to govern together, or neither lot of us is going to govern. We have exhausted all there is to be said. Meet again? We're in favour, but only if something worthwhile is to be achieved.'[67] At 1.15 a.m. the meeting broke up, all three leaders professing to the television cameras their willingness to meet again. But no date for a further meeting had been fixed. In fact they were not to meet again until after the first ballot in March – six months later.

The rank and file Left had watched these events unfold with deepening stupefaction. The final break caused such an explosion of confusion and dismay that both sides trod carefully as they attempted to arrange their troops in the new line of battle. The PCF attacked the PS for its 'swing to the Right'. The Socialists had gone over to the side of the big bourgeoisie and could, accordingly, no longer take the PCF's electoral co-operation for granted. Marchais attempted to deepen the contrast by launching the new watchword 'Make the rich pay'. Suddenly, without warning or Party consultation, the 'Union of the French people' was apparently tossed aside to enable the PCF to play to its hard-core support within the lower-income groups. If the Party could at least consolidate its hold over such milieux it would avoid complete disaster and split the PS away from some of its working-class support. It was, though, a desperate throw, for it meant writing off years of effort aimed at broadening PCF support beyond this traditional group. At the same time the PCF appealed endlessly to the PS and MRG to 'return to the Left' by meeting again to concede the PCF's demands. Mitterrand denied the Communist allegations, called for a PS campaign to win 7 million first-ballot votes, and announced that whatever the PCF did the PS would observe republican discipline and stand down on the second ballot for better-placed Left candidates, Communists included.

The possibility remained that a desperate PS might force Mitterrand's hand. Marchais' allegations that Fabre and Mitterrand had deliberately planned events in such a way as to be able to go into the elections with no programme, free to make any opportunist deal they wished, found at least some echo in the lively reservations the PS Left entertained about its leaders. The CERES group rose to this bait at the PS national conference in early November, calling on the leadership to soften its position towards the PCF. Mitterrand flatly refused but felt unable to oppose a subsequent motion – passed unanimously – calling for immediate new negotiations. A few days later a delegate from each of the Left parties met. It was mere ritual: there was nothing new to say and the meeting broke up in less than an hour.

After this the positions of the parties hardened fast, a process assiduously assisted by the state broadcasting services. The government, at first hardly able to believe its good fortune, quickly grasped the fact that it had everything to gain by ensuring Marchais had maximum exposure for his denunciations of his erstwhile partners. Suddenly, the PCF leader, bitterly accustomed to his treatment as almost a non-person by the television networks, found that all studio doors were open to him as he was repeatedly given opportunities to put his case at peak-viewing time. An infuriated Mitterrand began to speak of the PCF's 'objective alliance' with the Right. And, for the first time, he began to talk of the possibility that the Left might lose the elections. 'The PS holds the keys to victory,' he warned, but 'the PCF holds the keys to defeat.' Marchais was quickly back on the air to jeer that 'François Mitterrand is losing his *sang-froid* . . . François Mitterrand and Raymond Barre, yes, in a lot of ways they're tweedledum and tweedledee.'[68]

By the beginning of 1978 the question loomed whether the PCF would even agree to support better-placed Socialists on the second ballot in March. To maintain PCF candidates regardless, as the Party hinted it might do, would produce an automatic landslide for the Right, perhaps of 1968 proportions. On 7 January Marchais brought this spectre fully to life by announcing that the Party would only make its decision on this question in the light of the first-ballot results. The Party wanted 25 per cent of the vote. If it got under 21 per cent this would mean that it would have insufficient strength to ensure the bringing about of real change anyway. The implication was clear: if the PCF could not achieve sufficient weight to 'force' the Socialists to hold to their promises, then perhaps there was less than no point in helping the Left win at all. If Left-wing voters wanted a Left government badly enough, perhaps they could be blackmailed into voting Communist, all else having failed . . .

This was a cardinal error, for although the PCF continued to appeal to the PS and

MRG to meet without delay to reach agreement on (its version of) the Common Programme, Marchais had apparently now linked the Party's electoral co-operation not to the results of any such meeting, but to a purely arithmetical calculation about the first-ballot vote. The PCF henceforth spent much time denying this interpretation and on 23 January Marchais sought to correct the disastrous impression he had created by a notably more conciliatory tone ('We want to win with our Socialist comrades'). Thereafter the tenor of the PCF's propaganda continued to soften and any notion that the Party might refuse to observe republican discipline on the second ballot was quietly dropped.

Mitterrand was quick to notice the change. Earlier, on 4 January, he had given way on the Communist demand for a minimum wage of Fr. 2,400 a month – a concession whose inflationary implications had alarmed even some of the CFDT trade unionists who had demanded it of him. To make any further concessions would simply harm Socialist credibility. CERES were, of course, keen that the PS should take advantage of the PCF's new spirit of conciliation. They argued that Mitterrand's intention of deferring all further discussions on the Common Programme until after the second ballot (when, if the Left had won, he could deal from strength and in a practical political context) would needlessly humiliate the Communists. Their threat to maintain their candidates at the second ballot was clearly mere bluster and the satisfaction of making them eat their words was hardly worth the damage done to the Left by continuing dissension. Ultimately a compromise was reached: Mitterrand would refuse all further negotiation until after the first ballot.[69] This he announced in early February. The PCF grasped the straw and, within hours, announced that they were looking forward to a negotiation between the ballots. Henceforth the new PCF slogan became 'Vote Communist on the 12th for discussions on the 13th and victory on the 19th'. Marchais hinted broadly, indeed, that the PCF was dropping its detailed demands and would settle for a general agreement of principles. This was what the PS had hitherto demanded but Mitterrand stuck to his refusal to meet until after 12 March.

And so it was to be. The Left limped raggedly on towards the election, the unity it had so painfully and lengthily constructed now thrown to the winds and the Common Programme which it had made the centrepiece of its campaign since 1972 now more a sort of mutual altercation. It was a classic example of how defeat could be snatched from the jaws of victory – particularly when one took into account the multiple handicaps anyway suffered by the Left on the electoral field of battle.

# 10 The Field of Battle

Paris, in the cold spring of 1978, was a city waiting to have its future told. For several years sophisticated Parisian opinion had found the prospect of a Left victory exciting, even glamorous, and several successful futuristic novels appeared on the subject. The Left had enjoyed first celebrating and then anguishing over events in Portugal and Chile, debating with a pleasurable passion the likelihood and identity of a French Spinola or Pinochet. After a while, with the pre-electoral mood dragging on and on, the subject had become wearisome and had been dropped. The events of September 1977 produced a further lowering in the emotional temperature. At the same time the property market froze over, the stock exchange tailed lifelessly down and the franc trembled and fell – and trembled. The result was a strange atmosphere of lowered morale and dull, pervasive tension. Parisian sophisticates now volunteered statements reflecting their entire lack of interest in the election, their certainty that a Left victory would, boringly, change nothing very much, and their conviction that the French were hardly interested in politics anyway. (This a few weeks before two record voter turnouts in a row.)

There was also considerable bad temper and a general shortage of patience for, underneath, nerves had been worn extremely thin. 'Policitians' of all colours were targets for such feelings and so too were foreigners. An Englishman moving in any level of French society was likely to be besieged alternately by requests to help their hosts find schools and homes in England for their young to become proficiently anglophone, and by equally forceful resentments that this should be necessary to 'getting on'. It was, moreover, wickedly unfair that the British should have stumbled upon North Sea oil when France had no such asset. It was even unfair that the Gulf Stream had just given England, as always, a warmer winter than France. Stronger dislike still was evinced for the Americans and, above all, the Germans. The rise and rise of the mighty Deutschmark meant that a Frenchman had only to cross the border to feel a pauper. The Germans were becoming altogether too rich and powerful, and this too was hardly fair. The French, it was said, had lost their confidence and their élan, had every reason to feel sorry for themselves.

Such feelings were almost entirely lost on the large invading force of foreign academics, journalists, broadcasters and 'experts' of all descriptions who rolled into Paris for the election. Mainly, of course, this was because of the foreign academics' and journalists' habit of talking only to other foreign academics and journalists. Some, indeed, had little choice, speaking little French and having no previous acquaintance with the intricate workings of the French political sub-culture. In any case, many of them had not come to Paris to be seriously informed about this, but rather to describe in suitably vivid terms scenarios well fixed in their minds before they had set out. The Left would win and Mitterrand would be a Kerensky to Marchais's Lenin. The Left would win and there would be general economic chaos and a second snap election called by Giscard to throw the rascals out. Or the Left would win and the rascals would throw Giscard out. The Left would win and there would be a coup. The Left would win and . . . Everyone enjoyed such speculation, especially since the scenarios were invariably laden with doom.

Pardonably enough, the conviction that the Left would win stemmed from a source comprehensible even to journalists who had never covered a French election before, the unmistakable prognostications of such a victory by all the opinion polls. Even the most reputable of the polls, SOFRES and IFOP, who had never previously failed in their predictions, recorded the Left as hovering at the 50 – 53 per cent level, a good 5 per cent clear of the Right. This seemed, surely, to portend a landslide, however badly the Left might be split?[1]

The problem was that the Left would need to get well clear of 50 per cent to win, for the French electoral battleground is by no means a neutral no-man's-land between the parties. It is, rather, a steep uphill slope for the Left. Quite apart from such routine government advantages as its ability to make lavish use of state funds and patronage (large donations were handed out to UDF candidates from a paymaster actually stationed in the Elysée), the government was, as always, able to rely on the steady support of the State radio and television services. Although this weapon was less crudely used than in the past (its open abuse having proved counter-productive), government leaders were still able to acquire greater air-time and more or less sycophantic interviewers.

Moreover, the electoral system discriminates against the Left in a variety of ways. Most obviously, of course, the two-ballot system helps the Centre against extremes of any kind. In practice it hurts the Left most, given the unwillingness of many Socialists to vote Communist on the second ballot (where the first ballot has left the PCF candidate in a leading position on the Left). As a rule of thumb it was generally true that for a Communist to win a seat the combined Left score in a constituency had to be about 54 per cent at the first ballot. Naturally, the PCF argues strongly for a return to proportional representation and even the PS has, under Communist pressure, accepted this objective. Actually, almost *any* other system would have suited the Left better; had the election been fought on the Italian or German systems of PR the Left would have won, but so would it had the Anglo-American first-past-the-post system been employed.[2]

Second, constituency boundaries have remained virtually unaltered in metropolitan France since 1958. Over time population movements have produced a crazy patchwork of tiny rural (and Paris inner-city) constituencies (in 1978 the smallest had less than 26,000 voters) and vast urban seats overflowing with humanity (in 1978 the largest had over 181,000 voters). Since the Right predominate in the former and the Left in the latter type of seat the government, simply by doing nothing, has, over time, produced a built-in gerrymander to its own advantage. In all, this probably gave the

Right a start of some 15–20 seats over the Left in the 470 constituencies of mainland France.[3]

As the election approached, with the Left apparently riding a tidal wave of popularity, the government cast round, like not a few French governments before it, to see whether it could not take a rather more active role in electoral engineering. It was clearly best to leave well alone in mainland France, where masterful inaction had already produced such benefit; where attempting any change would only open Pandora's Box; and where any change that was less than grossly crooked was bound to help the Left anyway. Beyond the mainland the situation was more promising, particularly since changes there might escape the full glare of metropolitan attention.

First there was Corsica. Despite the fact that electoral corruption was a way of life on the island, Corsicans had in recent years allowed sadly to lapse their old status as a Gaullist fief, returning two MRG deputies and one RPR. Moreover, a strong movement for regional autonomy had sprung up on the island. Seizing on this latter fact, the government decided it must placate these regionalist forces (though not those in Brittany, Languedoc or anywhere else) by creating an extra seat. This, at least, had to be the official explanation since, with three seats for its 204,000 voters, Corsica was already somewhat overrepresented. An artful redrawing of the boundaries now saw the island return a solid block of four RPR deputies in 1978. Of all parties the RPR was, of course, the most severely opposed to demands for local autonomy . . . Thus the Left, which entered the election with a one-seat lead here, emerged from it with a 0:4 deficit. The Right thus enjoyed an effective net gain of five seats.

The overseas departments and territories (the 'DOM-TOM') came next. Electoral management in many of these far-flung remnants of empire required no great sophistication. Their Governors were chosen by the Minister in Paris with an eye to their political reliability and not much more needed to be said. Their colonial administrations were, after all, the largest single source of employment and patronage in their dependencies, and they controlled the police, the media and the postal service. Moreover, many of them were wonderfully small. Saint-Pierre-et-Miquelon had less than 4,000 voters and Wallis-et-Futuna under 5,500. This, too, facilitated control – Giscard had won no less than 95 per cent of the vote in 1974 in the latter constituency, and even this had represented something close to electoral insurrection when compared to De Gaulle's 99.6 per cent in 1965 (on a 98.5 per cent turnout). Only in the larger dependencies did the Left have much of a chance – in Martinique, for example, where the left-wing poet, Aimé Césaire, was returned yet again in 1978. But in general the DOM-TOM were a handy bonus for the Right which, in 1973, had won 14 of their 17 seats.

The problem here was that whatever shaky legitimacy the DOM-TOM seats possessed derived from the fact that a few of them, at least, were quite substantial territories, and since the last election two of the largest, French Somaliland and the Comores Islands, had become independent. In the latter case, something at least was saved, for when the other islands had taken their independence in 1975 (leading to a total and crippling cut-off of all French aid and technical assistance), France had hung on to the island of Mayotte (where she has a naval base), despite the furious indignation of the new Comorian Republic and the Organisation for African Unity (OAU).[4] Mayotte now became a new constituency in the French Assembly, dutifully returning a UDF deputy in 1978 with over 92 per cent of the vote on the first ballot – thus setting a new and dubious record in French electoral history.

This still left the DOM-TOM with only fifteen seats – two less than 1973. To remedy this deficiency, just three months before the election, in December 1977, the Right pushed through a law creating two new seats (both with less than 25,000 voters) in French Polynesia and New Caledonia. Virtue was again rewarded at the polls – indeed, in the new Polynesian seat the Right took 91.4 per cent of the vote at the first ballot. In the end the DOM-TOM returned 8 RPR deputies, 6 UDF, 2 Independents and 1 Socialist. Even if the Independents attended the National Assembly (which was doubtful)[5] and voted with the Left, the Right still emerged with a 14:3 lead from the DOM-TOM, a net advantage of 11 seats.

All told, these quirks of the electoral system were worth not less than 30 seats for the Right (15–20 in mainland France, 4 in Corsica, and 11–13 in the DOM-TOM). Not surprisingly, such facts lent further passion to the Left's demands for electoral reform. It was, after all, not a little provoking to have to endure all this at the hands of a president who had, while in office, authored a bestselling book entitled *French Democracy* and who lost few occasions to deliver lofty sermons on his vision of the modern liberal democratic society towards which he was guiding the French. Replying to this clamour in January 1977 Giscard declared loftily that 'In present circumstances I can see no advantage for the functioning of our institutions of a change in the electoral law'.[6]

Under the stimulus of the Left's municipal successes in March, however, the government began to see differently. The Empire might be shrinking still, but, quite apart from the DOM-TOM, there were still large numbers – some 875,000, it was thought – of Frenchmen scattered around the world, mainly in former French colonies: ambassadorial and consular officials, technical assistants, *colons* left behind after decolonisation, soldiers, businessmen, and simple emigrants who had retained French citizenship. In the old days of colonial representation in the National Assembly tiny electorates composed of such elements as these had sent a minor flock of conservative (mainly Gaullist) deputies and senators to Paris. Was there not some way in which this last reserve might be brought in to shore up the flagging fortunes of the Right?

The problem was that there was no postal vote, merely a complicated system where such overseas residents had to procure power of attorney to vote by proxy. This effectively discouraged most from voting – only 110,000 were registered. And this was a drop in the ocean in a total electorate of almost 35 million anyway. By July 1977 the government had cooked up a scheme to make these votes count, quietly tacking it on to a bill excluding from participation in the second ballot all candidates who failed to gain a vote equal to 12.5 per cent of the registered electorate at the first ballot.[7] Since this meant scything down the minor party candidates who were a nuisance to all the large parties, the bill sailed through. Only later, when a telegram from the Ambassador in Gabon to the Minister of Foreign Affairs, discussing how overseas voters might vote 'usefully', was leaked to the press, was the full cunning of the government's plan appreciated. For, under the new law, citizens resident overseas could register at their embassy to vote in the metropolitan constituency *of their choice*.[8] (This, it transpired, led a further 28,000 such citizens to register.)[9] It was not long before such citizens, 'guided' by a helpful ambassadorial corps, were transmitting their votes (via that same corps) to precisely those marginal constituencies where a mere few hundred votes would probably settle the result. These voters were further aided by a newly created *Rassemblement des Français à l'Etranger* (a title deliberately echoing the RPF and RPR), over which presided the Gaullist notable, Maurice Schumann, and Paul d'Ornano, the brother of one of Giscard's Cabinet Ministers. During the ensuing gale of protest a large number of legal actions were initiated, involving almost 17,000 of these ballots. In the end only 2,256 were invalidated, but the other 99 per cent (151,444) passed muster – in part because of the highly contradictory stances adopted by the hundreds of local tribunals adjudicating the matter. Many of the tribunals took the view, indeed, that the new law enabled overseas citizens not merely to vote their choice by proxy but to delegate their actual voting choice to others. Mitterrand called it a 'veritable racket'; *Le Monde* called it a 'legal fraud'; *Le Nouvel Observateur* pointed out that the result might be to tip the balance towards the Right in as many as twenty-five seats. Given that twenty-eight deputies were ultimately returned for the Right with majorities of under 1 per cent, this seems not impossible.

Faced with this imposing array of electoral hurdles carefully constructed in its path, the Left had one major consolation: the electorate was getting younger and the young were overwhelmingly on its side. Moreover, Giscard, shortly after his election, and keen to show progressive intent, had lowered the voting age to eighteen. This, in the eyes of the Right, had been a cardinal error. For if the young were left-wing (and 61 per cent of the 25–34 age group voted Left in the event), the youngest were even more so (of the newly enfranchised 18–20 year olds, 72 per cent finally voted for the Left).[10] As the baby-boom of the 1950s began to reflect itself in the swelling numbers of young voters, the Left felicitated itself on the fact that, given such trends, it was moving inexorably towards becoming a 'demographic majority'. By 1978 no less than 15 million of the potential electorate of 35 million were voters who had come of age since the Fifth Republic's foundation in 1958 and, at 44.4 years, the electorate's median age was lower than at any time since 1936.[11]

Much of this optimism reflected a rather hasty reading of the demographic facts. The young were certainly more numerous – but so were the (conservative) old. The over-65s, who had made up only 13 per cent of the electorate in 1936 and 17.3 per cent in 1958, constituted 19.5 per cent by 1977 and over 20 per cent in 1978.[12] Moreover, an increasing proportion of the old were women, an important political fact given the still noticeable feminine bias towards conservatism. Among those aged under fifty there was actually a male predominance, often of quite large proportions – there were, for example, 10 per cent more men than women in the 21–34 age group (in part, of course, this helps 'explain' the Left bias of the younger age groups). But among the older citizenry large differentials in mortality rates more than reverse the balance. This is, of course, true in class terms – among the over-40s workers have almost three times the mortality rate of managers and the professions. But it is also true in sex terms, and here the feminine advantage has been increasing steadily through the century. At the turn of the century women outlived men by an average of 3.3 years, in the 1930s by 5.7 years, in the 1960s by 6.9 years, and in the 1970s by 7.4 years. Hence the overall feminine predominance in the population, which had normally been understood as simply a legacy of the huge male death-rate in the First World War, has continued to erode only rather slowly. Women made up 53.5 per cent of the electorate in 1949, 53.2 per cent in 1960, 53 per cent in 1970 and still constituted 52.8 per cent in 1978. Among the over-65 age group there were no less than seven women for every four men.

Thus the high hopes placed by the Left on the electorate's rejuvenation were somewhat misplaced. In assessing the true social weight of the different age groups within the electorate it would would probably have been wiser to pay more attention to the fact that, despite the steep increase in the number of women going out to work, the 'actively employed' proportion of the electorate had actually continued to decline – from 58.6 per cent in 1954 to 57.1 per cent in 1975. (Indeed, contrary to what might have been supposed, the 'actively employed' have constituted a steadily shrinking fraction of the total population over the whole of the twentieth century. By 1978 this proportion had probably fallen under 40 per cent for the first time.)[13] This falling 'activity rate' in part reflected the large size of the very young age cohorts,[14] but it was also a powerful indicator of the increasing numerical importance of the old. In this respect, the fall in the median age of the electorate was also somewhat misleading, for the historically low figure of 44.4 years was entirely the result of the once-and-for-all addition to the electorate of 2,065,000 18–20 year olds. Without them the electorate's median age in 1978 would have been a historically rather high 46.3 years. So in effect the whole of the Left's demographic optimism rested on this latter group of the newly enfranchised young.

This was a rather fragile basis for such hopes. For, inevitably, unknown though certainly large numbers of the 18–20 year old group were not registered as voters. In general, registration of this group was highest in rural (conservative) areas where local village mayors were closely in touch with their communities and where an old-fashioned sense of civic duty frequently prevailed. In the big cities registration was often very low indeed. Isolated instances of high registration levels were achieved only in Communist municipalities where those in power had both the motive and the grassroots organisational strength to launch successful registration drives. Even so, getting the uninitiated young to the polling booths was something else again – post-election surveys showed this group to have had three times the abstention rate of the electorate as a whole; that is, a rate of about 50 per cent.[15] As a result the net advantage conferred on the Left by demographic trends was probably very small in 1978 – if it existed at all.

Other social trends were of equally ambiguous advantage to the Left. On the one hand several of the most politically conservative social groups have declined greatly in importance. Between 1954 and 1975 the number of peasants shrank by over 62 per cent, while the number of employers fell by almost 40 per cent as France experienced the same processes of urbanisation and business concentration seen elsewhere in Western Europe. But the number of industrial workers rose by less than 7 per cent in the same period and agricultural workers fell in number by 70 per cent. The real growth has been concentrated in the middle groups – lower white-collar workers (+60 per cent), middle white-collar (+97 per cent), and the professional and managerial class (+116 per cent).[16]

These trends have, moreover, been particularly pronounced in Paris, whose continuing centrality to all aspects of French life for long gave a particular importance to the strength of the Left (in effect, the PCF) in and around the capital. Like other great Western cities, Paris is shrinking: its population fell by 500,000 between 1962 and 1975. Its 2.29 million people constituted only 23 per cent of the population of the wider Paris region in 1978, against 40 per cent twenty years before.[17] As this process continues the capital's remaining population becomes older and older – and more middle-class. Between 1954 and 1975 the number of workers fell by 27 per cent while artisans and small shopkeepers fell by 42 per cent. At the same time, despite the large overall fall in population, there were actually large increases amongst lower white-collar workers (+10 per cent), middle white collar (+47 per cent) and the professions and management (+98 per cent).[18] Moreover, for some time now the same process of *embourgeoisement* has been visible in the *banlieu* encircling the capital, as middle-class commuters, particularly the young, spill out of the centre in search of housing they can afford.

At the same time the great Communist fiefs of the *banlieu* – whole Red cities like Seine-Saint-Denis with 1.25 million people (1968) and nine PCF deputies out of nine – were being transformed by a different sort of demographic change. For it is here, above all, that the great hosts of immigrant workers who have flooded into France in the 1960s and early 1970s have taken root.[19] Even by 1968 one person in every seven in the department of Seine-Saint-Denis was a foreigner[20] and thereafter numbers continued to increase to a point where it was a commonplace by 1978 to find working-class suburban towns one quarter or more of whose population was composed of foreign migrants.

This process of settlement left the Communists badly squeezed. They were, at once, aghast at the social dislocation created by the influx, convinced that the government (and Chirac's Paris) was deliberately unloading its social problems – with their resultant stresses and racial animosities – on to PCF municipalities, and yet unwilling to put themselves at the head of native working-class resentments against the alien invasion. This does not mean, however, that the PCF has succeeded, or even tried very hard, to integrate the immigrants into a united working-class community. The Party has been happy enough to enrol the immigrants into the CGT and willing to accept them as Party members – if they ask. But it has not pursued their membership or participation with any great zeal, arguing that this would be unfair to immigrants, who are dangerously dependent on the good will of their employers and their often reactionary home governments. (Moroccans who join the PCF are said to disappear without trace when they revisit Morocco.) While this argument is doubtless valid enough, it has also helped to rationalise a real ambivalence on the part of the PCF's native clientele. Even PCF militants are, in effect, content to accept a large measure of social segregation between themselves and the migrant working-class communities. Inevitably, this ambivalence has only increased with the coming of recession and unemployment steady over the 1 million mark.

There is no doubting the importance of the migrant worker phenomenon to the Left. Despite some departures after 1973 the number of migrants remaining in France by 1978 was variously estimated at 4 million and 4.5 million.[21] Unlike their counterparts in Britain, they have no vote. This inflicted a double political loss on the Left (particularly the PCF) which, at a stroke, counterbalanced all other demographic trends operating in its favour. First, by their very presence the migrants facilitate a greater degree of native mobility out of the working-class – which, in the long run, deprives the Left of votes. Second, there is the more direct loss in support stemming from the disenfranchisement of so significant a fraction of the working-class. There seems little doubt that the migrants, if enfranchised, would give the Left at least equivalent support to that which it receives from the native working-class.[22] If so, the 'disenfranchisement effect' alone probably costs the Left at least a net 750,000 votes.[23] Interestingly, however, while the Socialists have suggested that the immigrants should be given the vote at least for municipal elections, the PCF has condemned such proposals as 'demagogy'.

Thus the Left approached the confrontation of March 1978 on considerably less than equal terms, encumbered by an accumulation of disadvantages. Some of these were natural (though how 'natural' is a differentially high rate of working-class mortality?) but most stemmed, directly or indirectly, from the Left's long decades of political impotence. It was for this reason, too, that the Left's protests against such inequities were surprisingly muted. It has lived too long with the fact of its own powerlessness to react with other than a cynical shrug. The attitude is comprehensible. What rational attitude to take to the sudden pile-up of mountainous overseas votes in Corsica, where leaflets circulated linking the Left's candidates to the Red Brigades which had just murdered Aldo Moro, where some villages cast more votes than they have people . . . ? Even at its most serious a French election is always also a sort of brutal circus. A circus in reverse, where the ringmaster is cynically hilarious and only the clowns are solemn. Amongst the latter must be counted the ever-increasing number of (utterly hopeless) minor party candidates. In 1962 there were 2,228 candidates in all (4.6 per constituency), in 1967 2,256, in 1968 2,314, in 1973 3,087. If there was always one safe prediction to make about the 1978 election it was that there would be yet more candidates clambering into the ring.

There were. Even after numerous withdrawals there were no less than 4,268[24] of them, an average of 8.7 per constituency. The hoardings and hustings everywhere were swamped by the posters and slogans of parties and candidates representing every imaginable tendency, as well as others that it would have taken a bold man to imagine. Apart from the four big battalions (the RPR, UDF, PS and PCF) there were four varieties of Trotskyites (with *Lutte Ouvrière*, the most significant of them, putting up 468 candidates), five varieties of Maoism ('fighting for a united party'), the remnants of the PSU, running as the *Front Autogestionnaire*, and four different anarchist groups appealing to the Left not to vote at all. Women's Liberation candidates banded together under the rubric *Choisir*, while Homosexual candidates put up posters explaining that they didn't want any one to vote for them (though, oddly, some did). Two sets of Breton Nationalists ran, as did four groups of Occitanian regionalists, two groups of Left Gaullists, the Radicals of Right and Left, two social democratic parties, the Ecologists (a cartel of five groups, sometimes opposing one another), the Jobertistes (followers of Pompidou's former foreign minister), two varieties of the fascist Right, the *Union des Français du Bon Sens* (led by an anti-trade union bakery employer), and three groups of monarchists, one of them grouping young royalists who favoured a 'popular monarchy' and supported the Left. These latter announced solemnly that they put forward their candidates 'without illusions as to the game in which they are participating'. Bringing up the line of march were unattached centrists, *Modèrés*, MRPs, Christian Democrats, supporters of the 'Presidential Majority', those who advertised themselves merely as *'divers opposition'* or *'divers majorité'*, and independents pure and simple.

While there was scant chance of minority candidates surviving to the second ballot, they represented a serious menace to the four big parties all the same, for these latter were, the effect, engaged in 'primaries' on the first ballot, with only the leading Left and Right parties going through once their *frères-ennemis* had withdrawn. And even the small fractions of the vote taken by minority candidates could well decide the outcome of these primaries, which in turn could well decide the second ballot too. In particular, minority candidates menaced the more centrist of the big formations, the PS and the *Union Démocratique Française* [UDF]. A Left Gaullist or Ecologist, for example might shave just sufficient votes from either of them to leave them frustrated spectators of a second ballot run-off between the RPR and the Communists. Such an outcome, it should be seen, was desirable from the point of view of the latter two parties not merely in principle, but also tactically. For the PCF could rely on greater Socialist second-ballot solidarity against the RPR than against the UDF, while the RPR could hope to win seats against PCF opponents they were bound to lose if pitted against Socialists. Similarly, a Trotskyite candidate who took votes mainly from the PCF at the first ballot was an asset to the PS, while a neo-Fascist who stole votes from the RPR was a hidden ally of the UDF. Given the much greater solidarity of right-wing voters against the Red threat, such calculations were of particular importance on the Left.

Hence, almost certainly, a further reason for the inflated number of candidatures: not a few of the minority challengers were actually 'submarine' candidates, put up with the encouragement or connivance of the party or parties which might hope to benefit thereby. Certainly, if one examined those constituencies where primary battles were bound to be at their most intense in 1978, one was immediately struck by the exaggerated plethora of minority candidates fishing in these same troubled waters. In the event, the net effect of the Trotskyite and Maoist interventions was to take 6 seats from the PCF and hand them to the PS and MRG, as well as helping these latter win 3 seats the PCF might not have won.[25] The damage inflicted on the PS and MRG by minority candidates was even greater, costing them their lead over the Communists in no less than 45 seats.[26] In 13 of these cases the PCF went on to win (indeed, virtually all the PCF gains resulted from them) but in the other 32 it lost. Examination of these seats suggests that, on a conservative estimate, the PS and MRG might have won 14–20 of them.[27] As it was these were all lost to the Left altogether. Given that the PS would undoubtedly have won all the 13 seats taken by the PCF, the overall loss to the PS/MRG from such contests amounted to no less than 30 seats. It went without saying that the Left, already labouring under the accumulation of handicaps we have seen, could ill afford to indulge in such suicidal games as these. Even if the hopes, encouraged by the polls, of a virtual Left landslide had been fulfilled such tactics might still have cost the Left a working majority. But, as it was, such hopes were not to survive beyond 12 March.

# 11 The Battle

On 12 March France voted, concluding an election campaign which had, in effect, lasted ever since May 1974 had put the possibility of a Left victory on the agenda. Despite the Left's open disarray since September 1977, the opinion polls continued to the last to suggest that the balance of forces seen in the 1977 municipal elections still held. On that occasion the Left had beaten the Majority in the 221 large towns by 50.8 per cent: 41.9 per cent or, when Ecologist and other third-party votes were redistributed, by 53.6 percent: 46.4 per cent.[1] The last SOFRES poll in March 1978 showed the Left leading by 51 per cent: 45 per cent, while IFOP showed an even more handsome 53.5 per cent: 43 per cent lead.[2] It was known, of course, that the Left would need a handy lead to overcome the effects of unfavourable constituency demarcation[3] and the certainty of at least some PS/MRG defections on the second ballot in seats where withdrawals by their own parties had left them with a choice between a Communist or the Right. But both polls suggested that the Left had enough support for a majority, if not a landslide.

In a record turnout of 82.8 per cent the electorate confounded these prognostications. The exact dimensions of the Left's shortfall were not at first clear, for the only widely available global statistics were those rushed out by the Ministry of the Interior which, in time-honoured fashion, distorted the figures to the government's advantage. (During the 1977 municipal elections it had announced a Majority victory of 45 per cent: 42.9 per cent, even while admitting the Left's victory in three-quarters of the major towns.) This time the Ministry's figures showed the Majority gaining 46.5 per cent to the 45.2 per cent won by 'parties supporting the Common Programme'. The Ministry also triumphantly announced that the PS had failed in its bid to become France's largest party: it had got 22.58 per cent of the vote against the RPR's 22.6 per cent. Both sets of figures were, of course, crooked. Later, exhaustive calculations showed that the Left had taken 49.3 per cent to the Right's 47.7 per cent and that the PS had indeed beaten the RPR, winning 22.78 per cent to the Gaullists' 22.60 per cent.[4]

The Left did not need such statistical refinements to know that it had performed far below its hopes. Disappointment was particularly great among the Socialists and not a few of its leaders betrayed open pessimism about the final result as soon as the first-ballot figures were known. True, the PS had overtaken the PCF, regaining the primacy on the Left it had lost in 1945, and leaving the PCF as the strongest Left party in only one-third of France. Moreover, the performance of the MRG, which did well only in the absence of a PS candidate and derisorily when it faced one, suggested strongly that its votes really 'belonged' to the PS and could be added to theirs for all practical purposes. If this was done the PS total rose to 24.94 per cent and passed the 7 million vote target set by Mitterrand. But it was still a long way from the 28–31 per cent level predicted by the final polls. Moreover, it was immediately clear that a lot of the new PS votes were going to be wasted, for while the PS could boast proudly that it was the most national of the parties – with the most even geographical spread of support round the country – what this meant in practice was that it had gained most in hopelessly right-wing areas and often stood still or even lost ground in strong left-wing seats. Its main hope of victory had always lain in the prospect that it might overtake the PCF in large numbers of marginal but winnable seats on the first ballot, then going on to take them on the second ballot. But a glance at the first-ballot results showed that this had not happened. The PS or MRG had overtaken the PCF in 55 seats but in only 13 of these had the combined Left first-ballot vote exceeded 50 per cent and in only a single case (Béthune, in Pas-de-Calais) had the PCF formerly held the seat.[5] In the end these 55 seats were to yield only another 12 PS/MRG deputies.

The PCF, on the other hand, had grounds for discreet relief. True, the Party's score of 20.6 per cent[6] was not much above the disastrous level of 1968 – ten whole years of popular front campaigning had left it where it had started – but the worst had been averted. Above all, the Socialists were not ahead by the threatened 8–10 per cent, but only by 2 per cent. The fact that the Party was still losing ground geographically was extremely alarming: it was the leading Left party now in only 169 of the 474 metropolitan seats. But conversely the Party's increasingly dense concentration in the great urban and industrial centres meant that its vote was actually building up in the working-class areas safe for the Left.

Thus, if in the end the PCF's enormous organisational effort had not prevented the Party being overtaken by the PS, it had at least succeeded in another objective of at least equal importance: the retention of the PCF's primacy within the working-class. The Party had strained every nerve and muscle to achieve this, even mobilising the CGT Secretary-General, Georges Séguy, into quite unprecedentedly partisan activities on the Party's behalf. Séguy was, of course, a member of the PCF Politburo, but the Party had hitherto always been careful in its observation of at least the appearances of trade union political neutrality within the Left, which forms so central a part of French syndicalist tradition. Séguy's open campaigning for the PCF thus threw into jeopardy the entire balance of the CGT, whose large non-Communist membership had always taken on trust the non-partisan stance of the union's predominantly Communist leadership. It was quite certain that there would be a price to be paid for this departure from tradition – after the election. Meanwhile the PCF's willingness to risk even its industrial strength to shore up its electoral position was an unmistakable indication of just how desperately the Party was prepared to defend its 'home ground' predominance amongst the proletariat. A similarly tigerish battle was fought for the PCF's other redoubt: its primacy amongst the young. In both cases the Socialists had pulled ahead of the PCF in the most alarming manner. A SOFRES poll of June 1976 had shown PS support amongst workers at the unheard-of height of 36 per cent. Among the 18–24s the figures were even more staggering: 38.3 per cent for the PS/MRG, 15.7 per cent for the PCF and 8.1 per cent for the extreme Left.[7] It was such figures – suggesting nothing less than a general Communist rout – that the PCF had strained every sinew to reverse.

It worked. With only a month to go to the election the PS led the PCF 33:23 per cent among the 25–34 age group and, more strikingly still, in the light of all previous electoral history, by 28:26 per cent among the 18–24s. On election day, however, the PCF had pulled back, leading the PS by 26:24 per cent in the former group and 28:25 per cent in the latter.[8] Amongst the working-class the PCF's last-minute recovery was, as Table 11.1 shows, even more dramatic.

TABLE 11.1 Percentage Communist and Socialist support among industrial workers, 1967–78

|  | 1967 | 1968 | 1973 | Feb. 1 1978 | Feb. 1–March 1 1978 | Actual vote March 1978 |
|---|---|---|---|---|---|---|
| PCF | 31 | 33 | 33 | 29.5 | 34 | 36 |
| PS | 18 | 18 | 27 | 30 | 32 | 27 |
| TOTAL | 49 | 51 | 60 | 59.5 | 66 | 63 |

Sources: IFOP, Les Français et De Gaulle (Paris: 1971) pp. 234, 241; J. Charlot, 'Le déclin communiste', Le Point, no. 282, 13 February 1978; L'Express, 13–19 March 1978; J. Julliard, 'Comment les Français ont Changé de Cap le Dernier Jour', Le Nouvel Observateur, 24 April 1978. The figure for February–March 1978 averages the findings of three separate polls carried out in that period by the Institut Louis Harris-France. The actual vote of 1978 is obtained from the SOFRES post-electoral survey. All other polls used were carried out by IFOP.

Thus the PCF not merely won its battle with the PS for the working-class vote but in the end pushed its own score to a record level within its 'natural' class. The PS could congratulate itself on preserving, in the face of a bitter PCF campaign against it, the whole of the proletarian support it had won in 1973 only with the aid of the PCF's benevolent neutrality. But this was merely a consolation prize. In the last weeks of the campaign its working-class support had ebbed away to both Left and Right (as the fall in the total Left support from this group shows). In the long run this might be just as significant as how well the PS fared amongst the electorate at large, for it was difficult to see how the PS could sustain itself as the leading party of the Left in the long term unless it could dislodge the PCF from its stranglehold over the industrial labour movement. This it had signally failed to do. The new initiative of the Socialist sections d' entreprise may have helped the PS consolidate what it held, but the PCF's enormous counter-effort within the factories had more than held the line.

In immediate political terms the consolidation of the PCF's working-class support paid dividends, too, for in many of the most solid Socialist redoubts PCF candidates continued to close the gap on well-established PS deputies. Ironically, many of these safe seats were held by PS notables who, while leading their party to unprecedented national success, were having to glance nervously over their shoulder in their own constituencies. Thus Gaston Defferre, the mayor of Marseilles, saw his lead shrink to a point where any continuation of this trend would almost certainly cost him his seat, while Mitterrand was denied his normal first-ballot victory by the strong PCF advance in his fief of Nièvre. In 9 constituencies the PCF actually overtook the PS, and whereas the PS had overtaken the PCF mainly in hopeless areas, all 9 of these had been blue-chip safe seats for the PS. (In 7 of the 9 the PS had attempted to replace a sitting deputy, or was split, or both.) The PCF went on to win 6 of these – the other 3 going to the Right as PS voters revolted against having to vote Communist on the second ballot.

The greatest exception to this pattern – and one which hurt the Party's pride – was in the biggest working-class concentration of all, the Paris region, on which the PCF relied for a whole quarter of its vote. Here the PCF's vote fell sharply; indeed the losses here made up almost two-thirds of all the PCF losses nationally. Had the Party fared as poorly elsewhere as it did in this, its greatest redoubt, it would, indeed, have fallen nationally below the nightmare level of 19 per cent. Some, though by no means all, of these losses could be explained by demographic factors. Paris has become an increasingly white-collar and middle-class city. This process of *embourgeoisement* has affected many of the outer suburbs too; and here, of course, the large concentrations of voteless immigrant workers constituted a further indirect handicap for the PCF. Such explanations held little consolation for the Party, however, particularly in light of the prodigious advance of the PS both in the capital and the wider Paris region. Ultimately the PCF was to cling on – by wafer-thin majorities – to only 3 of the 31 Paris city seats. For the first time in half a century the Party was no longer the main left-wing force in the capital. Paris has returned at least some PCF deputies ever since the Party's inception, but the 1978 results suggested that this long political tradition was almost at an end.

Outside the great urban centres the PCF had to watch helplessly as the last vestiges of its Resistance heritage were washed away. In huge areas of rural and semi-rural France the Party fell back to the 3–5 per cent levels typical of Communist Parties in countries where Communism has never been a major force. It was galling enough to be trounced by the PS in such areas, but it was worse still to find that quite often the Party was trailing in behind Ecologist candidates whose movement had hardly existed as an electoral force before 1977. Moreover, the Trotskyite groups, particularly *Lutte Ouvrière*, often polled rather well in such areas, sometimes quite closely approaching the PCF. (In Ambert-Thiers, indeed, its leader, Mlle Arlette Laguiller, received 8.4 per cent of the vote – a record level for the LO.)

Superficially, indeed, the far Left had not done badly and the LO, with almost 500,000 votes was now clearly a force to be reckoned with. But while the far Left had kept the share of the poll it had achieved in 1974, it had entirely failed to expand – at a time when the Left overall was growing. Moreover, even its success was shot through with ironic contradictions, for the LO, in theory the most *ouvrieriste* of parties, had performed worst in the most proletarian area, the Paris region. Instead, it relied for almost 90 per cent of its support on isolated nuclei of radicals scattered through provincial France. Moreover, while the LO abominated the presidential system and the cult of personality, it was clearly and heavily dependent for much of its appeal on the striking personality of Mlle Laguiller, its 1974 presidential candidate. Arlette, as she was universally known, was a most accomplished TV politician, creating a further sensation in 1978 by using her air-time to go through the Prime Minister's tax returns. These returns, she hinted, hardly told the whole story, but they told of quite enough wealth, even so, to render quite grotesque M. Barre's calls to workers to tighten their belts. The broadcast caused a frisson of pure horror in every bourgeois home, where the idea of tax-inspectors combing through one's returns – let alone their wholesale filching by *gauchiste* militants – is nightmare enough. The problem for the LO, however, was that Arlette's prominence led the party to become, much against its will, a personalised section of the women's liberation movement, for while men predominated in the electorates of all the other Left parties – and increasingly so the farther Left one went – the LO's support was more feminine even than the Gaullists'.[9]

The PSU (i.e. the remnant which had not followed Rocard into the PS), fighting in 1978 under the *Front Autogestionnaire* label, was a mirror-opposite of the LO, losing most of its provincial support to the Ecologists and relying on the Paris region for a whole one-third of its 300,000 votes. Almost certainly a majority of these Parisian *gauchistes* were students, not workers. Thus the alliance which made the May Events had decomposed quite neatly into its constituent parts; the parts had shrunk; and they were isolated both from one another and the rest of the Left. In March 1978 May 1968 was a lot longer than ten years away . . .

The first-ballot results had been a grave disappointment to the Left, but not all hope was gone. A great deal would now depend on discipline within the Left at the second ballot. There were no less than fifty-seven seats held by the Right where the combined Left had totalled over 50 per cent on the first ballot. If the PS and PCF carried out mutual withdrawals and achieved a near-perfect transfer of votes behind the leading Left candidate in every seat, they might win most, perhaps all, of these. Beyond these were another forty-six Right-held seats where neither Right nor Left had totalled 50 per cent on the first ballot and where the Ecologists and other minor parties held the balance. Needing only another sixty-four seats for a bare majority in parliament, the Left thus still had a fighting chance – on paper – in almost twice as many (113) cases . . .

On 13 March, the day after the first ballot, delegations from the PS, MRG and PCF met for their climactic summit. Television cameras and journalists by the score gathered to record this tense and final moment of truth. The meeting was to be at the Socialist headquarters in Paris at the Place du Colonel-Fabien, a venue to which, fittingly enough, the Metro runs via Stalingrad and Jean-Jaurès. All day was spent by Socialists and Communists alike in conclaves of their own to discuss the results and the approaching meeting. Tension rose towards evening – the Communists must come soon. Marchais would now, at last, confront Mitterrand and Fabre. It was months since these generals of the Left had met face to face and much bad blood had flowed between them in the meantime.

But quite apart from such personal tensions, what chance was there of an agreement? Without one the Communists had vowed they would maintain their candidates even against better-placed Socialists. In which case the second ballot would be a St Bartholemew's Day Massacre of the Left. But how, after all that had passed, could there be an agreement? Only, surely, if Mitterrand was prepared to give way on all that he had steadfastly refused to concede since September? Mitterrand prepared for his Waterloo, carrying into the meeting with him a final list of further concessions with which to buy a compromise, notably an extension of the list of subsidiary companies to be nationalised. His lieutenants, led by Pierre Mauroy, mayor of Lille and the real boss of the PS organisation, readied themselves to bargain for their lives.

The Communists arrived at the Place du Colonel-Fabien just after 6 p.m.,[10] Marchais's entourage including Paul Laurent (the Politburo's main electoral analyst), Charles Fiterman, and, among the lesser lights, Philippe Herzog, the PCF economist whose costing of the Common Programme had cost the PS so much pain. Herzog would be a key man in any discussion of nationalisations or economic reforms. His presence suggested that the Politburo meant business. The Communists sat down as one man – everyone knew his right place without asking. There was, equally, no discussion about who should sit on either side of Mitterrand – Mauroy and Defferre – but there was a good deal of jostling amongst Fabre's retinue, with none of the MRG small fry willing to take seats at the bottom of the table.

Mitterrand began, introducing a simple resolution calling, without further negotiation, for 'a common majority around a common programme for a common government'. Fabre had brought along his own little resolution too but immediately shelved it, saying the PS version was just as good. It was now up to Marchais. His listeners could hardly believe their ears. The PCF wanted a short declaration outlining the principal objectives of a Left government, that was all. He would have liked to press the earlier negotiations to a conclusion, he said, but he knew his partners weren't ready and he would, accordingly, drop all such matters. He went on to read a bland PCF draft of the proposed declaration. Listening to the parade of uncontentious points which followed one PS delegate was so stunned as to interrupt: 'Subsidiaries? You said subsidiaries?' No, no one was talking about subsidiaries. All that the PCF wanted was maximum Left unity for the second ballot. The Party would – of course – accept the full requirements of republican discipline and withdraw its candidates wherever they had come behind the PS or MRG. Mitterrand, now wreathed in smiles, kept his list of concessions safely in his pocket and declared that he would happily accept the PCF text as the basis for such an agreement. Mauroy, less able to contain himself, observed curtly to Marchais, 'Pity that you didn't propose this to us in September.' The PCF delegates looked at one another – and burst into loud hoots of spontaneous laughter. For they were in high good humour . . .

With the PCF in genial, even jovial, mood it took only half an hour to go through the agreement. The PS wanted to extend the time it would take to increase family allowances? The PCF had no objection. The MRG wanted compensation for small and medium employers who had to pay the new minimum wage laid down in the declaration? By all means. A minor deadlock then loomed over the programme of legislation for a future Left government, with Mme Yvette Roudy, the PS National Secretary, arguing passionately for priority for a law on nursery schools. Mme Madeleine Vincent, her opposite number on the Politburo, shrugged her shoulders:

'Nobody knows what this is about. Go ahead, it's not very important.' The whole thing was over, signed and sealed, in a little over two hours – including the time it took to have the amended declaration retyped. While this was going on the delegates headed for the buffet where Mitterrand's economic adviser, Jacques Attali, buttonholed his opposite number, Herzog: 'What is going on, then? Are the subsidiaries no longer a problem?' Herzog's reply had nothing to do with nationalisations: 'We've done our count. The Left is going to be fifteen seats short in any case.' Mauroy summed the situation up succinctly: 'The Communist Party has got what it wanted. It has gone through the campaign with a state of super-competition existing between our two parties, blindly determined to keep the Blue Riband. Then, after the match, you find it in the changing-rooms ready for the handshakes . . .'

The problem for the Left was that Mauroy's perception was rather generally shared by the electorate. The terms of the 13 March agreement were such that it could easily have been reached at least in January and very probably in September. It now enabled the Left to conduct a united campaign for the second ballot and mutual withdrawals took place with perfect discipline. But the Left's sudden agreement failed to carry conviction. Either the disagreements within the Left had been real and substantive – in which case the agreement was a mere papering over of the cracks. Or agreement had always been possible and the Left electorate had been cynically manipulated by the artificial disagreements of their leaders. Whichever was the case, the credibility of a future Left government was hardly enhanced. Moreover, electors felt cheated. They had expected high drama and had been served up a low farce. They had been encouraged to view the altercation as a stern battle of principle but, in the event, as Mauroy's remark suggested, they had discovered they were only at a boxing match . . .

These considerations were of particular importance to the Left's external audience – the Ecologists (the so-called 'Greens') and other centrist voters – whose support the Left would now need. Had the Left won well over 50 per cent at the first ballot, it would have been freed of the necessity to play the time-honoured game of angling for centrist support at the second ballot. In the past enough of these votes had always crumbled to the Right in the end to produce conservative victories, but by 1978 the position was further tightened by the almost complete incorporation of the Centre (which had taken 13.2 per cent of the vote in 1973) into the Majority. In 1978 the Ecologists and others had taken only 3 per cent of the vote, but even this might be crucial. They were, accordingly, wooed by all the parties – who suddenly discovered a common preference for their campaign literature to be a brilliant shade of green. Socialists comforted themselves that many of the Ecologists – voters and candidates – came from the political family of the Left. And, indeed, at local level Ecologist candidates frequently passed word to their friends that they would favour a Socialist vote. But, to the great disappointment of the PS, none would do so publicly and their national leaders stuck stubbornly to their traditional anti-party line, calling down plagues on the houses of Left and Right quite indiscriminately.

The larger question remained whether the Left could really pull together after all the bad feeling of previous months. On the surface, at least, it appeared to do so, with leaders and press on both sides manfully swallowing their bile and calling on their supporters to rally behind the single Left candidate now remaining in contention in each constituency. It was possible in some constituencies to see even *Lutte Ouvrière* candidates trudging up to common platforms to call for a vote for an MRG candidate on the second ballot; only the Maoists called on their voters to abstain. Even at this level, however, Left unity had a peculiarly *nuancé* quality. *L'Humanité*, the PCF daily, for example, called for a mighty effort to elect 260 Left deputies – 112 Communists and 148 PS/MRG. Such a result, by happy coincidence, would produce an almost exact correspondence in seats to the ratio of votes received by the two sides on the first ballot. It was also decidedly odd: most calculations suggested that the Left could not reach 260 seats unless the PS/MRG won 160 of them . . .

Beneath the surface the nuances were altogether more pronounced. The PCF, with its vastly superior organisation, had no intention of using it to push home gratuitous extra dozens of Socialists. In constituency after constituency a small token force of PCF militants would be sent along to help the PS campaign, while the real weight of the Party machine was switched into neighbouring constituencies to help PCF candidates. Not infrequently, indeed, such militants took advantage of their anonymity in such constituencies to present themselves as Socialists eager to organise a united campaign behind their PCF comrades. Moreover, in not a few cases the word was quietly passed to militants and their families (constituting a possibly key group of several hundred voters in each constituency) that the Party would not exactly discourage them from voting for the Right to keep a Socialist from winning. Clearly, the argument went, they had to vote: the PS would quickly notice abstentions by PCF regulars; but if the PS won the seat it might not be long before it won the *mairie* too. Then they would find themselves living in a Socialist town, with the full weight of municipal patronage used to turn the balance against the Communists in whatever local outposts they held and, finally, in the local factories too. The Party would have used its strength to put the Socialists in but would thereafter shrivel into impotence; in effect it would have committed hari-kiri. Did they really want that? Similar calculations and similar tactics were, of course, being deployed on the PS side too, but were of much less significance. The PS simply lacked the organisational strength to make a great deal of difference, let alone to operate with such finesse on several different levels at once. In any case large numbers of PS voters were always certain to defect from the Left rather than vote for the PCF at the second ballot. The PS could thus rely on the spontaneous indiscipline of its own troops to limit the PCF's advance, though this did not, of course, prevent Socialists from giving discreet encouragement to this spirit of mutiny in local cases.

Such manoeuvres represented no more than submerged eddies in an already thoroughly muddied stream. Months of pre-election polemic and the disappointment of the first ballot gave the Left's campaign now a somewhat *triste*, bedraggled air – at a point when it needed, above all else, to mobilise its forces for the greatest possible turnout on the second ballot. The Right, after all, had done better than expected at the first ballot in part because it had mobilised its electorate's fears of a Left victory to produce a record turnout. It seemed entirely possible that in doing so it had already scraped the bottom of the barrel of its support. If so, a final Left effort aimed at maximising its turnout might still turn the tide.

It was not to be. If the government's propaganda machine had been in top gear before, it now went into overdrive, with a masterful and very professional anti-Communist campaign centring on the question of how many PCF Ministers Mitterrand would appoint and to which posts. For the many Right and Centre voters with an almost (or, in many cases, literally) religious horror of having Communists in government, the campaign successfully concretised a vague nightmare, as they were invited to speculate, for example, on the likely police deployments of a PCF Minister of the Interior. The campaign was clearly not without effect upon the rightward fringe of the Socialists, too – between the ballots two MRG candidates beaten on the first ballot suddenly declared for the Majority on the grounds that a vote for the PS was a vote for Marchais in the Cabinet. The renegades were generally dismissed as government 'plants', which they quite likely were, but their misgivings were not unrepresentative. Mitterrand had no real counter to this campaign: to minimise the future role of the PCF in government would have brought fresh Communist fury down on his head. Instead, he could merely point out that PCF Ministers had served unproblematically in De Gaulle's post-war government. Moreover, he asserted, since no one expected Barre to detail the members of his post-election Cabinet, so he too had the right to keep his cards to his chest about the personnel-selection of a putative Left government.

The campaign succeeded in its main aim, that of mobilising conservative supporters to vote, for turnout on the second ballot rose to the all-time record of 84.7 per cent. In some areas – Corrèze, Côtes du Nord, Tarn, the Dordogne, the Somme, Haute-Saône – the poll rose to over 89 per cent. Given the inevitable imperfections of the election register and the fact that the abstention-prone 18–21-year-olds were enfranchised for the first time, it seems clear that many constituencies experienced 'true' turnouts of near 100 per cent among the over-21s. What was quite clear was that much of this extra turnout represented the tapping of a yet further reservoir of conservative support. In seat after seat Left candidates managed to attract enough votes to have won outright on the first ballot – only to find themselves outdistanced, sometimes by several thousand votes, on the second round. Overall turnout rose by 280,000 over the first ballot, but while the Left's total vote fell by 10,000 between ballots, the Right's increased by 1.5 million. This time no manipulation by the Minister of the Interior was necessary to show that the Right had a majority. Perhaps the truest figure is achieved by reckoning together the results of the second ballot together with those seats settled on the first ballot, a statistical trick known as the *'tour décisif'*. On this basis the Right had won 14,541,448 votes (51.5 per cent) and the Left 13,685,794 (48.5 per cent). It was by far the Left's best legislative performance in the Fifth Republic but it had lost decisively all the same.

In terms of seats the Right had won not by inches but by a mile: 290 to 201. The PCF, with its usefully concentrated strength, made a net gain of 13 seats (to 86) but the PS had gained only 15 seats (giving it 104), while the MRG lost 2 (leaving it 10) and Left independents lost 5 of their 6 seats. The Communists had lost votes but increased their representation by one-sixth, while the non-Communist Left had increased their share of the vote by almost one-sixth but their representation by only 7 per cent. The hopes and expectations of several years lay in ruins. Utter delight on the Right was paralleled on the Left by anti-climactic demoralisation – and a mounting tide of bitter recrimination. Had the Left simply failed to garner enough votes at the first ballot? Or had the real disaster occurred only at the second ballot? And, above all, how and why had it happened?

# 12 Anatomy of a Defeat

> In again losing the elections in the face of a government already worn out by its own divisions and by the unpopularity of its economic policy, the Left has not merely lost a battle. An immense sense of hope has been shattered for, it is to be feared, a long time to come.
>
> Louis Althusser
> Etienne Balibar
> Guy Bois
> Georges Labica
> Jean-Pierre Lefebvre
> Maurice Moissonier
> (Open letter to *Le Monde*, 6 April 1978)

The election was over, the Left had lost. Another five whole years of Majority rule stretched ahead. Quite likely even more, for Giscard was, quite clearly, the single greatest victor of the contest and now seemed well poised for re-election in 1981. Indeed, if the Right, after twenty years of unbroken dominance, amidst record unemployment and inflation, and despite the unparalleled tide flowing to the Left – if, after all this, it could still win, when would it *ever* lose? For the Majority's heroic (Gaullist) age was visibly over. It had become corrupt, self-serving and complacent, a congealed mass of special interests, privilege, and insiders' deals. It was so used to stacking the cards in its own favour that its abuses of power had become shamelessly blatant. It displayed a clear lack of democratic sensitivity, indeed seemed at times almost to glory in its contempt for its opponents – as when the Prime Minister had told striking workers that he had no money for them 'and if I had there would be a lot of other ways in which I'd prefer to spend it'. (The same M. Barre, when challenged by Mitterrand on whether he believed in the alternation of governments at all had replied 'alternation yes – but not with just anyone', as if even reserving to himself the right to vet the alternatives.) Many on the Right, not least Giscard himself, were uneasily aware of the deep unpopularity the Majority had brought upon itself by its sheer grossness. Yet here was the electorate asking for more. The Majority was still a majority. With an opposition like this one could , it seemed, get away with anything. The Right, especially the newly powerful UDF, could almost be heard rubbing its hands with glee. The Stock Exchange took off like a rocket. It would, in every sense, be business as usual ...

On the Left the inquests began with, as we shall see, much sound and fury. Why had the Left lost; or, more precisely, whose fault was it? The argument, as is generally the case on the French Left, was couched in terms of large ringing abstractions about the class struggle, reformism, sectarianism, revolutionary identity, and so forth. It is, though, possible to answer the question more directly by looking at what actually happened. This is best done by examining two separate phenomena: the Left's shortfall from its predicted first-ballot vote, and the transfers of votes which settled the election at the second ballot.

## i THE FIRST BALLOT

The breakdown of the negotiations on the Common Programme in September 1977 led many commentators to conclude summarily that all prospect of victory for the Union of the Left had ended then and there. Such judgments were, however, apparently confounded by the continuingly strong indications of a Left victory in the opinion polls right up to the election. (The election was a minor Waterloo for the pollsters as well as a major one for the Left.) Examination of the trends of opinion over this period (see Table 12.1) suggests that the crucial damage to the Left did indeed occur in the autumn of 1977. The picture is clouded by the fact that it was only in October 1977 that SOFRES began to pose interview questions designed to elicit Ecologist preferences. It is, none the less, very striking that the poll of November 1977 foreshadowed the final result far more exactly than later surveys: in December 1977 SOFRES showed the PS/MRG recovering to 27 per cent and in January 1978 to 28 per cent, the Left total returning to 50 per cent and then 51 per cent as a result.[1] The trend of opinion up to September (on the eve of the Left's rupture) not only suggests that the preceding polemics had had no effect on the electorate at large but that the PS/MRG was actually continuing to attract new support. By November, however, the electorate had had time to assimilate the bombshell of September – confirmed by the final failure of early November[2] – and that month's survey captured the full depth of its impact. Thereafter the loyalties built over the preceding several years appeared gradually to reassert themselves, quite fully by March according to IFOP, partially but still impressively according to SOFRES. In the event, and under such pressures as the Right's hysterical campaign and Giscard's eve-of-poll broadcast[3], the configuration of the electorate's preferences returned to very much the same lines of fracture visible in November. From September on, the Left was – to use a closer analogy: a stricken ship, grievously holed below the waterline. In calm water the crew's frantic baling and the craft's own sheer momentum might keep it afloat, apparently little scathed. Once it encountered rougher water the gravity of the damage was exposed and, inevitably, it sank.

If this was the greatest effect of the rupture within the Left, it seems clear from Table 12.1 that it was not the only one. If the PCF's campaign against the Socialists allowed it to pull back a few votes in a leftward direction, its principal effect – perhaps surprisingly – was to repel away from the Left a large mass of voters on the rightward fringe of the PS. The sudden appearance of the Ecologists in the November survey coincided with this movement, giving rise to the suspicion that the PS's

TABLE 12.1 The evolution of opinion, January 1976–March 1978

| | Jan. 1976 | Oct. 1976 | May 1977 | Sept. 1977 | Nov. 1977 | March 1978 IFOP | March 1978 SOFRES | March 1978 Final Result |
|---|---|---|---|---|---|---|---|---|
| PCF | 20 | 21 | 20 | 20 | 21 | 20.5 | 21 | 20.6 |
| PS/MRG | 30 | 28 | 30 | 31 | 26 | 31 | 28 | 24.9 |
| Other Left | 3 | 3 | 3 | 2 | 2 | 2 | 2 | 3.8 |
| TOTAL LEFT | 53 | 52 | 53 | 53 | 49 | 53.5 | 51 | 49.3 |
| Ecologists and Others | – | – | – | – | 4 | 3.5 | 4 | 3.0 |
| RPR | 15 | 18 | 20 | 23 | 21 | 21 | 22 | 22.6 |
| Non-Gaullist Right | 32 | 30 | 27 | 24 | 26 | 22 | 23 | 25.1 |
| TOTAL RIGHT | 47 | 48 | 47 | 47 | 47 | 43 | 45 | 47.7 |

Source: J.-L. Parodi, 'L'Echec des Gauches', *Revue Politique et Parlementaire* (April–May 1978) p. 17; 1978 result figures from Professor Jaffré, CEVIPOF. All polls January 1976–November 1977 by SOFRES. The IFOP and SOFRES polls of March 1978 represent the last pre-election surveys of both organisations. 'Other Left' includes Left Gaullists and Independents as well as extreme Left; 'Non-Gaullist Right' includes the extreme Right as well as Centrists and Giscardiens.

support had hitherto been artificially inflated by the omission of this preference from survey questionnaires. While this was doubtless at least in part true, the fact remains that the PS was able to regain its old poll levels by March, even though in competition with the Ecologists. Moreover, while the previous electoral behaviour of the Ecologists might have suggested that their 4 per cent support in November was simply 'on loan' to them from the PS for the first ballot, in the event this group divided only evenly between Right and Left at the second ballot. That is, to the extent that they were indeed deserters from the PS in November, their defection represented a real net loss of support from the Left, not a temporary wandering. In practice, of course, there was no simple transfer of PS votes to the minority parties. The fluidity of electoral choice is invariably far more complex than such neat pictures might imply, and the ultimate propensity of Ecologist voters to behave like seasoned conservatives suggests strongly that many were merely 'homing' back to their original preferences.

One must, moreover, situate these developments in the context of two other factors. First, the events of September–November 1977 had a large impact on the Right, as well as the Left. As Table 12.1 reveals, Chirac's strategy of attempting to unite the Right around a revitalised RPR had achieved a large measure of success by September 1977. This strategy depended heavily on the strength and credibility of the 'danger' represented by the Union of the Left. As the threat loomed larger, so the RPR grew, passing the President's own *Parti Républicain* (the former *Republicains Indépendants*) in May 1977 (after the Left's municipal triumph) to recover its old primacy on the Right for the first time since 1974. By September the RPR constituted half of the whole Right as conservative electors looked increasingly to the militant and aggressive Chirac, rather than the President, as their most effective recourse against the Left. Once the Left had, by its fratricidal strife, weakened this threat the trend neatly reversed itself: Marchais's tirades against the PS were a disaster for Chirac just as much as they were for Mitterrand, for the Left's rupture threw into new perspective Giscard's earnest strivings for a more progressive Centrism. As the Left's threat grew conservative electors had increasingly taken the view that the President's espousal of such Centre-Left causes as a wealth tax constituted, at best, ineffectual dithering, at worst, a weakening of the Right's defences against the onslaught of the Left. With Left unity in ruins after September Giscard's stance, with its implied promise of rapprochement with the non-Communist Left, suddenly appeared a more constructive alternative to voters of both Left and Right.

This reinvigoration of Giscard's Centrist current has, in turn, to be placed against our second contextual factor, the elimination of an independent Centre after 1973. With Giscard's incorporation of all remaining Centrist elements into his 'new Majority' of 1974, it had seemed that the bipolarisation of French political life into Right and Left was complete. But many of the Centre's 1973 voters (13.2 per cent of the electorate) were unwilling to accept this incorporation. In 1974 enough of them had trickled across to the Left to bring Mitterrand in sight of victory and thereafter they provided the main source of recruits for the remarkable growth of the PS. Their attachment to the Left was, however, always extremely fragile. Most of these Centrists (a strongly Catholic group) had, after all, long expressed their true feelings precisely by their refusal of both Left and Right blocs, at least at the first ballot. The dependence of the PS on this new group of supporters meant that the party's vote was always extremely 'soft', easily prone to volatile fluctuation. The shock of the Left's internal quarrels was, naturally, felt most keenly by this always sensitive group. The result was the recreation of the old *marée* of the Centre, a milling confusion of moderate voters torn between their still very recent attachment to the PS, the 'non-party' relief of the Ecologists, and the progressive conservatism of Giscard and the UDF. In the event enough were to defect in the latter direction to shatter the dreams of the PS, defeat the Left, prevent Chirac from taking over the Right – and make Giscard the real victor of March 1978.

The dénouement of the polling organisations in March resulted from the subterranean nature of the damage being suffered by the PS. That is, many voters whose opinions were in the process of changing continued to attest to their newfound partisan (PS) loyalties when surveyed. The process was much clearer when questions not bearing directly on party preferences were posed. It is particularly clear if one examines Giscard's own popularity ratings. In April 1977, in the wake of the government's municipal debacle, a 43:42 per cent plurality were dissatisfied with him as President, and in May the gap widened to 46:40 per cent. With the beginning of the PCF campaign against the PS and Mitterrand, Giscard had recovered to a favourable 'satisfaction rating' of 46:45 per cent in June. In October, after the Left's split, this had widened dramatically to 49:36 per cent. In November, when, we have seen, the polls most accurately reflected the changing public mood, the proportion registering dissatisfaction with Giscard touched bottom at 35 per cent, while those satisfied became a majority (51 per cent) for the first time in many months. Thereafter, as partisan loyalties began to re-harden in the face of the approaching election, the proportions both of those satisfied and dissatisfied rose, leaving Giscard with a handsome 56:38 per cent lead on election eve.[4]

An equally striking indication was provided by the answers SOFRES received to their reiterated question, 'At heart, do you wish for the victory of the present Majority or the Left?' As the accompanying chart (Figure 12.1) shows, the damage done to the Left was, yet again, most dramatically visible in November 1977. It was, of course, always likely that there would be *some* late rally to the government by those unnerved by the prospect of the first left-wing government since the Liberation. There was certainly never a shortage of pundits willing to offer as a sort of eternal truth the adage that Frenchmen, with their hearts on the Left but their wallets on the Right, would never elect a Left government 'when it came down to it'. This adage (which was, of course, found wanting in 1936, repeatedly in 1945–6, and perhaps again in 1956) receives only limited support from Figure 12.1. To be sure, the Majority's fairly consistent advantage in fundamental preferences in this period contrasts markedly with their consistent disadvantage in the opinion polls recording party preferences. Doubtless this is at least partially explicable by the fact that a Left government was, for much of the electorate, an almost unimaginable alternative of which they had no recent historical experience; and it is certainly always safe in France to campaign against *'l'aventure'*. But the trend line in Figure 12.1 is clearly towards a roughly

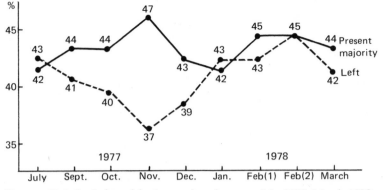

FIGURE 12.1 Evolution of fundamental preferences, July 1977–March 1978

'At heart, do you wish for the victory of the present Majority or the Left?'
*Source*: Parodi, op. cit., p.19 (Sondages SOFRES/*Figaro*).

equal distribution of preferences, save for the yawning gap of November 1977. It seems virtually certain that the sudden opening of this gap again in March resulted from the exertion of the extreme pre-election pressures on the same fault-line created by the fissure of six months before. It seems likely, moreover, that the gap between preferences continued to widen rapidly – perhaps all the way back to the extent seen in November – in the period which elapsed between the last SOFRES pre-election poll shown above (taken on 1 March) and election day itself. Some measure of this was, indeed, provided by a SOFRES post-election poll, taken a fortnight after the second ballot, which found only 35 per cent of voters saying they were disappointed by the result and 51 per cent saying they were pleased.[5] Allowing for the further evolution of opinion towards the Majority due to the post-election bandwagon effect familiar to all opinion analysts it seems likely that November's 10 per cent gap in preferences was almost exactly replicated by 12–19 March (i.e. the midpoint between the 2 per cent gap of 1 March and the 16 per cent gap of end-March). The most crucial damage may, however, have been done by 1 March, for a breakdown of that poll showed no less than 13 per cent of PS supporters saying that at heart they desired a victory for the Majority.[6] The defection to the Right of this group would almost exactly account for both the overall result and the shortfall in the PS vote.[7]

What was true of fundamental preferences was even truer of the electorate's belief in the likelihood of a Left victory, as Figure 12.2 shows. While the general shape of Figures 12.1 and 12.2 is the same, the oscillation is much wilder (doubtless because it was easier to say one would vote Left while believing it would lose than to claim one would vote flatly against one's fundamental preferences). In particular it is clear that the popular credibility of a Left victory was far more quickly, as well as more deeply, damaged than was the popular desire for such a victory. This was of no little significance given that the Left's major problem was always the weakness of public confidence in its ability to provide a credible alternative government. Even before

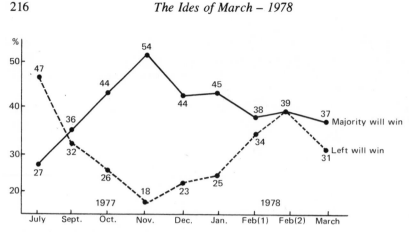

FIGURE 12.2 Belief in victory of Right or Left, July 1977–March 1978

'Who do you think will win the elections of March 1978?'
*Source*: Parodi, op. cit., p.20.

the breakdown of the Common Programme negotiations the PCF campaign against the PS had dramatically weakened this credibility (as witness the sharp drop by September 1977).[8] The breakdown did further enormous harm. In just four months the Left's nearly 2:1 advantage in public prognostications had been reversed to a 3:1 disadvantage. Thereafter the trend lines converge very much as in Figure 12.1, with the same sharp reopening of the gap eleven days before the first ballot. There is, of course, the same tendency in France, as elsewhere, for voters to wish to identify with the winning side. (Hence, for example, the invariable post-election bandwagon effect where more voters claim to have voted for the winners than actually did.) It would, therefore, be surprising if the weakened belief in Left victory did not also have its own depressive effect on Left partisanship. The Socialists were bitterly conscious of this; hence their accusation against the PCF that it had deliberately sought to damage the dynamism and élan of Left unity.

There is, then overwhelming evidence to attest the damage done to the Left by the PCF's campaign against the PS in July–November 1977. An element of apparent paradox remains, however. The PCF fell hard to the Left, attempting to pull with it elements from the left wing of the PS. Yet in the event the reaction produced was more like that of the 'cannoning' effect of billiard balls, with the more right-wing PS voters detaching themselves so that they in turn 'collided' with the Ecologists and the UDF, some of them doubtless even ending their trajectory in contact with the RPR. A point little noticed by commentators was that there had been an exact precedent for this phenomenon – a sort of dry run, as it were, two years before. At the time of the March 1976 cantonal elections the PS had led the PCF 30:21 per cent in the polls, giving the Left a comfortable 53:47 per cent advantage over a Right within which the Giscardian *Républicains Indépendants* were steadily losing ground. With the elections over, PCF criticism of the PS recommenced and in May the summit of the three Left parties broke down over the question of revisions to the Common

Programme. By June the PS had fallen to 28 per cent; the Left's lead over the Right was cut to 51:49 per cent; and the RI suddenly reversed its falling trend, clearly bolstered by defecting Socialist voters.[9] Essentially this process was simply reproduced – in magnified form – in 1977.

The explanation of this apparent paradox lay in the sociological characteristics of the more recent (and thus most marginal) PS recruits. Though spread across social classes, such recruits were disproportionately working-class;[10] tended to live in rural provincial towns; were both younger and more feminine (and thus, often, a more 'apolitical') group than the traditional Socialist electorate and; most significantly, they were, frequently, practising Catholics who had hitherto voted MRP or Centrist. Typically, such voters placed a high value on charitable good works and Christian endeavour as a means for tackling social problems, evincing a strong dislike for 'tougher' methods such as trade union militancy or power politics. Indeed, one of the strongest instincts of this group was that politics as a whole was 'dirty'.[11] Many such voters were attracted in 1974–7 to the PS and thus to the Union of the Left, which they conceived of in vague terms as a goodhearted campaign for social justice.[12] Such voters often swallowed whole the view of militant Left Catholics that socialism was merely Christianity in action. In general their political views were characterised by naive good nature and considerable hesitancy at their own boldness in moving to the Left. Such voters turned out in enthusiastic droves in March 1977 to vote Socialist mayors into power in such classically conservative and Catholic areas as Brest and Rennes.

This group was, however, particularly sensitive to any dimunition of the Left's ability to provide a credible alternative government, and the impact on them of the Left's rupture was correspondingly severe. Worse, as the Union of the Left took on the character of a fratricidal combat over electoral advantage, so it lost its crusading appeal, its sense of enthusiastic onward movement, so important to such voters. Instead it seemed to be 'dirty politics' at its dirtiest. Inevitably, such voters recoiled, some reluctantly, some with relief, towards Giscard's reassuringly lofty brand of humane conservatism. Hence the fact that women[13] and the young[14] predominated amongst the last-minute defectors from Socialist ranks, for they were often the most recently and marginally attached to the PS. Here, too, lies the explanation for the Socialists' ultimately disappointing showing among practising Catholics[15] – as also, conversely, for the remarkably strong PS performance in March 1978 in the Paris region[16] – where this type of voter was hardly to be found.

It seems unlikely that the precedent in the evolution of opinion March–June 1976 had escaped the notice of the PCF's analysts, who are nothing if not hard-nosed professionals; which is to say, that the PCF was very probably aware in September 1977 of the likely consequences of its stepped-up campaign against the PS. In theory the PCF's objective was merely to re-equilibrate the Left to its own advantage, leaving the PS as a large enough conservative rump to allow the Left the chance of victory. Doubtless, the Politburo would have been only too happy had their campaign resulted in such an outcome. But if this was impossible of achievement, and all the previous experience in 1974–7 suggested it was, the more negative objective of trimming the PS down in size was always within reach. Even if the party had not learned the lesson of March–June 1976, it could never have doubted that the reduction of the Left's governmental credibility would impact most strongly on the floating voters on the rightward fringe of the PS. Indeed, the PCF was not seriously to contest the view that the rupture of September had been disastrous for the Left, merely averring that the party was 'forced' to take the line it did by the Socialists' stealthy slide to the right. This view carried little conviction even for the party's own militants, whose anger at their leaders was patent even in September and exploded quite openly after the election, for the unitary current which had carried the Left to the verge of victory was still flowing with great strength – so great, indeed, as to constitute a major new constraint on the PCF leadership.

## ii THE SECOND BALLOT

If one focuses – as hereto we have – on the effect of the September rupture on the Left, one is struck by the remarkable magnitude of this self-inflicted wound. Equally remarkable, however – and an impressive gauge of the continuing strength of the *dynamique unitaire* – was the Left's steep and almost immediate recovery in the polls (visible in Figures 12.1 and 12.2). This recovery occurred, moreover, despite a mutual loss of confidence in each other's party by both PCF and PS supporters. In October 1974, with popular front sentiment at a peak in the wake of the joint effort behind Mitterrand's presidential bid, 68 per cent of Communists had said they had a 'favourable' image of the Socialists, though a similarly friendly view of the PCF was taken by only 51 per cent of Socialists. By December 1977, however, only 37 per cent of Communists thought well of the PS and only 31 per cent of the latter had a favourable view of the PCF.[17] Perhaps more damaging still, large numbers of Left voters had lost faith in the whole project of the Union of the Left. In mid-January one poll found that by a 3:1 margin (63:21 per cent) voters thought that the Left parties would not be able to form a durable government if they won the elections, even 56 per cent of Socialists sharing this view. Only among the Communists was there still a majority (58 per cent) refusing to give up belief in such a possibility.[18]

For the PCF here, indeed, was the rub. While it was the Politburo which was hinting openly of abandoning the unitary strategy (by refusing second-ballot withdrawals) and Mitterrand who was holding unconditionally to such a strategy (declaring that the PS would desist for better-placed Communists whatever the PCF did), everything suggested that voters in the two camps were disposed in quite precisely opposite directions from their leaders. While PS voters were now so distrustful of the PCF as to throw into doubt the viability of a unitary strategy, PCF voters clung passionately to such a strategy and to their enthusiasm for a Left government. This emerged with startling clarity when IFOP asked Left voters in November 1977 what they would do at the second ballot if there were indeed no withdrawals by their parties. Only 66 per cent of PCF voters declared they would stick by their party, while 23 per cent said they would, against Party orders, vote for the better-placed Socialist, and 10 per cent would abstain. PS voters, on the other hand, would remain overwhelmingly (85 per cent) loyal to their party's candidate in such an eventuality, and only 5 per cent would vote for the better-placed Communist.[19] Such figures foretold utter disaster for the PCF. The Party had hoped to brake the *dynamique unitaire* among its own supporters and cajole the PS into submission. Instead it had succeeded in alienating PS voters while failing to carry its own with it. If the Party attempted to carry out its threat a whole one-third of its legendarily monolithic electorate was planning to desert it at the second ballot – and the possibility loomed that many of these might even defect at the first ballot. Undoubtedly, if the Politburo was ever serious in its threat to refuse second-ballot withdrawals (which seems highly unlikely), such figures alone would have been enough to deter it. If even one-fifth of its electorate crossed to the PS the PCF might end up with 16 per cent of the vote and the PS with over 30 per cent, *and* with the Left losing the election: an outcome far worse than that which the threat was designed to avoid. Almost certainly it was figures such as these, together with the continuing and strong disaffection of many Party militants at grassroots, that lay behind the PCF's perceptible relaxation of tone towards the PS from 23 January on.[20] The Party simply had no choice. Mitterrand knew it too – and could afford to be intransigent.

Mitterrand's unconditional declaration in favour of mutual withdrawals had accurately judged the mood of the Left electorate. While much damage had been done and while it was clear that Socialists in particular would react strongly against the PCF if 'republican discipline' were not respected, it was also the case that almost all Left voters regarded such a prospect with horror. Most, indeed, had their hearts set on a Left victory and were greatly exasperated by the possibility that the antics of their respective party leaderships might deprive them of it. Even in the last week before the election – after months of intensive polemic and counter-polemic over the reasons of principle at stake – most voters still felt that the quarrel was simply the product of electoral rivalry, rather than over the substantive issues of policy a Left government might face. PCF voters were no better than evenly split on the question (44:44 per cent) while PS voters attributed the dispute to electoral rivalries by a 57:26 per cent margin.[21] Given this, it was hardly surprising, as Table 12.2 shows, that Left voters were strongly in favour of mutual withdrawals even should the parties fail to reach agreement on the Common Programme. As the election neared this dismissal of

TABLE 12.2 Preference for second-ballot mutual withdrawals, January–February 1978

| Partisanship | January 16 | | February 3 | | February 14–17 | |
|---|---|---|---|---|---|---|
| | *Yes* | *No* | *Yes* | *No* | *Yes* | *No* |
| PCF | 70 | 15 | 74 | 16 | 81 | 10 |
| PS | 68 | 18 | 73 | 13 | 78 | 10 |

'If the PS and PCF fail to reach agreement on the Common Programme would you still like mutual withdrawals for the second round?'
*Source*: *Le Nouvel Observateur*, 24 January and 27 February 1978 (SOFRES polls).

'merely' programmatic issues in favour of the more elemental solidarities of class and opposition strengthened steadily. A similar process was visible when voters were asked what sort of government they would like to see in power after the election. PCF voters, for all Marchais' tirades against the PS, were never in much doubt that they wanted a PCF-PS-MRG coalition. On 4 January 83 per cent said they wanted this and thereafter the number steadily climbed: to 87 per cent on 16 January, 90 per cent by 17 February [22] and, doubtless, virtually 100 per cent by election day. Among PS voters, of course, much greater ambivalence had always existed over the prospect of helping put the PCF into government and their doubts were greatly increased after September 1977. On 4 January SOFRES found that only 29 per cent of PS voters wanted a PCF-PS-MRG government, 40 per cent favouring a PS coalition with the Right (the remainder preferring a minority PS/MRG government).[23] By 3 February Socialists split almost evenly between these three alternatives and by 17 February still only 38 per cent wanted a government of the Union of the Left, though those preferring a PS coalition with the Right had fallen to 27 per cent.[24] Doubtless this trend continued up until election day, but it seems entirely likely that less than half of all PS voters went to the first-ballot poll certain that they wanted a united Left government.[25] It is little wonder that the Right centred its between-the ballots campaign on the question of PCF ministers in government, or that the campaign should have had such damning effect. None the less, the strong grassroots trend towards a generalised Left solidarity was extremely striking, particularly given the heavy countervailing pressures exerted by the open division between the Left's elites.

This trend was also very pronounced in the all-important matter of second-ballot transfer of votes from one Left party to another. The weakness of such transfers, particularly the disinclination of PS voters to vote Communist, has always been the Achilles' Heel of the Left in the Fifth Republic, but, as Table 12.3 shows, the events of 1977 further undermined the Left's cohesion. Left solidarity was at a peak in May 1977 in the wake of the municipal triumph, thereafter gradually falling away to disastrously low levels by late autumn.

The two electorates did not, however, respond in parallel. Despite the PCF's strong hints that it might wish to discourage the faithful from supporting Socialists at the second ballot, never less than two-thirds of the PCF electorate continued to declare it would do so. Indeed, one begins the better to understand the PCF's decision to stage the dramatic rupture of September 1977 when one observes that up until that point the Party's entire campaign against the PS had made no difference at all to the willingness of the PCF grassroots to support Socialists. Moreover, the impact of Marchais's bitter anti-Socialist polemics after September merely had the effect of pushing PCF voters into refusing to declare their intentions for the second ballot. Even this was true only for a month and by November the process had already begun to reverse itself, only to be swayed back again as the PCF organisation swung into full gear. None the less, after four whole months of such efforts all the leadership had done was to demonstrate the hopelessness of the task it had set itself. The grassroots were passionately attached to 'popular frontism' and while the Party leadership could rein in this enthusiasm to a limited extent it could not dismount from the tiger it had, with such different

TABLE 12.3 Evolution of second-ballot preferences of intending and actual first-ballot voters for the Union of the Left, February 1977– 19 March 1978

I COMMUNIST FIRST-BALLOT VOTERS

| | | *Where second-ballot alternative was:* | | |
|---|---|---|---|---|
| | | *PS/MRG* v. *Right* | | *Abstain/No Response* |
| February 1977 | | 88 | 8 | 4 |
| May 1977 | | 92 | 3 | 6 |
| June 1977 | | 85 | 7 | 8 |
| September 1977 | | 90 | 5 | 5 |
| October 1977 | | 77 | 7 | 16 |
| November 1977 | | 82 | 6 | 12 |
| 12–16 January 1978 | (i) PS *v.* UDF | 69 | 6 | 25 |
| | (ii) PS *v.* RPR | 70 | 3 | 27 |
| 30 January– | | | | |
| 1 February 1978 | (i) PS *v.* UDF | 71 | 8 | 21 |
| | (ii) PS *v.* RPR | 68 | 9 | 23 |
| 25–28 February 1978 | (i) PS *v.* UDF | 71 | 4 | 25 |
| | (ii) PS *v.* RPR | 73 | 5 | 22 |
| *Actual vote* | (i) PS *v.* UDF | 98 | 0 | 2 |
| 19 March 1978 | (ii) PS *v.* RPR | 94 | 3 | 3 |

II SOCIALIST/MRG FIRST-BALLOT VOTERS

| | | *Where second-ballot alternative was:* | | |
|---|---|---|---|---|
| | | *PCF* v. *Right* | | |
| February 1977 | | 59 | 20 | 21 |
| May 1977 | | 58 | 19 | 23 |
| June 1977 | | 56 | 25 | 19 |
| September 1977 | | 59 | 23 | 18 |
| October 1977 | | 51 | 28 | 21 |
| November 1977 | | 47 | 28 | 25 |
| 12–16 January 1978 | (i) PCF *v.* UDF | 53 | 22 | 25 |
| | (ii) PCF *v.* RPR | 46 | 18 | 36 |
| 30 January– | | | | |
| 1 February 1978 | (i) PCF *v.* UDF | 56 | 13 | 31 |
| | (ii) PCF *v.* RPR | 56 | 11 | 33 |
| 25–28 February 1978 | (i) PCF *v.* UDF | 44 | 21 | 35 |
| | (ii) PCF *v.* RPR | 47 | 20 | 33 |
| *Actual vote* | (i) PCF *v.* UDF | 65 | 23 | 12 |
| 19 March 1978 | (ii) PCF *v.* RPR | 73 | 10 | 17 |

*Source*: 'La Situation de l'Electorat' in SOFRES, *L'Opinion Française en 1977* (Paris: 1977) Tables 26, 27, p. 299; *L'Express*, 22–29 January 1978; *Le Nouvel Observateur* 6 February and 24 April 1978; *Figaro*, 3 March 1978. All polls were taken by SOFRES save that of 12–16 January, which was by the Institut Louis Harris-France. The poll of 25–28 February was the last legally publishable before the election. The 'Actual vote' above was that revealed in SOFRES's post-election survey of 28 March–5 April.

expectations, opted to ride seventeen years before. Once the leadership gave the go-ahead to a PS vote at the second ballot PCF voters fell so unanimously towards this course as to leave real doubt whether they would have acted very differently whatever directives the leadership had given.

Socialist voters were affected very differently. The onset of the PCF's campaign against the PS after the municipal elections had already, by June 1977, pushed a significant fringe of PS voters straightforwardly towards the Right (not into abstention). By the eve of the negotiations breakdown in September, however, such voters had begun to drift back again as the underlying *dynamique unitaire* reasserted itself. The breakdown turned the tide again, this time catastrophically, with the nadir reached in November, when Socialists were giving the PCF a net preference of only 19 per cent compared to one of 39 per cent in both February and June. In early 1978 the gap began to widen again, but with far less resilience than the PCF electorate showed. The proportion of Socialists willing to support the PCF at the second ballot stubbornly refused to move upward from its November level, the gap in net preferences widening merely on account of the retreat into non-response or abstention of many who had earlier been prepared to vote for the Right.

By this point the pollsters had begun to differentiate within the Majority between the UDF and RPR, something which had not been possible until the UDF was hurriedly brought to birth in the months before the election. Although at first voter perceptions of the new group were blurred and indistinct, it gradually became clear that Socialists were somewhat more willing to consider a second-ballot vote for the new group than for Chirac's RPR, which many considered to be the more reactionary and aggressive wing of the Majority. That is, the UDF's projection of itself as the Centrist reflection of Giscardian moderation gradually achieved a notable impact on its target group, the wavering Socialists of the Centre-Left. PCF voters, on the other hand, were marginally *more* repelled by the UDF than the raucously anti-Communist RPR, for such voters were, first and last, oppositionists and, Giscard being President, they disliked Giscardians most . . . In the event these discriminatory preferences between the two conservative parties were of considerable significance, particularly, as can be seen, for Socialists, who gave the PCF a net preference of 63 per cent against the RPR but only 42 per cent against the UDF.

In the end, of course, the most striking aspect of Socialist second-ballot behaviour was its collapse back towards 'republican discipline'. In fact, despite the deep wounds left by the PCF campaign PS voters were, at the crunch, more willing to support Communists at the second ballot than *ever* before (61 per cent had voted Communist at the 1973 second ballot, 66 per cent did so in 1978).[26] There was even a slight increase in the already overwhelming propensity of Communists to give second-ballot support to Socialists[27] – an impressive index of the underlying strength of the *dynamique unitaire*. The exact pattern of vote transfers is shown in Table 12.4.

In the context of previous French electoral history the most notable aspect of Table 12.4 is the relative simplicity of the ballot-to-ballot transfers, with each group of voters distributing its final preferences in a manner evenly, corresponding to its position on the Right-Left spectrum.[28] This simplicity is, in turn, merely an indicator of the ever greater polarisation of the political universe between Right and Left. The onward march of this process is, of course, inimical to those parties previously able to attract both their own hard-core electorate at the first ballot and large sections of the

TABLE 12.4 Transfer of votes, first to second ballot, 1978

| Of every 100 voters who on the first ballot, voted... | Second Ballot Vote | | | | | |
|---|---|---|---|---|---|---|
| | (i) *PCF v. Right contests* | | | (ii) *PS/MRG v. Right contests* | | |
| | *PCF* | *Right* | *Abstain* | *PS/MRG* | *Right* | *Abstain* |
| Extreme Left | 76 | 15 | 9 | 85 | 6 | 9 |
| PCF | 96 | 2 | 2 | 91 | 5 | 4 |
| PS | 66 | 16 | 18 | 95 | 2 | 3 |
| MRG | 61 | 21 | 18 | 82 | 11 | 7 |
| Other Left | 40 | 41 | 19 | 42 | 41 | 17 |
| Ecologists | 28 | 32 | 40 | 32 | 26 | 42 |
| UDF | 2 | 91 | 7 | 6 | 88 | 6 |
| RPR | 3 | 93 | 4 | 2 | 94 | 4 |
| Other Right | 2 | 79 | 19 | 12 | 81 | 7 |
| Abstain | 18 | 18 | 64 | 13 | 17 | 70 |

*Source*: IFOP polls, cited by J. Charlot, 'Rien N'est Changé, Tout Est Changé', *Le Point*, no. 287, 20 March 1978.

Centre at the second. The Gaullists were, until recently, past masters at this tactic and not a little of their decline has been due to Giscard's ability to surpass them at it. Certainly, the UDF was the more successful of the Right parties in this respect in 1978. The Socialists, on the other hand, were less successful than ever at playing both sides of the street. The party's unitary strategy has brought it extra support, but the price has been the increasing confinement of the party's appeal to a homogenised Left electorate. In 1978, as Table 12.4 reveals, the PS received precious little profit from Ecologist and even Other Left votes at the second ballot. At the same time Socialist voters increasingly define themselves as electors far enough to the Left to vote Communist (if necessary) at the second ballot. Those who do not accept the implications of the PS/PCF alliance have, more and more, refused to vote PS even at the first ballot. The result has been a steady narrowing of the differential between PCF and PS performance at the second ballot. In 1967 a Socialist standing at the second ballot received, on average, 9.9 per cent more of the vote than a Communist; in 1973 6.6 per cent more; and in 1978 only 4.1 per cent more.[29]

This narrowing differential had dire effects for the PS in terms of seats. In 1967, or even in 1973, it was virtually unheard of for a Socialist candidate to lose in a seat where the Left had totalled 50 per cent of the vote at the first ballot – often, indeed, 45 per cent might be enough if the Centrist vote broke favourably at the second ballot. The PCF, on the other hand, could seldom win a seat in which the Left had totalled under 54 per cent on the first ballot. Indeed, in areas such as the Nord and Pas-de-Calais, with a long history of internecine conflict between the PCF and the old SFIO, a Communist would do well to win even if the Left had approached 60 per cent on the first ballot.

By 1978 increasing polarisation had amended these old laws of electoral behaviour. The PCF managed to win eight seats where the Left had gained under 53 per cent on the first ballot – one of them, sensationally, where the Left had won under

49 per cent[30] – but the PS and MRG, to their great discomfort, found themselves losing in fourteen seats where the Left had gained over 50 per cent on the first ballot. Both sides, of course had their 'atrocity' stories where it was pretty clear that the other Left party had sabotaged their chances. In Gueret (Creuse), the PS mayor went down to a sensational defeat despite a Left first-ballot total of 53.9 per cent. (Indeed, although turnout rose 5 per cent between ballots his RPR opponent actually won with fewer votes than the Left had achieved a week before!) Given the legendary discipline of PCF voters it was virtually impossible to believe that the Party had not decreed this extraordinary defeat. The PCF, in return, pointed bitterly to their defeats in Senlis, Creil (Oise) where the Left first-ballot total had been 55.3 per cent and in the 19th *arrondissement* of Paris where their long serving deputy, Henri Fiszbin, was easily beaten despite a Left first-ballot score of 54.5 per cent. Given their supporters' legendary *in*discipline the PS could, however, throw up at its hands at such results and disclaim all responsibility.

Probably more significant than such scattered cases of overt 'sabotage' was the phenomenal ability of the PCF organisation to pull out a maximal Left vote for its own candidates while, relatively speaking, sitting on its hands in seats where the Left candidate was a Socialist. This was reflected in the fact that the PCF was able to pull home to victory no less than one-fifth of all its deputies on margins of under 1 per cent – while only one-tenth of PS/MRG deputies squeaked home this narrowly. On the other hand, only eight Communists lost by margins of under 1 per cent while eighteen PS/MRG candidates suffered this unhappy fate. As Table 12.3 reveals, the PCF was actually able to match the Right vote for vote in mobilising extra electors to turn out at the second ballot – something the PS signally failed to do.[31]

The polarisation of the French political system into Right and Left halves was thus a double-edged sword for the Left. Above all (as Table 12.3 again reveals), this process has produced a Right which exhibits much greater solidarity than the Left. Nowhere was this more apparent than in Nancy where, on the first ballot, the Radical leader, Jean-Jacques Servan-Schreiber ('JJSS') had only just edged ahead of his RPR opponent, and where the Left had totalled over 50 per cent of the vote. This left the RPR in an intriguing position, for little less than a miracle could save JJSS at the second ballot. He faced a popular PS opponent; his party was in ruins; his stock had fallen greatly since the days when he owned *L'Express* and was regarded as something of a French Kennedy – indeed, he had lost votes in Nancy continuously for over a decade. He had been ejected from the Cabinet at Chirac's furious behest after a ministerial career of only a few weeks, and he was hated by the Right. Chirac had repeatedly and publicly made clear his furious dislike of JJSS, even refusing to be in the same room with him. To make matters worse, the Monarchist who had taken 279 precious votes at the first ballot called on his followers to abstain rather than vote for the 'dangerous and wicked' JJSS. Despite all this the Right, including the RPR, united behind him to such effect that he not only received the whole of the Right's first round vote but surpassed it by 1,000, winning the seat by just 22 votes.[32] The Left talked more of solidarity, but the Right practised it . . .

In only a few constituencies did the Left provide a glimpse of what might have been. The most significant case concerned Prince Michel Poniatowski, Giscard's long-serving henchman. Poniatowski was execrated by the whole of the Left. He was a visceral anti-Communist who often seemed to glory in his reputation (by no means contradicted when, as Minister of the Interior, he had controlled the police) as the hard man of the Right. The PCF, the leading Left party in his seat (Pontoise in the Val d'Oise), was so set on beating him that they put up no candidate of their own, supporting a Left Gaullist instead. To their dismay this tactic failed. Instead an unknown young (thirty-two-year-old) Socialist easily ran ahead on the Left. With the Left totalling only 47.2 per cent of the vote on the first ballot, Poniatowski seemed set for yet another victory. But here the PCF set to work with a will it normally reserved for seats where its own candidates were running. At the second ballot Poniatowski was not merely beaten but lost by over 1,100 votes. It was a case which made it seem not impossible that the Left might have won the whole election despite the disappointment of the first ballot. But it was hardly typical, for here the Left parties' hatred of the Right surpassed even the enmity they felt for one another . . .

Perhaps the result which best exemplified the temper of the Left was that in Marchais's seat in Val-de-Marne, which bears the not inapposite name of Le Kremlin-Bicêtre. At the first ballot Marchais had run many lengths ahead of his PS challenger who, following republican discipline, withdrew in his favour. Since, however, no other candidate had mustered enough votes to qualify for the second round, Marchais's was the only name on the ballot paper – which meant he would be elected even if he alone voted for himself. With no alternative candidate to vote for, no less than 19,036 electors turned out all the same to spoil their ballots, among them not a few Socialists . . . [33] Such feelings of bitterness and resentment were to find many other outlets in the aftermath of the election, not only in the continuing feud between the Left parties but in major internal crises *within* them.

# PART FOUR

# The Left Since March 1978

# 13 The Reckoning

The defeat of March 1978 shattered the morale of (in Mitterrand's phrase) the people of the Left. On the parties and unions of the Left its effect was that of a fragmentation bomb, hurling each organisation centrifugally away from every other while simultaneously splintering them internally. This effect was visible within days – even hours – of the second ballot on 19 March. Michel Rocard, interviewed on television as the results rolled in, made little attempt to hide his view that the insufficiencies of Mitterrand's leadership were partly to blame for the PS disaster. 'Fortunately,' he added, 'it's only three more years from now to 1981.'[1] With this, the gauntlet was thrown down for a bitter struggle over the PS presidential nomination – and thus, inevitably, the party leadership. Robert Fabre, the MRG leader, was equally quick to react, declaring that the result freed him from all commitments he had made since signing the Common Programme in 1972. Drawing the lesson from the double defeat of the MRG and the Union of the Left, he would tender his resignation from the party's leadership. Giscard, never one to miss a chance of wooing over further fractions of the Centre-Left, quickly invited Fabre to the Elysée, an invitation which was as quickly accepted.

The PCF Politburo met on 20 March to declare that the Party bore 'no responsibility whatsoever' for the defeat (it even attempted at first to talk of a 'semi-success' but gave up when it became clear that PCF militants talked only of 'the defeat'). All blame was due to the 'turn to the right' by the PS. Notice was thus given that what Marchais called 'the ideological war' against the PS, relaxed briefly between the ballots, would now be resumed in top gear. The statement was also intended – rather wishfully – to stifle any expression of the bitter discontent simmering within PCF ranks. In fact this barefaced attempt at self-vindication merely helped provoke a quite unprecedented display of public disaffection and criticism by Communist militants and intellectuals. A similar wind of discontent gathered force within the CGT over Séguy's highly partisan behaviour during the campaign. The CFDT and FO, which had held their breath while the campaign lasted, now vented their fury against their former partner, reviling the CGT once again as no more than a tool of the PCF. Edmond Maire, the CFDT leader, went a step further by accepting, implicitly, the criticism levelled by *gauchistes* against the trade union movement since 1974, that they had sacrificed the workers' interests to political ends, toning down industrial militancy to help the Left's electoral image. Maire announced a new policy of *'recentrage'* towards pragmatic and autonomous trade unionism. Maire was almost as critical of the PS leadership as he was of the PCF. It was all very well, he pointed out with some asperity, their striking strong postures in their war with the PCF, but the

CFDT was the only real organisation of the non-Communist Left which had to meet the Communists head-on in the industrial front-line. It had tagged on behind the Socialists and put far too much faith in their promises of victory. After the election result, said Maire, he 'had to put his watch right'. He would deal with the devil if necessary and politics be damned. Raymond Barre, the prime minister, pricked up his ears at this and invited Maire to the Matignon. Maire had 'useful discussions', attempting to persuade Barre of the necessity of a Fr. 2,400 minimum wage. Barre's response was 'Well, yes . . . in stages'.[2]

In truth the government had little need for compromise. Its opponents were now so throughly beaten and bowed that they were competing with one another to accept its invitations (when Giscard, the prodigious victor of March, invited all the party leaders to the Elysée after the election, they all came – even Marchais). Giscard was now at the height of his power and had moved a long way towards becoming master of the Majority as well as the country. Chirac could bluster all he wished but he could not hold his troops. RPR deputies happily took office in Barre's new Cabinet, declared they would not be dictated to by the party high command, and – to Chirac's utter fury – defected in sufficient numbers to elect Giscard's nominee, Chaban-Delmas, as President of the National Assembly against Chirac's own choice, Edgar Faure.[3] Giscard's UDF spokesmen made it clear that the President viewed the future with lofty confidence. In 1958 France had put behind it colonialism and political instability; in 1968 it had refused revolutionary romanticism; now, in 1978, it had turned its back on class struggle. The way was now clear for Giscard to plan the France of the year 2,000 leading the country on to a new and liberal 'end of ideology'.

Viewed from the Elysée the contortions of the Left in the wake of March 1978 were at worst comic, at best frankly helpful. With Barre's government plodding painfully on towards ever-rising unemployment amidst recurrent commercial deficits and stubbornly high inflation, it was certainly more than Giscard could have hoped to find the pages of *Le Monde* filled mainly with accounts of the feud between Rocard, Mitterrand and Mauroy or the latest diatribe against Marchais by Althusser or Elleinstein. Even the desperate steelworkers of Lorraine had to stage not merely riots[4] but recurrent 'happenings'[5] to get noticed amidst the high drama of intellectual debate . . .

It is easy (and true) enough to say that 1978–9 simply saw the French Left back to its very bad worst. But there was more to it than that. Some settling of accounts was long overdue. Ever since 1971–2 all sections of the Left had papered over the cracks of rivalry and difference in the interests of unity. But, thanks to the success of the *dynamique unitaire* those same years had also seen profound changes in the nature of the Left: the PCF had 'gone Eurocommunist' and doubled its old membership, the PS had gone from being a clique of *Conventionnels* round Mitterrand and a few old municipal bosses to being the largest party in France. While the Left had been riding the escalator of electoral success neither party had found it necessary to come to terms with its new self. Now, in the aftermath of March 1978, both had to do precisely that. The significance of the intra- and inter-party strife of 1978–9 thus lies not just in the historical facts of those divisions but in the light they shone on the nature of the Left as it entered the 1980s.

## I THE COMMUNISTS

### i THE CRITICS

The days following 19 March were filled with the sound of a muffled but steadily growing uproar within Communist ranks. Some cells suddenly found that half or two-thirds of their members were staying away from meetings but others sat in almost continuous session for weeks on end, feverishly discussing the situation. Within a fortnight the surge of discontent had become too powerful for the leadership to contain as the dissidents, deprived of outlets in the Party press, burst into print in the 'bourgeois' press, most notably in the pages of *Le Monde*. The critics were strongly represented in the Party's middle ranks and among the intelligentsia, notably including many who staffed the Party's own intellectual journals (*France Nouvelle* and *Nouvelle Critique*) and its publishing house, Editions Sociales. Two voices quickly gained particular prominence, that of the philosopher, Louis Althusser (and the group around him),[6] and of the historian, Jean Elleinstein, the deputy director of the *Centre des Etudes et Récherches Marxistes* (CERM).

The Althusser group, finding their views debarred from expression in *L'Humanité*, launched an initial salvo in *Le Monde* on 6 April, protesting against the leadership's attempt to stifle discussion and demanding

a discussion and critique bearing on *all* aspects of the whole of the recent history of our policies, *without limitations or prior conditions*, and without prejudging the causes which lie at the root of the defeat or the rectifications which are called for.

Such a discussion should involve the leadership going humbly into the cells and federations of the Party and listening to the views of militants, and the full publication of all such views in the PCF press. Moreover the next (23rd) PCF Congress should be 'extraordinary in its form' – that is, democratic, with free elections and debates, and without screening or filtering of delegates or candidates. The Congress must be truly sovereign and there must be no resolutions announced in advance by the leadership.

Althusser followed this up with four long articles published in *Le Monde*[7] on 24–7 April to coincide with the meeting of the PCF Central Committee called to discuss the situation. He accused the leadership of neglecting even to consider its own responsibility for the defeat, of having taken at least one and probably several secret strategic turns, of having treated the Party faithful with crude manipulative contempt, of systematic 'pragmatism and authoritarianism' aimed only at narrow Party advantage. First, the Party had encouraged belief in 'the over-long, excessively technical and astonishingly cold Common Programme' and had then autocratically demanded equal support for a whole series of *voltes-faces* over *autogestion*, the nuclear deterrent, and so on. Policies simply 'fell from on high one after the other: the hour of the great parachute drops had come'. Such secret and autocratic methods derived from the 'whole Stalinist tradition surviving within the Party apparatus' and from the fact that the leadership had lost touch with the masses, with Marxist theory and, more simply, with the truth: truth now was simply what 'worked' (electorally).

This brought Althusser to the heart of the problem: the PCF's structure and mode of functioning. These, he argued, were modelled on the bourgeois state and military apparatus, with all initiative coming from the top, with vertical partitioning of the membership so that any horizontal contact between cells was viewed as 'factional activity', and a key cut-off level provided by the paid, full-time *permanents* whose whole careers depended on their loyal submissiveness to the leadership. These latter, argued Althusser (from the Sorbonne), might have been workers once but did not now 'come into any real contact with the masses'. Instead they served a collective leadership which carefully stage-produced its own unanimity, hiding the least disagreements from the membership. Even the purges of yesteryear (Marty, Tillon, Lecoeur, Servin, Casanova) had long ceased. (In a later article Althusser condemned such purges as 'Moscow trials right here in France'.) In a theoretical sense this leadership was virtually bankrupt – 'the world-wide crisis of Marxism leaves it cold' – and it made no effort to emulate 'the meritorious theoretical efforts of Maurice Thorez'. Thorez, Althusser pointed out – as of a promising but not very gifted student – 'still had the courage to present concrete analyses of class relations in France'. The Marchais leadership, on the other hand, simply hid behind a simplistic set of slogans about state monopoly capitalism which reduced French society to 600,000 'big bourgeois' and 50 million plus possible supporters of the PCF. This enabled the Party to argue smoothly that there was no longer any need for proletarian dictatorship – that it could simply glide into control of the already fairly appropriate existing state apparatus. The ambition was clear: the PCF had lost its sense of 'class independence' and was simply bidding opportunistically for the middle classes.

This pursuit, Althusser added bitterly, was doomed anyway: the petty bourgeoisie were not fools. Marchais could say what he liked but who could forget the 'massacre and deportation of recalcitrant peasants baptized as kulaks? What of the crushing of the middle classes, the Gulag Archipelago, the repression that still goes on twenty-five years after Stalin's death?' Moreover, who could believe Marchais on the subjects of freedom when there was so little room for it in the internal practices of the Party? 'What proof is there? Certainly not Georges Marchais's hair-raising maxim: 'The French Communists have never laid a finger on the people's freedom.' For everyone thought to himself: 'Too true, they've never had the chance!'. All that the PCF was doing, Althusser argued, was forsaking the path of class independence. Ahead lay the possibilities that it would either become a simple instrument of the bourgeoisie, espousing the cause of class collaboration, or that it would continue to 'reproduce within itself . . . the bourgeois practice of politics' – this latter being defined as the separation of the leadership from the militants.

Althusser's outburst was treated as a great intellectual event – extraordinarily, given that most of what he had to say had been said by the sociologist Roberto Michels seventy years before and by social democrats ever since. His attack was in many ways a boon to the leadership, for Althusser had been loud in his denunciations of the abandonment of proletarian dictatorship by the 22nd Congress and was regarded as the high-priest of the Party's conservative wing. Somewhat disingenuously Althusser's critique concealed the fact that he had been far happier with the PCF in its Thorezian (i.e. more Stalinist) phase. His main objection, in practice, appeared to be not that the PCF had broken with the PS in September 1977 but that it had disgraced itself by patching up a temporary truce with it on 13 March 1978: the bulk of the Party's dissidents felt precisely the opposite about these two events. Moreover, and perhaps a little incautiously, Althusser had leaked many of these post-election views to the PCI Left leader, Rossana Rossanda, in an interview given months *before* the election to *Il Manifesto*, which happily published them in April 1978 . . . Althusser here committed himself to the decidedly ghetto view that a Communist Party must never be thought of as 'a party of government' – 'though it may be necessary to participate in government from time to time' (!). Such statements were not only at flat variance with the desperate hope of most PCF militants – the more desperate now that it was dashed – of seeing the PCF in government at last, but also with Althusser's own urgings that the PCF should 'leave the fortress'. The PCF leadership happily denounced Althusser and tried for a while to identify all dissidents with those Stalinist backwoodsmen who had supported proletarian dictatorship.

Althusser had shot his bolt by April. In May he gave an interview to *Paese Sera* in which he urged militants not to resign from the PCF: 'that would be the best present one could give the leadership and Marchais, who ask for nothing better'. By June, perhaps a little daunted by *L'Humanité*'s repeated denunciations, Althusser gave a further interview, this time to *Nouvelles Litteraires*:

> Anything can happen . . . I'm excommunicated today, but I have no desire to be a martyr. I'm a philosopher. I'm not caught up by the effects of daily public politics . . . the Party has adopted a recruitment strategy of a military type: it thus provides itself with the possibilities of a recruitment so extensive that the Party is dying by its own treason.[8]

Althusser was clearly unprepared for the revelation of such overtly elitist views and immediately announced that he would sue the journal for not allowing him to vet its account.[9] By this time he had made himself so unpopular that stalls selling his books at the young Communists' Fête d'Avant-Garde were ransacked and overturned.[10] It was clearly time for philosophical writers to retire from the fray. While the Althusser group (Balibar, etc.) continued to express its criticisms, the great man himself dropped from sight.

Jean Elleinstein, though intellectually less distinguished than Althusser, was a far more significant critic. The author of a popular book (*'Le P.C.'*) interpreting the Party in its Eurocommunist phase, he had long been regarded as a conduit of views for the leadership's liberal wing and had been chosen as a parliamentary candidate in March in the Latin Quarter of Paris. He not only spoke for a far larger element in the PCF than

Althusser could ever hope to do, but continued to publish his dissident views quite prolifically in the 'bourgeois press' for well over a year.

Elleinstein was in agreement with Althusser's demands for greater democracy and openness throughout the PCF and an exhumation of all the Party 'trials' back to Marty and Tillon,[11] but whereas Althusser had opposed the changes of the 22nd Congress Elleinstein saw the 22nd Congress as merely a beginning. Althusser had proposed that the 23rd Congress should be 'extraordinary' by virtue of allowing free discussion. Elleinstein couldn't see why this should not be a permanent condition. Althusser believed the PCF must get back on the high road of Marxist theory and, above all, come up with a theory of the State. Elleinstein wanted the PCF to adapt its theory to contemporary facts and regard nothing as theoretically sacred. He was, he said, a Marxist – but not a Leninist. What on earth, he wondered (sacrilegiously) aloud, did Lenin have to offer the skilled and highly paid workers of the Paris belt, many of them now the owners of second homes?

Elleinstein was prompted by such thoughts to the belief that nothing less than the reconstitution of the PCF's identity was necessary. The 'old' Party had died at the 22nd Congress but the new one was still waiting to be born. No wonder the PCF had failed in its mighty efforts to win over intellectuals and petty bourgeois. Indeed, its problem was that it had less and less to offer skilled workers. It was actually losing ground in areas where the cultural level of the proletariat was highest (i.e. around Paris) and gaining only in declining and small town areas where it was lower. The old Thorezian notion of 'pauperisation' was dangerous nonsense and the PCF must face the fact that the more skilled and educated workers no longer thought of themselves as poor or felt at all pulled by the old *ouvrieriste* tradition. Such groups were increasingly concerned with qualitative, not quantitative demands – with problems of ecology, feminism, bureaucracy, urban decay, the role of the State, *autogestion*, and so forth. The PCF had seen 1968 as merely a case of *gauchisme* getting out of hand and had failed to take seriously these new 'quality of life' issues stemming from the Events or the workers' greatly deepened dislike of hierarchy of every sort. Not merely intellectuals and the bourgeoisie, but workers such as these had been repelled by the PCF's 'make the rich pay' campaign in 1977–8. Elleinstein attached such importance to the PCF's remaining in contact with the more affluent workers that such a line had, quite axiomatically in his eyes, been a disastrous error.[12]

But, said Elleinstein, a great deal more than that had been wrong. He accepted – as did all the dissidents – that the PS bore the major responsibility for the Left's rupture and defeat, but he could not entirely exculpate the PCF. It should have thrashed out whatever problems existed over the Common Programme long before the election – 13 March had shown that agreement was not difficult if there was a will to find one – and the Party should never even have mentioned the possibility of refusing second-ballot withdrawals for the PS. The Party should be frank about these errors as it should about the whole of its history. It should expunge its lingering Stalinist inheritance by a complete opening of its books, going all the way back to the 1930s and the (unmentionable) Nazi-Soviet Pact . . .

For Elleinstein the major present necessity was for the PCF to re-establish the

Union of the Left and to work out its problems with the PS in a fraternal spirit. For the PCF the 'historic compromise' would have to be with the PS, not with the Right (as in Italy). The PCF must move openly towards a synthesis. In order to know what it should keep and what it should reject of its old self it must continue a great debate with itself. Did it really want democratic centralism? In theoretical discussion the 'democratic' was emphasised, but in practice it was the 'centralism' that counted. What did it really think about the State, about liberty, even about socialism? The Althussers and Balibars must be heard – and at the Congress podium – even if they were wrong. Did Leninism really have any role in the PCF today? Should the Party defend philosophical materialism? Did Communists have to be materialists? or theists or atheists? Nothing should be sacred and nothing settled in advance. Why should Marchais announce the abandonment of proletarian dictatorship in advance of the 22nd Congress? Why did Althusser not get to speak at that Congress? Why did the PCF not publish the papers on the modern State produced by CERM in 1976? It was important that nothing – not the USSR, nor even the doctrine of revolution – be regarded as sacred:

> The conception of revolution itself can, in modern-day France, no longer be what it was hitherto. The world has changed and France has been transformed. It is a question of finding a new way which is neither that of traditional social democracy, nor the Communist orientation of Tours and the Comintern.[13]

The PCF, urged Elleinstein, must have the courage of its convictions, as expressed by the 22nd Congress. At first it had said it disagreed with the USSR but still espoused the 'Soviet model'; then it had rejected this model; now it must accept that the USSR was actually an 'anti-model'. It must *really* believe in a *socialisme aux couleurs de la France*. If this meant that the very name 'Communist' had to be discarded, well and good . . .

Thus Elleinstein in April 1978. Besides the furious condemnation of *L'Humanité* his views earned the warm commendation of the PS and a full-scale attack in the *Soviet New Times* – 'anti-Soviet, anti-Communist and an enemy of socialism . . . worse than Bernstein'. (Elleinstein retorted 'how many years in a concentration camp, how many years in a psychiatric hospital do I have to do?'[14] and claimed to detect a note of Soviet anti-semitism in the attack (Elleinstein is Jewish.)[15] Better still, Mme Vermeersch, Thorez's widow, gave a radio interview in June to protest that Elleinstein had not been expelled from the Party. The unthinkable thing, she said, was that such a 'dangerous' man had actually been a PCF candidate in March 1978. The leadership stood condemned for having nursed such vipers in its bosom. In her eyes, she added, it already stood condemned for having opposed the Soviet invasion of Czechoslovakia which she still believed to have been fully justified . . .[16] *L'Humanité*'s furious condemnation of Mme Vermeersch could not conceal the fact that many of the faithful, however much they agreed with Elleinstein on particular points, were beginning to wonder how long such a heretic could be tolerated. They were outraged that he should accept invitations to write for the PS newspaper and address PS symposia, to appear as a star of the annual *fête* of Krivine's Trotskyite *Ligue Communiste Revolutionnaire* (LCR),[17] and to travel abroad on the Anglo-American lecture circuit as a 'glamorous' dissident.

Elleinstein's return to the fray in July suggested a certain softening of his position under such pressures. Noting that Mme Vermeersch had refrained from criticising Althusser, he took the opportunity to side with the leadership against Althusser on several points. He strongly defended the PCF's *permanents* as the salt of the earth and now supported the doctrine of democratic centralism against Althusser. He was still a loyal Communist; he opposed social democracy; he was only writing for the bourgeois press because *L'Humanité* wouldn't publish him; it wasn't a matter of his defending obdurately fixed positions but of simply wanting a debate. The PCF, he argued, had wasted the whole period 1956–75 and was only now beginning the real debate. It was a jolly good debate, not one about personalities, as in the PS: 'This is only a beginning, let's continue to debate!'[18] was his final – and rather muted – warcry.

As the 23rd PCF Congress of May 1979 neared Elleinstein appeared to give up hope of making any impression, condemning the Congress in advance as one of 're-glaciation'. It was clear, he said, that the old Stalinist habits were too strong, that there would be no real debate, that the Party was turning back on itself. He complained bitterly that he himself would not be allowed to speak at it, even though Garaudy had been allowed that right in 1970.[19] (Garaudy had, though, been a Politburo member – which Elleinstein was not . . .) These complaints he carried further in several long articles in *Le Monde* in February 1979. It was already clear, he wrote, that the Congress would be 'one step forward and two steps back'. The PCF was still too pro-Soviet; it had still not come to terms with its failure to achieve a revolution in France; it still had not admitted its share in the responsibility for the defeat of March 1978 – let alone 'the mistakes, faults and inadequacies of the PCF leadership and of Georges Marchais personally these last ten years and more'.[20] Eurocommunism was dead and had been replaced with a narrow 'Gallocommunism' full of imprecations against a 'German-American Europe' which were deeply offensive to all principles of internationalism. At the same time, he pointed out bitterly, the PCF continued to applaud Soviet involvements in Africa as selfless internationalism, taking no account of the motives of 'hegemony and expansionism under the cover of anti-imperialist solidarity'.[21] Such remarks, particularly the personal attack on Marchais, were so deliberately offensive to all canons of Party behaviour that it seemed likely that Elleinstein was readying himself for a crashing personal condemnation by the Party Congress itself.

Althusser and Elleinstein were only the most prominent of the leadership's critics. Their significance derived simply from the fact that they, particularly Elleinstein, spoke for so many. Elleinstein, indeed, was the authentic voice of the many thousands of PCF militants who had known the Party *only* in a period of Popular Front, who had been pulled in by the vast recruitment effort of the 1970s on the back of the *dynamique unitaire*, a group whose confusion and demoralisation was now almost pitiful to see. He was not even the most radical of them. While the Politburo railed against *Le*

*Monde* as the instrument of the *haute bourgeoisie*, its continual revelations of the PCF's inner life were eagerly read by thousands of militants. Jean Kehayan, editor of the Marseilles PCF paper, *La Vie Mutualiste*, actually criticised Elleinstein for being too prudent. He was waiting, he said, for that 'fine day' when the PCF 'will call a cat a cat: the USSR is the antithesis of socialism'. Speaking of the climate within his (Bouches-du-Rhône) PCF federation, Kehayan added:

> I have the impression of being in Moscow during the Solzhenitzin affair. I was there. All Moscow talked of it and in *Pravda* there wasn't a line about this Solzhenitzin whom nobody had read because he wasn't published. What anathemas, what signatures, what taking of position there was by the Stalinist writers. In order to know more all the Moscovites listened to the BBC. With due regard for context, the debate going on inside the French Party reproduces that scene: *Le Monde* equals the BBC.[22]

This effervescence was neither localised nor restricted to intellectuals. As Antoine Spire, head of Editions Sociales and a prominent dissident, put it, 'The workers of the Paris suburbs are not the *moujiks* of 1917'.[23] Dissent and discussion were particularly intense in the Paris PCF federation where the federal secretary, Henri Fiszbin, braved the Politburo's wrath by his attitude of almost complete tolerance. Critical tumult was loud in the 11th *arrondissement* – one of the most proletarian in Paris[24] – as well as in Elleinstein's own Latin Quarter. In this latter *arrondissement* the situation was, as usual, particularly fraught, for many of the Althusser group as well as Elleinstein's partisans were cell members there. When Marchais' report to the Central Committee was discussed in this section Balibar put up a contrary motion which, it rapidly transpired, had majority support. The leadership's face was only saved when Balibar decided to withdraw his motion.[25] Not all militants suffered failures of nerve when faced with the leadership's wrath, however. One cell in Aix-en-Provence circulated a public petition denouncing the leadership for backsliding from the line of the 22nd Congress. By September 1978 it had attracted the signatures of over 1,500 Party members, including an ex-deputy and numerous leading intellectuals.[26]

A factor which gave a wholly new amplitude to the forces of dissent was the clear ambivalence, even sympathy, which large sections of the PCF's press betrayed for their cause. In all previous crises the leadership's complete control of the means of communication had enabled it speedily to isolate and marginalise the (rare) voices of rebellion. During the last great intra-party crisis – the Servin-Casanova affair of 1961 – Thorez, not content with the public support the Party media gave him against the rebels, had demanded to know what line was being taken by Party editors and writers within their own cell discussions – with the clear hint of sanctions against any who dared take the Servin-Casanova line even at this semi-private level.[27]

The situation now was very different. To be sure, *L'Humanité* and *L'Humanité Dimanche*, under Leroy's firm control, kept up a ceaseless pitch of denunciation of the dissidents to their mass audience. But Jacques Fremontier, the former editor of *Paris-Presse* and *Paris-Jour* as well as of the PCF's main factory-floor journal,

*Action*, resigned in fury in April 1978, accusing the leadership of having 'done everything to avoid' the Left's victory. Fremontier, a key election publicist for the PCF in 1978,[28] was a good deal more frontal and sweeping in his attacks than most others dared to be. He accused the Party of 'crocodile tears' over the Left's defeat. The reports that Marchais' post-electoral speech to the Central Committee had been unanimously accepted were, he suggested sarcastically, the final proof of how the capitalist press lied, for he knew a good dozen of its members who couldn't possibly have done so. Marchais' report itself was so lamentable, he said, that it was quite clearly a fabrication of the CIA . . .[29]

Fremontier's conviction that dissent reached right the way up to the top of the PCF was widely held and encouraged other Party editors to boldness. The organ of the PCF's Paris federation, *Paris-Hebdo*, gave almost completely free rein to the expression of dissident views until it was closed down for 'financial reasons' in April 1978 – in fact on the orders of a furious Roland Leroy.[30] The same fate met the PCF's Lyons paper, *Point du Jour*.[31] In April 1978 *Nouvelle Critique*, the party's 'intellectual' journal (edited by Francis Cohen, whose book, *L'URSS et Nous*, was the Communist literary event of the year), brought out an issue in which some (moderate) dissident views were expressed, earning it the censure of the Politburo.[32] Unabashed the journal brought out its October issue on the theme of 'pluralism', including similarly dissident views. This earned a second vote of censure from a furious Politburo – for the *Critique*'s editorial team had carefully omitted to inform it of their plans.[33] The journal was now brought to heel with several editorial 'resignations' and the pointed cancellation of a second issue on the same theme.[34] Dissident rumblings also came from *France Nouvelle*, whose editor, Maurice Goldring, actually broke ranks by airing his strong critical views to the 'bourgeois' press.[35] The October showdown over *Nouvelle Critique* seems, however, to have precipitated a general resolve on the part of the Politburo to put a summary end to any further display of insubordination within its media network. On the same day as the Politburo censure of *Nouvelle Critique* came news of mass sackings and redundancies both at Editions Sociales (Spire resigning) and at the Party's *Centre du Diffusion du Livre et de la Presse*. The dismissed workers – all Party members – were also members of the CGT local, which bitterly declared: 'We have witnessed a sad parody of "negotiations", of manoeuvres of every kind and finally of *diktat*, with methods of revolting hypocrisy.'[36]

Predictably, the wave of dissent had a quite special incidence within the PCF's youth movement, the *Mouvement de la Jeunesse Communiste Française* (MJCF), especially its student section, the *Union des Etudiants Communistes* (UEC). Many local sections of these organisations sided quite openly with the dissidents. (When the Politburo member, Guy Hermier, was sent to address the Paris UEC in May 1978 he received such a torrent of criticism that he threatened never to meet with it again.)[37] The UEC itself desperately petitioned the Party over its plight – speaking of itself as an organisation 'in crisis . . . isolated . . . [with] reduced influence . . . massive absenteeism'.[38] The MJCF was in almost equally dire straits. In April it distributed 200,000 tracts advertising a demonstration in Paris – to which only 1,000 turned up. . .[39] Its journal, *Avant-Garde*, found it could sell only 15,000 of its 150,000 weekly copies and in July 1978 it was closed down.[40] It was racked by disputes, absenteeism and lost members 'due to the disenchantment of militants in the aftermath of the elections', as it frankly reported.[41]

## ii THE LEADERSHIP RESPONSE

The intra-Party crisis which faced the leadership after March 1978 was different from all other crises the PCF had faced. In order to counter the rise of the PS, the PCF had been reconstructed as a mass party on the model of the PCI, with well over 600,000 members. PCI experience showed that it was not possible to deal with such an organisation as the time-honoured Leninist military *apparat*. It was, inevitably, ponderous, slow-moving and more pluralistic. By definition it included far more 'marginal' members from whom militant activism and tough discipline could not be (and were not) required. If the leadership wanted to retain this new type of Party it had to show a far greater sensitivity – almost a democratic accountability – to its views and feelings. This would have been true even if the membership had not been more educated and sophisticated than ever before – they were truly not *moujiks*: it was all the more true given the wholesale dismantling of traditional PCF ideology in the 1970s. With one doctrinal verity after another cast away the membership tended be both more confused and also more free-thinking than hitherto. If even the USSR and proletarian dictatorship were not sacred then surely nothing was. To these conditions for freer debate the leadership had then added large promises of democracy. It was a heady brew.

Then, backed into a corner in 1977, the leadership had resorted to precisely the sort of dramatic switch in line which it had been able to carry off many times before – when the PCF had been an *avant-garde* party. The response had been slow, grumbling, uneasy. But, at least while the election campaign was on, the traditional 'family loyalties' of members held – just. Once the election was over the real price of treating a mass party as an *avant-garde* elite had to be paid. The Politburo's initial attempt to foreclose all debate on 20 March suggested a nervous reflex in the direction of traditional 'tough' leadership methods: speedily to declare a new 'line' and then expel as heretics all who dared cross it. With quite surprising rapidity, however, the leadership realised that this time such tactics would simply not do. There was simply far too much dry tinder lying around and too great a danger that the multitude of vocally dissident intellectuals might ignite it. No doubt a tough line could be maintained – the organisation *would* hold – but only at the cost of losing a large part of the new membership and sullying the Party's new 'liberal' image beyond repair. In any case the Politburo was not united. The Leroy faction had enjoyed an increasing moral dominance as the Party's line hardened after September 1977 and was now ready to follow through with a tough disciplinary line against dissidents. But it had no clear majority in the Politburo, where the balance was held by a middle group in whom the rapid policy changes of 1977–8 had bred considerable hesitancy and confusion.[42] It was widely rumoured that Marchais had taken the 'liberal' view in favour of opening the Party press to the dissidents, but had been overruled by a majority vote.[43] Leroy, for his part, launched a ferocious campaign against the dissidents in *L'Humanité* – where dissenting journalists were swiftly silenced by threats of redundancy and dismissal.[44] Marchais then won the most important round of all, however, one which allowed him to declare on 4 April that 'Undoubtedly there are some of (the dissidents) who would like to be expelled from the Party. But it won't happen, there won't be a *single* expulsion. The time when we expelled people is definitely over.'[45] This set the tone for the operation which was to follow: the dissidents would be condemned, their numbers and significance minimised, individual critics 'marginalised', and the whole rebellion ended as quickly as possible. On this the leadership was as one. But there would be no (public) sanctions. The Party would 'contain' its quarrelsome family members and leave the invidious option of family disloyalty to them.

The leadership's attitude to the period ahead was spelt out by Marchais in his report to the climactic meeting of the PCF Central Committee called to discuss the post-election situation on 26 April. Acknowledging the intensity of the 'debate' within the Party he spoke of 'those comrades' who had aired their grievances outside normal Party channels: 'This behaviour provokes understandable resentment here and there in the Party'.[46] But discussion in itself was not unhealthy and the PCF's statutes would be amended to allow freer discussion in the Party press.[47] Too many, he said, now spoke as if the Left's victory in March 1978 had been a foregone conclusion. It had never been that and the limited gains made by the Left, especially the PCF's gain in seats, were not to be despised. As for the 13 March agreement with the PS, the narrowed gap between the PCF and PS on the first ballot had made that politically possible in a way that would not have been so had the PS retained the sort of lead it had had in September 1977. In any case, the choice had been that agreement or nothing. Those who decried it now would have been even more critical if the PCF had refused to make any agreement at all. As for the Party's 'soak the rich' line, this had been justified both by the electoral result and by the simple fact of extreme and growing social inequality.

For, Marchais made clear, the PCF would maintain its hard line against the PS. It had, he admitted, been a mistake not to publish his 1972 report until 1975. The Politburo had always been aware of the difficulties in collaborating with the PS and should have made them clearer earlier, for the 'betrayal' of the Common Programme by the PS should have surprised no one:

> the Socialist party did not truly change at Epinay. Underneath its leftist and unitary phraseology, which allowed it to win over people sincerely committed to unity and to change, it remained a social democratic party whose objective was not a real and democratic change. Its signature of the Common Programme allowed it to gain a certain credibility and to mask its basic orientation.[48]

With this the Common Programme was effectively declared to be dead. The PCF's task now must be to expose the PS at every turn, to demonstrate its culpable collaboration with Giscard and with the reactionary forces of German and British social democracy. At the same time the PCF must strengthen itself, particularly in the factories, by dint of a continuing membership drive and by the intransigent defence of workers' interest at every turn. This did not, however, mean that the gains of the 22nd Congress should be lost. Indeed the coming (23rd) Congress would extend that line and would, Marchais promised, be a veritable feast of democratic discussion.

All of which, Marchais averred, did not mean that either Althusser or Elleinstein were justified:

What is starkly clear when one acquaints oneself with the writings and proposals of these comrades is their political weakness and their total failure to understand the realities of struggle in the conditions of France today. That is why their moves – whether presented under the colours of the 'left' or 'right' have this in common, that they would lead the party towards liquidation. Accordingly, we reject them outright. We want neither the dessication nor the dilution of the Party, neither the ivory tower nor the quicksand . . .

'Some comrades', Marchais continued meaningfully,

would like to set in motion in the Party and its press a sort of permanent discussion on everything and anything. This we shall certainly not do . . . To have the greatest concern for the democratic life of the Party is one thing, to dismantle the Party in the name of petty bourgeois anarchism is quite another. It is clear to any common-sense mind, after all, that permanent discussion means, in the last analysis, the paralysis of decision and action. We are a democratic party. We are not a debating society.[49]

Many attacks, Marchais noted, had centred on the practice of democratic centralism and had criticised the leadership's use of this mechanism for not always being in perfect harmony with mass opinion:

one must be clear: the Communist Party is a revolutionary party, a party of the *avant-garde*. And there are some tendencies towards a cult of spontaneity, anarchistic tendencies, to which we cannot give way save at the price of renouncing the very existence of a party able to play its role of *avant-garde*. How then . . . do we take into account the opinion expressed by one comrade that, somehow or other, there must be no difference at all between the Party and the masses; that is to say, if one takes this reasoning to its logical conclusion, that on every point and at every level we must put an equals sign between these two realities? . . . The Communist Party does not seek to reproduce existing society and its workings within its own ranks . . . It is the instrument of combat of the *avant-garde* of the working class and its allies, and for that purpose it has furnished itself with structures, rules and a life which give the maximum effectiveness in that struggle.[50]

Still others, said Marchais (meaning Althusser), had tried to exploit the gap between the PCF's leadership and base by attacking the *permanents*, the Party's full-time officials. Unsurprisingly, Marchais defended his fellow *permanents* with furious vigour. Given the vast mass of functionaries in the service of the bourgeois State, the PCF had too few, not too many. Moreover, most *permanents* were workers. 'These comrades receive workers' wages, and we are ready to compare their incomes with those of their attackers.'[51] If the Party did not enrol this proletarian corps it would quickly be taken over by liberal professionals with the time, money and the ability to take sabbaticals from their jobs. This would negate the whole point of the PCF which was, first and last, a revolutionary party with workers at its head: 'This we shall keep to and nothing will make us give it up.'[52]

It is impossible to know how far Marchais was challenged on this shameless combination of traditional *avant-garde* rhetoric with his simultaneous proclamation of a PCF mass membership target of 1 million. So many members of the Central Committee put themselves down to speak that the session had, extraordinarily, to be prolonged over two days. No record of the debate was ever published. Mme Mireille Bertrand, a Politburo member, answering demands for publication from her constitutents in Essonne, was later to declare that the unity of the Party would be threatened were any full account of the meeting to be made public.[53] In the end, of course, the Committee accepted Marchais's report – unanimously, it was said – and its members fanned out across the country to mobilise the creaking PCF apparatus in support of the new line.

The effects were almost immediately obvious. Letters rained in to *L'Humanité* from those who had earlier signed dissident petitions, now dissociating themselves from them. Those who resisted such pressures found themselves increasingly isolated and shunned. The Party's media meanwhile kept up a ceaseless barrage of anti-Socialist propaganda, throwing all blame for the Left's division on the PS 'turn to the right' and seeking to lump the PS and Giscard together as supporters of the 'German-American EEC' which could only wreak further unemployment on French workers. (The open defection to Giscard of Fabre, the former MRG leader, in August 1978 was a boon to such propaganda.)[54] At the same time the Party's media issued appeal after appeal to the faithful to stand together against the 'new wave of anti-communism' to which, it added bitterly, the dissidents within the PCF were contributing. Gradually, incompletely, but still quite definitely, the Party's faithful began to fall into line behind such views.[55] Many dissidents began to waver. In May even Elleinstein came to a secret meeting with Marchais, admitting his faults on some points while maintaining his general critical position.[56] By June the leadership had clearly begun to gain the upper hand. Leroy announced that while the no-expulsion policy would be maintained, dissidents could expect a 'stronger and stronger political riposte'.[57] By mid-June Marchais was able to announce that every single PCF federation had accepted his report. The dissidents, he claimed, could muster only 5 sections out of 2,724; 65 cells out of 27,000; and only 1,000 members out of 630,000.[58] At the same time the Central Committee announced that 1978 had already seen the Party gain 100,000 new members, 80,000 before the elections and 20,000 since then. Even allowing for the normal high fall-out rate, membership should pass 700,000 by the year's end.[59]

The dissidents were certainly swimming against a powerful tide, but Marchais was exaggerating all the same. The leadership's 'victory' had been achieved only at the cost of massive disillusionment and apathy throughout the PCF. Sales of the Party press plummeted, attendance at cell meetings fell to derisory levels, and the annual *Fête de l'Humanité* in September showed a notable fall-off in interest, enthusiasm and attendance. True, some of the hard-line elements who had dropped disgustedly out of Party affairs in the wake of the 22nd Congress now began to resurface, attracted by the new tough line against the Socialists. But even for them the *Fête* – the PCF's major annual gathering of the faithful – was an uncomfortable affair, for the Politburo 'liberals' used it to launch a new bombshell – the book *L'URSS et Nous*, which attacked the PCF's old pro-Soviet stance head-on.[60] The book led to a virtual fracas at the *Fête* between furious pro-Soviet traditionalists and liberal elements, some of whom objected in round terms to the presence of journalists from the Czech paper *Rude Pravo*, on the grounds that the Czech leader, Gustav Husak, was no more than a 'Czechoslovakian Pétain'. Moreover, none other than Jean Elleinstein sat in another corner of the *Fête*, signing copies of his books – a sign of leadership tolerance which was ill received by the Leroy faction.[61]

Above all, though, dissent had not gone away. Elleinstein in particular continued to write critically and widely in the bourgeois press (welcoming *L'URSS et Nous* but querying whether the PCF was moving fast enough and repeatedly describing the USSR as 'fascist').[62] Moreover, polls showed that by a 57:25 per cent margin ordinary PCF voters regarded the problem of intra-party dissidence as 'not yet settled'.[63] As if to verify such opinions the *Nouvelle Critique* affaire then burst upon the Party.[64] The leadership reacted with a firmness born of exasperation and bore down with increasing toughness on the remaining dissidents. Dissidence was now defined solely as a problem between the PCF and its intellectuals. Marchais, angrily rejecting the charge of anti-intellectualism, called on Communist intellectuals to play a more active part *within* the Party. They could carry on their discussions all they liked provided they carried it on inside Party institutions and recognised the final authority of the Party. At the same time he invited any who wished to to come and see him – his door was open for any intellectual with 'problems'. Elleinstein, who had refused further meetings with Marchais after the latter had gone on television to give a highly partial version of their earlier encounter, was now solemnly condemned by his own (Montpellier) PCF section.[65] He was, none the less, amongst the 400 PCF intellectuals (also including Althusser, Balibar, Jean Rony, and Hélène Parmelin) convoked to a special two-day summit with the Politburo at Vitry on 9–10 December.

The Vitry meeting showed just how far the Politburo would have to go if the new 'no expulsion' policy was to be made to work. For two days, in a frosty and often bitter atmosphere, the Politburo, composed for the most part of working-class autodidacts, confronted many of the leading figures of French intellectual and literary life. Balibar denounced Marchais as a 'paranoiac'. Mme Parmelin inveighed against the 're-stalinisation' of the PCF and criticised Marchais for trying to treat the Party's intellectuals as a schoolmaster did his errant pupils. Rony concluded his speech with the declaration that 'Optimism is the opium of the imbeciles: vive Trotsky!' Elleinstein attacked the leadership's anti-intellectualism. At the end Marchais thanked them deeply for their criticisms and advice and pronounced the meeting a great success. To their pleasurable amazement the intellectuals found that the next day's *L'Humanité* devoted five pages to their debates, including all the main criticisms they had voiced. Truly, the Party had changed . . .[66]

With the Vitry meeting the Politburo had taken a giant stride towards the containment of the dissidents. Although voices of dissent continued to be heard the notion was now firmly established that further disputes would be 'within the family': Elleinstein was the only major figure who continued to publish his views in the bourgeois press. The Politburo had, in effect, used the Vitry meeting as a sort of 'mini-Congress' to vent discontent in advance of the real (23rd) PCF Congress to be held at Saint-Ouen in May 1979. Marchais had given a solemn promise that there would be lengthy and free preparatory discussions throughout the PCF and its press prior to the Congress, but it was clear that the Congress must put dissent behind it. Ahead loomed the major tests of the cantonal and European elections (March and June 1979, respectively). If the PCF was to succeed in pulling back the Socialist lead, its own house must be firmly in order. There could be no question of following the example of the CGT which, in November 1978, had held its freest and most unruly Congress in the thirty years since the Communists had gained control of it.

## iii THE CGT

The forceful intervention of Georges Séguy on the side of the PCF in March had probably saved the Party from the worst it had to fear. It had, though, been a fateful step, one at complete variance with the principles of non-political trade unionism and with the long-term trend, strongly encouraged by Séguy, towards greater CGT independence from the PCF. Even according to Séguy's own reckoning, no more than 500,000 of the CGT's 2.3 million members held a PCF card and only 60 per cent voted Communist.[67] Séguy had played his partisan electoral role only under strong pressure from his Politburo colleagues, for it was always certain that he would pay a heavy price in dissent not only from the CGT's non-Communists but even from many of its PCF members as well. Fearing the storm to come, Séguy had announced, immediately after the election, that although the CGT would attend the April 1978 congress of the (pro-Communist) World Federation of Trade Unions (WFTU) and maintain its representatives on the WFTU bureau, it would retire its representative, Pierre Gensous, from office as Secretary-General. The CGT had many reservations about WFTU, Séguy announced, particularly its failure to champion the right to strike in Communist countries. The astonishment with which the move was greeted in WFTU circles suggested strongly that this was an on-the-spot post-election decision. It was, though, hardly enough to placate the CGT's non-Communists, who pointed out that the CGT's Italian analogue, the CGIL, had withdrawn from WFTU altogether some years before.[68]

Séguy hastened to appeal to the CFDT, the FO and other[69] unions for a new 'unity of action' campaign. In part this echoed the new PCF line which, while rejecting any further Common Programmes or 'unity at the summit' with the PS, called for a new period of struggle founded on 'unity at base'. The appeal was coldly and universally rejected by other union leaders, who saw in it merely a hasty CGT attempt to recover (as Maire put it) its 'trade union virginity'. Maire's fury against Séguy was no less for the fact that it could not be openly expressed: to condemn Séguy's electoral campaign for the PCF would have infringed the principles of non-political trade unionism as much as the campaigning itself had done. But his loud, new emphasis on non-political trade union autonomy made the point clearly enough, as did his sensational refusal to take part with Séguy in the great annual trade union demonstration on 1 May (he was, he said, 'tired'.)[70]

There was little doubt that Maire was articulating the workers' popular mood. In one factory council election after another the CGT lost ground. The losses were often sharpest amongst white-collar, not manual, workers and there were some industries where the CGT actually gained ground (in some banks, Rhône-Poulenc, Moulinex); but the overall loss of solid, blue-collar support was unmistakable, even in the great bastions of CGT influence – the railways, the bus service, Renault, Peugeot, Air France, Michelin, shipbuilding, the Toulon arsenal, the State tobacco and matches industry and, most striking of all, in the northern coalmines and steel plants, where the CGT vote fell by up to one-third.[71] Séguy acknowledged the setbacks, putting them down to unemployment, a 'campaign of denigration and calumny against the CGT', the CGT's own organisational failings, victimisation by employers,[72] and 'the bitter disappointment which followed the great hope of a Left victory'.[73] None of this was untrue, but it was also clear that the CFDT had made at least some progress while the CGT was losing heavily. Even it, though, was handicapped by its strong involvement with the parties of the Left in 1974–8. The really striking gains were made by the FO and the autonomous unions – those who had stayed clearest of political commitment of any kind. The retreat into abstention or non-unionisation of other workers told the same story. The political failure of the Left, far from leading to an industrial 'long hot summer' (as had been so widely predicted), had simply produced a deep mood of proletarian disenchantment and even defeatism.

Faced with this deep malaise, Séguy announced that the CGT's 40th Congress at Grenoble in November 1978 would be unprecedentedly open and democratic. He was as good as his word. The CGT press (*Le Peuple* and the mass circulation *Vie Ouvrière*) was not only opened to all manner of dissenting opinions but even, obligingly, ran several special editions to encompass the outpouring of critical comment which followed. Week by week astonished factory militants were able to read letters and articles denouncing the CGT's subordination to the PCF, its responsibility for the Left's defeat, the lack of real democracy in its own ranks, and even personal attacks on Séguy, who found himself simultaneously accused of anti-Sovietism in regard to WFTU *and* of being Georges Marchais's lap-dog . . . The leadership, naturally, replied in kind, accusing the PS members within the CGT's bureau of attempting to create a new split and pointed out, truthfully enough, that they would be better represented if only it weren't so difficult to get Socialists to stand for election within the CGT. But overall the leadership – including not just Séguy but his more traditionalist deputy, Henry Krasucki – rejoiced in the simple fact of debate and pointed with pride to the extraordinary number (over 4,000) of animated meetings at every level of the CGT in preparation for the Congress. The Congress, promised Séguy, would see a major democratic renewal of the CGT; he hoped there would be full and lively debate – and he hoped that the days when all motions passed by unanimous vote were over, as were the days of uncontested elections to the executive. Meanwhile, although the CGT had earlier condemned the CFDT's policy of *'recentrage'*, he announced that he had no criticisms to make of other trade union federations – indeed, for the first time in French trade union history all the CGT's competitors would be invited to the Congress; even the students' union was welcome. The most important thing was to forget past quarrels and launch a new period of united action in harmony with the deep popular desire for unity. (The offer was, of course, indignantly repulsed by most of the invitees, but the point was that it had been made – at a time when the PCF was furiously cold-shouldering all PS attempts to renegotiate Left unity at the political level.)

The resulting Congress was a landmark in French labour history. One Socialist after another marched to the rostrum to vent his grievances against Séguy and the PCF in the most forthright fashion – and to demand that the free discussion in the union's press should now become a continuous phenomenon. The traditionalists were generally more silent, but shared the general mood of high enthusiasm engendered by the new spirit of democracy. Only after several days of such contumely did Séguy rise to reply. The leadership was, he knew, in no real danger; with 80 per cent of the CGT's federal and departmental unions in the hands of PCF cadres, that was hardly possible. Moreover, having allowed his critics to exhaust themselves in a torrent of (mainly destructive) rhetoric, Séguy was not only able to play on the strong loyalist reflexes of the movement but to enjoy a wave of affection and gratitude for his role as bringer of union democracy.

Séguy wished, he said, to offer the Congress his autocritique. The CGT had allowed itself to be pulled too heavily into the political campaign of the Left. It had given too much prominence to the Common Programme and had thereby 'distanced itself from the daily preoccupations of the workers'.[74] He could not apologise for having supported the PCF in March – the CGT had a right to state its views on the breakdown of the Common Programme which it had supported and he had a right to his political opinions like anyone else – but he conceded that his electoral intervention had not been properly 'explained' or 'understood'. He would, though, have to offer his (unthinkable) resignation if the Congress were to forbid him from holding political office. Meanwhile, he could promise the Congress that the CGT would play no part in the coming European elections.

The CGT, Séguy said, had reached 'a point of no return' in its democratic evolution. He knew that there were those who disliked this development but they would simply have to accept it: 'We must get used to listening to different opinions, even those couched in an outrageous or intolerant manner.'[75] For himself, he was delighted by the 'high quality' of the debates. To those who had argued that the CGT press should be permanently open to free discussion, Séguy replied 'Why not indeed?' He was pleased to see contested elections for the executive and hoped it would now become more representative (in fact the elections were carefully 'organised' to increase Socialist representation – though not enough to disturb the Communist predominance). Even Séguy's pious expression of hope that the Congress would avoid a monolithic unanimity was achieved, the executive's motions all passing with majorities of only 96 per cent . . .[76] The Congress, which had long seemed destined to be a funereal affair, had produced an extraordinary wave of enthusiasm – and a triumph for Séguy. The price of March 1978 was now clear: the CGT, though weaker, would have to resume, even accelerate, its movement towards greater independence from the PCF. And it would at least have to begin to live with democracy.

## iv THE 23rd PCF CONGRESS

What was sauce for the goose was not necessarily sauce for the gander: in the eyes of the PCF leadership the CGT Congress had provided some lessons it might wish to learn but also some which it wished at all costs to avoid. It was not even clear that the Politburo welcomed the trend of events within the CGT, for the idea was quickly floated, against Séguy's strong opposition, that the CGT should be more tightly bound to the Party by putting a third CGT leader (in addition to Séguy and Krasucki) on the PCF Politburo. And while the CGT felt that its gradual decline in strength relative to the non-Communist unions[77] gave it no option save that of renewed unity with them, the PCF had drawn the very opposite conclusion from its decline relative to the PS. Its only salvation,, it was sure, was to differentiate itself as sharply as possible from the Socialists, never again to allow its idiosyncratic appeal to be blunted and submerged beneath a common programme or too close a unity of any kind. It angrily rebutted all PS attempts to regenerate the old *dynamique unitaire* as mere 'dirty politics' and proclaimed that while the PS already only had eyes on the 1981 presidential election, the only sort of unity that Communists were interested in was 'unity at base'. And, on closer examination, the PCF wasn't too interested in that either . . .[78]

In any case the PCF had, with the Vitry meeting, largely overcome the 'problem' of the dissidents. The problem had been carefully narrowed down simply into one about the Party's relationship with its intellectuals – and the intellectuals had failed. They had failed for many reasons: above all because the whole structure of democratic centralism was against them; because the old habits of 'family loyalty' were too strong, both within the Party in general and in themselves; because they had been too easily flattered by the aristocratic embrace of the Politburo; because they were too divided amongst themselves;[79] and because almost to a man they had lacked the courage to call a spade a spade. In the last analysis their anger with the leadership stemmed from a deep-seated suspicion that the PCF had deliberately lost the election for the Left – and it was this suspicion that they found it quite impossible to articulate: the repudiation it required was simply too great. From the very outset Althusser and Elleinstein alike had genuflected to the notion of a sharp PS turn to the right and of an at least equal party responsibility for the Left's defeat. Neither they nor any of their supporters ever ventured further than to suggest that the PCF might bear *some* responsibility for the defeat. Most intellectuals had, in any case, been attracted to the Party precisely because they felt there was a distinction in principle between a Marxist party – however Eurocommunist – and the despised, provenly rotten alternative of social democracy. It would always sit hard with them to give the Socialists any benefit of doubt. It had been a significant moment at the Vitry meeting when Jean Rony had, quite alone, argued, obliquely, that the PS was not all bad, that some rapprochement might be possible. He had met frigid hostility not only from the Politburo (even though Laurent and, doubtless, Marchais, shared such a view) but from all his intellectual colleagues as well . . .[80] This failure of nerve had meant that the real debate, over electoral responsibility, had quickly turned into a protracted but essentially secondary debate about Party democracy. This demand the leadership could satisfy – by gestures, by promises and, above all, by the quite undemocratic expedient of the Vitry meeting where the intellectuals were not only able to air their views but were, in effect, treated as Party super-members. Vitry managed to satisfy the feelings of wounded self-importance of most who attended; thereafter Elleinstein held out virtually alone. The comedy was completed in January 1979 when Guy Konopnicki,[81] the only major intellectual figure to have resigned from the Party in the post-March furore, announced he was re-applying for membership. He would, he said, continue to feel free to criticise the leadership, fight for reforms within the Party and publish his views in the bourgeois press . . . His application, not surprisingly, was refused.[82]

Immediately after the Vitry meeting the PCF Central Committee met and resolved upon an energetic effort to correct 'deficiencies in the life of the Party'. These, it believed, were particularly flagrant in the Paris region – where the electoral results had been worst and where virtually all the dissidents were to be found. Some militants, the Committee declared in horror, were still blaming the PCF for the Left's defeat ('the campaign launched by our opponents has penetrated certain sections of the Party').[83] The Leroy faction in particular were outraged at the continuous indulgence extended to dissidents by the tolerant regime of Henri Fiszbin, the head of the PCF's Paris federation: how could he have allowed the federation's paper, *Paris-Hebdo*, so to err that it had had to be suppressed? Why had the Paris federation never formally condemned Elleinstein, one of its own members? Such questions were aimed in good part at the Politburo's leading liberal, Laurent, whose fief the Paris federation really was. With Fiszbin (Laurent's close friend and associate) in charge, it was pointed out, there was every chance that dissidents would be elected as delegates to the PCF Congress – which could then quite easily become a repetition of the bear-garden the CGT had just held. The near approach of the Congress now lent cogency to such arguments and in early February it was announced that Fiszbin had resigned as head of the Paris federation for 'health reasons'. The new first secretary in Paris, Henri Malberg, was a loyal *apparatchik* who helpfully produced a dissident-free slate of delegates – no mean feat in Paris.[84]

At the same time the Central Committee's motions for Congress debate were announced. Three changes of statute were proposed: an allowance of free discussion in the Party press whenever the political situation required it – since discretionary power remained with the leadership, a meaningless (but face-saving) change; attachment to philosophical materialism was no longer to be a condition of Party membership; and, more significantly, all the old disciplinary sanctions on members were to be abolished.[85]

The leadership's three central texts[86] spoke of the profound international crisis of capitalism and the consequent 'decline of France'. With each passing year the decadence of capitalism saw the abandonment of the old bourgeois virtues and the enthronement in their place of pornography, crime, corruption and an increasingly amoral attitude to the family, the environment and so forth. Responding to this crisis, the multinationals and the capitalist states of Europe, grouped under German-American hegemony, had come to rely 'deliberately and systematically' on the forces of social democracy to contain the inevitable mass reaction. Since 1974–5 social democracy, organised in the Socialist International under German leadership, had gone over to 'active participation in the strategic counter-offensive of the forces of capital'. Hence, in France, the turning back of the PS towards the ways of the old SFIO. The picture of international crisis was, however, lightened by the role of the Socialist camp. It was certainly true that the Soviet Union was far from perfect in many ways but there was also no doubt that the 'record of the Socialist countries is positive overall'. For France, though, there could be no question of simply aping the Soviet or any other model. The PCF wanted a democratic form of socialism, democratically achieved. It had no interest in simply replacing one centralised and authoritarian apparatus of bureaucrats and technocrats by another – hence its demand for *autogestion*. In any case 'our choice is national'. France must keep its sovereignty, its identity, its liberty. The PCF rejected all forms of homogenised, bureaucratised, and Americanised society. 'The attachment of our people to their independence and their patriotism constitute a precious basis of union, a force for renovation . . .'

The transformation that was required could not be the work of an 'active minority' or a revolutionary elite. True, the PCF would itself remain a revolutionary party of the *avant-garde*, but it would seek to win its objectives via mass struggle and Left unity. Despite the behaviour of the PS, which had 'created a new situation', some alliance with it was 'indispensable'. This could not, however, be done by way of a Common Programme which, history had shown, had simply created illusions amongst the masses and allowed the PS to hide its true motives in a cloud of leftist verbiage. Instead there would have to be 'unity at base' which successively forced the Socialists to live up to their promises in the context of concrete situations. In this way the present 'disequilibrium' of the Left might be reversed and the PCF, the party of Guèsde,

Jaurès – and Lenin – would lead the work of democratic, peaceful social transformation.

With the publication of these texts 'debate' was now open. That is, PCF cells and sections were free to air their views on the document provided by the leadership, and the Party press – even *L'Humanité* – carried fairly full (though always paraphrased, never directly authored) accounts of dissident opinion, enabling Marchais to boast that 'Without a doubt we have never seen so democratic a preparation for a Congress as this'.[87] This was, actually, true: the openness of debate in *L'Humanité* was a scandal in the eyes of hard-liners. But the conception of democracy held in some quarters of the Party was such as to make it a highly relative term. Many dissidents had, for example, demanded that the Congress should, this time, have other motions to debate than those handed down to it on tablets of stone by the leadership several months in advance. One cell – in, of all places, Leroy's federation – did defiantly put up its own motion,[88] annexing to it the letter it had received from Gaston Plissonnier (one of Leroy's faction in the PCF secretariat) explaining the Party's refusal to publish it. Plissonnier's reply was something of a collector's item:

> The method of preparing a Congress on the basis of a variety of texts is a restriction on the right of every member to participate fully and with full information in the determination of the Party's policy. For the member, in such a case, has to range himself behind one banner or another without knowing what his Party's definitive policy will be – for it will be the deals between factions in the corridors of the Congress which then make the decision.[89]

The effect of the Congress preparation on the Party was of a gentle purge as the leadership motions were determinedly forced through cells, sections and federations, with dissidents overcome and pushed towards resignation. At cell level the battle was usually won with the help of large-scale absenteeism – particularly marked amongst those who had joined the Party in 1972–8 under the heady spell of the *dynamique unitaire*. None the less signs of discontent were often quite clear at this level: some cells refused point-blank to put up Party posters for the European elections bearing the slogan 'NO to a German Europe';[90] others invited Elleinstein to address them – always against the 'advice' of the Party federation;[91] and in some areas, notably the Côte d'Or, anti-leadership votes of 25 per cent were not uncommon. (The leadership had demanded that one member of the Côte d'Or federal committee, Alain Caignol, be voted off for having voiced dissident opinions in the bourgeois press. The leadership won the day – but only by a vote of 77 to 71.)[92] Despite Fiszbin's departure the opposition was liveliest of all in the Paris region but finally Laurent and Malberg prevailed there, too. In the end Marchais was able to boast that 93 per cent of the federal conference votes had been cast for the leadership.[93]

The result was a normally serene Congress. Neither Althusser nor Elleinstein were among the delegates – though this did not prevent the Congress spending much of its time denouncing them *in absentia*. Marchais received the standard tumultuous ovation for his five-hour speech and the most controversial issue – the judgement of the Soviet record as 'positive overall' – was duly accepted. The Russians were pleased – Boris Ponomarev, attending for the CPSU (which had sent no delegate in 1976) actually addressed a political meeting at Bobigny (Saint-Denis) in order to express his approval of the PCF's foreign policy.[94] For the same reason, and despite the loud promises to continue the Party's evolution towards greater openness and democracy,[95] the Congress seemed to signal the ascendancy of the Leroy group.

At the very last moment Marchais struck. Just as delegates were about to leave, and with no word of explanation or commentary, the results were announced of the elections for the (21 member) Politburo and, within it, the 7-member Secretariat. Etienne Fajon, Guy Besse, Jacques Chambaz and André Vieuguet were dropped from the Politburo. The first 3, at least, had been part of the Leroy group. Kanapa had died so there were now 5 vacancies – and all 5 went to liberals or known Marchais supporters. (To Séguy's displeasure, René Le Guen, head of the engineering union, and now the third CGT secretary on the Politburo, was one of these.)[96] These changes gave Marchais a friendly, though still not cast-iron, majority on the Politburo. Then came the real bombshell: Leroy and his supporter, René Piquet, were dropped from the Secretariat – and replaced by Mme Maxime Gremetz and Mme Moreau, giving Marchais a solid majority of at least 5:2 there. The liberal Laurent thus became the PCF's effective No. 3, behind Fiterman and Marchais. It was a sensational palace coup. Later, Marchais explained that Leroy had been overburdened as both a Secretariat member and *L'Humanité* editor: now he could devote himself full-time to the latter job. Yet Leroy had combined the two functions for several years past . . . Leroy showed his own feelings the next morning when *L'Humanité* simply failed to carry the news of his demotion.

With this victory over the Party's conservatives under his belt Marchais was now free to complete the reconciliation of the dissidents – which might be of considerable help to the PCF's image in the June European elections. One name would count more than any other: Elleinstein. To the scandalised fury of the conservatives Marchais and Laurent now met with Elleinstein to negotiate the terms on which he would sign an appeal to vote Communist. On 29 May *L'Humanité* was able to publish just such an appeal, bearing the names of large numbers of former dissidents – including Elleinstein. The next day *L'Humanité* actually published an article by Elleinstein, who announced that, while he was still less than fully happy with PCF policy, he was pleased at the direction taken by the 23rd Congress and had been delighted to accept Leroy's invitation (!) to write for *L'Humanité*, especially now that the paper was open to everyone nowadays . . .

Thus the end – effectively – of the great rebellion. For while Elleinstein continued to maintain that he had the right to write in the non-Communist press and to voice periodic notes of dissent,[97] the fact that he was seen chatting amicably to Marchais at Party receptions and could boast of having friendly telephone conversations with him[98] meant that he became a figure of more ambivalent symbolic stature. When he next criticised the leadership he did so as an *ex*-dissident: the prefix was as powerful as the protest . . .

In just fifteen months after March 1978 Marchais had recouped to an astonishing degree. In the June 1979 elections the PCF vote held up exactly to its previous level: it had lost no support at all. Although apathy and discontent continued to rumble through the PCF, membership continued to climb. At the end of 1978 it stood at 702,864, 70,000 more than a year before.[99] Marchais was now able to launch the new target of 1 million members. His no-expulsion policy had proved effective and he had guided the PCF a little further down the democratic road. He had, moreover, made himself master of the Party to a far greater degree by winning a major battle against Leroy. A battle – but not the war. Leroy still represented too much to be unimportant: he remained a Politburo member and he controlled *L'Humanité*. In the month following the Congress Leroy actually consolidated his hold there, forcing Mme Lazard to resign her deputy-editorship (Marchais had promoted her to the Politburo partly with the aim of extending his control over the paper).[100] By September Marchais was complaining furiously to the PCF parliamentary group that Leroy and his collaborator, René Andrieu, were a law unto themselves and that *L'Humanité* was attempting to sabotage the decisions of the 23rd Congress.[101] The war, clearly, would continue.

## II THE SOCIALISTS

Socialists tended to watch the eruptions of the PCF with much the same mixture of alarm and fascination as rabbits might display observing a fight between two snakes. The PS, lacking the mass organisation and intense inner life of the PCF, experienced its own post-March reckoning in the more traditional style of ruling-class politics. The leaders of the party's regional clans and political factions, hotly supported by small bands of fervent clients, now clashed in a series of mannered but bitter confrontations, attaching passionate feelings to nuances and manoeuvres which only they and devotees of the political class understood. Far below, the party faithful, still cast down by the simpler emotion of electoral disappointment, regarded these arcane disputes with blank incomprehension, uncertain as to their necessity or significance. What was universally grasped, however, was that the election defeat was a major crisis for Mitterrand. The PS leader's popularity had reached record heights just before the breakdown of the Common Programme negotiations. It had then drifted down as it began to appear that he might not be the leader of a winning team after all. Then, after March, it plummeted as electoral disappointment was translated into personal disenchantment with the man who, in the eyes of most, had led the Left to its Waterloo. Between March and October 1978 he fell by no less than 22 points in his popularity rating with Left voters,[102] and by a similar amount among the electorate as a whole.[103] And while an overall majority of the electorate had said they would vote for him as President in September 1974, by September 1978 only 31 per cent could see him as future President.[104] Most of the disputes which racked the PS after March 1978 were traceable to this single perception: that François Mitterrand, after a long and resilient career, was reaching the end of the road.

## i THE DIFFICULTY OF BEING FRANÇOIS MITTERRAND

Mitterrand's record as a repeated loser hardly softened the blow of March 1978 for the PS leader. He tried to be philosophical, saying that he had expected the PCF's attack from the moment that the PS had drawn ahead on the Left. The only question had been whether it would come after or before the election.[105] But his mood was bleak. After his post-election audience at the Elysée he commented that 'Personally, I expect nothing, I ask for nothing, I refuse everything. I shall finish my days with no decoration'.[106] And he was bitter. Defending the strategy of Left unity, he maintained that it would have succeeded completely 'if there had been no treason. I was well able to understand the embarrassment of Napoleon at Leipzig when he saw (his own) Saxon troops turn their guns on him'.[107] (The Saxons had let Napoleon down because, in the last analysis, they weren't French. The PCF had been too often reviled as anti-patriotic to let this pass. *L'Humanité*, not unnaturally, pointed out that it revealed not a little of Mitterrand's pretensions that he should compare himself so artlessly with Bonaparte . . . ) Mitterrand felt an almost equal bitterness against Rocard, whom he could not forgive for his televised stab in the back of 19 March. But not the least difficult aspect of Mitterrand's wounded state was that it did not become the presidential austerity to which he aspired, to express his feelings too openly. Instead he gave the impression of a man who had set himself standards of self-restraint rather beyond what his emotions allowed him to sustain. Accordingly, his attempt to remain loftily above the battles between the PS and PCF and within the PS was punctuated with sudden displays of lost control and furious sensitivity. Rocard played on this weakness adeptly – as did Marchais more brutally, enlivening a PCF public meeting with an account of how, after the 1974 first ballot, he had seen Mitterrand break down in tears and had had to console him like a father. Mitterrand furiously retorted that the only time *he* had seen a French politician break down in tears was when Marchais, harrassed by a right-wing press campaign depicting him as a wartime collaborator, had sobbed in open court as he described the miseries he had endured under Nazi forced labour. In the wake of March 1978 there was little that was regarded as sacred.

Mitterrand's dilemma was strategic as much as personal. He had identified himself utterly with the strategy of Left unity symbolised by the Common Programme and after March both were in ruins. The predominant emotions now within the PS were a revulsion against the PCF and a feeling that the party had become too submerged in the Common Programme, that it must now strike out strongly to establish its own autonomous policies and appeal. Rocard, who had never had any time for the Common Programme anyway, was well placed to articulate these feelings most fully. From 19 March onwards Rocard denounced the PCF quite flatly, arguing not merely that the Party bore total responsibility for the Left's defeat but that, in any case, it 'serves no purpose': it was neither revolutionary, nor pro-Soviet, nor democratic, and it simply did not want to win. As it stood it was simply a blight on the working-class. Some alliance with it was 'a necessity of the French situation', but it was worth having only because the workers would judge the PCF so hard when they saw the cost of defeat in higher unemployment, that the Party would never again dare to repeat what it had done in March.[108]

Such rhetoric confirmed Rocard in the PCF's eyes as their bitterest enemy (Fiterman described him as 'the only Stalinist in France');[109] it nourished a reawakening enthusiasm within the PS for a Third Force strategy;[110] and it considerably embarrassed Mitterrand. For, having staked all on alliance with the PCF, Mitterrand could not afford to attack his erstwhile partner too strongly for fear of admitting that his strategy had been mistaken after all. Moreover, he knew – as did every PS member at heart – that there could be no turning back now: all over France PS deputies, mayors, and local councillors owed their seats to PCF votes. The fact that the municipalities the Left had won in 1977 were now a ceaseless battleground of PS-PCF rancour was neither here nor there. The PS could not go back to Third Force politics now without effecting an electoral hara-kiri.

The true problem, Mitterrand was bitterly aware, stemmed from his own success in rebuilding the PS as the largest party in France, thus making of it an eminently desirable vehicle for those with presidential ambitions. Within the PS leadership all eyes were already fixed on the question of the party's candidacy for 1981. Already voices could be heard doubting the wisdom of nominating Mitterrand yet again. Quite apart from his losing record, he would be nearly sixty-five in May 1981 or, if he won, nearly seventy-two when he finished his term in 1988. True, De Gaulle had been President at the age of seventy-nine, but Pompidou had been only sixty-three when he died in office. A third Mitterrand candidacy was still possible – but would lack lustre and perhaps even credibility against Giscard who, though ten years younger than Mitterrand, would have seven years in the Elysée already to his credit. Not surprisingly, Mitterrand reacted angrily to the hints that it was time for him to quit. As far as he was concerned the succession wasn't open – yet. When questioned as to who might assume the PS leadership in the event of an accident to himself he had generally indicated that Pierre Mauroy, mayor of Lille and the PS 'organisation man', was a likely choice – but 'then there is Michel [Rocard] too . . . ' He had sought by such allusions to prevent any single *dauphin* from emerging. In practice this had meant witholding his blessing from Rocard who, though fourteen years his junior, was the only PS leader with a large independent following to rival his own.

Mitterrand's hostility to Rocard derived in past from the latter's sheer glamour, youth and brilliance and his habit of maintaining a large Parisian brains' trust of his own;[111] in part from Rocard's scathing criticism of 'old-fashioned socialists' who wishfully neglected the irreversible integration of France within a world market economy; and in part it was simply that Rocard threatened to do to him what he, in 1972, had done to Savary. For just as Mitterrand had used his team of loyal *Conventionnels* as a Trojan Horse to carpetbag him into the PS leadership at Epinay, so Rocard had maintained his own clan of CFDT and ex-PSU followers within the PS. Not a few of these were Catholics – leading Mitterrandistes to mutter angrily of 'a Catholic plot'[112] (though Rocard himself was a protestant, and divorced). But what infuriated, and fascinated, others was that the Rocardians were fashionable, 'smart' Parisians; that Rocard and his closest friends were *Enarques* (graduates of the elite

*Ecole Nationale d'Administration*); that their chic, metropolitan sophistication barely concealed a laughing contempt for dowdy provincials. CERES, in particular, nursed a lively hatred of Rocard. How could one trust a man who had worked as an *Inspecteur des Finances* with Giscard; who still had some influence in the Elysée; whose economic liberalism now marked him out, for all his *gauchiste* past, as the French Schmidt? Above all, they could never forgive the fact that Rocard's accession to the PS secretariat had been effected at the price of their own expulsion from it. The PCF, CERES felt, was not far wrong in dating its analysis of the PS 'rightward turn' from that point.[113]

But in the wake of March neither CERES nor Mitterrand could prevent the onward march of the Rocard phenomenon, for while Mitterrand's popularity had dropped steadily from September 1977 on, Rocard's had, as steadily, risen. By the autumn of 1978 a plethora of polls began to show that Rocard had not merely caught Mitterrand but had now far surpassed him in popularity. By December 40 per cent of the electorate thought that Rocard would be the best Left candidate for 1981, against 27 per cent for Mitterrand.[114] Particularly galling for Mitterrand was the fact that, while Rocard was overwhelmingly favoured over him by right-wing voters (2:1 by RPR and 3:1 by UDF supporters), he was also regarded by left-wing voters as being further to the Left than Mitterrand.[115] Rocard, playing cleverly on his PSU past *and* his present position on the PS right wing, had become all things to all men. He now stood perfectly poised to expropriate the PS from Mitterrand's grasp just as the PS had finally fulfilled its old dream of outscoring the PCF in a national election. For Mitterrand it was just too much.

## ii PRELIMINARY SKIRMISHES

Seeking to head off this challenge Mitterrand took two rapid steps straight after the election. First, conceding to the demand for a more 'autonomous' PS programme, he agreed to set up party policy commissions. These, he knew, would grind on for many months, even years, before giving fruit – by which time they might well be rendered obsolete by a fresh opportunity for alliance with the PCF. Second, he let drop the notion that the task of the next PS Congress would be to select the party's candidate for 1981. It took two years, he suggested, for a candidate to play himself in – one to pull the party together, another one to campaign nationally. While he refrained from actually declaring his candidacy ('It is a problem which preoccupies me not at all. We shall see. Don't they say third time's lucky?'),[116] it was clear to one and all that his present dominance within the party would make any other choice unthinkable once he put himself forward.

This latter move, he quickly realised, was a mistake. He had intended to head off any challenge to his leadership within the PS by becoming its candidate – and therefore above criticism. In this way he would simply tide over the present period of difficulty and hold the fort until he could hand over the PS to the new generation of personal protégés he had 'brought on', notably Pierre Joxe, Lionel Jospin, and Jean

Poperen. Rocard's booming popularity in the polls torpedoed this strategem, making it painfully clear that, if the main preoccupation of the PS was to win in 1981, perhaps the party's first task should be to change its leader. Mitterrand hurriedly reversed himself. The two-year campaign argument was, he knew, nonsense. He had emerged from relative obscurity and considerable success after a short campaign in 1965 and had done even better with an even shorter campaign in 1974. In any case, after the enormous exposure of these two campaigns the one thing Mitterrand hardly needed was a long introduction to the voters – it was his rivals who needed that. His problem was that he was already overexposed. Accordingly he now took the line that the PS should concentrate on the immediate task of consolidating the position it had won and defer all discussion of the potentially divisive candidacy issue till much later. If the party delayed long enough, he knew, no successor could possibly establish himself, and the nomination – if he wanted it – would be his by default. This strategy had the extra merit that if the polls suggested an easy win for Giscard he could bow out and leave Rocard to blight his career by losing badly. In effect this new strategy meant that Mitterrand would defend his castle within the PS organisation and dare his rivals to attempt to take it by storm or siege. Given the enormous authority he enjoyed with PS members grateful for the restoration of their party's fortunes, this should not be an impossible defence to conduct.

But victory was not a foregone conclusion either. Mitterrand's great weakness was that the real heart and sinews of the PS still lay in the huge federations of Bouches-du-Rhône, Nord and Pas-de-Calais. Mitterrand, hailing from Nièvre, had no substantial bloc vote behind him. The real power-brokers, history suggested, would be Defferre (Bouches-du-Rhône) on the one hand, Mauroy (Nord) on the other – particularly since such regional bosses had a habit of sweeping neighbouring federations along with them. But all such calculations came into play only when it was a matter of voting at party congresses. And, since Epinay, Mitterrand had been careful to avoid any such thing, proceeding instead by a steady policy of co-optation of leaders (Defferre, Mauroy, CERES, then Rocard) into the secretariat, leaving congresses the job merely of ratifying such deals with sweeping majorities. This had enabled Mitterrand to disguise his own numerical weakness in terms of regional support and, along the way, to recruit a quite unrepresentative number of his own protégés into the PS leadership. CERES, since its eviction from the secretariat, had naturally inveighed against this situation and demanded greater democracy within the party. Mitterrand had been able to ignore such demands as long as Rocard, Defferre and Mauroy – the party's three great barons – had desisted from rocking the boat while the ascent of the PS continued. Things would be different now . . .

Immediately after the election the Rocardians began circulating critiques of Mitterrand's leadership (particularly the 13 March accord with Marchais), calling for greater party democracy and the summoning of an early Congress. The cry was taken up, anomalously, by Rocard's sworn enemies in CERES and by Alain Savary, still thirsting for revenge for Epinay. At much the same time the MRG met to elect a new leader and chose Michel Crépeau[117] over Jacques Maroselli. Maroselli had fought strongly for the MRG to distance itself from the old Union of the Left and had proposed standing as a separate MRG presidential candidate in 1981. With all ten MRG deputies owing their seats to PS and PCF votes, the victory of Crépeau (who favoured a continuation of the united Left) was hardly surprising. It was not, though, very welcome news to Mitterrand, for Crépeau was a vocal admirer of Rocard. The outlines of a threatening anti-Mitterrand coalition were rapidly taking shape.

In early May a PS national convention met. CERES led the attack on the leadership 'oligarchy' and reminded Mitterrand that there were far more deputies on the nineteen-member *comité directeur* than the 20 per cent the PS statutes allowed, most of them Mitterrand's yes-men. Mauroy, taking Mitterrand's side, urged that the statute be not yet applied. As the vote was passed a CERES delegate observed bitterly, 'OK, here is the leadership violating the statutes once more.'[118] Mitterrand and most of his supporters walked out in a huff, leaving the meeting in a state of angry turmoil, with Pierre Joxe accusing Rocard of being 'childishly aggressive' and others criticising Mitterrand bitterly for his pretensions to 'presidentialism'.[119]

The critical fact of the May meeting had been Mauroy's willingness to lend his weighty support to the Mitterrand camp. The Mitterrandistes were more impressed, however, by the clear threat of a wholesale purge against them. Foolishly, they now overplayed their hand, circulating a signed 'contribution', eulogising Mitterrand and warning that the PS must not now allow itself to be seduced by 'modernistic language' – a hardly veiled attack on Rocard.[120] By collecting no less than thirty signatures of leading PS figures for the document the Mitterrandistes hoped to isolate Rocard beyond recall and to close off all further debate on the leadership question. The next step, clearly, would be to expel Rocard from the PS secretariat altogether.

The storm broke when the secretariat met in July. Mauroy exploded with indignation against the 'contribution', suggesting that the leadership compromise which had run the PS since 1975 was now in ruins. If the party was not to tear itself to pieces the only thing to do was to have an early Congress and direct leadership elections. The 'contribution' must be withdrawn. There could be no question of expelling Rocard from the leadership; indeed, it should be made more collegial and democratic, bringing CERES back in too. He was strongly supported by Defferre – leaving the Mitterrandistes entirely isolated.[121]

In part Mauroy's exasperation reflected the concern of a party 'organisation man' at the threat posed to the *apparat* by the emergence of warring clans. But he also shared the general resentment of Mitterrand's high-handedness – he exploded with fury against him again a few weeks later when Mitterrand blithely told the press of plans for a new PS newspaper without even bothering to acquaint the PS *comité directeur* with the idea.[122] Beyond that Mauroy, like Defferre, had a healthy self-conceit for the status to which his powerful regional base entitled him within the party. The two men stood for much; above all the continuity of the old SFIO inside the PS. Mauroy was pure SFIO: a teacher and the son of a teacher, born and bred in the SFIO bastion of the Nord. He had been brought up within the SFIO from earliest youth – by 1950 he was already national secretary of the SFIO's *Jeunesse Socialiste*, a position he held (in true SFIO style) for eight years. Rocard had been a brief shooting star beneath him (he had been secretary of the SFIO student section in 1955–6) and had still been a political nobody when Mauroy took over the leadership of the SFIO Nord federation in 1961. Mauroy was aware, inevitably, that though he was twelve years Mitterrand's junior he had deeper roots in French Socialism than his new leader could ever hope to have.

Mauroy, like Defferre, had made room for Mitterrand at the helm of the PS and had rejoiced in the party's progress under him. But he was, he felt, a power apart. In the old days he had been the major support of Mollet's failing leadership. Mollet had held on as long as he had because he had been able to maintain the loyalty of the Nord to his neighbouring Pas-de-Calais federation. But when Mauroy had decided, in 1969, that enough was enough, his control of the Nord had meant that Mollet had had to go. Neither Mauroy nor Mitterrand had forgotten that the mayor of Lille had un-made the last great leader of French Socialism. He was a power to be reckoned with.

Mauroy's normal calm and self-esteem had been badly dented by his having been badgered and forced into a tactical corner by members of Mitterrand's personal entourage (who had attempted to twist his arm to sign their 'contribution'). He had long felt uneasy at the power of these clan-followers and placemen within the PS organisation which he, above all, had been concerned to rebuild. He greatly resented the fact that the Mitterrandistes had created, and then kept as their own organisational fief, the PS *sections d'entreprise*. The aim, clearly, was to create an independent base to compensate – perhaps to more than compensate – for Mitterrand's weakness *vis-à-vis* the old regional blocs. Since the election Mitterrand and his followers had laid great stress on their objective of increasing the number of SEs from 1,200 (October 1978) to 2,000 by the end of 1979.[123] If this occurred – and if Mauroy failed to bring the SEs within the ambit of the normal PS organisation – they might play a crucial role in a future leadership election.

If, meanwhile, Mitterrand's protégés succeeded in ejecting Rocard from the secretariat, then Mauroy would find himself more outweighed than ever by the Mitterrandiste 'clan'. All hope of forcing a more collegial form of leadership on Mitterrand would be gone. But who were these upstarts that they thought they could summarily close off the leadership question in such a manner? In any case, if the leadership succession was open Mauroy was not going to let his own candidacy go by default. For, partly as a result of his own considerable media exposure as the PS's key middle man, Mauroy's stock had begun to rise in the polls, too . . .[124]

Mitterrand, with Defferre's support, sought to conciliate Mauroy. The 'contribution' was condemned and withdrawn and a promise given that the PS presidential candidate for 1981 would be chosen by a free vote of all party militants. Meanwhile, Mitterrand promised, his entourage would be reined in from further attacks on Rocard and, specifically, there would be no move to expel the latter from the Secretariat. As for Mauroy's substantive demands about party democracy and organisation, well Mitterrand wanted time to think about them . . . This 'compromise' left Mitterrand in control, with his protégés where they were.

This was hardly satisfactory to Rocard, who set off on a nation-wide speaking tour to cultivate support amongst the PS federations – a dangerous tactic (for federation bosses resented such poaching if it deprived them of the ability to wield power via their bloc votes) but, for Rocard, a necessary one. For, like Mitterrand, Rocard possessed no substantial regional base (he represented Conflans, in the Paris suburb of Yvelines, where the Right held seven out of eight seats). He returned to Paris in September to a chorus of denunciation of his 'personal campaigning' from the Mitterrandistes – and to a public opinion poll showing him pulling ahead of a slumping Mitterrand. Rocard's somewhat provocative comment was that, naturally 'A good poll gives one pleasure' but that the real meaning of the poll was that 'a sort of political archaism stands condemned'.[125] Mitterrand responded bitterly that 'one is always someone else's archaism' and that 'if I needed reassurance I would only have to look at the names of those who have overtaken me [in the poll]'.[126] With this exchange the simmering rivalry between the two men broke into open war. Rocard was clearly not prepared to allow matters to rest with the one-sided July 'compromise'. He had gone out of his way to make clear his opinion that Mitterrand was now a man of the past, and to pose his own presidential candidacy, bidding over the head of the PS *apparat* to all on the Left who simply wanted a winner. While Rocard was careful to say that he would not run if Mitterrand were a candidate in 1981, his bid inevitably provoked a strong reaction from the Mitterrandistes – who spoke of finding an alternative candidate to Rocard even if Mitterrand did not stand.

The strongest reaction against Rocard came, however, from Defferre, who angrily suggested an early party congress to re-elect Mitterrand, so that 'the case of Rocard would be settled'.[127] 'Michel Rocard', he argued, 'is neither a new man nor a young one. I cannot agree that Rocard has anything new to say, for on an economic level his speeches seem mainly to resemble the classic oration of the *Inspecteur des Finances* who talks of balancing the budget'.[128] If anyone wanted this sort of thing, Defferre added with passion, they already had Messrs Barre and d'Estaing: worse, it was the old policy of Pierre Laval in modern form, a truly archaic policy.

The ferocity of Defferre's counter-attack – soon answered with equal bitterness from Rocard – was, on the face of it, hard to understand. Defferre, after all, had once tried to impose himself on the party as a presidential candidate of the Centre-Left – which was just what Rocard was attempting now. The idea of Gaston Defferre attacking any PS leader from the Left was in itself intrinsically comic. The root of the matter, as so often, lay elsewhere. The fact was that Defferre's regional base was in a state of dangerous decay. In the old days the Marseilles mayor had controlled not merely the massive Bouches-du-Rhône federation but such neighbouring federations as Vaucluse, Var and Gard as well. Not only was this no longer true, but Defferre now found himself in acute and embarrassing difficulties within Marseilles itself. Throughout the Provence-Côte d'Azur region, and particularly in Marseilles, the continuing erosion of Socialist strength to the benefit of the PCF had given rise to strong discontent among PS militants, many of whom blamed Defferre's 'bossism' for their woes. The convention of the Bouches-du-Rhône PS federation in November echoed with loud protests against Defferre's autocratic and highly personal style.[129] For the first time in Defferre's long reign (he had been mayor since 1953) he faced a major challenge to his authority in which the question of his succession was openly mooted.[130] It was in these extremely troubled waters that the Rocardians had been fishing – to some effect. (A petition signed by many leading PS figures in the region was circulated protesting against Defferre's attacks on Rocard and Defferre's most likely successor, Charles-Emile Loo, went some way towards associating himself with the Rocard camp.)[131] Defferre was forced to retreat under such heavy pressure, giving a public promise to distance himself from national politics in future (i.e. to stop attacking Rocard) and to devote himself entirely to Marseilles; but his fury against the Rocardians knew no bounds. One of the great unwritten laws of the PS was that no one – not Mitterrand, Mauroy, nor even CERES – ventured into Defferre's fief to disturb the even tenor of the *'système Defferre'*. Indeed, Defferre had been known even to adopt a protective paternal attitude to the CERES leaders for their acceptance of this rule of the game.[132] But Rocard, quite alone, was openly contemptuous of the idea that the giant 15,000-member Bouches-du-Rhône federation was sacred ground. Defferre concluded not only that Rocard was at the root of his local problems, but that anything less than the maintenance of the Mitterrandiste *status quo* within the national PS would gravely endanger the already fragile balance within his federation. The fact was, of course, that Marseilles Socialists, locked in their long and habitual feud with the PCF, provided a natural reservoir of support for anyone bidding for power on the PS Right. Rocard could hardly afford to ignore them, especially since they constituted a whole one-twelfth of the PS membership.[133]

Thus by November 1978 the following situation had been reached: Defferre was determined on the maintenance of the Mitterrand-Mauroy leadership but was opposed to Rocard; Mauroy was keen to placate his old friend Defferre but could not tolerate Rocard's exclusion from the leadership; Rocard could not afford Mauroy's 'compromise' because it would leave Mitterrand in control; and CERES hated Rocard (referring to his faction as 'the American Left') and wanted to rejoin the leadership itself. This left Mitterrand with two alternatives: either he could maintain the Nantes majority – excluding CERES but including, uncomfortably, his bitter rival Rocard; or he could build a new coalition with Defferre and CERES – which meant risking the threat of a powerful Rocard-Mauroy combination against him. He chose the latter: Rocard must be crushed, whatever the cost. The crucial trial of strength would come at the long-awaited PS Congress at Metz in April 1979.

### iii THE CONGRESS OF METZ

In late November Mitterrand let it be known that he would regard the deposition of a separate motion before the Metz Congress by anyone within the PS leadership as an act of treachery, incompatible with their continued presence within the leadership.[134] Rocard responded by putting forward his own 'contributions' for discussion by the PS *comité directeur* and launching a series of public meetings to propagate his views. Rocard had been deeply stung by Defferre's attacks and, at a meeting of the PS leadership in December, demanded a 'jury of honour' to clear his name.[135] Mitterrand claimed that he had been equally injured by personal attacks, all coming 'from one particular source'.[136] Mauroy sought desperately, and unsuccessfully, to moderate the conflict between the two men. He had been shocked to hear that feelers had already gone out from Mitterrand towards CERES with the constitution of a new leadership coalition in view. He could, he warned Mitterrand, 'never' tolerate such a deal. On a whole series of issues – the PS's promised 'rupture with capitalism', the question of responsibility for the Left's divisions, and in its nationalist rejection of the EEC – CERES was simply aping the PCF. Had not Mitterrand himself observed of Chevènement, the CERES leader, that in his regard for the PCF 'he confuses love with striptease'? On a purely ideological level, he pointed out, there was little to choose between himself, Mitterrand, Rocard, or even Defferre. The differences between CERES and any one of the other factions were far greater; to bring the former into the leadership would split the party and lead it down a dangerous road. A synthesis between the positions of the three major PS leaders would not be hard to achieve; only personal rivalries stood in its way. These could be ironed out via a straightforward vote by proportional representation for a new *comité directeur*.

Mauroy's position was logical – but naïve. As Savary (supporting Mauroy) put it, the 'presidential contagion' had thoroughly infected the PS, giving personal rivalries a far greater weight than ideological differences. In any case, the PS was fast reverting to the old party games of the SFIO, with factions and clans proliferating at every turn: by the end of 1978 at least fifteen were bidding for recognition.[137] At the PS *comité directeur* on December 20 Mitterrand contemptuously swept away all Mauroy's pleas for compromise, rejecting outright his plans for the democratisation of the PS organisation. Under Mitterrand's guidance the *comité* voted simply not to consider any of Rocard's 'contributions', taking instead as its basic text two of Mitterrand's recent speeches . . . Rocard walked out – to the jubilation of Defferre and CERES, the latter now gleefully anticipating its return to the leadership, having suddenly rediscovered Mitterrand's virtues after a gap of three years. All that Mauroy had achieved was that henceforth every faction, while presenting its own unalterable demands, deplored the intransigence of other fractions in preventing the 'synthesis' which all good men desired. Mauroy found himself simply towed along in the wake of his two powerful colleagues, alternately embarrassed by Rocard's aggression[138] and Mitterrand's flinty determination to be rid of his rival.

What made the situation finally impossible was the opinion polls. These rated the leaders in two ways. On questions concerned simply with the expression of favourable opinion ('Who do you want to see play an important role in the years to come?') Mitterrand did not fare too badly. Here Rocard led him by 1 point in October 1978, by 6 in December and by 13 in January–March 1979. Only in this latter period, though, did Rocard actually enjoy an advantage among PS voters. Much worse for Mitterrand was the question 'Who would be the better presidential candidate?'. Here Rocard led him by 7 points in October 1978, 13 in November and 22 in January 1979. On this basis, moreover, Rocard's advantage was just as strong among PS voters as with other electors.[139] Findings like these made it impossible that Rocard should give up his bid – and vital that Mitterrand should stop him.

Mauroy's suggestion that Mitterrand would, if he persevered, split the party, rested on the assumption that the PS first secretary would find himself embarrassed, perhaps even defeated, if he forced into opposition both Rocard, with his wide support throughout the party, and Mauroy, with the mighty Nord-Pas-de-Calais bloc vote behind him. The great revelation of spring 1979 was just how strong Mitterrand's hold over the PS was. As the Metz Congress approached Mitterrand's motion attracted the support of over half of the PS deputies and of 58 of the PS federation first secretaries (Mauroy was supported by 15, Rocard by 11).[140] Mauroy, who had done so much to build the PS organisation, found his creation slipping ineluctably away from him. Worse, far worse, was the fact that he could not even hold the Nord and Pas-de-Calais solid. Mitterrand had carefully cultivated the support of Mauroy's principal local rival, Arthur Notebart, who actually put up a motion aganist Mauroy. Moreover, it now became plain that many old Mollet supporters (on whom Mauroy was relying) were essentially just leadership loyalists, unwilling to back even Mollet's natural successor, Mauroy, against the central *apparat*. In the last few weeks before the Congress there was a great rush of waverers toward the Mitterrand bandwagon. Mitterrand now disdainfully rejected the idea of 'synthesis' and the Rocard-Mauroy forces went down to painful defeat. In January even Chevènement, although anxious to minimise the strength of the Mauroy-Rocard faction and exaggerate that of Mitterrand, had predicted that the former would obtain 40 per cent of the Congress vote to the latter's 35 per cent.[141] In the event Mitterrand took 47 per cent, Rocard 21.3 per cent, Mauroy 16.8 per cent and CERES 15 per cent.[142] A few days later, with the Rocard and Mauroy factions not deigning to take part in the vote, the CERES-Mitterrand alliance was reconsecrated. A jubilant CERES re-entered the PS secretariat, from which Rocard and Mauroy were unceremoniously bundled out. Chevènement triumphantly claimed Metz as a major watershed. The PS had been launched on its upward ascent by the 'line of Epinay', based on a CERES-Mitterrand alliance; it had run into trouble once this line was abandoned, but now the advance could begin again, based on the new 'line of Metz'.

Rocard had not anticipated such a stinging defeat. Only a month before Metz he had announced himself happy that the Congress should adopt a clear-cut line – and declared that if he lost at Metz or if the PS adopted a policy with which he disagreed, then plainly there was no question of his presidential candidacy. PS policy should, he argued, be·hammered into definitive form by a meeting of all the parties and trade unions of the non-Communist Left – thus bringing in his CFDT friends and his many admirers within the MRG and PSU, where he still enjoyed some affection. A week before the Congress, with the Mitterrand bandwagon gathering speed, Rocard had suddenly rediscovered his enthusiasm for compromise with the first secretary – too late. In fact Rocard had not done badly to take over one-fifth of the vote. Lacking any substantial regional base he had none the less almost matched the combined forces of the two greatest regional bosses, Mauroy and Defferre. His bid had failed partly because of a large slippage of CERES support to Mitterrand, who, with only a 35 per cent vote otherwise, might have been forced to compromise; and because Mauroy, whose tactics had been surpringly amateurish, had turned out to be a hollow man.

In the wake of this crushing defeat Rocard's poll ratings slumped. His lead over Mitterrand as 'best candidate' fell from 22 points in January to 11 in April. His lead in the more general ratings (as a man the electorate wanted to see play a major role in the future) fell from 13 points to 1 – while among PS voters alone Mitterrand surged ahead.[143] The Rocardian camp fell silent and let it be understood that the point of the exercise had not necessarily been to displace Mitterrand as the PS candidate in 1981, but to put down a marker for the future, much as Rocard had done by running as PSU presidential candidate in 1969.

Perhaps the most potent single argument in Mitterrand's favour had been the good PS results in the March 1979 cantonal elections which, coming just before Metz, had convinced waverers that the PS still had a promising future under Mitterrand. In June came the extremely disappointing results of the European elections, with a fall in the PS vote and a sharp diminution in the PS lead over the PCF. Hostilities immediately recommenced, with both Mauroy and Rocard criticising the PS campaign and the party's ambivalent attitude to the EEC. At the PS *comité directeur* meeting called to discuss the election result Mitterrand and CERES were astonished to discover that afternoon's *Le Monde* carrying a lengthy account of their debate, particularly Mauroy's contribution to it. Mauroy's leak – he could not deny it – had been extremely inept, for the debate had not yet taken place . . . Nor did it, for a furious Mitterrand immediately suspended the *comité* and summoned a national convention of the PS in its place.[144] Mauroy and Rocard boycotted the meeting but were bitterly condemned in their absence. Mitterrand then met with his two opponents, hoping to detach Mauroy from Rocard. For Rocard, he implied, the only road back lay via total submission to the leadership; if he continued to refuse to accept the verdict of Metz the penalty would simply be his own isolation and marginalisation. The meeting resulted, predictably, in stalemate.[145]

Mitterrand's position was not as impregnable as his lordly behaviour suggested. He was greatly embarrassed when, in August, a police raid on the PS pirate radio, Radio Riposte, resulted in charges against him and several other PS leaders. Although Mauroy and Rocard rallied loyally to his defence and although his protests that radio piracy was justified by Giscard's abuse of the state radio monopoly carried some weight,[146] his image was badly dented. He had, after all, led the PS in voting for a law against pirate radio as recently as June 1978 and polls showed that (by 45 per cent to 33 per cent) voters thought he had been wrong to break the law.[147]

Moreover, the same poll carried an even more shaking message for Mitterrand: Rocard's ratings had recovered sharply from their post-Metz slump and were now again soaring ahead. 55 per cent of voters said, damningly, that they saw Mitterrand as 'a man of the past', and by 46:25 per cent they thought Rocard would be the better candidate. PS voters shared this view by a crushing 52:33 per cent, as did PCF voters by 42:28 per cent. Even amongst Mitterrand's supporters more than half thought of Rocard as his eventual successor.[148] The Mitterrandistes were visibly panicked by these results. The point of Metz had been to kill off the Rocard phenomenon – but it clearly hadn't worked. On the other hand the price of that hollow triumph now had to be paid in good money – to CERES. Ever since Metz Chevènement, taking advantage of his new foothold in the PS secretariat, had taken charge of the work on the party's new policy document, the *Projet Socialiste*. When he produced the fruit of his labours in autumn 1979 the Mitterrandistes were aghast. The rupture with the PCF was now to be regarded as merely a regrettable accident. The PS would help bring peace to Europe by reliance on the tradition of Franco-Russian friendship. It would install 'working-class hegemony'. It would make France more self-sufficient by retreating from international trade and taking its distance from the EEC. And so on. This produced hurried confabulation between Rocard, Mauroy and Mitterrand – and a new spirit of conciliation between them. In the end a number of amendments were moved and the document passed, Chevènement announcing himself still well pleased with it. In truth it contained much which the Rocardians could not really accept but which they were frightened to reject for fear of ruling out a Rocard candidacy.

Thus the PS eighteen months after its emergence as the 'first party of France'. The party had come a long way. It was badly split between a leader who, after a long career in conservative governments, had in middle age discovered he was a Marxist; and a challenger who had moved with equal agility from the fringes of the extreme Left to the right wing of the PS. Strange ideological alliances had been contracted for purely personal ends. The old anti-clerical *canard* had been raised again, with factions within the leadership talking of 'throwing out the Christians'.[149] The party's chief organisation man had been revealed as a tactical greenhorn. Its greatest regional figure was reeling under furious assaults on his 'bossism'. He had clung on to his eroding position thanks to alliances with the party's leader (whose united Left tactics he had for long opposed) and with the party's extreme Left (who, in principle, reviled all he stood for). This latter group had, as happily, accepted his support in order to scrabble back into the party leadership. Within a few months of voting to outlaw pirate radio stations the party had gone into business to set one up and its leader had become involved in a minor scandal over it. The leader had held on under challenge, displaying an almost royal vanity, an entourage to match, and a lively suspicion of democratic practice. The party's most popular figure had been kicked out of the leadership and a party platform drawn up with the precise intention of preventing him from running on it. This tactic he had outwitted by accepting it just the same, regardless of his principled disagreement with it. This in turn had afforded the leader the semblance of a united leadership front at last, thus providing him with the base for yet another presidential candidacy. The party's voters who, the polls showed, thought him a poor choice of candidate, were confused and disenchanted. Party members, too, were disoriented. The party had ceased to grow – membership stagnated around the 180,000 mark,[150] even while PCF membership was climbing over 700,000 and the RPR's (it claimed) to 760,000.[151] Even the PS's greatest moral asset – its martyrdom to the PCF's ambition – had been heavily obscured, for its leadership now contained a faction eager to throw responsibility for the rupture of Left unity back on their own party. The new preponderance of presidentialist factions over the old regional blocs made it impossible to say precisely that the PS was turning back into the SFIO, but in all other respects the resemblance was uncanny – and unnerving.

# 14 Towards 1981

Rocard's observation as the 1978 second-ballot results rolled in, that 'fortunately it's only three more years from now to 1981', had got him into hot water, but the thought was general. The PS was, in the last analysis, a party that lived only for and through elections. Hardly had the party lost one election before it was locked in internecine strife over its candidacy in the next one. The priorities of all sections of the PS leadership were only too clearly displayed by this conflict. The PCF, for its part, immediately made clear its intention to run its own candidate in 1981. It had learnt too painful a lesson about the power of presidential coat-tails ever to think of leaving a clear field to its rivals again. But on the Left as a whole the sense of disappointment engendered by March 1978 was so strong that the temptation to think about 'the next time' was simply irresistible.

First, however, there was unfinished business left over from March. The Constitutional Council heard petitions concerning alleged electoral irregularities in 61 seats. It dismissed 8, retaining the cases of 18 RPR, 14 UDF, 11 PS and 10 PCF deputies. The Council, which is one-third appointed by the President and two-thirds by the legislature, was entirely composed of Majority dignitaries and presided over by Roger Frey, a former Gaullist Minister. It was thus without surprise that the Left heard its initial decision, annulling the elections of two Socialists and one Communist. After a period of ruminative delay the Council then announced two further annulations – that of Christian de la Malène (RPR), Chirac's right-hand man in the Paris *mairie*, and Jean-Jacques Servan-Schreiber (UDF). Despite the list's inclusion of JJSS, Giscard's long-time friend, the Council's decision provoked considerable cynicism. The majority of cases had concerned right-wing deputies but the Council had speedily struck down three on the Left. Then, as if to balance the books, it had added two from the Right, the delay allowing its deputies to defend their seats in the autumn when their (middle class) supporters were back from holiday. The move against de la Malène was a major blow to Chirac and confirmed the state of bitter cold war between the RPR leader and Giscard. They, too, both had their eyes on 1981 and Giscard's determination to harass and crush Chirac before then was quite patent. Chirac certainly saw the attempt to dispose of his deputy-mayor in this light and suggested bitterly that JJSS had only been added to the list so as to give an impression of impartiality. It had been necessary to find one UDF deputy somehow and JJSS had been thrown to the wolves because the fury he aroused in the RPR had made him, at last, an embarrassment to his former patron in the Elysée. When, despite the RPR's desperate efforts,[1] de la Maléne went down to crushing defeat, Chirac's fury against the Constitutional Council knew no bounds: 'If I respect the institution I

265

do not necessarily respect the men who sit on it or the man who presides over it,' adding, a little opaquely: 'I'm very moderate in relation to what I think of M. Roger Frey.'[2] Frey, together with the other Council members, was to be found that evening dining in luxurious style at the Elysée with Giscard who (naturally) deplored 'partisan divisions' over the Council's role and spoke of his sacred duty to defend the Republic's institutions . . .[3] The spectacle of the Council attending a thinly disguised and vindictive celebration of an election defeat they had brought about – as the guests of the chief beneficiary of that operation – stirred somewhat coarser sentiments in other quarters.

If the by-elections had been intended to embarrass the Left amidst its division and disappointment, the tactic failed. It held all its own seats with ease and the PS captured the other two with an enormous swing of votes. Taking the five by-elections together, the Left had gained nearly 5 per cent, achieving a level of support which would have ushered them triumphantly into power a few months earlier. The PS had particular cause for satisfaction. Announcing that it regarded the annulments in Left seats as fraudulent, the party refrained from challenging the PCF in the seat it had held, calling instead for a united vote even on the first ballot to re-elect the Left's 'legitimate' deputies. The PCF, on the other hand, seized the chance to carry the battle to the PS in its own seats, announcing that it would 'give a lesson to the PS' and use the by-elections to wage a 'campaign of clarification' of the PS's responsibility for the March defeat. The tactic was a disaster. In its own seat the PCF's vote held up but elsewhere it fell heavily, sometimes by over half. The Politburo took the unusual step of offering a public *mea culpa*, admitting that it had erred badly in not accepting unitary candidatures.[4] It seemed possible, moreover, that the PCF was suffering for its internal dissensions even if the PS was not. The old pattern of PS advance and PCF decline had been immediately re-established.

Hardly pausing to draw breath from the election campaign, the PCF strove furiously to reverse this trend, falling back hard on to its traditional role as 'tribune'. Despite the internal criticism engendered by the Party's sharp switch of line before the election to a soak-the-rich populism, the line was continued and intensified after March. Brushing aside all talk of the Left's reunification, the PCF endlessly denounced the PS for its rightward turn, its responsibility for the Left's defeat, and its complicity with the Schmidt-Giscard axis which was leading Europe into mass unemployment. The Party energetically sought to place itself at the head of every social struggle and strike, behaving as a sort of super-trade union and presenting itself as the only organised force of opposition able and willing to defend the under-privileged in the harsh climate of the post-election economy. While it paid lip-service to the cause of future Left unity, it rejected 'unity at the summit' with the PS leadership, saying it wanted only 'unity at the base'. By this it meant that PS members were welcome to lend their support to local or industrial actions initiated and led by the PCF – no more. At the same time the PCF pursued two other themes: the development of the 'Eurocommunist' strain of the 22nd Congress, and a bitter, populist nationalism directed principally against the EEC – and thus against the (more pro-European) PS.

The PCF was nothing if not energetic in this role. It championed each and every new group of discontents to appear, whether Lorraine steelworkers or the wine and fruit farmers of the South-West alarmed at the prospect of under-cutting competition from their Spanish, Portuguese and Greek counterparts if their countries were admitted to the EEC. In its campaign against a 'German Europe' the PCF exploited quite shamelessly the old embers of the Resistance movement in the South-West and – to the distress of Elleinstein, who had much fellow feeling for the Spanish Communist Party (PCE) leader, Carillo – brutally ignored the PCE's pleas in favour of the (even poorer) Spanish peasantry. At the same time the great drive for Party membership continued – especially in the factories, as the Party sought to seal off its proletarian base from further PS or CFDT contamination. It even found time to conduct a major sociological enquiry into its burgeoning membership.[5]

In one sense the PCF was batting on a friendly wicket, for the Barre government, with its typical mixture of ruthlessness and complacency, was producing no shortage of discontents. Unemployment, which had risen steadily every year since 1973, was growing at an annual rate of 100,000–150,000, and inflation remained stubbornly in double figures. Barre, who had adroitly pulled unemployment down below 1,050,000 by March 1978, let it soar by 300,000 in the nine months following the election. Thereafter the figure rose rapidly towards 1.5 million – while the government sought simultaneously to widen business profit margins, depress wage increases, and implement large-scale redundancies in the steel and other industries. The PCF, as also the PS, railed against the government as the most reactionary France had known in decades, but Barre appeared to be hardly listening. When Marchais rose to speak in the Assembly's main economic debate in October 1978, Barre simply got up and left the Chamber, saying, 'I am going to work.' His junior Minister stayed to explain that the premier had not stayed to listen to what was, after all, the chief working-class spokesman in the Assembly because he was 'certain he'd learn nothing'.[6] The Communists, for their part, seldom acted as if the government was as important an audience to them as was the Left electorate. In February 1979 the Minister of Labour, Lionel Stoléru, called in the trade unions for strictly confidential talks on his plans for the repatriation of migrant workers from France. The CGT immediately published his plan, denouncing it as 'racist' – leading a furious Stoléru to ban the CGT from further meetings.[7]

The PS reeled under the PCF onslaught. In this sort of war, whatever the PS's feelings of angry self-justification, the PCF invariably had the upper hand. Enjoying complete hegemony over the main (Marxist) socialist tradition in France, the PCF had a clear, tough, logical line. The PS had to invent its own, felt its own left wing already tugged away by the Communist undertow, and was uneasily aware that the only alternative tradition on which to fall back was the discredited Third Force politics of *Molletisme*. The party as a whole – and Mitterrand in particular – were furious with the PCF, but were bound to it by hoops of steel and had no alternative save further alliance with it. Moreover, the PCF possessed a propaganda machine and an organisational and industrial strength with which the PS simply could not compete. The PS leadership not only lacked any organic links with the labour movement but were frequently out of touch even with their natural ally, the CFDT. Thus in October 1978 PS deputies joined happily with the PCF in voting against government proposals for conciliation boards in industry. This produced a cry of rage and grief from the CFDT leader, Edmond Maire, who had won Barre's concession of such boards in their post-election talks. Even those PS deputies closest to the CFDT such as Rocard were openly surprised at his reaction, for they had not ever been aware that Maire had favoured the measure . . .[8] Such reforms had been critical to Maire's new policy of *'recentrage'*, which had already encountered stiff internal opposition within the CFDT (at the CFDT Congress at Brest in May 1979 Maire's report was passed only on a 57 per cent vote – a far lower figure than normal). Maire, who already found himself the target of bitter PCF and CGT attacks, reacted with understandable exasperation against the PS leadership which, he said, was already dreaming of 1981 and even 1983 (the next parliamentary elections). Referring to the Left's long history of illusory hopes, Maire noted bitterly that now one had to learn 'to conjugate May '68 with March '78'.[9]

Mitterrand's response to the PCF assault was tempered by a healthy respect for his adversary's brute strength. The PCF was, as he put it, 'heavily armoured', though he reminded Marchais that it was through the weight of their armour that the French had lost at Agincourt.[10] But he could also hardly afford to depict the PCF as impossible partners for the future, not only because to do so would invalidate his past strategy, but because he retained the conviction that a united Left could win, but that a divided Left would always lose. Only in May 1978 did he concede, reluctantly, that the Common Programme had 'run its term'. Apart from occasional musings that Elleinstein would be happier in the PS and Chevènement in the PCF, he refused to provoke the PCF by commenting on its internal dissensions. Over the EEC he back-pedalled before the PCF's nationalist onslaught, defining the PS stance as acceptance of the Treaty of Rome but not a single step more. In September he appealed forlornly to the PCF for a 'non-aggression pact' and in December suggested the calling of the old liaison committee of the three Left parties to organise a concerted response to the government's 'anti-social' policies. Marchais brushed all such suggestions aside, saying that what was needed was 'not sonorous proclamations but powerful and concrete mass action at the base'.[11] The PCF was eager to create the largest possible mass movement against the government and was not particularly interested in a special relationship with the PS. Even to suggest the need for a non-aggression pact was a slander on the PCF, which was not aggressive at all. As for the suggested meeting of the Left's liaison committee, this was just another of Mitterrand's 'intrigues'. Given Mitterrand's 'grave responsibility' for the rupture of the Left it would be absurd to meet . . .[12]

Marchais could well afford such an attitude. The PS would be there when he needed it. If necessary the PCF could hold the PS at arm's length till the second ballot of May 1981 – they'd come begging for its support all right then, regardless of whether they were running Rocard or Mitterrand. Meanwhile, all the evidence was that the Socialists were more reliant than the PCF on the *dynamique unitaire*, so it was merely common sense to deprive them of it. But it would not do to trample too hard on the still strong *unitaire* sentiment amongst the PCF rank and file and in the long run the PCF had no alternative to a united Left strategy, so the door to unity had to be kept open in principle though closed in practice. The PS might then lose the momentum of its advance, while the PCF, exploiting to the full the oppositional opportunities which Barre was providing in such measure, might regain its old supremacy on the Left. The strategy was not wholly implausible. The Party was still gaining members and was solidly dug in at local level: its strength and resilience were not to be doubted. Indeed, despite its parliamentary by-election disasters, the cantonal by-elections of March–December 1978 showed the PCF gaining slightly (+ 1.3 per cent) and the PS losing (– 0.4 per cent). Moreover, the Vitry conference of December 1978 had effectively brought to an end the period of PCF internal dissidence, allowing the Party to advance relatively united towards the fresh electoral hurdles of 1979.

As the first of these approached, the cantonal elections of March 1979, Marchais was able to point to the divisions of the PS, professing himself astonished at 'the absence of democracy . . . the struggle of men, of tendencies, of groups and of fractions which, at bottom, reveal personal ambitions [only]. With us Communists, everything happens in a completely different way.'[13] At the same time, however, he quietly conceded that the PCF would unconditionally desist at the cantonals' second ballot for better-placed Socialists. There would be no re-run of the dramas of March 1978 on this cardinal point. The electoral pattern of 1973–7 was thus resumed.

The results also resumed the pattern of that period, with the Left almost stable in its old winning ways, as if 1978 had never happened. The total Left vote, which had been 53.9 per cent in the 1973 cantonals and 56.4 per cent in 1976, was now 55.1 per cent. The PCF now won 22.5 per cent (22.7 per cent in 1973, 22.8 per cent in 1976) and the PS 27 per cent (21.9 per cent in 1973, with a quarter less candidates, and 26.5 per cent in 1976).[14] The only real trend was the continuing decline in the vote of the other fragments of the Left. The most striking aspect of the results was simply the fact that the PS's divisions and Mitterrand's tarnished image had made not the slightest difference to the party's electoral position. Regionally the most notable trend was the PCF's continuing large losses in the Paris area, counter-balanced by its gains in the troubled steel belt of Lorraine, the equally depressed Somme and Nord, and in rural areas of the Loire and Midi, where its campaign against EEC enlargement was having some effect.

The cantonal elections (in which 10.7 million had voted) had been friendly terrain for the Left, with its many hundreds of well-entrenched representatives at grassroots. Everyone knew the European elections in June would be a far harder and more significant test, particularly since they would provide the last great test of opinion before 1981. All parties saw them as little less than a full-scale rehearsal for the presidential contest, especially since they were fought on a national PR basis, making the parties' entrenched positions at local level virtually irrelevant. Realising that the vote would exactly resemble the 1981 first ballot in form, the PS, PCF and RPR hastened to put their party leaders (i.e. their putative presidential candidates) at the head of their lists. Giscard alone could not do this, instead choosing the formidable Mme Simone Veil to head the UDF list. It was a canny move, designed to create the maximum difficulties for the RPR and PS, both of whom regarded her as virtually 'unattackable',[15] for polls had long shown her to be easily the most popular politician in France, with an essentially apolitical image of integrity and compassion.[16] The PCF brought off a notable coup too, including on their list the redoubtable Emmanuel Maffre-Baugé, veteran leader of the Midi wine-growers, who was also a Catholic and a spokesman for Occitanian regionalism. He had, he said, been won over by the PCF's 'No, frankly No' attitude to the EEC and its enlargement, as compared to the UDF's 'Yes, frankly Yes', the RPR's 'No, but . . .' and the PS's 'Yes, but . . .'

Giscard was fighting on extremely favourable ground – French public opinion has always been overwhelmingly favourable to the EEC[17] – and seized the chance to do the maximum damage to his most dangerous opponent, Chirac. The whole weight of the State propaganda machine, so long fashioned as a Gaullist weapon, was now turned against the Gaullists. Chirac was carefully depicted as irrational and intemperate (a by no means difficult feat), while Barre appeared repeatedly to give prime ministerial broadcasts – in support of the UDF list. Meanwhile the mayor of Toulouse was threatened with a cut-off of funds to his city if he accepted nomination on Chirac's list, while other intending candidates found themselves threatened with loss of jobs or promotions for themselves or their families.[18] Prudent conservatives tiptoed away from the RPR. Even Edgar Faure, whom Chirac had so strongly supported for the presidency of the National Assembly, now deserted to run on the UDF list. Chirac, furious and badly rattled, inveighed bitterly against Giscard, calling on all true Gaullists to resist the new takeover by the 'American' Centre they had defeated in 1965 (i.e. by the defeat of Lecanuet, now Giscard's right-hand man and a leading figure on the UDF list). Chirac was fighting for his political life[19] and now faced polls showing the UDF at 35 per cent, the RPR at 14 per cent.[20] He railed desperately against the 'Veil-Lecanuet' list (Mitterrand called it the 'Barre-Veil' list), suggesting that anything less than a 50 per cent vote for it should be seen as a defeat and a clear sign that Giscard would lose in 1981.

Marchais was under only slightly less pressure. At the end of April IFOP was predicting only 18 per cent for the PCF and 28 per cent for the PS/MRG.[21] As the election neared he sought desperately to woo back the Party's liberal wing which, at heart, still blamed the PCF for the breakdown of Left unity before March 1978. Hence the desperate importance of acquiring Elleinstein's public support for the PCF list and Marchais' speech at the PCF Congress (on the eve of poll) in which he suddenly departed from the 'unity at base' line to declare that he did not rule out 'unity at the summit' either. The Rocardians regarded the polls with equal gloom, for a PS lead of 10 per cent over the PCF would consolidate Mitterrand's position beyond further challenge.

In the event the UDF took 27.5 per cent, the RPR 16.2 per cent, the PS/MRG 23.6 per cent and the PCF 20.6 per cent. None of the other lists did well enough to qualify for seats (the Trotskyites took 3.1 per cent, the Ecologists 4.4 per cent and three other lists 4.6 per cent between them). The somewhat odd result was that the Left, having been beaten by 48.3 per cent to 47.3 per cent overall,[22] had actually won the contest between the four big lists, taking 41 seats to the Right's 40 (UDF 25, RPR 15,

PS/MRG 22, and PCF 19). This outcome infuriated Giscard, the more so since it resulted essentially from a successful act of revenge by Servan-Schreiber. JJSS had run his own list against the UDF, stealing just enough votes (1.9 per cent) to cost the UDF the extra seat it had needed for Giscard to enter the run-up to 1981 with a clear-cut victory over the Left to boast about. Although the election had been a disaster for Chirac – who immediately faced a major crisis within the RPR[23] – the 41–40 tally in seats appeared to justify his claim that Giscard, by concentrating his fire on the RPR, would lead the Majority to defeat. Equally provoking, it would allow Mitterrand – now clearly Giscard's most likely Left opponent in 1981 – to disguise the major setback he had just suffered with the boast that he had led the Left to its first overall majority in seats at a national election.

It was not to be tolerated. The police raid on Radio Riposte followed almost immediately and although (of course) the Elysée maintained an Olympian silence over the affair, it was clear that Giscard's hand lay behind the move: Mitterrand was to be harrassed, dragged through the courts, and brought down a peg or two. But that was not enough. The election law provided for the official *Commission de Recensement* to verify the exact electoral result in detail within four days of the ballot. After a long (and illegal) delay of ten days, which itself bespoke abnormal controversy within its ranks, the Commission delivered its bombshell: Giscard had won after all. Many thousands of electors had failed to use the voting slips required by law and had simply put party propaganda sheets into the ballot boxes. The law specifically forbade that these should be regarded as valid votes but the Commission decided that it would disregard the law and count them after all. It now obligingly provided a whole new set of election statistics, subtracting votes from the PCF, PS and RPR but giving another 78,958 to the UDF – just enough for the UDF to relieve the PS of the one seat required to give the Right a 'winning' 41–40 margin.[24] Mitterrand furiously resigned his own European seat in protest.[25] When it was revealed that the Radio-Riposte raid had been launched at the initiative of the State Procurator, he also refused to accept his summons to further court proceedings.

Mitterrand had a far greater cause for disquiet, however. For the first time the PS had visibly fallen back. Taking its vote together with the MRG it had lost 1.1 per cent since March 1978. The PS angrily blamed MRG defections for this trend but more profound causes were clearly at work. PS losses were spread evenly around the country and the party had held on to its March 1978 level of support only in the areas most hopeless for the Left. True, the PS had overtaken the PCF in two of its parliamentary seats, but it had been overtaken by the PCF in eleven of its own. Without much doubt the endless and bitter divisions within the PS leadership had contributed to the party's loss of momentum. The PS had suffered notably large losses in all the constituencies held by its top leaders: $-2.5$ per cent in Rocard's seat, $-3.7$ per cent in Mitterrand's, $-4.1$ per cent in Defferre's, $-5.0$ per cent in Chevènement's and $-5.5$ per cent in Mauroy's.

Marchais greeted the results with joy: 'We have begun to reduce the gap which separates us from the PS.'[26] This was true – though only at the cost of an overall decline in the Left's vote. The PCF's vote had merely held steady – though once again the Party had lost ground in the Paris region, making it up only with widespread gains throughout the South and West. There seemed little doubt that the Party's vehement anti-EEC enlargement campaign (and Maffre-Baugé's candidacy) had paid off. But throughout the industrialised northern half of the country the PCF had stagnated or lost ground, including a notable slide in Lorraine.

The Lorraine result was perhaps the most significant, especially since the PS had lost there too, so that the Left as a whole had fallen back badly in the working-class area most affected by the economic crisis. The fact was that the Left's, particularly the PCF's, attempts at populist exploitation of the steel crisis had backfired badly: even the CGT was almost openly critical of the PCF's energetic opportunism. In one sense the campaign had been a success, for the government had tried to interest Ford-Europe in opening a new plant in Lorraine. Renault and Peugeot-Citroen panicked at the thought of a major competitor thus being installed in their backyard and drew up plans to create 6,000 new jobs in the area by 1983. The Lorraine workers were greatly relieved, dismissed the PCF's campaign to fight to the end for their steel jobs and accepted voluntary redundancy in their thousands. Even with the Renault/Peugeot plan unemployment would still rise, but the workers were now too exhausted and demoralised not to be grateful for small mercies. In the end the government which had inflicted misery upon the area was rewarded by an electoral swing *towards* it there . . .

This, rather than any number of seats at Strasbourg, was the real significance of the election for the Left. The SOFRES post-electoral poll contained some consolation for the Left in its revelation that the Left had been the main sufferer from the relatively low (61 per cent) turnout. The social groups most favourable to the Left – the 18–34 age group and industrial workers – had been almost twice as likely to abstain as the groups that typically supported the Right.[27] The PS had been particularly badly hit, with its voters more than 30 per cent more likely to abstain than their UDF or RPR counterparts.[28] The PCF, with its vastly superior organisation, had got more of its voters to the polls but even so its sympathisers had still been more than 10 per cent more likely to abstain than had the Right.[29] In one sense such figures could be taken to mean that the Left – particularly the PCF – had done well, for it had 'won' the election even without the benefit of this potential reservoir of extra support. The polls had shown no less than 60 per cent of the electorate expressing no interest in the June campaign,[30] after all. Surely the Left's deserters would come flocking back when drawn by the excitement of the 1981 election?

This argument consisted in making a virtue out of the demobilisation of the Left electorate. It sat ill with the fact that frequently the abstainers came not from abstention-prone marginal voters, but from the Left's hard core. The UDF, for example, had had no difficulty in pulling out an extraordinary number of women to vote for it, even though they typically had a higher abstention rate. There was even a sizable preponderance of women in the PCF's electorate in June.[31] At the same time the PCF was losing more than 5 per cent of its industrial worker support (compared to March 1978) but actually outscoring the PS amongst the peasantry and farmworker group.[32] Most significant of all was the evidence of a clear loss of working-class support by the Left since March 1978 and an overwhelming UDF predominance amongst the very poorest voters.[33] It was impossible to imagine any clearer indication of the demoralisation and demobilisation of the 'people of the Left' than that.

There were other signs too. *Le Nouvel Observateur*, though friendly to the PS, estimated in October 1979 that the party's membership had fallen to under 100,000 in real terms.[34] The PCF's numbers continued to mount but actual membership activity was at a new low. It had become all but impossible to find militants willing to sell *L'Humanité-Dimanche* on Sundays and the paper had seen a calamitous fall in circulation as a result: from 400,000 in 1974 to around 200,000 in 1979. Moreover, the hitherto apparently bottomless reservoir of young militants had dried up: the *Jeunesse Communiste* continued to suffer even worse than its parent from apathy and absenteeism. Even more significant was the clear phenomenon of 'de-syndicalisation'. Until 1977 the CFDT had grown steadily by 4 per cent every year for a decade. In 1978 its membership had receded by 3 per cent and the trend continued into 1979. The CGT's position was even worse. In 1978 it had lost 13.8 per cent of its membership, with the same trend again visible in 1979. In the key iron and steel industry sector the situation was particularly dramatic. The CGT's membership there had fallen from 420,000 in 1974 to 370,000 in 1977 to 320,000 in 1978. The 1979 figure seemed likely to be around 285,000, representing a fall of a whole one-third since 1972.

Both the Left parties were acutely conscious of this malaise – but drew different conclusions from it. Mitterrand regarded it as an urgent necessity to halt all further quarrels within the PS leadership and to renegotiate some form of alliance with the PCF: only this could stop the clear PS slide. The PCF was conscious that the malaise hurt the PS more than themselves in the end. It was the price the Left as a whole had to pay for the re-establishment of PCF pre-eminence – and the June vote showed that the tactic had begun to work. The Party determined to launch a new campaign of 'tribune' politics – and to keep the PS at arm's length.

In early August Marchais returned, unseasonably soon, from a holiday as Tito's guest in Yugoslavia and, to the general astonishment, launched a series of major attacks on the government in the middle of this 'dead' political month. Announcing that the rise in unemployment over the 1.4 million mark marked a major crisis for the French working-class, Marchais declared that he was ready 'to unite with the devil' to fight 'the most ferocious class politics applied in France in a long time'.[35] At the same moment Séguy announced that the CGT would lead a great mass movement against the government, centring on a 'week of action' in early September.

With Mitterrand still on vacation, the PS was caught off-guard. Jean Poperen, the senior PS man left in Paris, quickly echoed Marchais's attacks and announced that Mitterrand would shortly take an initiative to relaunch the Union of the Left. The PCF – whose manoeuvre had been staged precisely in order to pre-empt such an appeal by Mitterrand – poured scorn on the idea of the PS leader making such moves while on holiday. Marchais quickly condemned the PS initiative in advance, arguing that the PS leadership was only interested in 1981, anyway. If they were serious in their concern for the workers why were not their friends in the FO and CFDT joining in the CGT's week of action? Because, the leaders of the latter bitterly replied, when they had met with the CGT on 9 August Séguy had failed entirely to mention the great campaign he was to launch just forty-eight hours later. Séguy merely responded that the situation was far too urgent to have wasted time in laborious negotiations with the CFDT which, he was sure, would have led nowhere . . . With this it became nakedly apparent that the PCF and CGT had concerted their efforts to throw the rest of the Left off balance, putting themselves forward as the only real defenders of the working-class. All others were invited to fall in as infantry behind the PCF's cavalry charge. Only unconditional recruits would be welcome – how could one take seriously those who talked of pacts, agreements, or conditions of alliance in the hour of battle? Marchais fell straightforwardly into the old language of the tribune as he put himself forward as the Left's general: 'Our sole aim as Communists is to defend the world of work. Anything else is just dirty politics *(la politique politicienne)*'.[36]

Mitterrand returned hurriedly from holiday to declare that the PS would associate itself with any trade union or party in the struggle against the government-produced economic crisis, though he could not see the point of futile acts of protest (i.e. the CGT's week of action). The PS would, he said, move 'step by step' towards unity, making a PCF refusal of unity more and more difficult. But if the PCF wanted 'unity at base', well the PS was ready to accept that right away. The most important thing, he announced, in an unwise and perhaps Freudian slip, was to enlarge the audience of the Left so as to put a PS candidate in the best possible position for the second ballot in 1981. Meanwhile he was ready to meet Marchais at any time to help reconstruct Left unity.

Marchais was thrown on to the defensive and seized on Mitterrand's mention of 1981 to 'prove' that the PS was not really interested in the workers' problems save for the purposes of gaining eventual electoral profit from them. As for a meeting with Mitterrand, Marchais simply blustered:

> I don't know at all, but all that is secondary! The problem posed – in the hypothetical case that there were a meeting – is what could come from such a meeting? While that is still so unclear, I can answer neither yes nor no to the question you put to me.[37]

In the end the PCF consented to a meeting on 20 September – though with neither Marchais nor Mitterrand in attendance. The PCF loudly announced in advance that the meeting was bound to be a failure – and, of course, it was.

Perhaps more significant was the meeting the day before of the CGT and CFDT. Although the PCF kept up a furious barrage of attacks against the CFDT (which it saw as representing the real core of PS working-class support), the CGT had begun to sing a very different song. Its week of action, aimed particularly at gaining new white-collar members, had been an almost complete flop and Séguy was, like Maire, deeply disturbed by the continuing trend towards 'de-syndicalisation'. Maire, for his part, was keenly aware of the continuing resistance within the CFDT to his policy of *recentrage* and the corresponding enthusiasm for a renewal of the old (1974) 'unity of action' pact between the two organisations. Accordingly, the two leaders found themselves able to agree without difficulty on a new unity pact. The result was distinctly odd: a continuing and bitter war of words between the CFDT and PCF and amicable relations between the CFDT and CGT. Maire tolerated the situation – even Séguy's occasional, if somewhat watered-down, echo of the PCF line – partly because he had no alternative and partly because he wished to encourage Séguy's bid for independence from the PCF. The PCF tolerated the situation partly because it could not ignore the damage being done to the CGT – its own real industrial base – by continuing disunity, and partly because it was pushing ahead so vigorously with the expansion of its own factory cells that it looked increasingly to the day when it might not need to rely so openly on the CGT anyway. If all went according to plan the PCF would develop such a commanding presence on the factory floor that it would in any case be in a position to call the tune to the CGT from its own grassroots up, for amidst the general organisational malaise of the Left the PCF provided the only bright spot. It might have difficulty in obtaining the old level of devotion from its members, but it was still having no problem in signing them up. The PCF happily announced that the two-day *Fête de l'Humanité* in September 1979 had drawn an attendance of 1 million and 10,200 new PCF members.[38]

The PCF might criticise Mitterrand for being already preoccupied with 1981 but by October 1979 the same thought was in every mind. At the 20 September meeting of the PS and PCF it rapidly became clear that the real anxiety of the PCF representatives centred merely on the possibility of an early declaration of candidacy by Mitterrand. Should this occur the PCF might find its voters rallying to his standard before Marchais' hat was in the ring, making the Party's already uphill task even harder. The Party decided to take no chances, almost immediately launching a campaign encouraging workers to write personally to Marchais recounting their struggles, woes and ideas for the future. Even Fiterman admitted that this attempt to depict Marchais as the father of his suffering people was not unconnected with the presidential contest.[39] Marchais was known to be an enthusiastic candidate: his private conversation, when not about Leroy's obstructive tactics at *L'Humanité*, already revolved largely around his eager entry into the political big-time of the presidential arena.[40] When polls were published showing Mitterrand losing to Giscard in 1981 and Marchais going down 64:36 per cent in the event of a Giscard-PCF run-off, Marchais could hardly contain his excitement. Jeering at Mitterrand as a three-time loser, he added: 'The PCF *will* have a candidate – it may not be me – but look, I've never been a presidential candidate before and already I'm given 36 per cent. The future belongs to me!'[41]

Neither Mitterrand nor Marchais wished to declare too soon, but others wasted no time. In early September Chirac announced (from the safe distance of Réunion) that no 'great party' could afford to be absent from the 1981 contest – an almost open declaration of candidacy. The PSU quickly followed by announcing it would designate a candidate of its own at its November 1979 Congress. In early October the ex-PCF Politburo member Roger Garaudy announced his candidacy 'on a programme much wider than the Ecologists' '. The Trotskyites began discussions aimed at presenting a single candidate between them in 1981. Most significant of all, the MRG announced in mid-October that it would have its own candidate, too – possibly in concert with the Ecologists. This was a major blow to the PS, which feared that such a candidate could steal enough votes from it to put Marchais ahead on the first ballot. The MRG leader, Michel Crépeau, still held out the possibility that the MRG would stand down – if Rocard were the PS candidate. The Mitterrandistes reacted furiously by threatening the MRG with heavy reprisals in the 1983 legislative elections.[42] It was, however, unclear how many of these minor party candidatures would finally materialise, for the new (1976) election law had made it forbiddingly hard to achieve a place on the ballot paper. In 1981 candidates would have to present petitions in their support signed by 500 national or local representatives from 30 departments (instead of, previously, 100 from 10 departments.) This left many of the minor parties pondering what (literally) the price of a local councillor's signature would be. It also opened up a whole vista of entertaining possibilities for 'submarine' candidates. Would PCF councillors decide that it was in the interests of democracy to have an MRG on the ballot? Would the PS sponsor a Trotskyite? Would Chirac even sponsor JJSS to hurt Giscard?

Equally fascinating were the range of possible unholy alliances. Chirac's best interests would be served, for example, if a Socialist actually beat Giscard – making the RPR the only recourse of the Right. Giscard, on the other hand, had everything to gain from Marchais winning through to the second ballot: the President would then win easily and would hardly need Chirac's votes. The PS would hope Chirac did well against Giscard on the first ballot: either Mitterrand or Rocard could beat Chirac at the second ballot and, short of that, both stood to gain from whatever damage Chirac might do to the cohesion of the Right by a rough first-ballot campaign. The PCF, on the other hand, would hope Chirac did badly. If he did well he might pull Giscard to the Right and leave a larger Centrist vote available to the Socialist. So it was in the PCF's interest that Giscard should do as well as possible. Hence the 'objective' alliances were between the PS and the RPR on the one hand and Giscard and the PCF on the other. But if the party leaderships had begun to feel the pull of the new logic of quadrilateralism, the voters clung fast to the older logic of polarisation. In the end the electorates of Left and Right would demand some semblance of unity from their respective leaders. But victory – for either side – might now have to depend in part on voters' defiance of those leaders. It was a curious and dangerous game in which the Right's greater and more spontaneous solidarity appeared to give it the advantage yet again. But the Left, having failed to sweep to victory on its own *dynamique unitaire*, had little choice. It would advance towards 1981 either praying for defeat or hoping for a victory bestowed by its worst enemy, Jacques Chirac.

# Conclusion: A March Without End?

'One must learn', Edmond Maire had said, 'to conjugate May '68 with March '78.' That the defeat of 1978 could so quickly gain stature alongside the explosion of *les évènements* was a not inaccurate measure of its significance. But the road travelled by the French Left winds back much further than that. As the Left entered the 1980s it was still deeply marked by the great schism of 1947–8 and by the continuing impact of the new political world inaugurated by De Gaulle in 1958. It had indeed been a long march, a story of travail, bitterness, hope – and defeat.

None the less, Maire's formulation has the merit of isolating 1968–78 as a period with, it already seems clear, an importance and historic unity all of its own. The May Events, for all that they produced an immediate landslide to the Right, inaugurated a period of transformation and great opportunity for the Left. The Events effectively brought down the curtain on the high age of Gaullism and resulted, after only brief delay, in the exit of De Gaulle himself. While his towering figure had dominated centre stage the Right had, in effect, been invulnerable. Once he had gone the Left could dare to hope. Second, the Events saw the definitive *ralliement* to the Left of the CFDT. The ensuing decade, which saw a marked decline in the conservative pull of traditional Catholicism, did much to fulfil the symbolic promise of that event. Moreover, the events also witnessed – for many they were almost synonymous with – the eruption of a new generation into the political arena. The ensuing years not only saw the *enragés* gain a permanent, if marginal, place in French political life in the form of a powerful Trotskyite movement; they saw a sweeping rejuvenation of the Socialist Party and the conversion of even the PCF to the demand for *autogestion*, which was the political self-definition of the 'generation of '68'. By 1978 the overwhelming left-wing preference of the young had become a potent force in French politics, one enhanced both by demographic change and by the introduction of the eighteen-year-old vote. Finally, 1968 saw the French working-class stake its claim for full citizenship in the social and political nation. This was the most fundamental fruit of May and nothing contributed more powerfully to the new political mood of 1968–78, the decade of *après-Gaullisme*.

The context of this new mood was provided by the overall decline of Gaullism and the Left's new unity. Within those parameters it was, though, a complex and mobile thing. Its keynote was, indeed, fluidity. Gaullism was not merely declining but changing (as it lost its more 'popular' element) and losing shape as it merged into an increasingly formless Majority. The progressive incorporation of the Centre into the

Majority – which should, logically, have strengthened it hugely – was accompanied by such powerful counter-flows of electoral support that the Majority continued to lose ground overall. This fluidity extended to the Left, too. Above all, the PS was gaining many new converts. But so too, to a lesser degree, were the Trotskyites. Even the PCF was making some gains from the PS in proletarian strongholds while losing ground elsewhere. A period which began with the Gaullists and the PCF taking two-thirds of the vote between them (in 1968) ended with their combined strength at only 43 per cent (in 1978): a whole one quarter of the electorate had moved.

In considerable part this fluidity was created by the erosion of the old bedrocks of the Right: the supra-political mystique of Gaullism and the power of the religious cleavage. The former process was well illustrated by a 1977 poll asking voters to compare the three presidents of the Fifth Republic. By a 68.26 per cent majority voters thought De Gaulle had been 'the President of all Frenchmen' rather than just 'the President of those who voted for him'. The same view was taken of Pompidou, though only by 51:41 per cent. The opposite view was taken of Giscard by a huge 60:30 per cent.[1] The declining power of religious conservatism was equally unmistakable and, by the late 1970s, had helped the Left to lighten its greatest traditional handicap, its disproportionately male bias in a society where men were heavily out numbered by (religiously more practising) women. In 1952 this bias had been so pronounced that although men made up only 48 per cent of the population they had provided 61 per cent of the PCF and 59 per cent of the SFIO electorates.[2] By 1979 women made up 53 per cent of the PCF and 48 per cent of the PS vote.[3] The femininisation of Left politics was striking at leadership level, too. Women had begun to make their appearance near the top of the PS; there were four women on the PCF Politburo; and the leaders of both the Trotskyites (Mlle Arlette Laguiller) and the PSU (Mme Huguette Bouchardeau) were women.

As the parties discarded old habits and the party system drifted free from its moorings, new issues inevitably surfaced. There was a new concern for ecology, for feminism, for 'quality of life' issues, and for a (vaguely conceived) 'social justice'. There was, in particular, a new focus on the brutal facts of inequality in French life – a concern which sprang at bottom from the new push of the working-class towards its own greater integration into bourgeois society. With the removal first of De Gaulle and then, progressively, of Gaullism, the old obsessions with grandeur and stability became less central and the middle ground of politics was taken over by a vague social liberalism. In this atmosphere, not surprisingly, the Socialists and the Giscardians thrived. The Gaullists and the PCF tried hard to ride the new wave, too, the PCF strenuously attempting to turn itself into a Eurocommunist party committed to pluralism and human rights; their failure to blossom in the climate of the 1970s was hardly mysterious. It was an atmosphere which suited their respective opponents far better than them (and their opponents' very success further reinforced this climate, of course). Strain as they might, there was no changing that.

The spirit of hopeful reformism filled the sails of the renascent PS, pushed even the PCF towards liberalism, and was assiduously cultivated by Giscard. It was, though, riddled by contradiction. This was true at the level of attitudes: there was (for example) an enhanced liberal concern with the plight of the hitherto largely ignored immigrant workers. When IFOP polled the electorate for its views towards these new *misérables* it was so staggered by the breadth of hostility it discovered that it actually falsified its results to hide the fact.[4] But it was true at a structural level, too. The Left's onward sweep produced a tremendous strengthening of the class alignment, with the working-class achieving an unprecedented solidarity and political unity behind the Common Programme. It was, moreover, a class bloc concerned with class issues: when young voters were asked in 1977 what aspect of French life they most disliked, 'social inequalities' was by far the most common response. In a period of record youth unemployment more than eight times as many young voters were concerned with social inequality as with unemployment amongst their own age-group![5] Yet – and this was the conundrum which defeated the Communists – it was a period of declining, not increasing class-consciousness. Only two-thirds of the electorate identified with any social class; only 56 per cent of workers thought they were working-class (although far more than that were supporting the Left); and the young voters who were, of all groups within the electorate, by far the most likely to support the Left, were also the least likely to identify with any social class. The most class-conscious group were the over-65s, who had lived through Depression, war and the Resistance: 76 per cent of them identified with one class or another. As they passed out of the electorate, however, their place was being taken by younger age cohorts who were far less class-conscious. Only 70 per cent of the 25–34 age group identified with a class and only 59 per cent of the 18–24s did so.[6] Moreover, while the Left was united in its determination to achieve what even the Socialists termed 'revolutionary' social change with a clean 'rupture with capitalism', no social group believed in revolution. By a 3:1 majority the electorate as a whole thought that change would come by 'peaceful and progressive reform' rather than by 'a sudden and violent crisis'. Even workers, the 18–24 age group, and Communist supporters held this view by 5:3 majorities.[7]

Thus while there was no doubt of the fading power of the old religious cleavage, the class alignment was only replacing it at a purely 'electoral' level. The spirit of the age was, rather, hostile to the formation or even maintenance of either of these older solidarities. Indeed, the new popularity of sexual politics and 'quality of life' issues stemmed in part from an increasing privatisation of life at every level. In this climate *every* political party found itself suffering a *crise de militantisme* and, even as voters were being polarised as never before into Left and Right camps, general sentiment against *all* politicians was extremely strong.[8] The 1970s introduced into every politician's vocabulary the ritual denunciation of *la politique politicienne*'.

Apoliticism and anti-politicism were, none the less, only minor eddies in a stream where the real thrust was provided by the confluence of two mighty currents: the polarisation and quadrilateralisation of political life.[9] The first of these was hardly mysterious. Thanks in large part to the institution of direct presidential elections France was divided ever more clearly and evenly into the great camps of Right and Left. This had two principal effects. The clash between Right and Left grew in intensity with the battle nowhere fiercer than in the competition for the allegiance of the diminishing no-man's land of the Centre and Centre-Left. Second, polarisation led to simplification and homogenisation within each of the major camps. For most voters the principal question was simply whether one favoured *la gauche* or *le Majorité*. On the Right the clearest signs of this process were the sheer amorphousness of the Majority, the ease with which Giscard captured its allegiance from the Gaullists, and the near-military discipline of conservative voters at the second ballot. On the Left it was noticeable as early as 1967 that young voters were beginning to plump at the first ballot for the Left party they expected to be supporting at the second ballot anyway. The politicians carried the process further with the construction of *la gauche unie* and the Common Programme. But the clearest indication of homogenisation was the gradual narrowing of the PS-PCF differential at the second ballot.[10] To some small degree this was due to improved Communist turnout for Socialists but far more to the contrary process. As the PS moved into closer alliance with the PCF a Socialist voter came increasingly to be defined as one who accepted that alliance and with it the potential necessity to support a PCF candidate at the second ballot. After 1978, though, the continuation of this trend was an open question.

If presidentialism meant that there had to be only two large camps, the retention of double ballots at both presidential and legislative elections allowed for each camp to enjoy the luxury of 'primaries' between its component elements at the first ballot: hence 'quadrilateralisation'. This process was long masked by the electoral dominance of Gaullism, though even by 1967 the Left camp had fallen fairly neatly into two roughly equal halves. With the institution of Majority primaries in 1973 and the rapid decline of Gaullism thereafter, the political system began to reshape itself into four roughly equal quadrants. By 1978 this process was apparently complete, with all four major parties gaining 20–25 per cent of the vote.

But there, however, was the rub. The logic of quadrilateralisation was *not* towards four equal quarters but towards the 'rise of the central blocs', for the system clearly privileged those parties best able to pick up extra Centre support at the second ballot: that is, the PS and the UDF. The tendency of the system, expressed in crude terms, was thus towards two 30 per cent parties of the Right and Left Centre, flanked by two 15 per cent parties on extreme Right and Left - the PCF and RPR. Much of the political life of the 1970s was determined, in effect, by the furious resistance of the PCF and RPR to being thus cut down to size. The fact that both had enjoyed a long historic dominance within their respective camps made their resistance the more bitter; the fact that they possessed the only effective mass political organisations in France made it the more effective.

Gaullist resistance to this process came late – the RPR was only founded in December 1976 – and was muffled by its absolute need to support the President against the Left. The PCF was under no such constraint and, as we have seen, its furious reaction to the threat of marginalisation was the pivot on which French politics turned in the 1970s. The crisis of French Communism thus became the central fact of political life.

The more conservative elements within the PCF argued, of course, that the Party's crisis was largely the result of the leadership's mistaken enthusiasm for popular frontism. It is certainly true that the PCF learned the wrong lessons from 1936. Then they benefited electorally from a Popular Front because Left unity was seen to be the product of their sacrifice; it was a one-election phenomenon; and it was essentially negative in intent – the point being simply to 'bar the road to fascism'. In the 1970s these conditions were exactly reversed. It was Socialist concessions which made Left unity possible, and the demands of the Fifth Republic were for a sustained movement of opposition able to offer a positive alternative to the Majority. In the end the Socialists were bound to be more credible than the PCF, for only through them could the Left hope actually to win power.

To admit this much, however, is to suggest that the causes of the Communist crisis were more fundamental than the mere strategic errors of the leadership, even when these errors were compounded by the Party's failure to achieve an earlier and more complete de-Stalinisation. The PCF's decision to seek alliance with the Socialists was not, after all, a merely tactical matter, and it was taken long before the birth of the Fifth Republic imposed new, systemic constraints on the Party. Rather, it reflected the PCF's acknowledgement from at least 1944 on that proletarian revolution was no longer possible and that the PCF could not remain for ever in the ghetto. For decades the tribune politics of the ghetto had seemed to provide a viable half-way house, but by the 1960s such a posture was becoming less tenable with every passing year. Even before 1968 the PCF could feel the groundswell of the workers' determination to leave the ghetto. In 1968 the groundswell mounted into actual waves. After that the Party was left with very little choice in the matter – indeed, the problem was whether it could run hard enough even to stand still. As Marchais put it in 1979, surveying the PCF's difficult relationship with the young, 'if we have advanced in the recent period, the problems have advanced more quickly than us'.[11]

On the surface the PCF, as it emerged cautiously from the ghetto, suffered simple stagnation. Closer analysis – as fascinating to the analyst as it was disturbing to the leadership – showed that the Party was actually subject to a far more complex social process. The best way to understand this process is, perhaps oddly, by an analogy from astronomy. As a large ('red giant') star burns itself it consumes the matter at its core and thus collapses inwardly, creating a much smaller, denser and hotter 'white dwarf'. The dwarf's great heat causes expansion back towards red giant size, occasioning further inward collapse and so on. The PCF behaved in similar fashion, losing volume as it concentrated more densely than ever round its proletarian core – actually increasing its working-class vote while it lost elsewhere. At the same time its support showed signs of inward collapse at the very centre – in the Paris region – leading the PCF to attempt desperate but superficial expansion outwards towards discontented peripheral groups – the peasantry of the South-West and those suffering the immediate impact of economic crisis in Lorraine and elsewhere.

Simultaneously the PCF sought to hold its ground by a prodigious organisational effort. This produced a series of peculiar contradictions. It was not merely that membership doubled while electoral support stagnated or fell, so that the Party became a mass party only as it declined. For those familiar with the PCF's early history two other details caught the eye. In late 1922 Trotsky, then the Comintern specialist on

French affairs, discovered by accident and to his 'complete stupefaction' that the PCF was honeycombed with freemasons, whose orders provided the natural milieux of the French anti-clerical Left. Trotsky, both furious and scandalised by this discovery, had launched a complete and immediate purge of the masons, including the PCF's secretary-general, Frossard, and his deputy, Ker.[12] Thereafter, the 'Bolshevisation' of the PCF had proceeded apace, with a heavy but often unsuccessful emphasis put on the constitution of factory (rather than neighbourhood) cells. The 1970s provided a curious echo of these events. On the one hand it became clear that there was, once again, some degree of overlapping membership between the PCF and the masonic lodges,[13] perhaps not a bad index of how far the Party had begun to emerge from the ghetto. On the other hand, however, the Party was simultaneously 'Bolshevising' itself to a quite unprecedented extent, with the number of factory cells reaching new record levels. Thus, as the PCF became more 'bourgeois democratic' in its posture, it simultaneously became more Leninist in its structure. As the intra-Party dissidence of 1978–9 showed, the PCF leadership had hardly solved the problem of maintaining Leninist habits of obedience and organisation in the newly 'democratic' Party of the 1970s. Liberalisation increased its difficulties not only because the leadership found itself under pressure to live up to its democratic promises, but because it involved the wholesale jettisoning of traditional doctrine. As the PCF's supporters saw even fundamentals discarded they naturally grew more open and questioning about everything else as well. Thus the phenomenon of 'collapse at the centre' was not restricted to the PCF's electorate alone – it was true of the *apparat* too. So much so that by late 1979 the Party faithful were goggling at the unheard-of sight of the PCF secretary-general entertaining friendly relations with the Party's leading critic (Elleinstein) while engaging in virtually open polemics against the editor of the major PCF newspaper (Leroy).

As it grappled with the Party's crisis the Communist leadership had one major ally – the Right. Even at a tactical level the bitter Socialist claim of an 'objective alliance' between the PCF and the government often seemed valid. The Right might dislike the PCF more than it did the PS but it was the electoral competition of the latter which posed the greater threat in the end. Hence the recurrent attempts by the Right in both presidential and legislative elections to help the PCF into the second ballot. This 'objective alliance' existed at a deeper level as well, for both the Right and the PCF had reason to fear for the future if the working-class should succeed in its bid to leave the ghetto. The PCF pressed on towards liberalisation in the uneasy awareness that should its strategy fail there might be no natural 'Red base' to which to return. The Europe of the inter-war years had seen a revolutionary Left encamped in several great proletarian redoubts – the Independent Labour Party on Clydeside, the KPD in Hamburg and Berlin, the PCI in Milan and Turin – and the PCF round Paris. The existence of such redoubts had depended upon a degree of mass poverty, proletarian alienation and political parochialism on which it had become increasingly unsafe to rely. Workers were now better educated, more affluent, and more nationally conscious. In its great urban redoubts loyalty to the PCF persisted through a lingering, though now much weaker, sense of alienation and, often, sheer habit. In the Paris region of the 1970s this was beginning to be no longer enough.

The Right's problem was the other side of this coin. In principle, at least, both Giscard and Chirac rejoiced in the embourgeoisement of the proletariat – and their regret at the Majority's loss of working-class votes was nothing if not sincere. Giscard in particular was keen to remain in tune with the reformist social-liberal spirit of the age, taking up the causes of divorce reform, abortion, and a wealth tax (the UDF frequently described itself as social democratic at heart). Even Chirac attempted to play this card from time to time.[14] But beyond the level of rhetoric and posture this never amounted to much. As Mitterrand observed of Giscard:

> One cannot say he has failed in his reform of society. He hasn't tried. It wasn't in his blood and no one truly expected it of him. There have been little tea-time speeches, the verbal confusion of a moment – but that's all.[15]

The fact was simply that the Right was never remotely willing to pay the cost in greater social and economic equality which the true emancipation of the proletariat from its traditional ghetto would entail. Giscard's lofty and abstract talk of 'reform' was barely tolerated by the bourgeoisie at the best of times. There was never any doubt that to meet the rising challenge of the Left in 1973–8 the government would have to rely chiefly on the hysterical anxieties of the bourgeoisie – indeed, to stoke the fires higher at every opportunity. The further social and economic emancipation of the working-class was simply incompatible with such a strategy; indeed, it was probably incompatible with the maintenance of the Majority in power, pure and simple. The Right wanted the workers to feel less alienated and hoped that gradual social change might achieve that end – but it was willing to pay no immediate price for that result and wanted, at all costs, to win. In that sense, at least, the Majority's victory in 1978 signalled a successful resistance to the workers' attempt to leave the ghetto. This, together with the harsh economic policies applied after the election, reproduced yet again a situation in which the PCF could in 1978–9 throw itself back into its old tribunitial role in defence of the ghetto. This, we have seen, the PCF did to some effect. To understand the dynamics of the 'objective alliance', one only has to imagine how much harder it would have been for the PCF to seek this escape route had the Left won the 1978 election.

The 1978 defeat was thus the close of an era of great opportunity for the Left. In large part the opportunity had been squandered. At the end of the period it seemed that if the workers were to leave the ghetto they would have to do so via piecemeal social change on terms acceptable to the bourgeoisie, not by their own victorious efforts. At the end of the 1970s the Left was weaker industrially and more divided politically than it had been at the start of the decade. A whole new generation of Socialists had, through the PCF's behaviour in 1977–8, been introduced to the same visceral anti-Comunism which had marked their SFIO elders. There were clear signs of the erosion of Left unity at the grassroots. Although 91 per cent of PCF voters remained in favour of a united Left by March 1979, only 34 per cent of PS voters felt the same: two-thirds of all Socialists preferred alliance with the Right or had no other viable solution.[16] Communist voters alone – despite their leaders' refusal of Left unity – remained pathetically willing to believe in the benefits of a united Left government: Socialists were apathetic or cynical even at the prospect.[17]

For the greatest assets which had been wasted were those of hope and belief. In the first decade and a half of the Fifth Republic the chief burden under which the Left had laboured was simply that of hopelessness. Nobody – even on the Left – believed that the Right could be beaten. The Left could not mount a credible alternative to the Majority because its challenge was not, in a strict sense, credible. Only gradually did this feeling disappear. Pompidou's dire warnings during the 1973 election campaign that he would not appoint a government of the Left whatever the election result had had no precedent in the 1960s. At last the prospect of a Left victory could not be entirely ignored. The chief significance of the 1974 presidential contest was the razor-thin majority it produced. Thereafter no one could doubt the plausibility of a Left victory. It was only as this lesson sank in that the standing of both Mitterrand and the PS began to soar in the opinion polls: the strength of the Socialists made them credible – which made them stronger still. With the joining of that virtuous circle the possibility of Left victory was at last in sight.

March 1978 not only shattered these hopes but suggested that it might be impossible for the Left *ever* to win a legislative majority. It was not just that constituency gerrymandering and the unwillingness of many PS voters to vote Communist at the second ballot meant that the Left needed more than 50 per cent of the vote to win. It now became clear that, to win, the Left had to stay united – which in turn depended on the achievement of a balance within the Left not too unfavourable to the PCF. Put together, these two requirements seemed virtually incompatible. Poll simulations in 1978 showed that if the PCF won 22 per cent of the vote the Left as a whole would need 52.9 per cent to win. If the PCF won 21 per cent the Left would need 52 per cent; if the PCF were reduced to 19 per cent the Left could win with 'only' 51.2 per cent.[18] But on the evidence of 1977–8 Left unity could not be maintained if the PCF seemed likely to poll only 19 per cent – in which case the Left would lose anyway . . .

In the wake of March 1978 these calculations seemed almost otiose. Such was the demoralisation induced by division and defeat that many were ready to conclude that the Left could *never* win, that Giscard could already begin to celebrate his re-election in 1981. This conclusion was certainly too hasty. In 1981, after all, a PS candidate on the second ballot would not have to worry about constituency gerrymandering or the unwillingness of Socialist voters to vote Communist: a simple majority of the popular vote would do. Moreover, while a Left government elected in March 1978 would have had an almost impossible job in attempting to dislodge Giscard from the Elysée, a Left President elected in 1981 could call fresh legislative elections and hope to coat-tail in a more friendly majority. Nor could Giscard be regarded as invulnerable. By September 1978 the brief post-election boom in his popularity ratings was already over. Voters professed themselves 'satisfied' with him by only a 50:38 per cent margin – which almost took him back to his record low rating of September 1977

(49:40 per cent). At the same time a record 58:31 per cent majority professed themselves 'dissatisfied' with Barre.[19]

The Left had other grounds for hope, too. Whatever the immediate bitterness of the PS-PCF feud no one seriously doubted that Left unity of a sort would continue. The PCF has nowhere else to go and, now that the alliance had been extended all the way down to municipal grassroots, nor has the PS. Probably only a change in the electoral system towards proportional representation could loosen the bonds now.[20] Moreover the PCF is unlikely to dare to repeat its strategy of pre-election rupture – it paid too high a price in post-election dissidence to risk that again.

Finally, there is no doubt that demography and social change are still working in the Left's favour. The Left has drawn considerable advantage from the large numbers of young voters born in the post-war baby boom entering the electorate after 1967, but this process still has some way to go: the number of such voters will go on steadily increasing until 1990.[21] Second, the religious cleavage may be expected to erode further with the steady onward march of secularisation.[22] Potentially, at least, the process holds the promise of a further wave of recruits to the Left.

After 1978, though, few on the Left were willing to draw much solace from statistics such as these. Demography could not explain why, if the Left was always gaining, it was never winning. With 1978 something very deep had died. A new period of ashes and iron, a new climate of apathy and distrust had begun. The question now seemed more whether the Left could even keep the gains it had made. Every further inch of fresh progress would have to be dearly won indeed. Nothing would come easily now.

Among the Left's leaders, however, hope had not entirely died. It was easier for the Communists: their position condemned them always to hope and to live without it, too. The Socialists stood in greater need of assurance. If, as cynics suggested, the party could always win the local elections but never the national ones, a large fraction of the party would be tempted to make their peace with Giscard (or, perhaps, the RPR) whatever the price. But nothing could be settled before 1981. By October 1979, after all, polls were showing that Rocard could reduce Giscard to a 50:50 per cent dead-heat in 1981, while even Mitterrand (trailing 52:48 per cent) was far from being a certain loser.[23]

But even for the leaders 1981 seemed a desperate, all-or-nothing affair. Defeat then would end the career of Mitterrand, jeopardise the strategy of Left unity with which he was associated, and might destroy the fragile unity of the PS. With that even such hope as now remained would die. The road travelled had already been too long, too hard. If the Left could not keep hope alive its long march might well become a march without end.

# Notes

## PREFACE

1 Throughout this book I have, for simplicity's sake, used the term 'Right' to denote the whole conservative half of the French political spectrum. Historically the term has been used in France only of the extreme Right. Only in the 1970s has this more Anglo-Saxon usage become current in France as the bipolarisation of political life proceeds.
2 Both figures here – and all electoral statistics cited subsequently in this book – refer only to metropolitan France (i.e. leaving out of consideration the Overseas territories and departments which are, for a number of reasons (see below, pp. 192–3) not usefully comparable with the metropole).
3 *New Left Review*, no. 109 (May–June 1978) p. 1.
4 L. Trotsky, *The Spanish Revolution: 1931–39* (New York: 1974) p. 117.

## 1 SCENES FROM FRENCH LIFE, 1977–9

1 See A. Percheron, 'La Politique Jugée par Vos Enfants', *La Nouvel Observateur*, 19 February 1979.
2 My account of this meeting relies heavily on P. Gilles, 'Avril-Septembre 1977: L'Escalade de la Désunion' in *Le Matin*, *Le Dossier des Législatives 1978* (Paris: 1978).
3 Cited by Gilles, op. cit.
4 Ibid.
5 On Dassault see A. Sampson, *The Arms Bazaar* (London: 1977) especially pp. 108–12, 300–5.
6 Cited in ibid., p. 111.
7 Ibid.
8 Renault died in prison after the Liberation, awaiting trial, and his firm was confiscated permanently by the State. Berliet refused to recognise legal actions against him and was allowed to keep his family business. In the end – staggeringly – no businessman was ever brought to trial for collaboration and even the extent of State action over illicit war profits gained through collaboration remains, to this day, a government secret. See R. Paxton, *Vichy France: Old Guard and New Order: 1940–1944* (London: 1972) p. 343; also Sampson, op. cit., p. 109.
9 De Bénouville had played a key role in bringing about the downfall of his fellow general, Stehlin. Ironically, they sat for closely neighbouring constituencies, de Bénouville for the 12th *arrondissement* of Paris, Stehlin for the 16th. Neither this, nor their comradeship in arms, nor any fellow feeling as Majority stalwarts, counted for anything compared to the fact that they were on the payrolls of two rival armaments companies.
10 Cited by F.-M. Benier, 'Marcel Dassault ou Tout est Normal', *Le Monde*, 4 April 1978, on whom I have relied for an account of this interview.
11 Secretary-General of the CFDT (*Confédération Française Démocratique du Travail*), the largest non-Communist trade union federation and second biggest overall after the (pro-Communist) CGT, led by Georges Séguy.

12 Rocard, a farmer leader and (in 1969) presidential candidate of the tiny ultra-Left *Parti Socialiste Unifié* (PSU), had joined the PS and become one of its leaders in 1974. For long the head of the economic forecasting bureau in the Ministry of Finance under Giscard, Rocard had become a spokesman for 'economic realism' and strongly resistant to those who saw nationalisation as a panacea. During the 1978 election campaign he had attempted to dissuade his friend and fellow PS leader, Pierre Mauroy, the *député-maire* of Lille, from promising that no steel jobs would be lost under a Left government. Lille being virtually part of the Lorraine steel belt, such 'realism' had seemed entirely unrealistic to Mauroy.

13 Average salaries for the heads of small French companies at end-1978 were £30,260 p.a.; for large companies the corresponding figure was £50,470. These salaries were unmatched in *any* European country: see *The Economist*, 27 January 1979. M. Barre and the rest of the political elite have also not hesitated to discard the Protestant virtues of deferred gratification they preach to others, for French parliamentary salaries are amongst the highest in the world, despite the fact that parliamentary sessions are shorter and less frequent than in any other democratic country. In 1979 a deputy's basic salary was £22,280 p.a., plus an annual allowance of £15,360, plus loans provided at privileged rates to buy houses, plus free telephones, travel, stationery, postage, eighty free internal air tickets a year and eight free international tickets: see R. Jackson and J. Fitzmaurice, *The European Parliament: A Guide to Direct Elections* (London: 1979) p. 168. Moreover, deputies paid only 4.3 per cent of their salary in tax so that, even on the basic salary (disregarding allowances), they were receiving post-tax incomes which exceeded those of their German, Dutch and Danish counterparts by 20 per cent, 31 per cent and 186 per cent respectively, even though Germany, Holland and Denmark all have higher average *per capita* incomes than France: See 'European Elections', *Which?*, April 1979.

14 The following account of events relies heavily on the excellent and very full coverage provided by *Le Monde*, February–March 1979.

15 Cited in *Le Monde*, 25–6 February 1979.

16 *Le Monde*, 9 March 1979.

## 2 THE LAST LEFT GOVERNMENT

1 *Le Nouvel Observateur*, 2 April 1979.

2 As a provisional government until November 1945, an elected one thereafter.

3 F. Claudin, *The Communist Movement from Comintern to Cominform* (London: 1975) p. 343. On the achievements and de-merits of *tripartisme* see also B. Graham, *The French Socialists and Tripartisme: 1944–1947* (London: 1965); A. Werth, *France 1940–1955* (London: 1956) especially pp. 284–316; and G. Elgey, *Histoire de la IVè République: La République des Illusions: 1945–1951* (Paris: 1965). For an illuminating account by one of the PCF Ministers in the government, see F. Billoux, *Quand Nous Étions Ministres* (Paris: 1972).

4 By the early 1950s French conservatives commonly claimed that summary executions by the Resistance plus the workings of official justice had led to 50,000–120,000 deaths (the far Right Action Française said 500,000). Werth estimates summary executions to have reached 10,000 at the very most and, although 6,710 persons were also officially sentenced to death, only 767 were actually executed. Of 79,000 sentenced to prison only 11,570 were still there in 1952. These figures seem small when one considers that the infamous Vichy Milice was regularly able to call on 45,000 Frenchmen as volunteers. (Those who saw the 1970 documentary on Vichy, *Le Chagrin et la Pitié* (made for, but never shown on, French television), will remember its account of the Milice putting out their victims' eyes, then sewing the lids shut with live cockroaches placed inside the victims' eye-sockets.

Barbarism of this kind earned the Milice a hatred which exceeded even that felt for the Gestapo.)

Beyond the Milice wide sections of the French Establishment collaborated by no means unenthusiastically in the deportation to forced labour of millions of French workers, the murder of 90,000 French Jews (rounded up, frequently, by French police), the parallel murders of thousands of Communists, Socialists, gipsies and freemasons, and so on. At the Liberation 10 per cent of the magistracy was suspended for its role in the application of Vichy justice – often amounting to judicial murder – but most were reinstated. The number of collaborators punished in France was, in fact, proportionately far smaller than in other occupied countries such as Holland, Belgium and Norway: see Werth, op. cit., pp. 284–90. For the peculiar moral climate of the post-Liberation era and the startling speed with which French conservatives emerged to denounce 'Resistance crimes' in a mood of self-righteous (and anti-Communist) hysteria, it is still difficult to better the literary account provided by Simone de Beauvoir's *The Mandarins* (London: 1954), particularly when set against her Resistance novel, *The Blood of Others* (London: 1945).

5 Werth, op. cit., p. 299.

6 See, for example, Claudin, op. cit., pp. 316–43, 'The Revolution Frustrated (France)'.

7 For all his later fulminations against the 'Iron Curtain', these were all Churchill's suggestions. Stalin, Churchill recalled,

> took his blue pencil and made a large tick upon it . . . The pencilled paper lay in the centre of the table. At length I said, 'Might it not be thought rather cynical if it seemed we had disposed of these issues, so fateful to millions of people, in such an offhand manner? Let us burn the paper'. 'No, you keep it,' said Stalin [cited in G. Kolko, *The Politics of War* (London: 1969) pp. 144–5].

8 As late as May 1944 the Resistance had only 35,000–40,000 'well-armed' men, of whom only 10,000 had munitions for more than one day's fighting. On the other hand there is no reason to doubt the Allies' D-Day estimate of 3 million potential Resistants, a figure which included 350,000 activists in the *maquis*, the *Armée Sécrète* and the Communist *Francs-Tireurs-Partisans*, and the several million trade unionists – particularly the railwaymen and postmen – who, thanks to the PCF, were almost invariably ready to respond to Resistance appeals: Werth, op. cit., p. 168.

9 The Belgiam case is worthy of note. The strong (80,000-man) Resistance, dominated by the Communist *Front de l'Indépendance*, furiously resented the Allied imposition of the conservative (London) government led by Hubert Pierlot and, even more, the restoration of the monarchy despite its open collaboration with the Nazis of Leopold III. Eisenhower and Pierlot demanded that the FI surrender its arms. The FI refused, suggesting the government should deal with collaborators first. The (British) Allied Commander, General W. E. Erskine, then threatened forcibly to disarm the FI. Its leaders gave way but the rank and file rebelled, leading to the police shootings on 25 November 1944. The Allies then helped break the general strike called by the FI, after which the Resistance collapsed. Churchill told the Commons that such repressive measures had been necessary to avert 'a bloody revolution', an extreme Tory view of the situation given that the mere concession of a republic would have satisfied most of the FI: see Kolko, op. cit., pp. 96–8.

10 The most visible evidence of such misgivings was provided by the heat of Thorez's denunciations of the 'Hitlero-Trotskyites' who wished to push the Left towards 'Blanquisme'. At the 10th PCF Congress in June 1945, Thorez spoke of reactionaries who 'were trying to push the most advanced elements of the working class into adventures, in order to divide the people': cited in the official PCF history, *Le Parti Communiste Français dans la Résistance* (Paris: 1967) p. 336, which, however, like the official *Histoire du Parti Communiste Français: Manuel* (Paris: 1964) otherwise draws a veil over those doubtless fascinating debates. Only in 1952 was further light shed, when the top Politburo members,

André Marty and Charles Tillon (the former head of the *Francs-Tireurs-Partisans*), were expelled from the Party, accused of having favoured a revolutionary insurrection in 1944–5, though both denied the charge.

11 See M. Thorez, *France Today and the People's Front* (London: 1936).

12 The PCF supported French nationalist demands for the dismemberment of Germany, the internationalisation of the Ruhr and French control of the Saar – all firmly opposed by the USSR. Thorez, in a Reuter interview published in the London *Daily Mail* on 15 December 1946, admitted this difference with 'our Soviet friends', adding that 'We must find a compromise formula': cited in Claudin, op. cit., p. 340.

13 Eisenhower cut off arms supplies to the French Resistance operating on German territory, transferred a French division to De Gaulle to maintain internal order, promised two more when De Gaulle asked for extra help to deal with the Communists in the Toulouse-Limoges area, and worked to facilitate the enrolment of Resistance militants into the new regular French army. Some 137,000 *maquis* were thus enrolled. They 'were given a high proportion of outmoded equipment and assigned the most menial tasks, many in isolated regions far from the front, bases which many bitterly dubbed "concentration camps" ': Kolko, op. cit., p. 93.

14 Kolko, op. cit., p. 95.

15 Interestingly, it was at precisely this time that Orwell gave his famous warning:

> The weakness of all left-wing parties is their inability to tell the truth about the immediate future ... The British people have never been warned, i.e. by the Left, that the introduction of Socialism may mean a serious drop in the standard of living. Nearly all left-wingers, from Labourites to Trotskyites, would regard it as political suicide to say any such thing ... Socialism is a *better* way of life but not necessarily, in its first stages, a more comfortable one [London Letter, *Partisan Review*, August 1945, in *The Collected Essays, Journalism and Letters of George Orwell*: 3: *As I Please* (London: 1970) pp. 448–50].

16 P. Williams, *Crisis and Compromise: Politics in the Fourth French Republic* (London: 1964) p. 24.

17 See Elgey, op. cit., especially pp. 136–41.

18 This was perhaps just as well, for even leading American spokesmen evidenced an extremely crude view of Communism. Senator Vandenberg, the Chairman of the Senate Foreign Relations Committee, for example, attended a dinner in Paris in 1946 where Thorez was also a guest. The Senator's eyes never left Thorez's ample form and he repeatedly demanded of fellow guests, 'How can such a healthy man be a Communist?': Elgey, op. cit., p. 246.

19 Ibid., p. 248. Billoux's ministry was an almost complete fiction, for three non-Communist Ministers – for Air, the Army and the Navy – were appointed to relieve him of all his functions. Gaullist personnel such as General Billotte used to send back his letters with the inscription 'Sender Unknown'. When he left the government his ministry's non-existence was acknowledged by simply abolishing it.

20 This network was maintained until 1956, then abolished, and subsequently resurrected by Chaban-Delmas, the Defence Minister, in January 1958. Directed by his fellow-Gaullist, Léon Delbecque, it was to play a key role in De Gaulle's coup of May 1958: Elgey, op. cit., p. 262.

21 The Embassy seems to have worked particularly closely with the army chief, General Revers, who, nearly twenty years later, was able to recall most of the Embassy staff by name: Elgey, op. cit., p. 278.

22 Elgey, op. cit., pp. 284–5.

23 Ibid., p. 290. Marcel Naegelen, a Socialist Minister, retorted 'that promises well for the day when you are prime minister!'

24 Mollet had enjoyed a meteoric rise within the post-war SFIO. Of working-class parents, he had become secretary of the teachers' union in 1932 and enjoyed a considerable career within the CGT. He had been a leading Resistance figure in his Pas-de-Calais region, Mayor of Arras, and secretary of the powerful SFIO federation there. Earnest, bespectacled and hesitant in speech, he was very much the working-class intellectual and – in 1947 – was still on the far Left wing of the SFIO.

25 Cited in Elgey, op. cit., p. 290. Teitgen was an MRP leader.

26 Duclos had been a PCF founder-member in 1920 and a leader of the ex-servicemen's organisation (he had been wounded himself at Verdun). A PCF deputy in 1926 and Politburo member since 1931, he was already a veteran militant in 1947. During the war he had been the effective leader of the PCF Resistance effort, Thorez being in exile in Moscow.

27 Cited in Elgey, op. cit., p. 292.

28 Werth op. cit., pp. 357–8.

29 Ibid., p. 366.

30 Ibid., p. 380.

31 Ibid., p. 366.

32 Ibid. See also J. Fauvet, *Histoire du Parti Communiste Français: II: Vingt-Cinq Ans de Drames: 1939–1965* (Paris: 1965) pp. 201–4.

33 Werth, op. cit., p. 314.

34 J. Davidson, *Correspondant à Washington: ce que je n'ai jamais câblé* (Paris: 1954) pp. 15–16; cited by Werth, op. cit., p. 314.

35 Ibid.

36 Werth, op. cit., p. 413. The AFL was a major conduit of CIA funds to the anti-Communist side of the European labour movement in these years, notably through the 'effective and witting' collaboration of George Meany, the AFL President, Jay Lovestone, the AFL Foreign Affairs chief and head of the CIA labour operations branch, and Irving Brown, the AFL European representative. For Brown's operations in recruiting strong-arm squads in Mediterranean ports see V. Marchetti and J. Marks, *The CIA and the Cult of Intelligence* (London: 1974) p. 77. See also F. Hinch and R. Fletcher, *The CIA and the Labour Movement* (London: 1977).

37 In 1955 Thorez attempted to show that real wages were still 30 per cent below their 1938 level; Werth suggests 20 per cent; the Ministry of Labour 13.5 per cent. This was despite a 21 per cent rise in real wages in 1949–54. In 1955 49 per cent of unskilled and 31 per cent of skilled workers were still earning less than 30,000 old francs (= £30.67 = $85.28 at 1955 exchange rates); 57 per cent were working forty-five or more hours a week; and 52 per cent of unskilled and 40 per cent of the skilled had experienced unemployment: see Werth, op. cit., pp. 633–6; and R. Hamilton, *Affluence and the French Worker in the Fourth Republic* (Princeton: 1967) pp. 71–3.

38 Jouhaux, a veteran and conservative syndicalist (he was sixty-eight in 1947) had been the CGT General Secretary continuously since 1909. Frachon, who had been made joint secretary-general with him in 1945 (during Jouhaux's absence in Germany) had a 2:1 majority behind him and was the real CGT head from then on. Frachon was a PCF veteran – he had headed the Communist CGTU (*Confederation Générale du Travail Unitaire*) in 1933–5 until its fusion with the CGT – and during the war had acted as effective co-leader of the PCF Resistance in France (with Duclos).

39 Elgey, op. cit., p. 341.

40 Ibid., p. 377.

41 Ibid., pp. 363–4.

42 Ibid., pp. 365, 375–7.

43 In 1953 Meany told the Washington Press Club,

> We also have a great part to play abroad, as important, if not more important, than that of the State Department. I am proud to tell you – for we may reveal this now – that it was

thanks to the money of American workers – the workers of Detroit and elsewhere – that we were able to create a split, important to all of us, in the French CGT, by creating the *Force Ouvrière* Federation [cited by Werth, op. cit., p. 385].

44 Throughout the strikes the French chief of staff, General Revers (who directed the deployment of troops and police against the strikers), maintained daily contact with General Tate, the Military Attaché of the US Embassy. Tate, later savouring the conspiratorial intimacy of these meetings, said that 'you could have believed you were in a Communist Party in time of war': Elgey, op. cit., p. 358.

45 Cited in Fauvet, op. cit., p. 209. Dulles had been attending a Four Power Conference on the future of Germany in London.

46 See Werth, op. cit., pp. 418–21.

47 *Combat*, 19–29 February 1948; cited in Werth, op. cit., p. 420.

48 Elgey, op. cit., p. 399.

49 *Esprit*, January 1949, pp. 123–4; cited by Werth, op. cit., p. 404.

50 Werth, op. cit., p. 404; J. Bruhat and M. Piolot, *Esquisse d'une Histoire de la CGT* (Paris: 1967) p. 216.

51 Cited by Elgey, op. cit., p. 403.

52 Ibid., p. 404.

## 3 THE ICE AGE OF THE LEFT, 1947–58

1 P. Williams, *Crisis and Compromise: Politics in the Fourth French Republic* (London: 1964) p. 176. The UDSR was something of a rag-bag of Gaullists (including André Malraux and Jacques Soustelle) and liberals like Mitterrand, its leader from 1953. The only common factor was that its members were ex-Resistants who, even at the Liberation, had opposed cooperation with the PCF.

2 For details of this case see Williams, op. cit., p. 506.

3 The other leading candidate for such a role, General Revers, had been dismissed in disgrace in 1950 for his part in the (still mysterious) 'Generals Affair': see P. Williams, *Wars, Plots and Scandals in Post-War France* (London: 1970) Chapter 3.

4 The Madagascar massacres of 1946, the Indo-China War of 1945–55, the repression in West Africa (1948–50), Tunisia (1952–6), Morocco (1944–52) and Cameroun (1955–60) and the Algerian War (1954–61).

5 See E. Mortimer, *France and the Africans: 1944–1960* (London: 1969) p. 157.

6 A. Werth, *France 1940–1955* (London: 1956) pp. 617–18.

7 See P. Williams, *French Politicians and Elections: 1951–1969* (London: 1970) Chapter 6.

8 See Williams, *Crisis and Compromise*, pp. 49–51.

9 See A. Kriegel, *Les Communistes Français* (Paris: 1968) pp. 150–6.

10 Cited by J. Fauvet, *Histoire du Parti Communiste Français: II: Vingt-Cinq Ans de Drames: 1939–1965* (Paris: 1965) p. 232.

11 Cited in ibid., pp. 259–60.

12 Ibid.

13 See above, pp. 32–3.

14 Cited by Fauvet, op. cit., p. 223.

15 Ibid., p. 230.

16 Cited in ibid., pp. 227–8.

17 Ibid.

18 *Le Populaire*, 12 October 1950.

19 Fauvet, op. cit., p. 257.

20 In 1945–6 Marty had opposed Mme Vermeersch's candidacy for the PCF in one of its

Paris seats on the grounds that Parisians had a right to be represented by someone who had fought in the city's Resistance, not someone (like Mme Vermeersch) who had spent the war in Moscow. Given that Marty was himself sitting for a safe Paris seat after having spent the war in Moscow too, this agreement had not been well received. Tillon's position was better based. When Mme Vermeersch had attempted to lead a discussion on the PCF's (wartime) clandestine action, Tillon had shut her up with the remark, 'How do *you* know, since you weren't there?' Coming from the former leader of the Partisans, this might have been regarded as forgivable, but Mme Vermeersch was hardly a forgiving lady. Both remarks were used as evidence against Marty and Tillon. See Fauvet, op. cit., p. 251.

21 'It [*Le Monde*] worries us far more than the Communists do', a US Embassy official told Werth. op. cit., p. 395.

22 Werth, op. cit., p. 394.

23 Ibid., pp. 554–5.

24 Eisenhower had departed to accept the Republican nomination. Ridgeway had been head of the UN forces in Korea where, the PCF claimed, he had employed bacteriological warfare – hence his nickname, 'The Bacterial General'.

25 See Werth, op. cit., pp. 575–80.

26 Marty, now labelled a police spy, died in 1956, a broken-hearted and totally isolated old man. Tillon was still alive in 1979 and dissident voices within the PCF were strongly championing the cause of his rehabilitation.

27 Fauvet, op. cit., p. 264.

28 It seems possible that Thorez knew what was coming and was hoping (in collusion with Molotov and the CPSU Stalinist diehards?) to head it off: note Stalin's promotion in this phrase to the place normally occupied by Lenin in such eulogies.

29 Fauvet, op. cit., p. 284.

30 A peasant, he was born in 1905 and attended the Lenin school for CP cadres in Moscow 1929–30. The PCF agricultural specialist, he was the central committee alternate in 1936 and a full member 1945. He was one of PCF deputies arrested during the war, and was transferred to Algeria, but escaped and spent rest of the war in London. A Politburo member 1950, he was appointed to the Secretariat in 1959 and became joint Secretary General (and thus Thorez's official successor) in 1961; he was PCF leader 1964–70.

31 G. Elgey, *Histoire de La IVè République: La République des Illusions: 1945–1951* (Paris: 1965) p. 27.

32 Fauvet, op. cit., pp. 285–6.

33 Ibid., pp. 288–9.

34 Ibid.

35 Ibid., pp. 286–7.

36 Ibid., pp. 294–5.

37 Ibid., p. 259.

38 This extraordinary story was revealed only in 1978 by the Soviet dissident historian, Zhores Medvedev. See his Postscript (pp. 101–3) to K. Coates, *The Case of Nikolai Bukharin* (Nottingham: Spokesman Books, 1978). In 1979 Bukharin and his fellow victims remain unrehabilitated.

## 4 TOWARDS LEFT UNITY, 1958–72

1 The fundamental law of revolution . . . is as follows. It is not enough . . . that the exploited and oppressed masses should understand the impossibility of living in the old way and demand changes; it is essential for revolution that the exploiters should not be able to live and rule in the old way . . . It follows that for a revolution it is essential . . . that the ruling classes should be passing through a governmental crisis . . . [V. Lenin, *Selected Works*, vol. III, (Moscow: 1960) pp. 430–1].

2 Casanova had been brought in as a loyal *apparatchik* to replace Tillon in 1952. He was

Thorez's only close personal friend on the Politburo. Also disgraced were two editors of Party journals, Jean Prouteau of *Economie et Politique* and Maurice Kriegel-Valrimont of *France Nouvelle*.

3 See J. Fauvet, *Histoire du Parti Communiste Français: II: Vingt-Cinq Ans de Drames: 1939–65* (Paris: 1965) pp. 311–16. Servin (though not the rest) ultimately acknowledged his errors in the requisite cringing fashion, speaking of the 'deserved lesson' he had been taught. The PCF students and their paper, *Clarté*, were criticised but not punished. The estrangement of the PCF leadership from Leftist student milieux – the seeds of May 1968 – dates from this period, which witnessed a prodigious growth in Maoist, Trotskyite and other *gauchiste* groups.

4 See P. Williams and M. Harrison, *De Gaulle's Republic* (London: 1965) pp. 174–9 and, by the same authors, *Politics and Society in De Gaulle's Republic* (London: 1971) pp. 136–8.

5 P. Williams, *French Politicians and Elections: 1951–1969* (London: 1970) p. 103.

6 *Union pour la Nouvelle République*. The Gaullists ran under this label in 1958 and 1962 (Giscard's affiliated Independent Republicans running as UNR–RI); in 1967 under a *Vè République* label; in 1968 and 1978 as the *Union pour la Défense de la République* (UDR); in 1976 they were rechristened by Chirac as the *Rassemblement pour la République* (RPR).

7 At legislative elections candidates could win single member seats by gaining an absolute majority at the first ballot or a plurality on the second, a week later. Typically contests were settled by the pattern of preferential withdrawals for the second round, with the first round front-runners' chances depending on the breadth of their appeal to first-round losers. In the Fifth Republic minor parties who attained the support of less than 10 per cent of the registered electorate at the first round (from 1978, 12.5 per cent) were prohibited from entering the second round – thus removing their bargaining power. Direct presidential election (brought in in 1962) worked on similar lines, with the extra proviso that only two candidates could stand at the second round.

8 See Williams and Harrison, *De Gaulle's Republic*, pp. 173–4.

9 Williams and Harrison, *Politics and Society in De Gaulle's Republic*, p. 133.

10 Williams, *French Politicians and Elections*, p. 141.

11 Resolution of the PCF Central Committee, 13 December 1962: cited by G. Lavau, 'Le Parti Communiste dans le Système Politique Français' in Fondation Nationale des Sciences Politiques, *Le Communisme en France* (Paris: 1969) p. 33, f. 49; emphasis added.

12 The PCF claimed that 53 out of 64 SFIO deputies had been elected thanks to their support: H. Simmons, *French Socialists in Search of a Role: 1956–1967* (London: 1970) p. 121; Williams, *French Politicians and Elections*, p. 143.

13 Williams and Harrison, *Politics and Society in De Gaulle's Republic*, p. 44.

14 With parliament now a mere rubber stamp, opposition leaders lost almost all interest in it. In the whole of 1967 it sat for only 551 hours: Williams and Harrison, op. cit., pp. 220, 229.

15 D. Goldey and D. Bell, 'The French Municipal Election of March 1977', *Parliamentary Affairs*, XXX, 4 (autumn 1977) p. 408.

16 Williams and Harrison, *Politics and Society in De Gaulle's Republic*, p. 121.

17 See Williams, *French Politicians and Elections*, pp. 178–81.

18 A. Kriegel, 'The PCF and the Fifth Republic', in D. Blackmer and S. Tarrow (eds), *Communism in Italy and France* (Princeton: 1975) p. 76.

19 See P. Williams, *Wars, Plots and Scandals in Post-War France*, (London: 1970) pp. 74–7.

20 There was no doubt that this had been the case in general, but a closer analysis of the two precedents might have provided food for thought. The SFIO had increased its share of the poll in 1936 despite the defection of almost a quarter of its deputies (the Neo-Socialists) with some 450,000 votes at their command. Thus the small gains of the SFIO in 1936 concealed a major real success. The real losers were the Radicals, who lost 360,000 votes

despite the addition of the Neo-Socialists to their strength. A not dissimilar pattern was discernible in 1945 – until the 'special' factor of De Gaulle's personal appeal shattered the SFIO. See G. Dupeux, *Le Front Populaire et les Elections de 1936* (Paris: 1959) especially pp. 81, 85, 138–9. In the Fifth Republic, too, Left unity led some right-wing Socialists to hive off. These losses too were easily made up; and once again the Radicals were the main losers as Right-Left bipolarisation increased.

21 Roger Garaudy, then leader of the Politburo's faction (he was expelled from the Party in 1970), later recounted how he had demanded a motion going beyond one expressing mere 'reprobation' to a full-scale condemnation of the Soviet system. Waldeck-Rochet, steering a middle way between the factions, refused and revealed to him that a survey of militants had been conducted showing only 15–20 per cent agreeing with such a position, but 30 per cent supporting Mme Vermeersch and 50 per cent the official line. Not the least interesting aspect of this story is that, in determining a vital area of policy, the PCF leader had been reduced to following the results of a poll whose very existence had been kept secret from at least some other Politburo members: *Rouge*, 25 May 1978.

22 A. Kriegel, *Les Communistes Français* (Paris: 1968) p. 218.

23 F. Wilson, *The French Democratic Left: 1963–1969* (Stanford: 1971) p. 182.

24 R. Debray, 'A Modest Contribution to the Rites and Ceremonies of the Tenth Anniversary', *New Left Review*, 115 (May–June 1979) p. 55. Debray argues that the Events actually constituted a major psychological watershed via which France passed from authoritarian conservatism of a traditional type to a modern, technocratic and more permissive capitalism – that the whole process was not a revolutionary moment but a necessary catharsis en route to a more sophisticated and subtle form of bourgeois rule.

25 See D. Goldey, 'The Party of Fear: The Election of June 1968', in Williams, *French Politicians and Elections*, p. 267.

26 Wilson, op. cit., pp. 183–4.

27 Williams and Harrison, *Politics and Society in De Gaulle's Republic*, p. 130.

28 Poll data here is taken from Institut Français d'Opinion Publique, *L'IFOP et le Scrutin Présidentiel du 1er Juin 1969*, IFOP communiqué, 3 June 1969.

29 V. Wright and H. Machin, 'The French Socialist Party in 1973: Performance and Prospects', *Government and Opposition*, vol. 9, no. 2, (spring 1974) pp. 127–8.

30 See below, p. 157.

31 See Debray, op. cit., p. 59.

32 As the Left slowly and painfully realised. Garaudy recounts (in an interview with *Rouge*, 25 May 1978) that Marchais, then Waldeck-Rochet's dauphin, had led the Politburo's panicky reaction to the May–June strikes and demanded of Séguy that he use the CGT's muscle to put a stop to them. Séguy replied that he could do this all right but 'we'll lose some feathers'. A year later Marchais, surveying the dismal calm and docility of the working-class, mused aloud to the Politburo, 'Perhaps we stopped the strikes too soon.' Séguy exploded: 'But it was you who got the Politburo to force me to do it.' It is events such as this which have caused the CGT to seek (and acquire) a growing industrial autonomy from PCF control. See G. Ross, 'Party and Mass Organization: The Changing Relationship of PCF and CGT' in Blackmer and Tarrow, op. cit.

33 Goldey and Bell, op. cit., p. 409.

34 Ibid.

35 Ibid., p. 418. Estimates of the Left vote in the large towns vary according to whether PS-led third-force coalitions are counted with the Left, but however they are counted the Left's recovery from its 1968–9 level remains striking.

36 At Epinay CERES had 8.5 per cent of the delegates, at the Pau Congress of the PS in February 1975 it had 25.4 per cent: *Le Monde, Les Elections Législatives de Mars 1978: La Défaite de la Gauche* (Paris: 1978) p. 13.

## 5 GAULLISM AND THE RIGHT: THE SOCIOLOGY OF POLITICAL DECLINE

1  This and all subsequent electoral percentages cited are, except where noted, taken from the Annexes (pp. 198–209) of F. Bon, *Les Elections en France: Histoire et Sociologie* (Paris: 1978) and refer only to voting in metropolitan France.

2  J. Charlot, *The Gaullist Phenomenon* (London: 1971; Paris: 1970) p. 181.

3  Ibid., p. 83.

4  See D. Goldey and R. W. Johnson, 'The French General Election of March 1978: The Redistribution of Support Within the Between Right and Left', *Parliamentary Affairs*, vol. XXXI, no. 3 (summer 1978).

5  *Le Monde*, 12 June 1979.

6  S. Rokkan and J. Meyriat, *International Guide to Electoral Statistics* (The Hague: 1969) pp. 160, 229.

7  IFOP, *Les Français et De Gaulle* (Introduction and commentary by Jean Charlot) (Paris: 1971) p. 26. Among De Gaulle's partisans in April 1947 21 per cent saw him as a man of the Right, 2 per cent as a man of the Left, and a prodigious 71 per cent refused to identify him with a party tendency.

8  The hard core of true believers was, unsurprisingly, even quicker to emerge: the February 1946 poll also asked whether voters thought De Gaulle would become head of the government again one day and found 21 per cent willing to believe in what then seemed a most unlikely event. IFOP, op. cit., pp. 174, 197.

9  Ibid., p. 174.

10  Ibid. Gaullist support was strongest of all among liberal professionals and in business circles at this point.

11  Ibid., p. 176.

12  The 35 per cent who declared themselves willing to vote for a Gaullist party in October 1946 were the same 35 per cent who, in September 1946, had told IFOP they would prefer De Gaulle as president against all other candidates. Blum and Thorez received only 11 per cent support each and Bidault 10 per cent (seven other candidates sharing the remaining preferences). Thus the three leaders of the tripartite coalition, whose parties had taken over 75 per cent of the vote three months before, could not, even when taken together, equal De Gaulle's support on a personal level: IFOP, op. cit., p. 198.

13  In November 1946 only one-third of MRP voters had decided firmly to stay loyal to their party in the face of De Gaulle's opposition to it: IFOP, op. cit., p. 35.

14  P. Williams, *Crisis and Compromise: Politics in the Fourth French Republic* (London: 1964) pp. 32, 139. In May 1947 and October 1948 IFOP asked voters how they would vote if forced to choose between only two blocs, the Gaullists and the anti-Gaullists: 40 per cent and 43 per cent respectively chose the Gaullists. If one omits 'Don't knows' and non-respondents these percentages rise to 54.8 per cent and 55.8 per cent respectively. These levels of support correspond fairly exactly to those we have argued (see p. 74) to be typical of conditions of maximal polarisation. For the RPF the problem was that, out of power, it had no means of making this hypothetical question a real one.

15  My calculations. Sixteen of the eighteen polls showed affirmative responses within the 31–38 per cent band: IFOP, op. cit., p. 199.

16  By 1952 polls showed the MRP enjoying the support of no less than 54 per cent of all regular churchgoers. At the same time its support became heavily localised in the traditionally conservative regions of the West and East: Williams, op. cit., pp. 109–10.

17  P. Williams, *French Politicians and Elections: 1951–1969* (London: 1970) p. 106.

18  In December 1955 IFOP found only 1 per cent of the electorate wanting the return of De Gaulle at the head of the government. This figure then rose to 5 per cent (April 1956), 9 per

cent (July 1956), 11 per cent (September 1957) and 13 per cent (January 1958). Charlot, op. cit., p. 45.

19 This is not to suggest that all 46 per cent voted Gaullist at the 1958 second ballot. In fact examination of constituency results (Williams, *French Politicians and Elections*, Table 21) suggests that the second ballot support of 1958 was very comparable with that of 1962 when the Gaullists took 35.7 per cent of the vote.

20 IFOP, op. cit., p. 180. These proportions were preserved in the actual election where 56 per cent of Gaullist voters were women, 44 per cent men: Charlot, op. cit., p. 68.

21 Williams, *French Politicians and Elections*, p. 139.

22 IFOP, op. cit., p. 225. Only 17 per cent said they wanted a deputy who would oppose De Gaulle, the rest refusing to reply. Thus slightly over 42 per cent of those who offered a response wanted a deputy who supported De Gaulle.

23 IFOP, op. cit., p. 72.

24 See above, n. 14.

25 Charlot, op. cit., p. 45.

26 Williams, *French Politicians and Elections*, pp. 202–3.

27 Charlot, op. cit., p. 48.

28 Ibid., pp. 46–50. Charlot assembles the 123 polls taken on 'satisfaction with the President' in 1958–69 and groups them in four-point ranges. If one averages all 123 – including the abnormally high ratings of 1958–62 – the median figure is 58–59 per cent.

29 I have reckoned together in the Left bloc the PCF, SFIO, and those Radicals, UDSRs and Social Republicans who ran as part of the 'Republican Front'.

30 The data that follow are taken from IFOP, op. cit., p. 73.

31 Charlot, op. cit., p. 74.

32 Charlot in IFOP, op. cit., p. 52.

33 Data for the following analysis is taken from Charlot, op. cit., p. 74, and IFOP, op. cit., pp. 73, 241, 245.

34 IFOP, op. cit., p. 245. Even in defeat, though, De Gaulle retained majority (53 per cent) support amongst women. He had never enjoyed such support among men. In an all-male electorate Mitterrand would have beaten him in 1965 by 52 per cent: 48 per cent.

35 The PDM, a breakaway from Lecanuet's *Centre Démocrate*, shortly afterwards rechristened themselves the *Centre Démocratie et Progrès* (CDP).

36 IFOP, op. cit., p. 245. The 25 per cent RI support made up only 2.1 per cent of the electorate, but UDR defectors made up 6.2 per cent. De Gaulle lost by 3.2 per cent.

37 'L'IFOP et le Scrutin Présidentiel du 1er Juin 1969', roneo (Paris: 1969) p. 2.

38 IFOP, op. cit., p. 245.

39 The *Réformateurs* were really two distinct parties, Lecanuet's *Centre Démocrate* and the right-wing Radicals led from 1971 on by Jean-Jacques Servan-Schreiber. JJSS (as he was known) was a notoriously unreliable political gadfly, hated by the Gaullists for his continual irreverence at their expense and his repeated attacks on 'the UDR State'. For Giscard this was merely another reason to befriend him . . . Giscard also sought links with the only other non-Gaullist conservatives, the old *Centre National des Paysans Indépendants* (CNPI).

40 See D. Goldey and R. Johnson, 'The French General Election of March 1973', *Political Studies*, vol. XXI, no. 3 (1973) pp. 325, 331–7.

41 My calculations. The tally in votes probably did not distort the real strengths of the parties except for somewhat exaggerating that of the UDR – which held on to the lion's share of URP nominations. Opinion polls at the time showed the UDR with a steady 22 per cent support: see J. Charlot, 'The End of Gaullism?' in H. Penniman (ed.), *France at the Polls: The Presidential Election of 1974* (Washington: 1975) p. 110.

42 See Goldey and Johnson, 'The French General Election of March 1973', pp. 333–6.

43 Such assistance did not amount to ballot-rigging (except in Corsica and the overseas seats – see below, pp. 192–3), but was considerable, none the less. The Ministry of the Interior and the prefecture actually arranged the mechanics of elections, including the siting

and collection of ballot boxes. The Ministry issued the voting figures. The police conducted their own opinion polls. The prefects arranged details of ministerial election tours, contacting mayors and Gaullist organisers to ensure a good turnout, etc. Not unnaturally UDR militants had come to look to the prefects to provide a general impulsion and coherence to their local efforts.

44  J. Charlot, 'The End of Gaullism?', p. 109.
45  Ibid.
46  Ibid., pp. 110–11.
47  A. Lancelot, 'Opinion Polls and the Presidential Election of May 1974' in Penniman, op. cit., p. 184.
48  Charlot, 'The End of Gaullism?', p. 108.
49  On the first ballot Giscard and Chaban together received 48 per cent of the white-collar and 30 per cent of the industrial workers' vote. Despite the addition of second-round support from the 5.1 per cent of voters who had supported other right-wing candidates on the first ballot, Giscard's ultimate tally was only 47 per cent white-collar and 27 per cent of the workers' vote: Lancelot, op. cit., pp. 192, 202.
50  Giscard received 51 per cent of the votes of regularly practising Catholics at the first ballot, Mitterrand and Chaban only 19 per cent each. At the second ballot this group divided 77 per cent: 23 per cent respectively between Giscard and Mitterrand: ibid.
51  J.-L. Parodi, 'L'Echec des Gauches', *Revue Politique et Parlementaire* (April–May 1978) p. 17. In June 1974 the UDR had sunk to only 13 per cent and in January 1976 it still stood at only 15 per cent in the polls.
52  Williams, *Crisis and Compromise*, pp. 139–40.
53  Charlot, *The Gaullist Phenomenon*, pp. 130–1.
54  This figure contrasts strangely with the English Conservative Party, for example, 60–65 per cent of whose members are women. For the RPR's structure and membership see A. Passeron, 'Le RPR: Un Néo-Gaullisme Populaire', in *Le Monde, Les Elections Législatives de Mars 1978: La Défaite de la Gauche* (Paris: 1978) pp. 10–1, and F. Bon, 'Le Réflux du Gaullisme', in *Le Matin, Le Dossier des Législatives 1978* (Paris: 1978) pp. 11–2.
55  The PR claimed 90,000 members in March 1978. Of the other constituent parties of the UDF (*Union Démocratique Française*), JJSS's Radicals claimed 60,000 members and Lecanuet's *Centre des Démocrates Sociaux* (CDS – a reunification of the CD and CDP) claimed 30,000. All these figures – particularly the Radicals' – were large exaggerations. Other fragments of the UDF – the CNIP and the *Mouvement Démocratique Socialiste de France* (MDSF) – effectively had no members at all. In 1978 UDF candidates typically had to rely on paid help even to get their posters put up.
56  In 1975 four-fifths of all centrist voters evinced strong hostility towards the Gaullists. The pivotal Centre-Left – PS voters who felt unhappy with the Union of the Left alliance – were 'characterised by a strong allergy to the Communist Party, tempered only by a still greater hostility to the UDR': J. Charlot, 'La Fluidité des Choix Électoraux', *Project*, 100 (December 1975) p. 1178. The RPR not only inherited these hostilities but frequently deepened them.
57  Parodi, op. cit., p. 17.
58  Both figures were deliberately inflated by the Ministry of the Interior in its habitual style. Strictly speaking, candidates who adopted UDF insignia before (rather than after) the election won only 18.6 per cent of the vote. On a similar basis of calculation the UDF won only 124 seats – but Giscard was rightly confident that he could effectively count most of the 'other Majority' deputies as safe supporters.
59  *Le Matin, Le Dossier des Législatives 1978*, p. 10.
60  Giscard's list was headed by Mme Simone Veil and called itself the *Union pour la France en Europe* (UFE). Chirac headed the RPR list, the *Défense des Interêts de la France en Europe* (DIFE).

61 Cited by A. Passeron in *Le Monde*, *Les Elections Législatives de Mars 1978*, p. 11.
62 Parodi, op. cit., pp. 16–17.
63 A difficult calculation: the RPR failed to field candidates in 73 of the 474 metropolitan seats but was allowed to run without challenge from the UDF in another 93: see Goldey and Johnson, 'The French General Election of March 1978', pp. 301, 304–8.
64 D. Lindon and P. Weill, *Le Choix d'un Deputé* (Paris: 1973).
65 Charlot, 'La Fluidité des Choix Electoraux', p. 1177.
66 See J. Julliard, 'Comment les Français ont Changé de Cap le Dernier Jour', *Le Nouvel Observateur*, 24 April 1978.
67 Ibid. See also Goldey and Johnson, 'The French General Election of March 1978', pp. 304–6.

# 6 THE CHANGING POLITICS OF FAITH AND INFIDELITY

1 M. Brulé, 'L'Appartenance Réligieuse et le Vote du 5 décembre 1965', *Sondages*, XXVIII (1966) 2, pp. 15–19.
2 G. Michelat and M. Simon, *Classe, Religion et Comportement Politique* (Paris: 1977) p. 377.
3 Ibid.
4 This should be continuously borne in mind for the analysis which follows in this chapter. I have concentrated attention upon the regularly practising group merely in order to provide a clear-cut case. But all that can be said of its behaviour can be said – in shades of grey, rather than black and white – of the irregularly practising group.
5 Brulé, op. cit., p. 16.
6 It also produced a number of valuable and more detailed studies. See, in particular, M. Dogan, 'Une Analyse de Covariance en Sociologie Électorale', *Revue Française de Sociologie*, 9, 4 (1968) pp. 537–47; E. Aver *et al.*, Pratique Réligieuse et Comportement Électoral', *Archives de Sociologie des Réligions*, 29 (1970) pp. 27–52; F. Isambert, 'Signification de Quelques Correspondances Empiriques entre Comportements Politiques et Réligieux', *Archives de Sociologie des Réligions*, 33 (1971) pp. 49–70; and, above all, the work of Michelat and Simon cited above.
7 See above, pp. 54–5.
8 The percentage of children attending church schools fell from 20 per cent in 1959 to 17 per cent in 1964 to 15 per cent in 1973: J. Ardagh, *The New France* (London: 1970) p. 567; *Le Monde*, 6 November 1973.
9 *Le Monde*, 7 February 1973.
10 Militants of the *Jeunesse Ouvrière Chrétienne*, whose rural counterparts were found first in the *Jeunesse Agricole Chrétienne* ('Jacistes') and then in the *Central National des Jeunes Agriculteurs*. The Jocistes, who were in competition with the strong Marxist traditions of the urban working-class, achieved considerable prominence but never the formidable power of the Jacistes – whose opponents were merely traditional rural conservatives.
11 The *Confédération Française Démocratique du Travail* (formerly the *Confédération Française des Travailleurs Chrétiens*) moved steadily leftwards through the 1960s – especially after 1958. In 1970 the CFDT Congress adopted the doctrine of class struggle and took as its objective the overthrow of capitalist society in favour of a socialism based on planning, workers' control, and the public ownership of the means of production.
12 Cited by R. Rémond, 'Forces Réligieuses et Participation Politique', in R. Rémond (ed.), *Forces Réligieuses et Attitudes Politiques dans la France Contemporaine* (Paris: 1965) p. 77.
13 R. Rémond, *Les Catholiques et les Elections* (Paris: 1960) pp. 99–100. Charlot argues that twice as many (1 million) Catholics moved Left. See his contribution to M. Duverger *et al.* (eds), *Les Elections du 2 janvier 1956* (Paris: 1957).

14 Lijphart's figures show indices of +15 for class voting and +59 for religious voting – compared to +37 and −1 for Britain (1959): A. Lijphart, *Class Voting and Religious Voting in the European Democracies* (University of Strathclyde Survey Research Centre: Occasional Paper no. 8, 1971) pp. 8, 20.

15 Ironically, two editions of the same book – D. Butler and D. Stokes, *Political Change in Britain* – best reflect this turn-around. In the first edition (London: 1969) there is heavy stress on the fundamental strength of the class alignment; in the second edition (London: 1973) the stress is on the aging and erosion of this alignment.

16 The following account relies heavily on the valuable series of articles to be found in *Autrement*, no. 8, February 1977 and *Le Nouvel Observateur*, 23 January 1978.

17 The *Jeunesse Etudiante Chrétienne*. *Jécistes* first came to the fore during the Algerian War when a number of them played important roles in UNEF, the national students' union, in opposition to the war. Most later gravitated to the PSU.

18 CERES was not, though, the wholly Catholic affair it was often depicted as. A survey of delegates to the 1973 PS Grenoble Congress found that 16.8 per cent of CERES delegates were practising Catholics, compared with 9.8 per cent of mainstream (*Mitterrandiste*) delegates. E. Feuilloux, '40 Ans de 'Main Tendue' et Ceux Qui l'ont Prise',*Autrement*, no. 8 (February 1977) p. 100.

19 Feuilloux, op. cit., p. 94.

20 Ibid.

21 Ibid.

22 Ibid., pp. 93–4.

23 *Le Monde*, 30 May 1973.

24 Feuilloux, op. cit., pp. 93–4.

25 J. Charlot, 'La Gauche Ne Séduit Plus les Catholiques'*Le Point*, no. 280, 30 January 1978, p. 38.

26 Ibid.

27 Julliard, 'Comment les Français ont Changé de Cap Le Dernier Jour', *Le Nouvel Observateur*, 24 April 1978.

28 W. Bosworth, *Catholicism and Crisis in Modern France. French Catholic Groups at the Threshold of the Fifth Republic* (Princeton: 1962) p. 329.

29 Ibid.

30 M. Dogan, 'Political Cleavage and Social Stratification in France and Italy', in S. M. Lipset and S. Rokkan (eds), *Party Systems and Voter Alignments: Cross-National Perspectives* (New York: 1967) p. 163. The average could have been higher than 40 per cent, given the predominance of women in the overall population.

31 SOFRES, *L'Opinion Française en 1977 (Paris: 1978) Annexe I.*

32 For comparable British data, for example, see R. Currie and A. Gilbert, *Churches and Churchgoers* (London: 1978). British Catholicism suffered as heavily as its French counterpart: A. E. Spencer, writing in the Jesuit journal, *The Month* (April 1975), estimated a drop-out rate of 250,000 per annum in 1965–71 from a Catholic population of only 7 million.

33 Michelat and Simon, op. cit., p. 377.

34 'Un Siècle de Catholicisme', *Le Nouvel Observateur*, 23 January 1978.

35 Moreover, ordination of priests continues to fall near to vanishing point. In 1965, 646 were ordained; in 1974, 170; in 1976, 136; in 1977, only 99: *Le Nouvel Observateur*, 23 January 1978; *The Times*, 1 November 1978.

36 *Le Nouvel Observateur*, 23 January 1978.

37 *Le Monde*, 16 August 1977. The major effects of this aging process lie ahead in the 1980s. In 1965 there were 34,000 priests aged under 65; by 1975 the number had fallen to 27,000; by 1988 the number will fall far more sharply, to 18,000. *The Times*, 1 November 1978.

38 Ibid.

39 SOFRES, op. cit., Annexe I.

40 A. Woodrow, 'Prêtres de Campagne et Campagne sans Prêtres', *Le Monde*, 16 August 1978.
41 Ibid.
42 Ibid.
43 Ibid.
44 Ibid.
45 Feuilloux, op. cit., p. 95. To produce an average figure of 22 per cent support for the Left, at least 90 per cent of the older clergy must have supported the Right . . .
46 Ibid., p. 94.
47 Julliard, op. cit., p. 59.
48 SOFRES, op. cit., Annexe I.
49 Woodrow asked Abbé Camper (see above, p. 114) how he explained the large swing to the Left of his Breton flock in the 1977 municipal elections. 'For him the gains made by the Left were explicable simply in terms of the opposition of Bretons to the central government, whatever its complexion. And he cited a recent declaration of the *Front de Libération de la Bretagne* which described the forces of the Left as 'for the moment the sole opposition to the government in power': Woodrow, op. cit.

## 7 CLASS, INEQUALITY AND THE POLITICAL ORDER

1 In 1978 the author attended a meeting in a Paris suburb where a Giscardian candidate, inveighing against the Common Programme, asked of her (largely working-class) audience where people could safely put their money if the Left nationalised the banks. Amidst gales of laughter came the immediate crowd response: *'En Suisse, en Suisse'*.
2 H. Kahn *et al.*, *The Next 200 years* (London: 1977) pp. 189–90.
3 M Sawyer, 'Income Distribution in OECD Countries, *OECD Economic Outlook* (Paris: July 1976) p. 16. Table 7.1 may actually *under* estimate the extent to which France exceeds other nations in income inequality. In 1967 the UN Economic Commission for Europe provided data on the share of total income received by the poorest 40 per cent of the population in Canada, Norway, the USA, Sweden, the UK, Japan, Holland, West Germany and France. In France this group received (in 1962) only 9.5 per cent of all income. In *all* the other countries studied the comparable figure fell with a range of 15.4–20 per cent: A. B. Atkinson, *The Economics of Inequality* (London: 1977) pp. 26–7.
4 Sawyer, op. cit., p. 27. Sawyer notes, however, that the trend is also partly explicable by the semi-technical factor of changed pension scheme arrangements. He adds that the same trend towards greater equality was visible in all the OECD countries studied and suggests that such a trend may merely be a concomitant of the type and stage of economic development being experienced by the block as a whole. But see below, n. 8.
5 J. Marceau, *Class and Status in France: Economic Change and Social Immobility 1945–1975* (Oxford: 1977) p. 30.
6 In 1967 87 per cent of all French farmers still owned less than 100 hectares (= 247 acres). In 1970 48 per cent of all French farmers declared annual incomes of less than Fr. 6,500 (£600) and 21 per cent less than Fr. 3,000: Marceau, op. cit., pp. 30, 49. The barefaced dishonesty of these latter figures should not be allowed to conceal the fact of real rural poverty.
7 The 1901 40.9 per cent of the population was urban (i.e. lived in towns of 10,000 or more inhabitants); in 1946 54.7 per cent; in 1962 64 per cent; in 1968 66.2 per cent. The projected figure for 1985 is 77 per cent: Marceau, op. cit., p. 37.
8 A. Babeau and D. Strauss-Kahn, *La Richesse des Français* (Paris: 1977) p. 164 provide income distribution figures for 1975 showing the bottom 30 per cent receiving 9 per cent (OECD 1970=8.1 per cent), the richest 20 per cent receiving 48 per cent (OECD

1970 = 47.6 per cent) and the richest 10 per cent 33 per cent (OECD 1970 = 29.3 per cent).

9  In only one other OECD country, Australia, did the income of the poorest 20 per cent not vary with tax effects – though here the poorest group, receiving 6.6 per cent of total income, was still 50 per cent better off in relative terms than its French counterpart: Sawyer, op. cit., pp. 19–20.

10  Sawyer, op. cit., pp. 21–2.

11  Babeau and Strauss-Kahn, op. cit., p. 164.

12  Atkinson argues that Britain probably heads the wealth inequality league with a distribution significantly more unequal than that found in the USA, West Germany, Denmark and New Zealand, for example. Such comparisons are normally based on the Gini coefficient scale, running from 0 (= perfect equality) to 1 (= perfect inequality – all wealth held by a single household): Babeau and Strauss-Kahn calculate a Gini coefficient for France (1975) of 0.54–0.55. This runs quite close to the official Inland Revenue estimate for Britain (1970) of a Gini coefficient of 0.65. A. B. Atkinson, *Unequal Shares*: Wealth in Britain (London: 1974) pp. 19–20, and his *The Economics of Inequality*, pp. 121–42; *Le Monde*, 18 April 1978. Babeau and Strauss-Kahn believe the level of inequality of wealth in France to be less than that of the UK or the USA but comparable to that of Canada or West Germany: op. cit., pp. 166–7.

13  In 1949 one-third of the French population lived in owner-occupied homes; in 1975 one half did so. In the same period the proportion owning second homes went from 3 per cent to 10 per cent: *Le Monde*, 18 April 1978.

14  A. Babeau in *Le Monde*, October 1977.

15  Ibid.

16  R. Lattès, *La Fortune des Français* (Paris: 1977), reviewed in *Le Monde*, 15 December 1977.

17  *Le Monde*, 18 April 1978, handily summarises the report of the CREP (of which Professor Babeau is the head). Plausibility is lent to the notion of stabilisation only since 1968 by the fact that the home-ownership boom begun in the early 1960s reached its zenith only after 1968, with a further 10 per cent of the population becoming home-owners in the 1968–75 period.

18  *Le Monde*, 18 April 1978. This conclusion is debatable. Most students of wealth inequalities have preferred to base comparisons on the second and ninth deciles of the population rather than, as here, the first and tenth, arguing that the top-most and bottom-most groups are misleadingly extreme cases.

19  Ibid.

20  Research in Britain, for example, has shown that poor housing conditions are probably the greatest single determinant of working-class educational underachievement: see J. W. B. Douglas, *The Home and the School* (London: 1969) especially pp. 60–7.

21  Marceau, op. cit., p. 70.

22  Ibid., p. 70.

23  *Le Monde*, 7 March 1973.

24  M. Parodi, *Low-Income Groups and Methods of Dealing with their Problems* (Paris: OECD, 1966) p. 16.

25  M. Parodi, *L'Economie et la Société Française de 1945–1970* (Paris: 1971) p. 222.

26  Marceau, op. cit., pp. 70–1. Again, it is worth noting the findings of British social research which suggest that overcrowding has particularly pernicious effects on the life-chances of children, resulting, on average, in a nine-month retardation in reading age, together with similar disadvantages in arithmetical ability and general social adjustment. More routinely, of course, lack of amenities and overcrowding are closely associated with poor physical and psychological health, higher mortality rates and so on. See R. Davie *et al.*, *From Birth to Seven: The Second Report of the National Child Development Study* (London: 1972) pp. 50–7.

27  Marceau, op. cit., p. 107.

28 J. Charlot, 'Les Elites Politiques en France de la IIIe à la Ve République', *Archives Européennes de Sociologie*, XIV (1973).

29 Cited by Marceau, op. cit., p. 83.

30 Ibid.

31 D. Hall and G. Amado-Fischgrund, 'The European Business Elite', *European Business*, 23 (1969) p. 52. For the best overall study see E. Suleiman, *Elites in French Society: The Politics of Survival* (Princeton: 1978).

32 B. Wood, 'Urbanisation and Local Government' in A. H. Halsey (ed.), *Trends in British Society since 1900* (London: 1972) p. 251.

33 See above, n. 7.

34 In Britain in 1931 6.7 per cent of the employed population were engaged in agriculture (including fishing) and another 5.2 per cent in mining; 42.9 per cent in manufacturing and 45.2 per cent in services (mainly transport and domestic service). In 1951 the figures were agriculture 5.5 per cent, mining 3.1 per cent; manufacturing 45.5 per cent and services 45.9 per cent. A perhaps more telling statistic is that in 1911 74.6 per cent of the occupied British population were manual workers and even in 1966 so were 58.3 per cent, at which point less than 3 per cent worked on the land: my calculations from B. R. Mitchell and P. Deane, *Abstract of British Historical Statistics* (London: 1962) p. 61, and G. Bain *et al.*, 'The Labour Force' in Halsey, op. cit., p. 113.

35 See D. Butler and D. Stokes, *Political Change in Britain* (London: 1969), especially pp. 66–94.

36 The classic case is perhaps that of Jacques Doriot ('Le grand Jacques'), who continued to hold the Paris working-class seat he had won as a leading member of the PCF even after his defection in the 1930s to form a Fascist Party, the *Parti Populaire Français* (PPF). See G. Allardyce, 'The Political Transition of Jacques Doriot', *Journal of Contemporary History*, vol. 1, no. 1 (1966) pp. 56–74.

37 In 1956 66 per cent of industrial workers voted for the Left – 49 per cent for the PCF, 17 per cent for the SFIO – and even this level of class alignment must have been exceeded in the Left's halcyon days of 1945–6. See M. Dogan, 'Political Cleavage and Social Stratification in France and Italy' in S. M. Lipset and S. Rokkan (eds), *Party Systems and Voter Alignments: Cross-National Perspectives* (New York: 1967) pp. 140–1.

38 *Centre d'Etudes des Revenus et des Coûts* (CERC), 'Ce Que les Français Savent de Leur Revenu', *Economie et Statistique*, 54 (1974), cited in Marceau, op. cit., p. 185.

39 D. Goldey, 'A Precarious Regime: The Events of May 1968' in P. Williams, *French Politicians and Elections: 1951–1969* (London: 1970) p. 246.

40 Ibid.

41 See above, pp. 61, 64.

42 See F. Ridley, *Revolutionary Syndicalism in France* (London: 1970) and T. Zeldin, *France 1848–1945: I: Ambition, Love and Politics* (Oxford: 1973), especially Chapter 10, 'Workers'.

43 Few immigrants entered France in 1945–56. Thereafter immigration increased fast to 1958, fell off until 1961, and thereafter increased rapidly again. By 1964–5 the annual rate of entry had reached 150,000; by 1970 it had surpassed 170,000: S. Castles and G. Kosack, *Immigrant Workers and Class Structure in Western Europe* (London: 1973) pp. 32–4.

44 Ibid.

45 Such, at least, was the round figure put on the immigrant population by the press during the 1978–9 debates over immigration control. This number apparently makes allowance for the considerable number of illegal immigrants.

46 A story, which stands for much, is told of how several students, finding themselves under fierce CRS pressure at the barricades in the early hours of the morning during the May Events, telephoned Georges Séguy, the CGT leader, to ask for help – only to be told that 'One does not mobilise the working class at this hour'.

47 In Britain the high point of the electoral class alignment was reached in 1966, when 58.5 per

cent of the skilled and 65.2 per cent of the unskilled working-class (61.5 per cent of the combined group) voted Labour: D. Butler and A. King, *The British General Election of 1966* (London: 1966) p. 264. A roughly similar level of working-class alignment with the Left was reached in the 1972 West German election: see R. Irving and W. Paterson, 'The West German Parliamentary Election of November 1972', *Parliamentary Affairs*, vol. XXVI, no. 2 (spring 1973). It is doubtful, in fact, whether the French level of 73 per cent working-class support for the Left in 1973–8 has ever been equalled elsewhere.

## 8 COMMUNIST TRIBUNES AND SOCIALISTS BORN AGAIN

1 J. Fauvet, *Histoire du Parti Communiste Français: I De la Guerre à la Guerre: 1917–1939* (Paris: 1964) pp. 280–1.

2 Ibid. Fauvet gives a figure of 340,000 for 1937 but I have preferred the lower figure provided by the PCF's own analyst, Jean Elleinstein. Numbers cited in all cases are those for Party cards actually placed with members and not the always larger numbers reported as delivered to Party secretaries: see. J. Elleinstein, *Le P. C.* (Paris: 1976) pp. 96–7.

3 The secretary of the Pas-de-Calais PCF federation records how he was quite unable to gain a hearing even from militants – who used meetings as public occasions on which to tear up their membership cards. Retiring to a Party café, run by Thorez's uncle, himself a regional figure in the PCF, he found that while Thorez's picture still hung on the wall, his uncle had scrawled insults on the portrait, which now sported swastikas for eyes. Disaffection could run no deeper: Fauvet, op. cit., pp. 254–5.

4 Elleinstein, op. cit., p. 96.

5 Ibid. An estimate. In 1961 407,000 cards delivered to Party secretaries saw 300,000 placed with members. In 1956 430,000 were delivered which, *pro rata*, suggests 317,000 placed.

6 My calculations. Men made up 60 per cent of the PCF electorate in 1951 but only 47 per cent of the overall electorate: M. Dogan, 'Political Cleavage and Social Stratification in France and Italy', in S. M. Lipset and S. Rokkan (eds), *Party Systems and Voter Alignments: Cross National Perspectives* (New York: 1967), p. 161.

7 J. Fauvet, *Histoire du Parti Communiste Français*, II: *Vingt-Cinq Ans de Drames: 1939–1965* (Paris: 1965) p. 166.

8 Ibid., pp. 167–8.

9 J. Ranger, 'L'Evolution du Vote Communiste en France Depuis 1945', in Fondation Nationale des Sciences Politiques, *Le Communisme en France* (Paris: 1969) p. 243. Percentages are proportions of the actively employed electorate only.

10 Fauvet, op. cit., II, p. 338.

11 Elleinstein, op. cit., p. 102, n. 2.

12 Ibid., p. 216.

13 Ranger, op. cit., p. 242.

14 Fauvet, op. cit., II, p. 216.

15 Ibid.

16 Ibid., pp. 274–5.

17 Percentages of actively employed electorate only: Ranger, op. cit., p. 243; Dogan, op. cit., p. 151.

18 Dogan, op. cit., p. 156. In practice the spread of proletarian support was uneven; in the most working-class districts of Paris and Marseilles the PCF took 75 per cent or more of the proletarian vote: Fauvet, op. cit., p. 337.

19 Dogan's definition of the working class is sensibly broader than that employed in most French sociological research, and includes retired workers, public service workers, and workers' wives. On the narrower definition, excluding these categories, 47 per cent of the

PCF electorate in 1948 had been proletarian: Ranger, op. cit., p. 243. This comparison exaggerates PCF gains among the working-class. A better indication is given by the fact that the Party recaptured in 1956 the ground lost in 1951 in the (proletarian) Paris region, though not in the countryside. But the real compensation for the peasant losses came through the increasing proportion (22 per cent in 1948, 27 per cent in 1952) of the PCF electorate which was not employed. Clearly, the Party was recruiting new, young members of the labour force while holding the allegiances of many retired workers.

20 The Party published no membership figures for 1956–9 – itself no accident. But it had claimed 389,030 cards delivered (not placed) for 1955 but the figure for February 1957 was officially only 287, 552 – a fall of over 26 per cent: Fauvet, op. cit., II, p. 298.

21 Ibid. The PCF actually gained some ground in municipal by-elections in 1957. See also Ranger, op. cit., pp. 232–4.

22 See above, p. 75.

23 Cited by Charlot in IFOP, *Les Français et De Gaulle* (Paris: 1971) p. 63.

24 Ibid.

25 Ranger, op. cit., p. 239.

26 Ibid., pp. 235–7.

27 Thus in May 1964 a survey found 61 per cent of PCF voters favouring direct suffrage presidential election, even though the Party had galvanised such voters against precisely this proposal in the October 1962 referendum: Ranger, op. cit., p. 240.

28 In this and subsequent paragraphs I have, in essence, followed Ranger's analyis, op. cit., pp. 234–45.

29 See above, pp. 75, 77–8.

30 Ranger, op. cit., pp. 242–3.

31 The PCF apparently recouped a good part of its 1958 losses by the time of the March 1959 municipal elections; in the Paris region it recovered over half its total losses. The referenda of 1961–2 and the 1962 election saw these 'floaters' defect again to the Gaullists, however. The Gaullist impact was also visible in the rising proportion of PCF voters refusing to respond to pollsters in this period, as also in the significant proportions of even loyal PCF voters surveyed willing to profess admiration for De Gaulle and the new prosperity and stability his regime had brought: Ranger, op. cit., pp. 238–40.

32 In 1936 the SFIO proper had received 20.8 per cent of the vote but the Neo-Socialists who had recently broken away (and were still the well dug-in men in possession in a number of SFIO areas), took 7.6 per cent. By 1945 these latter had vanished, utterly discredited, and the SFIO might reasonably have expected to recapture this lost ground. This would have given it 28.4 per cent of the vote, not the 23.4 per cent it actually received. See above, p. 59, n. 20.

33 B. D. Graham, *The French Socialists and Tripartisme: 1944–1947* (London: 1965) pp. 230–1.

34 Ibid.

35 See above, p. 75.

36 Graham, op. cit., pp. 178–80.

37 P. Williams, *Crisis and Compromise: Politics in the Fourth French Republic* (London: 1964) pp. 94–5. According to a 1952 survey industrial workers made up 35 per cent of the SFIO's actively employed electorate and farmworkers another 12.5 per cent: Williams, op. cit., p. 509.

38 The SFIO in 1952 had about as many peasant supporters as the PCF, but only half as many farmworkers: ibid.

39 Williams, op. cit., pp. 94–6.

40 Ibid.

41 H. Simmons, *French Socialists in Search of a Role: 1956–67* (London: 1970) p. 278.

42 Williams, op. cit., pp. 94–6.

43 Cited in P. Hardouin, 'Les Charactéristiques Sociologiques du Parti Socialiste', *Revue*

*Française de Science Politique*, vol. 28, no. 2 (April 1978) pp. 222–5.
44 Association Française de Science Politique, *Les Elections du 2 Janvier 1956* (Paris: 1957) Table XI.
45 Williams, op. cit., p. 95.
46 Ibid., p. 96.
47 Ibid., p. 95.
48 In a 1952 survey SFIO voters were more prone than any other group to cite family and kinship reasons for their party choice: Williams, op. cit., p. 510.
49 A 1952 figure: Williams, op. cit., p. 509.
50 Hardouin, op. cit., p. 225.
51 The September 1952 poll, cited by R. Remond, *Forces Réligieuses et Attitudes Politiques dans la France Contemporaine* (Paris: 1965) p. 78.
52 M. Fichelet *et al.*, 'L'image du Parti Communiste d' après les Sondages de l'IFOP', in Fondation Nationale des Sciences Politiques, *Le Communisme en France* (Paris: 1969) Table 24, p. 268.
53 Cited by Williams, op. cit., p. 101.
54 Simmons, op. cit., p. 120.
55 Ibid., Appendix A.3.
56 See above, pp. 55–6.
57 Simmons, op. cit., Appendix D, p. 278.
58 Ranger, op. cit., p. 240. See also Williams, op. cit., pp. 178–82.
59 In particular Mitterrand received considerable support from voters of the Far Right who had favoured Tixier-Vignancour on the first ballot: Williams, op. cit., pp. 198–9.
60 See above, p. 120.
61 V. Wright and H. Machin, 'The French Socialist Party in 1973: Performance and Prospects' *Government and Opposition*, vol. 9, no. 2 (spring 1974)p. 133.
62 See above, pp. 140–2.
63 Ranger, op. cit., p. 246.
64 See G. Lavau, 'Le Parti Communiste dans le Système Politique Française', in Fondation Nationale des Sciences Politiques, *Le Communisme en France* (Paris: 1969), and also his 'The PCF, the State, and the Revolution: An Analysis of Party Policies, Communications, and Popular Culture' in D. L. M. Blackmer and S. Tarrow, *Communism in Italy and France* (Princeton: 1975). Lavau's acute analysis is presented as a timeless sociological paradigm. This I have largely followed, attempting merely to situate it within a historical context.
65 Lavau, 'Le Parti Communiste . . .'. p. 18.
66 Ibid., p. 28.
67 Ibid., p. 19.
68 I.e. behaviour of an expressive kind, focused on achieving the representation of the voters' feelings, grievances and unmediated interests – frequently by means of 'actual representation' by deputies socially typical of their electorates. Such behaviour may be contrasted to more instrumental forms of action aimed at securing particular policy outcomes.
69 By the imposition of a qualifying barrier to the second ballot (on which see above, p. 54 and n. 7) and the effective institution of 'primaries' which penalised those who voted without tactical sense even at the first ballot (see below, pp. 191, 198–9).
70 I.e. the legislative elections of 1958, 1962, 1967 and 1968, the presidential elections of 1965 and 1969, and the referenda of 1958, 1961, April 1962, October 1962, and 1969 – at all of which the life of the government was quite explicitly at stake. In the same period in Britain and the USA there were three and six national elections respectively.
71 See above, pp. 52–3.
72 Cited by Lavau 'Le Parti Communiste dans le Système Politique Français', p. 29 (with his emphasis added). Lavau also notes that the pro-Communist farmworkers' organisation is

called the Mouvement pour la *Défense* de l'Exploitation Familiale, in Blackmer and Tarrow, op. cit., p. 100, f. 15.

73 M. Fichelet *et al.*, op. cit., Table 24, p. 268. The Party's other main preoccupations in the electorate's mind were equally defensive. 27 per cent thought it the party most concerned for the 'defence of the lay school'and 22 per cent saw it as the party most concerned with 'the struggle against the OAS' – although the UNR easily surpassed it (with 37 per cent) on this latter issue.

74 Ibid., Table 25, p. 269.

75 Lavau, op. cit., p. 30.

76 A. Kriegel, 'The French Communist Party and the Fifth Republic', in Blackmer and Tarrow, op. cit., p. 76.

77 P. Williams, *French Politicians and Elections: 1951–1969* (London: 1970) pp. 215–16.

78 Cited by J. Simmonds, 'The French Communist Party in 1978: Conjugating the Future Imperfect', *Parliamentary Affairs*, vol. XXXII, no. 1 (winter 1979) p. 79.

79 In 1962 the SFIO had received 12.5 per cent of the vote, the Radicals 7.7 per cent. A number of right-wing Radicals refused to join the FGDS – which nevertheless polled 18.9 per cent in 1967.

80 A November 1962 poll showed that voters associated both the SFIO and the Radicals with the 'defence of the lay school' more strongly than with any other issue, but only 9 per cent thought the SFIO (and 3 per cent the Radicals) to be the party most concerned with national economic development. By 1966 the FGDS was still rated most highly for its concern with education, but it was rated almost as highly in its concern over housing, wage-levels, the problems of small business and a wide range of other issues. In its concern with economic development and the construction of Europe it was rated twice as highly as the PCF. Fichelet *et al.*, op. cit., pp. 268–9.

81 See above, p. 66.

82 See above, p. 63.

83 In fact the PS emerged from Epinay with 74,598 members: the 60,869 above; 3,813 new members; and 9,916 CIR members brought in by Mitterrand: *Le Monde*, *Les Forces Politiques et les Elections de Mars 1973* (Paris: 1973) p. 13.

84 Wright and Machin, op. cit., p. 133, suggest this figure was probably an underestimate.

85 Wright and Machin, 'The French Socialist Party: Success and the Problems of Success', *Political Quarterly*, vol. 46, no. 1 (January – March 1975) p. 42.

86 *Le Matin*, *Le Dossier des Législatives 1978* (Paris: 1978) p.17.

87 Wright and Machin, 'The French Socialist Party: Success . . . ', p. 42 Wright and Machin give 589 *sections* for October 1974, but I have preferred the (official) figure given by R. Cayrol, 'Le Parti Socialiste à l'Entreprise', *Revue Francaise de Science Politique*, vol. 28, no. 2 (April 1978) p. 297. The 1976–7 figures are from Elleinstein, op. cit., p. 55.

88 Hardouin, op. cit., p. 227.

89 Ibid., p. 229.

90 Ibid., p. 231.

91 Wright and Machin, 'The French Socialist Party: Success . . . ', p. 42.

92 Wright and Machin, 'The French Socialist Party in 1973 . . . ', pp. 127–8.

93 *Le Matin*, op. cit., p. 67. Of the 45 new PS deputies in 1978, 26 were in their thirties, and 2 in their twenties.

94 R. Cayrol, 'La Direction du Parti Socialiste', *Revue Française de Science Politique*, vol. 28, no. 2 (April 1978) p. 216.

95 Ibid., p. 219.

96 Cited in P. Bacot, 'Le Front de Classe', *Revue Française de Science Politique*, vol. 28, no.2 (April 1978) p. 283.

97 Cited in ibid., p. 284.

98 Ibid., p. 283.

99 Cited in ibid., p. 285.

100 P. Garraud, 'Discours, Pratiques et Idéologie dans l'Évolution du Parti Socialiste', *Revue Française de Science Politique*, vol. 28, no. 2 (April 1978) pp. 262–72.

101 Ibid.

102 The resemblance to the UNR electorate of 1962 is near-perfect, save for the latter's more feminine base. See J. Charlot, *The Gaullist Phenomenon*, (London: 1971) Table 12, p. 68.

103 Hardouin, op. cit., p. 245. In 1973 there were some 6,000 higher education teachers in the party's total membership of 110,000 and this category was twice as likely to join the party as schoolteachers.

104 Hardouin, op. cit., pp. 223,228.

105 Kesselman's study suggested that in 1970 less than 10 per cent of party members were women. This was the proportion in the Isère federation in 1969; by 1975 it was 23 per cent. The feminine proportion in the Paris federation progressed from 19 per cent in 1969 to 23 per cent in 1972 and 28 per cent in 1974: Hardouin op. cit., pp. 226–8.

106 Ibid., pp. 238–9.

107 Ibid., p. 245.

108 Ibid., pp. 251–2. To some extent the PS was the party of the first generation upwardly mobile from the working-class: 37 per cent of all members had working-class fathers. At *comité directeur* level over 63 per cent had received higher education but 28 per cent had working-class and 32 per cent lower civil servant fathers.

109 Hardouin, op. cit., p. 250.

110 My calculations, based on *Le Matin, Le Dossier des Législatives 1978* (Paris: 1978) p. 68.

111 R. Cayrol, 'Le Parti Socialiste à l'Entreprise', p. 297.

112 Ibid., p. 299.

113 Ibid., p. 303.

111 Ibid., p. 305.

115 Ibid.

116 J. Charlot, 'Vote des Français: Qui, Comment, Pourquoi?', *Le Point*, no. 279, 23 January 1978. During the 1973 campaign the author heard of cases where voters, uncanvassed by the (threadbare) PS organisation, had been assisted by (ubiquitous) PCF canvassers in making touch with the PS and even helped to acquire application forms for PS party membership. Such solicitude was clearly ordained by a PCF leadership eager to help revive a credible Socialist partner for themselves. With the major working-class party exhibiting such unwonted generosity towards it, PS gains among the working-class were easily come by.

117 Garraud, op. cit., p. 265.

## 9 TOWARDS THE IDES OF MARCH

1 Born 1926. A railway worker, he was Secretary of the PCF's Seine-Maritime Section, and was elected as a PCF Deputy 1956, at the age of thirty, when he was also elected first as a substitute and then as a full member of PCF Central Committee. He was promoted to the Secretariat in October 1960 and to substitute Politburo membership in May 1964 (two months before Thorez's death). He was an official full Politburo member from January 1967. As deputy he holds a rock-solid seat at Rouen in Seine-Maritime, still his fief.

2 See above, p. 67.

3 The PCF insisted that Mitterrand should not be designated the 'sole candidate' of the Left, as in 1965, but merely its 'common candidate', arguing that the first formula suggested that other Left parties were merely deferring to the PS's choice of candidate.

4 Lancelot, 'Opinion Polls and the Presidential Election', in H. Penniman (ed.), *France at the Polls: the French Presidential Election of 1974* (Washington: 1975) pp. 193, 203.

5 Post-electoral polls showed that 90 per cent of 1962 PCF voters (21.8 per cent of the electorate) had voted for Mitterrand on the 1965 first ballot. This suggests that his 32.2 per cent score was composed of a 19.6 per cent PCF and a 12.1 per cent non-Communist bloc. On the same basis his 1974 first ballot score was composed of a 19.9 per cent PCF and a 23.5 per cent non-Communist bloc. These figures suggest that, had the PCF opposed Mitterrand in 1974, the result would have been a virtual re-run of the Poher-Duclos contest of 1969. Such a calculation flatters the PCF, however. Even against Poher large numbers of its voters seemed likely to defect up to the last moment (see above, pp. 62–3). Against Mitterrand the slippage of PCF votes would have been far greater – and more lasting.

6 J.-L. Parodi, 'L'Echec des Gauches', *Revue Politique et Parlémentaire* (April–May 1978) pp. 16–17.

7 *Le Monde, Les Elections Législatives de Mars 1978: La Défaite de la Gauche* (Paris: 1978) p. 15.

8 That is, Marchais, his 'dauphin' (and ex-secretary), Charles Fiterman, the ultra-liberal Paul Laurent, and the CGT leader, Séguy. In addition Marchais could normally count on the loyalties of 'pure' *apparatchiks* such as Jean Kanapa – a stereotype Stalinist who had once 'explained' André Gide's defection from Moscow as 'due to the absence of pederasts in the Soviet Union'. (Kanapa had served for many years as *L'Humanité* correspondent in Moscow – a post in which blind loyalty was *de rigeur* and real blindness a positive asset.) Outside the Politburo the young historian, Jean Elleinstein, was often regarded as a spokesman for this tendency.

9 That is, Leroy; old-timers such as Etienne Fajon and Gaston Plissonnier; Guy Besse and Jacques Chambaz (guardians of the Party's intellectuals); Séguy's deputy, Henri Krasucki, and Claude Poperen (whose brother, Jean, an ex-PCF member, was, confusingly, a key protégé of Mitterrand on the PS executive).

10 *Le Monde, Les Elections Législatives de Mars 1978*, p. 15.

11 'Rome' could be read as a reference either to the PCI or to the Treaty of Rome. In the 1978 campaign the PCF used a poster which read: 'Not in Moscow... Nor in Washington... Nor in Bonn... but here in France we shall decide the future of Frenchmen.'

12 J. Elleinstein, *Le P. C.* (Paris: 1976) p. 171. The contrast with the real measure of internal democracy apparent in both the PCI and PCE again underlines the difficulty of assimilating the PCF to any general 'Eurocommunist' model. At the PCE Congress in April 1978 Senor Carrillo, the party leader, faced strong opposition to his move to discard the PCF's 'Marxist-Leninist' label, winning the vote by 968 to 248, with some 200 abstentions. He also faced open opposition to his own re-election as secretary-general by delegates vocally critical of his 'authoritarianism'. Such scenes would be unimaginable within the PCF. See the International Edition of *Newsweek*, 1 May 1978, p. 14.

13 For further discussion of this point see below, pp. 277–9.

14 Elleinstein, op. cit., pp. 96–7

15 D. Blackmer, 'Continuity and Change in Postwar Italian Communism', in D. Blackmer and S. Tarrow, *Communism in Italy and France* (Princeton; 1975) p. 35.

16 See above, p. 137, n. 5.

17 These and subsequent membership figures cited are, unless otherwise attributed, taken from Elleinstein, op. cit., pp. 96–7. All figures relate to party cards actually placed with members, not the much higher numbers delivered to party secretaries.

18 Elleinstein, op. cit., p. 98.

19 1977 figures from *Le Monde, Les Elections Législatives de Mars 1978*, p. 14; 1978 figures from *Le Matin, Le Dossier des Législatives 1978* (Paris: 1978) p. 19.

20 Elleinstein, op. cit., pp. 44–45; *Le Monde, Les Elections...* p. 14; *Le Matin, Le Dossier...* , p. 19. '

21 Between November 1977 and January 1978 urban residential cells fell by 26 to 10,785 and rural cells by 342 to 5,588.

22 J. Charlot, 'Le Déclin Communiste', *Le Point*, no. 282, 13 February 1978; J. Julliard, 'Comment les Français ont Changé de Cap le Dernier Jour', *Le Nouvel Observateur*, 24 April 1978.

23 Elleinstein, op. cit., pp. 54–5.

24 Ibid., p. 56.

25 Ibid., p. 108.

26 Ibid. Of the 20,000 delegates attending the PCF's federal conferences in 1976, 16 per cent came from rural cells but only 3.3 per cent were peasants.

27 Ibid., p. 20.

28 Ibid., p. 97, n. 1.

29 *Le Monde, Les Elections* . . . , p. 14; Elleinstein, op. cit., p. 108.

30 *Le Monde*, op. cit., p. 14.

31 A figure supported by Elleinstein's analysis of Paris region membership, where 40.6 per cent of post-1973 recruits were women: op. cit., p. 109.

32 Ibid., p. 200.

33 A. Kriegel, *Les Communistes Français* (Paris: 1968) pp. 92–128. The Trotskyite groups in France, as elsewhere, clearly rely on the same through-put of transitory youthful recruits.

34 Elleinstein, op. cit., p. 109.

35 Ibid., p. 111.

36 Kriegel, op. cit., p. 264, n. 13.

37 Elleinstein, op. cit., p. 92.

38 *Le Monde*, op. cit., p. 14.

39 Elleinstein, op. cit., p. 97.

40 Ibid., pp. 98–9.

41 Dues (1 per cent of a member's income) produced Fr. 45 million in 1975; special subscriptions (on occasions such as the annual *Fête de l'Humanité*) Fr. 40 million; levies on deputies, senators, councillors, etc., a further Fr. 25 million. (All Communists elected to public office receive only a skilled worker's wage, with the remainder going to the Party – in a deputy's case three-quarters of his salary.) Elleinstein, op. cit., pp. 88–9. (At end 1978, £1 = Fr. 8.45 = \$2.)

42 Most of these are publishing concerns, some of which (e.g. *l'Humanité*) do not make profits.

43 Elleinstein, op. cit., p. 90.

44 Ibid., p. 111.

45 Ibid., p. 110.

46 Ibid., p. 113.

47 During the 1978 campaign the author witnessed a revealing argument between a PCF candidate and his young *suppléante*, who insisted on spending her afternoons at home with her children. All the older man's remonstrations that this was not how a *militante*, let alone a running mate, behaved in mid-campaign were brushed aside.

48 Interestingly, not a few of the PCF old guard have a more than grudging respect for the still intense militancy of the young Trotskyite activists. When, as often happens, these latter gravitate in time into the PCF, their zealous activism means they have more in common with the old guard than does most of the younger membership.

49 See Elleinstein, op. cit., pp. 103–8.

50 Parodi, op. cit., Table V, p. 17 (SOFRES polls of June and October 1976).

51 A. Lancelot, 'Le Rouge et le Vert: Les Élections Municipales des 13 et 20 mars 1977', *Projet*, no. 116 (June 1977) p. 109.

52 Parodi, op. cit., Table V, p. 17 (SOFRES polls of May–June 1977).

53 See Lancelot, 'Le Rouge et le Vert', p. 706.

54 J.-L. Parodi, 'Apres les Élections Municipales: La Fin de la Transition?', *Revue Politique et Parlementaire* (April–May 1977) p. 18.

55 Ibid.

56 In 1962 the UNR's 31.9 per cent of the vote had won it 229 metropolitan seats. With 30 per cent of the vote (and the creation of a further nine metropolitan seats since 1962) the PS could afford to dream beyond even the 210-seat figure.

57 P. Gilles, 'Avril-Septembre 1977: L'Escalade de la Désunion' in *Le Matin, Le Dossier* . . . , p. 82.

58 Ibid.

59 *Le Point*, 11–17 September 1978.

60 Dassault, Roussel-Uclaf, Rhône-Poulenc, ITT-France, Thomson-Brandt, Honeywell Bull, Péchiney-Ugine-Kuhlmann, Saint-Gobain-Pont-à-Mousson and Générale d'Electricité.

61 Denain-Nord-Est-Longwy, Marine-Wendel, Empain-Schneider, and Chiers-Châtillon in steel; Compagnie Française des Petroles and Total in oil; Peugeot and Citroen in automobiles (Renault being already nationalised).

62 Gilles, op. cit., p. 82

63 D. Buffin and A. Liebaert, 'Septembre 77-Mars 78: La Mort du Programme Commun', in *Le Matin*, op. cit., p. 84.

64 Parodi, 'L'Echec des Gauches', Table V, p. 17. The September SOFRES poll gave the PCF 20 per cent, the PS/MRG 31 per cent.

65 *Le Monde*, 31 October 1978.

66 Ibid.

67 Buffin and Liebaert, op. cit., p. 84.

68 '. . . dans beaucoup de domaines, c'est bonnet blanc et blanc bonnet'. Both citations above are taken from Buffin and Liebaert, op. cit., p. 84.

69 I have followed the interpretation of Buffin and Liebaert, op. cit.

## 10 THE FIELD OF BATTLE

1 The requirements of good faith compel the author to admit that he, too, placed too much faith in the polling organisations' strong previous record and was wrong in his expectations of the result. The paragraph above is, accordingly, part *autocritique*.

2 I.e., assuming that the distribution of the vote (49.3 per cent to the Left, 47.7 per cent to the Right) was that actually seen at the 1978 first ballot. PR on a German basis would have given the Left a 250:241 majority over the Right, on a Fourth Republican departmental list basis a 249:239 lead. (See F. Mayer, 'Et Si la France Avait Voté à la Proportionelle' in *Le Matin, Le Dossier des Législatives 1978* (Paris: 1978) p. 27.) Straight application of the 'cube rule' to the Left's 1.6 per cent vote advantage suggests a twenty-seat majority for the Left in a first-past-the-post system – though, of course, in such a system everything would depend on the pattern of candidacy.

3 On a strict quota basis there should have been 72,556 voters per constituency in March 1978. There were 24 (15 of them in Paris) with less than 40,000 voters, in fact. Of these the RPR held 14, the UDF 8, the PS and PCF 1 each. If one assumes that these were amalgamated into 12 homogeneously Right-held seats the Left would end up a net 8 seats better off. There were also 47 seats with over 100,000 voters, of which the Left won 28 in 1978 (16 PS, 12 PCF) and the Right 19 (RPR 6, UDF 13). These, redistributed, would produce some 75 seats of which, on a proportional basis, the Left could expect to win 45, the Right 30 – a further net gain of 6 seats for the Left. Beyond these extreme cases the bias against the Left was not sufficiently great for redistribution to produce more than a handful of net gains. It will be noted that the RPR would be the one clear, large loser from such a redistribution, almost all its losses concentrated in Paris. It is a curious fact that depopulation of the inner city has produced solid pocket-boroughs for the Left in Britain and the USA, for the Right in France.

4 An OAU report accused the French of a great variety of atrocities in their attempt to retain Mayotte, including the forcible marriage and concubinage of local girls with Foreign

Legionnaires to 'whiten' the island. *The Africa Contemporary Record: 1976–77*, without further explanation, terms the report 'rather exaggerated'. See 'Comoro Islands' in C. Legum (ed.), *A.C.R. Annual Survey and Documents* (London: 1977) p. B172.

5  M. Roch Pidjot (New Caledonia) and Aimé Césaire both demand independence for their territories, an objective they regard as compromised by undue attendance in Paris. Leaders of nationalist movements seldom get far in the DOM-TOM, however, as witness the curious case of M. Francis Sanford, champion of autonomy for French Polynesia, elected by a landslide in 1973, only to resign his seat to his *suppléant* on appointment to a government post. In 1974 he supported Mitterrand, carrying the island for him on a wave of opposition to French nuclear testing in the Pacific. He then lost his post; his *suppléant* obligingly resigned; and Sanford won the 1976 by-election with a hugely increased majority. The next year he made his peace with Giscard, became a vice-president of the council of government and again resigned his seat. In 1978 he was not a candidate, instead supporting a Giscardian. Unfortunately for the latter, Sanford's political credit was now exhausted and he lost his seat to the RPR.

6  Press conference, 18 January 1977.

7  I.e. on an (average) 80 per cent turnout a candidate would need 15.63 per cent of actual votes cast to go through to the second round. No less than 69 per cent of all candidates were eliminated by this rule in 1978.

8  The only restrictions were that they had to register in one of the 221 towns of over 30,000 inhabitants, and that overseas voters should not make up more than 2 per cent of the electorate in any constituency. (In light of the motives behind the law such concentration might have been deemed wasteful in any case . . .)

9  *Le Nouvel Observateur*, 11 March 1978.

10  J. Julliard, 'Comment les Français Ont Changé de Cap le Dernier Jour', *Le Nouvel Observateur*, 24 April 1978.

11  *Le Monde*, 26–7 February 1978.

12  For the demographic information in this and the subsequent paragraph I have relied on my own extensive calculations based on data handily summarised in *Le Monde*, 13 November 1973; *Le Monde* 26–7 February 1978; J. Alia, 'Les 'Bleus du Scrutin', *Le Nouvel Observateur*, 11 March 1978; and J. Charlot, 'La Relève Demographique Favorise la Gauche', *Le Point*, no. 280, 30 January 1978. Those wishing to consult the master source in these matters should direct themselves to the monthly and annual bulletins of the Institut National d'Etudes Demographiques, Paris. See, in particular, their bulletin, *Population et Sociétés*, no. 110, February 1978.

13  In 1906 51 per cent of the population were actively employed; in 1926 50.5 per cent; in 1946 48.5 per cent; in 1954 45.5 per cent; in 1962 42.5 per cent, and in 1968 41 per cent: J. Marceau *Class and Status in France: Economic Change and Social Immobility, 1945–1975*, (Oxford: 1977) p. 26.

14  In common with other industrialised nations France has, since the mid-1960s, experienced a steep and sustained fall in the birth rate. The youngest cohorts remain large partly because this decline was at first a very gradual one from historically high levels, and partly because the parental cohort, the children of the first post-war 'baby boom', is itself so large that even with a diminished birth rate its progeny are inevitably very numerous in absolute terms.

15  Julliard, op. cit.

16  *Le Nouvel Observateur*, 11 March 1978 (my calculations).

17  *Le Point*, no. 285, 6 March 1978.

18  J. Ranger, 'La Gauche Piétine à Paris' in *Le Matin, Le Dossier des Législatives 1978* (my calculations).

19  See above, p. 131.

20  *Le Monde*, 28–29 October 1973. At the same date a staggering 41 per cent of the department's population was aged under twenty-four years.

21  Uncertainty over the number of illegal immigrants blurs the figures. In 1970 there had been

3.4 million migrants in France. In 1971 a further 145,000 and in 1972 a further 105,000 entered; 1973 was probably the last year in which immigration was in six figures, though the net migratory flow has probably been positive since then (*Le Monde*, 13 November 1973). Account must also be taken of the immigrant community's youthful age structure (in 1978 it included 1,086,000 children aged 0–19) and rapid natural increase (80,000 births a year): *Le Monde*, 16 December 1978.

22 The author received some rough indication of this in the course of repeated visits to one of the constituencies on the edge of the Paris 'Red belt', where the PCF candidate was kind enough to allow him to examine the accounts of his campaign fund. In 1967, 1973 and 1978 some 60 per cent of the total revenue came from donations by workers at the local Citroen plant. In 1967 only 15 per cent of the workers at the plant were immigrants, by 1973 over 80 per cent. That is, large numbers of immigrant workers were making donations (in 1978 averaging over £1 ($2) per head) to PCF funds, even though they could not vote for the Party.

23 A conservative estimate. If one assumes a migrant population of 4 million with 3 million members over eighteen and a turnout rate of 80 per cent (below the native-born turnout rate), this produces 2.4 million voters. If these had divided in the same 69:31 per cent proportions for Left and Right as did the native working class in 1978, the Left would have gained 1,656,000 extra votes and the Right 744,000 – a net Left gain of 912,000. Of these extra 1,656,000 Left votes it seems safe to assume that a majority would go to the PCF, for the immigrants are heavily concentrated in the low-income groups where the PCF is strongest. It is worth remembering, too, that many of the immigrants come from countries such as Portugal and Algeria where they have already had exposure to leftist politics, and that high proportions work in industries such as construction and automobile manufacture where CGT and Communist influence is often particularly strong.

24 All candidate figures from J.-L. Parodi, 'L'Echec des Gauches', *Revue Politique et Parlémentaire* (April–May 1978) Table 1, p. 12.

25 All told, the Trotskyites robbed the PCF of its lead over the PS/MRG in 24 seats. In 9 of these the PS/MRG went on to win, but in 3 of these the Left's total first-ballot score was 53 per cent or less – the cut-off point at which a seat usually becomes unwinnable by the PCF.

26 That is, the vote cast for Ecologists, Left Gaullists, etc., in these seats exceeded the margin by which the PCF led the PS/MRG on the first ballot.

27 In 7 such cases the combined Left first-ballot vote was over 51 per cent. In a further 7 it was in the 48–50 per cent range, in yet another 7 it was 47–48 per cent and in 3 between 45–47 per cent. Given that, by definition, the potentially pro-PS vote available for redistribution on the second ballot was particularly large in such seats, virtually all of them should have been within range of a PS or MRG candidate.

## 11 THE BATTLE

1 A. Lancelot, 'Le Rouge et le Vert', *Projet*, No. 116 (June 1977) pp. 705–6. This was not a bad indicator: almost a third of the electorate lives in these towns and nearly 70 per cent of them voted. Lancelot found that 38 per cent of third-party voters had favoured the Left on the second ballot.

2 J.-L. Parodi, 'L'Echec des Gauches', *Revue Politique et Parlémentaire* (April–May 1978) pp. 16–17.

3 See above, pp. 191–2.

4 Figures provided by Professor J. Jaffré of CEVIPOF, Paris.

5 Here the PCF had unwisely replaced a well-established sitting deputy with a younger man who found himself the outsider against a popular Socialist mayor.

6 Or 20.8 per cent if one counts the votes cast for the two Left Gaullists and two PSU

candidates who were given official PCF support in lieu of straightforward Party candidates. But the PCF total is always somewhat inflated by the Party's habit of presenting candidates in almost every seat. In 1978 it had candidates in 470 out of 474 metropolitan seats, compared to the PS's 442 candidates and the RPR's 401. If this factor is taken into account then the RPR was indeed still the largest French party.

7 SOFRES post-electoral poll (after the cantonal elections), *Le Nouvel Observateur*, 21 June 1976.

8 The earlier figures average the findings of the three Harris-France polls of 1 February – March, *L'Express*, March 13– 19, 1978; the latter are from the SOFRES post-electoral survey, *Le Nouvel Observateur*, 24 April 1978.

9 Claude Leleu's study of the poll in Vienne (Isère) (*Le Monde*, 1 April 1978) shows that while women made up only 44 per cent of PCF and 48 per cent of PS voters, they constituted 55 per cent of the LO's support (and 51 per cent of the RPR's).

10 In the account which follows I have relied upon the very full report in *Le Nouvel Observateur*, no. 696*b* (special number) 16 March 1978.


## 12 ANATOMY OF A DEFEAT

1 J.-L. Parodi, 'L'Echec des Gauches', *Revue Politique et Parlémentaire* (April–May 1978) p. 17.

2 See above, p. 188.

3 A post-electoral SOFRES survey found that 5 per cent of voters claimed to have changed their preferences in the preceding few weeks, 1 per cent moving towards the Left, 4 per cent towards the Right, producing a (decisive) net gain of 3 per cent for the Right. Of these 'switchers' 87 per cent changed only during the last few days of the campaign, 50 per cent on the last day; 15 per cent of switchers cited Giscard's speech but doubtless it had at least a subliminal effect on a much larger group: J. Julliard, 'Comment les Français ont Changé de Cap le Dernier Jour', *Le Nouvel Observateur*, 24 April 1978.

4 Parodi, op. cit., p. 13.

5 Cited by Julliard, op. cit. The survey was made between 28 March and 5 April 1978.

6 J. Jaffré, (Special number) 'La Paille Dans les Sondages', *Le Nouvel Observateur*, no. 696 *b*, 16 March 1978.

7 The 1 March SOFRES poll showed the PS at 26 per cent (and MRG at 2 per cent. If all 13 per cent of PS supporters desiring victory for the Right had defected, the PS would have received 26 per cent, less 3.4 per cent = 22.6 per cent. In fact it received 22.78 per cent.

8 When the pollsters tested respondents with a hypothetical re-run of the 1974 presidential contest they also found that a major slide away from Mitterrand had occurred as early as September 1977. In December 1976 he had led Giscard 40:32 per cent on a putative first ballot, and 52:48 per cent on the second. By September 1977 Giscard led him 52:48 per cent on the second round and by no less than 42:30 per cent on the first: Parodi, op. cit., p. 21.

9 SOFRES polls from Parodi, op. cit., p. 17.

10 If one examines the crucial group of electors who, having voted for Giscard in 1974, defected to the Left in the 1977 municipal elections, one finds that 36 per cent were workers although only 20 per cent of Giscard's electorate had been working-class. No other group was similarly overrepresented. The movement of these workers to the Left contributed heavily to the resurgence of the class cleavage in this period. See J. Jaffré and J. Ozouf, 'Les Élections Municipales des 13 et 20 mars 1977', Table 6, in SOFRES, *L'Opinion Française en 1977* (Paris: 1978) p. 37.

11 See J. Duquesne, 'La gauche ne séduit plus les catholiques', *Le Point*, no. 280, 30 January 1978; and G. Michelat and M. Simon, *Classe, Réligion et Comportement Politique* (Paris:

1977) especially their section 'Le refus de la politique et la vision du corps social', pp. 26–33.

12 Significantly, it was the Right in this period which was more associated with 'dirty politics' than the Left – probably as a result of Chirac's fractious manoeuvres within the Majority. One indicator of this was the response received by SOFRES in March 1977 when it asked voters whether they regarded De Gaulle, Pompidou and Giscard as 'presidents of all the people' or merely the presidents of 'those who voted for them'. The former view was taken of both De Gaulle and Pompidou by 68:26 per cent and 51:41 per cent majorities respectively, but only 30 per cent saw Giscard as a non-partisan president and 60 per cent said he represented only his voters: A. Duhamel, 'Le Consensus Français', Table 8, SOFRES, *L'Opinion Française en 1977*.

13 Of last minute switchers 59 per cent were women. Indeed, it was women who won the election for the Right. Men divided 52:48 per cent for the Left, women 54:46 per cent for the Right: Julliard, op. cit.

14 Overall the Left fell some 3 per cent short of what the polls had predicted but in the 25–34 age group the shortfall was 6 per cent. See above, p. 202.

15 See above, p. 109.

16 In Paris the PS vote increased by one-fifth, in the *banlieu* by over two-fifths. Had such trends been seen nationally the Left would have won the election quite easily.

17 Jean Charlot in *Le Point*, no. 278, 16 January 1978 (IFOP polls).

18 Institut Louis Harris-France poll of 12–16 January, cited in *L'Express*, 23–29 January 1978.

19 I have used the 'worst case' figures of PCF voters facing a choice between their own minority candidate, a leading PS and an RPR, and of PS/MRG voters facing a choice between their own minority candidate, a leading PCF and a UDF: J. Charlot, 'Le Déclin Communiste', *Le Point*, no. 282, 13 February 1978.

20 See above, p. 189.

21 *Le Nouvel Observateur*, 4 March 1978.

22 SOFRES polls, *Le Nouvel Observateur*, 17 and 24 January and 20 February 1978.

23 Ibid. The poll gave respondents the choice between a straightforward PS coalition with the Majority, and one with the Majority minus the RPR. Above, I have amalgamated these two alternatives.

24 Ibid.

25 This was a great fall-off from 1973. A month before that election polls had shown fully three-quarters of Socialists believing the PCF would be a reliable partner in government: D. B. Goldey and R. W. Johnson, 'The French General Election of March 1973' *Political Studies*, vol. XXI, no. 3 (1973) p. 339.

26 For 1973 see Julliard, op. cit.; for 1978 see Table 12.4. In one sense the transfer of Socialist votes to the PCF was less impressive than it seemed. As Table 12.3 showed, intending PS voters in February–May 1977 favoured the PCF by a 3:1 margin in a simulated second ballot. But at that point intending PS voters were a 30–31 per cent group including many ex-Centrists, and their answers were given outside the campaign period when polarisation would undoubtedly have 'firmed up' their options. By March 1978 only a hard core of 24.9 per cent was voting PS/MRG. On the showing of the 1977 polls one might have expected pro-PCF transfers of 75–85 per cent from this group – under 'ideal' conditions.

27 Transfers in excess of 90 per cent must, though, be regarded as virtually perfect, given the normal vagaries of electoral fluidity. The high level of PCF transfers to the PS/MRG does not necessarily contradict what has been earlier said of localised PCF sabotage tactics against the PS. PCF militants sophisticated enough to campaign openly for the PS while voting against them in the polling booth were quite sophisticated enough to misinform pollsters.

28 The only exception to this general rule being the extreme Left's greater willingness to vote PS rather than PCF. Almost certainly the explanation of this apparent paradox lay in the

Left Catholic origins of many *gauchistes*, especially the PSU. While *gauchiste* dislike of the PCF may be expressed in terms of Trotskyite principle, the real roots of this repugnance may not infrequently lie in a lingering heritage of religious anti-Communism . . .

29 That is, if we take as the baseline the total Left first-ballot vote, we find that Socialist candidates exceeded this by an average of 8 per cent in 1967, 2.8 per cent in 1973 and 0.6 per cent in 1978. PCF candidates under-polled this level by − 1.9 per cent in 1967, − 3.8 per cent in 1973 and − 3.5 per cent in 1978. In 1978, it should be noted, the differential was least in marginal seats (where the Left had achieved 45–55 per cent on the first ballot). Here, on average, the PCF dropped only − 2.0 per cent from the total Left's first-ballot level − clearly an indication of the Party's supreme organisational effort in such seats. The PS, however, gained only 0.35 per cent in such seats on average − a pretty clear indication of how little effort the PCF was making to help them.

30 In Abbeville (Somme). It remained true, of course, that socialists could win seats where communists could not. The PS/MRG won 16 seats where the Left first-ballot total was under 50 per cent, and the PCF lost in 23 seats where the Left had had a first-ballot majority.

31 In marginal seats the PCF almost certainly more than matched the Right in its ability to mobilise first-ballot abstainers into voting. See above, p. 223, n. 29.

32 But see below, pp. 265–6.

33 Marchais' was not the only such case. In Pas-de-Calais, bitter battleground of the PS and PCF, Maurice Andrieux (PCF) and Henri Darras (PS) were elected despite 13,600 and 10,400 spoilt ballots being cast against them respectively.

## 13 THE RECKONING

1 *Le Monde*, 21 March 1978.

2 *Le Monde*, 15 April 1978. He was as good as his word. On 1 May the (monthly) minimum was raised from Fr. 1,750 to Fr. 1,810 − a 4 per cent increase at a time when inflation was running at 10 per cent.

3 Chaban beat Faure by 153 votes to 136, even though the RPR had 30 more deputies than the UDF. In fact Faure won over around 10 UDF deputies but Chaban won thanks to some 30 RPR defections: *Le Monde*, 4 April 1978.

4 The unrest described in Chapter 1 continued through spring 1979, with the steelworkers' march on Paris organised by the CGT in March that year producing the most serious street fighting seen in the capital since 1968 (Mitterrand and Marchais, clearly anticipating such scenes, were carefully absent). Despite the desperate efforts of the CGT and the ready violence of the police, swift recourse was made to the now familiar steel bars, Molotov cocktails and gas-canister bombs. On the Boulevards of Montmartre, Capucines and Italiens a large number of shops, banks and even restaurants were broken into and sometimes looted. The exact identity of the rioters remained unclear − they were generally young *'autonomes'*, a self-described anarchist-nihilist group. *Le Monde* (25–26 March 1979) describes how CGT stewards called for CRS assistance against the *autonomes* and beat them up themselves when they didn't get it, dragging their bodies along the Rue Sainte-Apolline and sending crowds of frightened prostitutes fleeing before them. One of the *autonomes* thus apprehended by the CGT turned out to be carrying a police identity card, leading the CGT to allege that *agents provocateurs* were behind much of the trouble. The Prefect of Police ridiculed such a suggestion, pointing out that those employed as *provocateurs* would never be allowed to carry such incriminating documents . . .: ibid.

5 Following their adventures with Johnny Hallyday (see Chapter 1), CFDT militants at Longwy stole the French football cup from F. C. Nantes in August 1979 and attempted to blackmail the soccer authorities into arranging a charity match in their benefit. This plan failed due to the absence on holiday of the president of the football federation, though the

cup was proudly paraded through Longwy's shopping centre by masked CFDT militants before being handed back. The football authorities then agreed to make a donation to Longwy funds from a special levy on gates at a regular fixture match: *Le Monde*, 11–12 August 1979.

6 Etienne Balibar, Guy Bois, Georges Labica, Jean-Pierre Lefebvre and Maurice Moissonier.

7 These articles were subsequently reprinted in book form by Maspero and, in English, in *New Left Review*, no. 109 (May–June 1978). All quotations here are taken from this latter version.

8 *Nouvelles Litteraires* 8 June 1978.

9 *Le Monde* 11–12 June 1978.

10 The *Mouvement de la Jeunesse Communiste Français* (MJCF) had originally shown strong sympathy with the dissidents and had its journal closed down as a result. It invited both Althusser and Elleinstein to its *fête* and then hurriedly rescinded the invitations under Politburo pressure: *Le Monde*, 1 and 6 June 1978.

11 Tillon (see above pp. 47–9), though excluded from the Politburo in 1952 had only been expelled from his cell in 1970. He now re-emerged to denounce democratic centralism as 'the spirit of Stalinism on the political and organisational level' (*Le Monde*, 1 June 1978). A considerable campaign for his rehabilitation was now mounted by both Althusserian and liberal dissidents. This came to nothing. Tillon then greatly embarrassed his sponsors by giving an interview to (the Maoist) *L'Humanité Rouge*, in which he suggested that socialism was no longer even potentially on the agenda in the USSR; that whatever the PCF might say it remained pro-Soviet at heart and would support the Russians in a war; and that the PCF had unbrokenly been in receipt of Soviet support 'which always allows it to live beyond it means' (*Le Monde* 17 May 1979). For a former Politburo member to allege 'Moscow gold', put him for ever beyond the pale with the PCF – as did his public support for the PS in the June 1979 European election.

12 Consistently (and not in this case heretically!) Elleinstein was strongly against the extension of the franchise to immigrant workers – a move which could only tow the PCF back towards the intransigent defence of a ghetto proletariat. For Elleinstein's main arguments see *Le Monde*, 13–15 April 1978.

13 *Le Monde*, 13 April 1978. The PCF was founded when the SFIO split at Tours in 1920.

14 *Le Monde*, 26 May 1978.

15 Elleinstein was particularly shocked by articles in *Komsomskaia Pravda* attacking Zionism and freemasonry as both Jewish-inspired. See Elleinstein in *Paris-Match*, 13 October 1978.

16 *Le Monde*, 30 June 1978.

17 In *Critique Communiste* no. 25 (November 1978) Elleinstein now also announced himself in favour of the rehabilitation of Trotsky who, he said, had been correct in his analysis of fascism and bureaucracy.

18 *Le Monde*, 5 July 1978.

19 Ibid., 26 April 1979.

20 Ibid., 21 February 1979.

21 Ibid., 22 February 1979.

22 Ibid., 20 April 1978.

23 Ibid., 6 April 1978.

24 Ibid., 10 May 1978.

25 Ibid., 10 May 1978.

26 Mme Charbonnel (who had held a seat in Aisne), the writers Helene Parmelin and Pierre Barberis, the Africanists Yves Benot and Catherine Coquery-Vidrovitch, Paul Meier of *La Pensée*, the historian Albert Soboul, Laurent Heyneman, producer of the film *La Question*, notably figured on this list.

27 *Le Monde*, 21 April 1978.

28 Fremontier, the noted author of *Forteresse Ouvrière: Renault* (Paris: 1971) had been quite a 'catch' for the Party. In March he had brought out 6 million copies of *Action*, a similar number of *Femmes Aujourd'hui-Demain*, and 8 million copies of a special election pamphlet, *Vivre*. *Vivre* had upset PCF hard-liners by carrying a photograph of a PCF deputy shaking hands with the Soviet dissident Leonid Pliouchtch.

29 *Le Monde*, 10 May 1978.

30 Ibid., 10 February 1979.

31 Ibid., 27 April 1978.

32 Ibid., 17 May 1978.

33 Ibid., 22–3 October 1978.

34 Ibid., 28 October 1978.

35 Ibid., 14 April 1978.

36 Ibid., 21 October 1978.

37 Ibid., 10 May 1978.

38 Ibid.

39 Ibid., 27 April 1978.

40 Ibid. A relaunch was attempted in November 1978.

41 Ibid., 17 October 1978.

42 Ibid., 21 April 1978.

43 Marchais favoured free discussion provided it was 'situated within the framework of the Party's strategy'.

44 *Le Monde*, 21 April 1978.

45 Ibid., 5 April 1978.

46 Ibid., 29 April 1978.

47 Marchais had claimed that the PCF press could not, by statute, be open to free discussion save in the period before a Congress. In fact no such statute exists. The relevant clause in the PCF constitution simply records that the Party press is under the control of the Central Committee.

48 *Le Monde*, 29 April 1978.

49 Ibid., 29 April 1978.

50 Ibid.

51 Ibid.

52 Ibid.

53 Ibid., 17 May 1978.

54 Fabre accepted a presidential commission to study unemployment – most sensitive of all issues to the Left. He was universally condemned as a sell-out by the Left, including the MRG's new leader, Michel Crépeau. Marchais pointed out that Fabre had been first to walk out on the Common Programme negotiations in September 1977, first to abandon the Programme in March 1978, and first to accept Giscard's invitation on the Elysée. On all three occasions, Marchais claimed, he had blazed a path for Mitterrand to follow and was now doing so again: *Le Monde*, 6–7 August 1978.

55 In March 1978 37 per cent of PCF voters had blamed the PS for the Left's divisions, and 39 per cent both parties equally. In May 1979 the corresponding figures were 48 per cent and 34 per cent: *Le Nouvel Observateur*, 7 May 1979.

56 *Le Monde*, 19 August 1978.

57 Ibid., 1 June 1978.

58 Ibid., 17 June 1978.

59 Ibid., 22 June 1978.

60 F. Cohen, A. Adler, M. Decaillot, C. Frioux and L. Robel, *L'URSS et Nous* (Paris: 1978). The book frankly admitted Stalin's large influence on the PCF, which had led the Party into all manner of errors and to ignore the works of Trotsky, Gramsci, Bukharin, and Rosa Luxemburg. But the authors also wondered aloud whether Marxism-Leninism itself was any longer a useful formula – after all not even Marx or Lenin had been infallible . . . The

book also pointed an accusing finger at Thorez for having failed to follow Togliatti's example in 1956 and traced in painful detail the PCF's continuing subservience to Stalinist myths into the 1960s, claiming that this had lain behind the Party's failure to grasp the true significance of May 1968. It had, said the authors, taken the Prague invasion of 1968 finally to dispel the scales from the Party's eyes.

61  *Le Monde*, 12 September 1978.
62  *Paris-Match*, 13 October 1978.
63  IFOP poll of August 24–29 in *Le Point*, 4 September 1978.
64  See above, p. 238.
65  'Is a Party card merely Elleinstein's visiting card or, rather, his passport to open to him the columns of the non-Communist press?' etc. *Le Monde*, 31 October 1978.
66  For a fuller account of the meeting see *Le Monde*, 12 December 1978.
67  Of the CGT's 2.3 million members 280,000 were actually retired workers maintaining their subscriptions. Séguy reckoned that while only some 30,000 members held a PS card, with roughly the same number belonging to Catholic groups such as *Action Catholique Ouvrière* (ACO), the PS took 30 per cent of the CGT vote: *Le Monde*, 21 October 1978.
68  Ibid., 15 April 1978.
69  I.e. the still-Catholic CFTC, the white-collar *Confédération Générale des Cadres* (CGC), the teachers' *Fédération d'Education Nationale* (FEN) and the Autonomous unions.
70  *Le Monde*, 3 May 1978.
71  *Le Monde*, 5 January 1979. At the Creusot-Loire Dunkerque plant the CGT actually lost control outright to the CFDT.
72  Of the 3,000 shop-floor representatives sacked by management each year between 1974 and 1977, half were from the CGT, compared to 16 per cent from the CFDT and 5 per cent from the FO: *Le Monde*, 5 January 1979.
73  Ibid.
74  Ibid., 28 November 1978.
75  Ibid., 1 December 1978. See also *Le Nouvel Observateur*, 4 December 1978.
76  Ibid., 2 December 1978.
77  Although the CGT's relative decline had been particularly marked after 1968 and after September 1977, an obstinately long-term trend has also been responsible for the repeated failure of the CGT's campaign to reach 3 million members. An analysis of blue-collar factory council voting over the whole decade 1966–76 shows the CGT proportion falling at a steady 1 per cent a year (from 57.8 per cent to 47.9 per cent of all such votes) with *all* other unions gaining at its expense: *Le Monde* 8–9 October 1978 and 25 November 1978.
78  Thus in the 18th *arrondissement* of Paris a broad Left committee was set up in June 1978 to agitate for a new hospital, grouping local Communists, Socialists, *gauchistes* and feminists. The PCF authorities refused to sanction this near-perfect example of 'unity at base', saying they had no interest in 'unity for unity's sake'. The local Communists – workers, not intellectuals – refused to accept this interdiction and wrote angrily to *Le Monde* to make their point: *Le Monde*, 14–15 January 1979.
79  See, for example, the article by two leading dissidents, Gérard Molina and Yves Vargas in *Le Monde*, 14 October 1978, where they speak contemptuously of 'Jean Elleinstein, all ready to propose miracle solutions to every question. Elleinstein is very comfortable with party crises ... [he thinks] they are settled if his problems are settled.'
80  *Le Monde*, 12 December 1978.
81  Konopnicki had authored a satirical work commemorating the PCF's hundredth anniversary (in 2020), in which the PCF finally published Khrushchev's secret speech in 1986, rehabilitated Tillon in 1994, and just lost the elections of 2018 (the PS swerving to the Right at the last moment again) ... Konopnicki described his own role as 'an agent of the Zionist conspiracy'. The Politburo were not amused.
82  *Le Monde*, 26 January 1979.
83  Ibid., 10 January 1979.

84 *Le Monde*, 10 February 1979. Fiszbin was rehabilitated in November 1979 – when his illness was admitted to have been a fiction.

85 The old hierarchy of punishment had run from internal reprimand, public reprimand, deprivation of Party functions, temporary exclusion, to permanent expulsion. See *Le Monde*, 15 February 1979.

86 For a fuller account see *Le Monde*, 14 February 1979 and 10 May 1979.

87 Ibid., 29–30 April 1979.

88 The Pablo Picasso cell of the Montivilliers section in Seine-Maritime; its motion attacked both Left and Right wings of the PCF.

89 *Le Monde*, 3 March 1979.

90 Ibid., 16 March 1979.

91 Ibid., 2 March 1979.

92 Ibid., 25 April 1979.

93 Ibid., 3 May 1979.

94 Ibid., 10 May 1979. The Russians' attitude was the more notable given that *L' URSS et Nous* had earlier received heated condemnation in the Soviet press. See, e.g., *Kommunist* (an organ of the CPSU Central Committee), December 1979.

95 Public credence in such promises was, however, in decline – see the SOFRES poll of 9–12 April in *Le Nouvel Observateur*, 7 May 1979.

96 The others were Pierre Juquin (49), an academic; Philippe Herzog (39), an academic and Marchais' personal economic adviser; Mme Francette Lazard (42), an academic and a deputy editor of *L' Humanité*, and Mme Gisèle Moreau (38), a bank employee. Thus the Politburo became notably more middle class and its women members increased from two to four.

97 See his interview with *Le Nouvel Observateur*, 8–14 October 1979.

98 *Le Monde*, 19–20 August 1979.

99 Ibid., 10 January 1979. The number of cells had risen by 1,300 (to 28,000), and there were now over 10,000 factory cells. In fact 133,312 new members had joined during the year – which meant that the Party was now having to recruit two members to make a net gain of one.

100 Leroy was able to use the same argument that had been used against him – that Mme Lazard should not simply add her new (Politburo) duties to her old ones. She was replaced by François Hilsum, former head of the MJCF – a compromise in Leroy's favour since Hilsum had already worked under him before and, not being a member of the Central Committee, was a far junior figure: *Le Nouvel Observateur*, 1–7 October 1979.

101 During the run-up to the Congress Leroy had made his own views clear: the 22nd Congress had gone 'too far'; the dictatorship of the proletariat should never have been abandoned; and the Party should now admit that the Common Programme had been a complete mistake: *Le Nouvel Observateur*, 21 May 1979 and 1–7 October 1979.

102 *Le Monde*, 8–9 April 1979.

103 Ibid., 19 September 1978.

104 Ibid.

105 Ibid., 3 May 1978.

106 Ibid.

107 Ibid.

108 Ibid.

109 Ibid., 31 March 1978.

110 Charles Hernu, the mayor of Villeurbanne, and one of the most dynamic young hopes of the PS, flatly declared that it was hypocritical of the party to deny the social democratic label. Were it not for the necessity of the PCF alliance the PS would, he declared, happily accept the term. The PCF did not look this gift-horse in the mouth.

111 All told, Rocard had a team of around fifty, with an inner group of eight – mainly economists and media-men, including one whose task it was to improve Rocard's image

by supervising his clothes-buying, haircuts and style of speech. It was Rocard's proud boast that there wasn't a single schoolteacher on his team – 'There are too many of them in the PS'. See *Le Point*, no. 316, 9 October 1978.

112 *Le Monde*, 25–6 June 1978.

113 Chevènement's diatribes against the 'takeover of the PS by the petty-bourgeoisie' since 1975 and his insinuation that Rocard's handling of the nationalisations issue lay behind the breakdown of the Common Programme were triumphantly quoted by Marchais and Fiterman to 'prove' the PCF case. This hardly increased the popularity of CERES with the rest of the PS.

114 *Le Monde*, 1 December 1978.

115 To the horror of the PCF even Communist voters shared this opinion (by 38:26 per cent). A campaign of 'rectification' was speedily launched: *Le Monde*, 1 December 1978.

116 *Le Monde*, 13 June 1978.

117 Born 1930, A lawyer, he has been mayor of La Rochelle since 1971 and its deputy since 1973. The only Radical to hold an urban seat, his popularity owed much to his imaginative application of his strong ecologist views.

118 *Le Monde*, 3 May 1978.

119 Ibid.

120 Ibid., 25–26 June 1978.

121 Ibid., 7 July 1978.

122 Ibid., 11 July 1978.

123 Ibid., 10 October 1978.

124 He remained some way behind, however. A SOFRES poll of 25–30 November 1978 showed 46 per cent holding positive opinions of Rocard, 40 per cent of Mitterrand and 30 per cent of Mauroy: *Le Monde*, 10–11 December 1978.

125 *Le Monde*, 19 September 1978.

126 Ibid.

127 Ibid., 4 October 1978.

128 Ibid., 24 November 1978.

129 Defferre's power was cemented not merely by his control of the local press (*Le Provençal* and *Le Méridional*), his large private fortune and the immense patronage afforded by his administration of the city and (especially) the port, but by the unique concentration in his hands of control over PS candidacies in the region. The convention witnessed a major revolt over this latter issue, for it meant that Defferre could not avoid personal responsibility for the poor PS results in Marseilles in 1978: *Le Monde*, 26–27 November 1978 and 1–2 April 1979.

130 Defferre had carefully avoided making any allowance for the succession. His *suppléante* as deputy was a woman of his own age while his first deputy mayor was simply the wife of the secretary-general of the *mairie*: *Le Monde*, 1 December 1978.

131 Loo actually entered his own motion against Defferre's at the January 1979 meeting of the PS *comité directeur* and consorted openly with Mauroy and Rocard: *Le Monde*, 9 January 1979. This was an unheard-of step. Bouches-du-Rhône (of which Loo was the federal first secretary) normally spoke with a single voice – Defferre's.

132 *Le Monde*, 1–2 April 1979.

133 A proportion kept at this inflated level by Defferre's habit of distributing party membership cards with a whole year's subscription paid in advance: *Le Monde*, 1–2 April 1979.

134 *Le Monde*, 26–27 November 1978.

135 Rocard was particularly incensed by the comparison between himself and Laval – who had been executed for treason for his role as Vichy prime minister. Rocard's father, a Sorbonne physics professor, had been a major Resistance hero. See R. V. Jones, *Most Secret War* (London: 1979) pp. 337–8, 405, 623–4.

136 *Le Monde*, 15 December 1978.

137  Many of these were makeweights or lesser regional leaders bidding for prominence. They included three separate CERES factions, two sets of Mitterrandistes, Defferre, Loo, a feminist group and even an anti-Savary group: *Le Monde*, 9 January 1979.

138  Mauroy and Rocard agreed that in order to avoid any PS leader enjoying Mitterrand's overwhelming dominance again there must be a rigorous separation between the posts of PS first secretary and of PS presidential candidate. In January 1979 Rocard suggested Mauroy as candidate for the first secretaryship (i.e. and himself for presidential nominee). An embarrassed Mauroy retreated denying that he was after Mitterrand's job.

139  J. Jaffré in *Le Nouvel Observateur*, 15–21 October 1979.

140  *Le Monde*, 18–9 February 1979.

141  Ibid., 26 January 1979.

142  Ibid., 10 April 1979.

143  J. Jaffré in *Le Nouvel Observateur*, 15–21 October 1979.

144  *Le Monde*, 21 June 1979.

145  Ibid., 29 June 1979.

146  Radio Riposte was only one of several political pirate radio stations. Radio Verte Fessenheim had been broadcasting happily from Alsace since 1977 without police harrassment and relayed the transmissions of the Longwy CFDT. The most successful station was run by the Longwy CGT from their 600-watt transmitter in a local church under the title Lorraine – Coeur d'Acier. The Longwy station (heavily guarded by CGT militants) had achieved a wide local popularity with its mixture of pop music and often very salty live interviews. The local police chief had rigged up a special aerial the better to receive it and special loudspeakers relaying it were erected in the Longwy steel plants. On the night of 17/18 May there was a major riot after the authorities began jamming the transmissions. Most of the city centre was sacked and many were hurt and wounded: *Le Monde*, 19–21 May 1979.

147  Louis Harris poll of 12–19 September 1979 in *L'Express*, 29 September 1979.

148  Ibid.

149  *Le Monde*, 11–12 February 1979.

150  According to Mauroy there were 181,503 members at the end of October 1977, 180,751 a year later (though these figures conflict with those on p. 158 above). At end-1978 the party claimed 188,216 members: *Le Monde*, 28 November 1978 and 9 January 1979.

151  The RPR, like the PCF, had set itself the target of 1 million members. Chirac had claimed 650,000 members in March 1978. (All figures above refer to end-1978.) By comparison the UDF, at its first (February 1979) Congress, claimed 245,000 members at end-1978, made up of 142,000 PR, 30,000 CDS, 20,000 Radicals, 28,000 members of the (Giscardian) *Club Perspectives et Réalités*, 4,700 MDSF and 20,000 simple UDF members: *Le Monde*, 26 January and 17 February 1979.

## 14 TOWARDS 1981

1  There was a large-scale and well-organised first ballot vote for the PCF by RPR militants in a (vain) attempt to prevent the more dangerous PS candidate from reaching the second ballot: *Le Monde*, 30 September 1978.

2  Ibid.

3  Ibid.

4  Ibid., 6 September 1978.

5  The results made interesting comparison with those of the last such enquiry in 1966–7, when the PCF had been exactly half its 1978–9 size. In particular, the Party's feminine membership had risen from 25.5 per cent to 35.7 per cent. In 1978–9 51 per cent of members were blue-collar, 28 per cent while-collar, 13.5 per cent 'intellectuals', and less than 3 per cent peasants. More than 10 per cent of the membership was made up of housewives not employed outside the home – more than twice the proportion of either

migrant workers or unemployed. Two-thirds had belonged to the PCF less than ten years and over a quarter were under thirty. See *Le Monde*, 29–30 April 1979.

6 *Le Monde*, 13 October 1978.
7 Ibid., 15 February 1979. Stoléru's plan envisaged the repatriation of 200,000 workers a year by withdrawing the five- and ten-year residence permits from African and Algerian workers, exempting those from the EEC, Greece, Spain and Portugal.
8 *Le Monde*, 14 October 1978.
9 Ibid., 10 May 1979.
10 Ibid., 24 June 1978.
11 Ibid., 17–18 December 1978.
12 Ibid., 19 December 1978.
13 Ibid., 3 February 1979.
14 Ibid., 21 March 1979.
15 Ibid., 26 April 1979.
16 Mme Veil owed this reputation essentially to the fact that she was attractive, a token woman, and to her detention in Auschwitz and Belsen as a teenager. She was, in all other ways, a perfect exemplar of the 'UDR-State', serving as assistant public prosecutor for the Ministry of Justice, on the board of the State radio and TV services in its high period of use as a UDR propaganda instrument under Pompidou, and as Chirac's Minister of Health from 1974 on. Her last act prior to leaving that Ministry for the Presidency of the European Assembly was to introduce sweeping increases in social security contributions, constituting a large cut in working-class incomes. She is married to the millionaire director of the State airline, UTA.
17 A SOFRES post-electoral poll showed that 49 per cent of voters thought French participation in the EEC a good thing, only 9 per cent a bad thing. Only PCF voters disapproved – by 33:23 per cent; PS voters were favourable by 49:8 per cent; UDF voters by 71:3 per cent and RPR voters (to Chirac's chagrin) by 68:5 per cent: J. Julliard, 'Les Transfuges et les Déserteurs du 10 juin' *Le Nouvel Observateur*, 23–29 July 1979.
18 *Le Monde*, 26 April 1979.
19 He had had a bad car accident at the end of 1978 and had attracted much public derision by the stream of invective against the Elysée he had delivered from his hospital bed. His poll ratings had fallen sharply. He had lost the presidency of the Corrèze *conseil général* in the cantonal elections. As mayor of Paris he was being harrassed and starved of funds by the government. He was under attack from leading Gaullists for his autocratic control of the RPR through his personal team, the 'gang of four' – losing one of them, Yves Guéna, a former UDR secretary-general, in March. Guéna resigned, attacked Chirac, and began to put himself forward as a potential RPR candidate for the presidency.
20 IFOP/*Le Point* survey of 12–15 May 1979.
21 IFOP survey of 27–30 April 1979.
22 I.e. if one allocates all list votes save that of the Ecologists to Right or Left. All figures refer to metropolitan France only, and are the original figures provided by the Ministry of the Interior, not the later ones provided by the *Commission de Recensement*.
23 RPR deputies were appalled at the result: the UDF had run ahead of the UDF in all but seventeen of its parliamentary seats. They blamed Chirac quite squarely and demanded the departure of the remaining three of the 'gang of four': Charles Pasqua, Pierre Juillet and Mme Marie-France Garaud. (So did Mme Chirac, who threatened to leave her husband unless he got rid of them, particularly Mme Garaud: see *Elle*, 17 September 1979.) Chirac dismissed Garaud and Juillet. Pasqua stayed, organised the election of a new RPR political council, but was then forced out by indignant RPR deputies, Chirac accepting defeat and annulling the election. He then wooed RPR deputies by promising a more withdrawn and dignified attitude in the future. Robert Poujade, a former UDR secretary-general, summed up the attitude of RPR deputies: 'Chirac is at once impossible and irreplaceable and we must live with that' (*Le Monde*, 14 June 1979).

24 The Commission 'discovered' that there were more registered voters than had been thought (+7,955) but 19,285 fewer actual voters. It validated 108,309 blank or nul votes, giving it 89,024 votes to distribute amongst the parties. Even so, the PCF somehow 'lost' 802, the PS 1,315, the RPR 151, and JJSS 56. Apart from the UDF's gain of 78,958 votes, the only other beneficiaries were parties too small to win a seat. The Commission's new total of votes for all parties did not add up to the new figure for total votes it provided.

25 In October 1979 the *Conseil d'Etat* quashed the Commission's finding and handed the extra seat back to the PS. But the point had been served: it was four months too late for Mitterrand to get the 'Victory to the Left' headlines he had wanted. Giscard avoided the embarrassment of having a UDF European deputy lose his seat by quickly appointing one of the UDF Strasbourg delegation as Secretary of State for Agriculture and thus creating a 'routine' vacancy.

26 *Le Monde*, 12 June 1979.

27 J. Julliard, 'Comment les Français ont Changé de Cap le Dernier Jour', *Le Nouvel Observateur*, 24 April 1978.

28 The calculation is complicated by the fact that although 39 per cent in fact abstained, only 21 per cent of poll respondents admitted to having done so. The figures cited here refer to admitted abstentions only, an accurate enough reflection provided that the propensity to lie to pollsters did not vary between different groups of the electorate: Julliard, op. cit.

29 Ibid.

30 Ibid.

31 The UDF electorate was 57 per cent feminine, the PCF's 53 per cent: Julliard, op. cit.

32 In March 1978 only 9 per cent of this group had voted Communist. In 1979 14 per cent did, against 13 per cent for the PS: Julliard, op. cit.

33 In households with monthly incomes under Fr. 2,000 the UDF won 38 per cent of the vote, the PCF 20 per cent, the PS 20 per cent, and the RPR 14 per cent. In those with incomes of Fr. 2,000–3,000 the UDF won 36 per cent, the PCF 27 per cent, the PS 18 per cent, and the RPR 10 per cent: Julliard, op. cit.

34 *Le Nouvel Observateur*, 22 October 1979. Other figures in this paragraph are drawn from the same source.

35 *Le Monde*, 12–13 August 1979.

36 Ibid., 16 August 1979.

37 Ibid., 4 September 1979.

38 Ibid., 14 September 1979.

39 Ibid., 10 October 1979.

40 Ibid., 17 October 1979; *Le Nouvel Observateur*, 22 October 1979.

41 *Le Monde*, 25 September 1979.

42 Crépeau, who had originally opposed such an initiative, was pushed towards it by the right wing of his party, by his own anger at the meagre places offered to the MRG on the PS European list in June 1979, and by the looming threat that if the MRG did not run, Fabre (with Giscard's support) very well might, thus emerging to federate the Centre under his control after 1981.


## CONCLUSION: A MARCH WITHOUT END?

1 A. Duhamel, 'Le Consensus Français', Table 8, in SOFRES, *L'Opinion Française en 1977* (Paris: 1977).

2 P. Williams, *Crisis and Compromise: Politics in the Fourth French Republic* (London: 1964) Appendix VII, p. 509.

3 J. Julliard, 'Les Transfuges et les Déserteurs du 10 juin', *Le Nouvel Observateur*, 23–29 July 1979.

4 The poll, commissioned by the Secretary of State for Immigrant Workers, found that 77.1

per cent wanted to see a reduction in the number of such workers, but IFOP published (in *Le Quotidien de Paris*, 11 October 1977) a figure of 57 per cent instead. *Le Canard Enchainé*, which uncovered the story, suggested that IFOP did not wish to upset the Secretary of State: *Le Canard Enchainé*, 3 January 1979. IFOP refused all comment.

5 Of this group, 25 per cent disliked social inequalities most, 3 per cent youth unemployment: J.-P. Blanchet and J. Daniel, 'Les Jeunes et la France ou Les enfants d'Après-mai', Table IX, in SOFRES, *L'Opinion Française en 1977* (Paris: 1977).

6 Duhamel, op. cit., Tables 9 and 10.

7 Ibid., Table 15.

8 Among the young voters previously mentioned dislike of politicians came second after social inequalities, with 18 per cent, dislike of the government and government policy (an answer reflecting some of the same sentiments) third, with 16 per cent: J.-P. Blanchet and J. Daniel, 'Les Jeunes et la France ou Les enfants d Après-mai' in SOFRES, *L'Opinion Française en 1977* (Paris: 1977) Table 9.

9 In fact anti-political feeling is probably best understood as a protest *against* the compression of political life into a mere two camps. The rise of the Ecologists and the ever-increasing proliferation of minor party candidates probably bespeaks the same urge to refuse the polarised reality of political life.

10 See above, p. 223 and n. 29.

11 *Le Monde*, 23 June 1979.

12 G. Walter, *Histoire du Parti Communiste Français* (Paris: 1948) pp. 118–23.

13 PCF members were visible within the *Grand-Orient de France* order, though not in the *Grand Loge de France* or the third great order, the *Grand Loge Nationale Français*. Although only 400 of the *Grand-Orient*'s 30,000 members were known as PCF members, by 1978 these latter headed a whole one-fifth of the order's 400 lodges, leading to talk of a deliberate PCF effort at infiltration (though all three orders remained under Socialist control): *Le Point*, 11–17 September 1978; *Le Monde*, 2, 12 and 14 September 1978.

14 After the RPR's setback in June 1979 Chirac talked of the need to bring Gaullism closer to 'the people' and 'the working class', called on Giscard to condemn the 'New Right', attempted to relaunch the Left Gaullists and spoke of the desirability of a wealth tax, higher family allowances, etc.: *Le Monde*, 25 September 1979.

15 *Le Monde*, 6 January 1979.

16 The poll of 9–10 March by Louis Harris-France in *Maintenant*, 19 March 1979.

17 On the crucial issue of unemployment only 42 per cent of workers and 46 per cent of PS voters thought there would be less unemployment under a united Left government; 76 per cent of PCF voters held this belief, however: SOFRES poll of 27 October – 2 November 1978 in *Le Nouvel Observateur*, 4 December 1978.

18 These calculations depended on 90 per cent of PCF voters voting PS at the second ballot and 70 per cent of PS voters voting Communist: IFOP simulation in *Le Point*, 16 January 1978.

19 *France Soir*-IFOP poll of 5–12 September 1978, *Le Monde*, 16 September 1978.

20 PR, strongly urged by the PCF, to whom it would give more seats, had been gradually accepted by the PS. Ironically, PR would free the PS from the need for PCF electoral support – which was why Giscard continually toyed with the idea of introducing it at least for municipal elections.

21 *Le Monde*, 26–27 February 1978.

22 An August 1979 survey made for the Catholic periodical *La Vie* showed that the number of regular *pratiquants* had fallen by a further 1 per cent from 1977 to 12 per cent. Perhaps most significant was the finding that among the critical group for the future, young women aged 18–34, only 9 per cent were regular *pratiquantes*. Even this group was hardly solid: a quarter of them professed to have little or no interest in the Church's teaching on abortion and contraception and 80 per cent said they expected 'no help from the Church in their personal, family, social or professional life': *La Vie*, no. 1772, 16–22 August 1979.

23 Public S.A. poll, *Paris-Match*, 18 October 1979.

# Index